HUMANISM, MACHINERY, AND RENAISSANCE LITERATURE

This book explores how machinery and the practice of mechanics participate in the intellectual culture of Renaissance humanism. Before the emergence of the modern concept of technology, sixteenth- and early seventeenth-century writers recognized the applicability of mechanical practices and objects to some of their most urgent moral, aesthetic, and political questions. The construction, use, and representation of devices including clocks, scientific instruments, stage machinery, and war engines not only reflect but also actively reshape how Renaissance writers define and justify artifice and instrumentality – the reliance upon instruments, mechanical or otherwise, to achieve a particular end. Harnessing the discipline of mechanics to their literary and philosophical concerns, scholars and poets including Francis Bacon, Edmund Spenser, George Chapman, and Gabriel Harvey look to machinery to ponder and dispute all manner of instrumental means, from rhetoric and pedagogy to diplomacy and courtly dissimulation.

JESSICA WOLFE is Assistant Professor in the Department of English at the University of North Carolina, Chapel Hill.

HUMANISM, MACHINERY, AND RENAISSANCE LITERATURE

JESSICA WOLFE

University of North Carolina at Chapel Hill

PUBLISHED BY THE PRESS SYNDICATE OF THE UNIVERSITY OF CAMBRIDGE
The Pitt Building, Trumpington Street, Cambridge, United Kingdom

CAMBRIDGE UNIVERSITY PRESS
The Edinburgh Building, Cambridge, CB2 2RU, UK
40 West 20th Street, New York, NY 10011–4211, USA
477 Williamstown Road, Port Melbourne, VIC 3207, Australia
Ruiz de Alarcón 13, 28014 Madrid, Spain
Dock House, The Waterfront, Cape Town 8001, South Africa

http://www.cambridge.org

First published 2004
Reprinted 2005

Printed in the United Kingdom at the University Press, Cambridge

Typeface Adobe Garamond 11/12.5 pt.   *System* LaTeX 2$_\varepsilon$ [TB]

A catalogue record for this book is available from the British Library

Library of Congress Cataloging in Publication data
Wolfe, Jessica.
Humanism, machinery, and Renaissance literature / Jessica Wolfe.
p.   cm.
Based on the author's thesis (Ph. D., Stanford University).
Includes bibliographical references and index.
ISBN 0 521 83187 3
1. English literature – Early modern, 1500–1700 – History and criticism.   2. Humanism in literature.
3. Machinery in literature.   4. Mechanics in literature.   5. Renaissance – England.
6. Humanists – England.   I. Title.
PR428.H8W65   2004
820.9'384 – dc22   2003055396

ISBN 0 521 83187 3 hardback

To my parents

"pregnant rules avail much, but visible examples amount incredibly . . ."
Gabriel Harvey

Contents

vii

Illustrations

Acknowledgments

The contours of this book have been shaped by dogs and the people who love them. The project was born in 1995, in the eaved study of a San Francisco Victorian house shared by Catherine Magid and Blackjack, who each in their own way provided a perfect antidote to the prospect of writing a dissertation. I made my final revisions in December 2002 while huddling by the fire during the aftermath of an ice storm, insulated by many blankets, my husband, and our two dachshunds, Tilly and Ginger.

Over the course of those seven years, my skills and my sense of purpose as a scholar have grown from the wisdom and kindness of many teachers, colleagues, and friends. At the University of North Carolina, Chapel Hill, an exceptional group of Renaissance scholars, including Alan Dessen, Ritchie Kendall, Megan Matchinske, Peter Kaufman, Lance Lazar, Mary Pardo, Michael Cole, Barbara Harris, Lucia Binotti, and Dino Cervigni have been generous with their advice and encouragement. John Headley deserves special mention for having fortified me with extraordinary support for my work as well as with camaraderie over kir *ordinaire*. An exemplary scholar, a conscientious citizen of the University of North Carolina community, and a devoted friend, Darryl Gless has helped me to complete this book in so many different ways, though none more delightful than companionship over a plate of *lardo*. As past and present chairs of the University of North Carolina English Department, Bill Andrews and James Thompson have both worked to cultivate the ideal conditions for making a happy and productive scholar and teacher out of me, and I am thankful to them and to the department as a whole for having confidence in me.

At Stanford University, David Riggs taught me to wear my love of the archive with pride, while Seth Lerer demonstrated how exemplary teaching and superlative scholarship can and do come in the same package, particularly when both are nurtured by an unabashed enthusiasm for the life of the mind. Thanks are also due to Ron Rebholz, Patricia Parker, Jennifer Summit, Ania Loomba, Suvir Kaul, Terry Castle, and Bliss Carnochan, to my fellow graduate students in English and Comparative Literature, and last but not least to Stephen Orgel. I am very grateful to Norman Fiering and the entire staff at the John Carter Brown library, where I was a doctoral fellow during fall of 1996, for the opportunity to tinker with working paper astronomical instruments and to enjoy the crisp tranquility of a Providence autumn, where I also had the pleasure of discussing my discoveries with Karen Newman and Stephen Foley.

Thanks to a Mellon Dissertation Fellowship, a travel grant from Stanford University, and John Kimbell, I was able to spend many months at the British Library at the beginning of this project; towards the end, thanks are also due to Nigel Smith and Kate Flint for the use of their home in Oxford, which allowed me to get to know Henry Savile and John Dee when the Bodleian was open, and the delights of Great Tew and the Vale of the White Horse when it was closed. On this side of the Atlantic, family and friends have offered plenty of love and wisdom to offset the challenges of writing this book. Michael and Belinda McFee, Al and Janet Rabil, and Tom and Margaret Stumpf have all helped make Carolina feel like home, while Erin Carlston, George Lensing, Tom Reinert, Jane Thrailkill, Rashmi Varma, and Joe Viscomi have offered with their friendship a healthy balance of incisive critique and frivolous diversion. I am also grateful to my editors and anonymous readers at Cambridge University Press for their valuable advice and careful work on the typescript, and especially for their much-needed urging to trim the book of its gratuitous bulk and its infelicities of style, much too much of which, I am sure, still remains despite my efforts. Most of all, I am grateful to my family, who taught me the value of keen analysis, carefully crafted prose, and lively debate, and who have been proud and supportive of my academic successes since the early days of gold stars and fingerpainting.

This book simply would not exist without the love, exuberance, erudition, and occasional cajoling of one extraordinary person, Reid Barbour, who has proven not only to be an ideal intellectual companion, but also the most sympathetic, dedicated, and downright fun husband I could possibly have imagined. From our shared interest in Cistercian abbeys, Lucretian atomism, and the poetry of Herrick to our mutual love of Slurpees and carnival rides, life with you brings back the Renaissance spirit of the *gioco-serio*. Our life together has been, and will continue to be, a recreation in the fullest, seventeenth-century meaning of the term.

Jessica Wolfe
Durham, North Carolina, April 2003

Introduction: Subtle devices: Renaissance humanism and its machinery

> [Tener ingenios auxiliares] Provide yourself with auxiliary wits [engines]. To enslave our natural superiors by cunning is a novel kind of power, among the best that life can offer.
>
> Balthasar de Gracián

This is a study of the ways in which Renaissance writers understand machinery and the practice of mechanics before the rise of the mechanical philosophy. By the middle of the seventeenth century, the discipline of mechanics and machines themselves begin to be understood as participants in, and exemplars of, a cohesive set of scientific theories and a corresponding set of political, ethical, and intellectual convictions. Yet in the century before Descartes and Gassendi, the meanings which scholars and poets attach to mechanical objects and practices are radically different from, and less systematic than, those of their successors. Rather than view machinery as the regulative model of a monolithic natural philosophy in harmony with particular ethical and metaphysical doctrines, sixteenth-century humanists endorse no single mechanical philosophy. Instead, they ally machinery with competing doctrines and attitudes, so that the practice of mechanics becomes capable of confederacy with a dazzling array of concerns distinctive to the intellectual culture of the period.

Humanism, Machinery, and Renaissance Literature argues that sixteenth- and early seventeenth-century culture embarks upon a widespread reconsideration of its attitudes towards instrumentality and artifice stimulated in part by a volatile and conflicted relationship to machinery and to the practice of mechanics. The construction and use of devices including clocks, stage machinery, war engines, and astronomical instruments, as well as representations of these devices in literature and in art, not only reflect but also actively reshape how Renaissance writers define and justify machination as an intellectual or political tool. Rather than focus upon the purely scientific applications of mechanics during the period, this book exposes how machinery plays a central and transformative role in the way Renaissance humanists reassess their understanding of all manner of instrumental means, from rhetoric and pedagogy to courtly dissimulation and diplomacy.

By humanists, I mean those writers whose interests and methods are primarily grounded in the *studia humanitatis* – in rhetoric, history, and moral philosophy, rather than in the systematic disciplines of logic or theology. Yet the scholarly activities of many of the writers studied in this book demonstrate that any categorical distinction between humanism and science during the period is precarious at best. Poets including George Chapman and Edmund Spenser reveal a profound interest in mechanics as an instrument of moral discipline or as a tool with which to redefine the relationship between nature and art. From Angelo Poliziano to Henry Savile, some of the most capable scholars of mechanics are steeped in the methods and concerns of humanistic scholarship and vice versa. Bernardino Baldi translates ancient Greek works on mechanics but also writes a laudatory history of the dukes of Urbino, while Francis Bacon writes history and court masques as well as works of natural philosophy.

Renaissance humanists recognize the profound applicability of mechanical practices and principles to extra-scientific questions. These include: the relative merits of theory and practice; the practicality of philosophical ideas such as Stoic *apatheia*, and above all the moral and epistemological challenges posed by instrumentality – the reliance upon instruments and tools, mechanical or otherwise, to effect a particular end. For the several generations of scholars and poets studied in this book, humanistic disciplines and the discipline of mechanics shed mutual light upon each other and are defined by a shared set of concerns and aims.

The applicability of mechanics to the intellectual culture of Renaissance humanism is in part due to the dominant understanding of mechanics during the period as a science of "means and instruments." In his 1612 treatise *Metallica*, the English clockmaker and natural philosopher Simon Sturtevant repeatedly defines mechanics as "Instrumentall means," a definition that implicates mechanics in a broader theory of means that extends to political and intellectual instrumentalities as well as to machines. After establishing the "powerfull efficacie and meanes of his dexterous prerogative instruments," Sturtevant identifies several subcategories of "mechanick invention," distinguishing between "impersonall" and "personal" instruments, or between machines and servants, the living instruments upon whom rulers rely.[1]

Inasmuch as it treats mechanics and politics as sister arts both involving the effectual use of instruments, Sturtevant's definition offers a novel, persuasive model of instrumentality applicable to political and intellectual methods alike. In the preface to *Metallica*, Sturtevant compares his "Litteral" and "Mechannicall" projects to each other, likening his work on mechanics to his "Scholasticall engin *Aucomaton*," a Hebrew and Chaldean dictionary entitled *Dibre Adam*.[2] Sturtevant regards his dictionary as an "aucomaton" – a conflation, in all probability, of *automaton* and *auctor* – in that it offers the scholar the effectual means to translate ancient languages. Sturtevant's perception that *Dibre Adam* is a philological "automaton" is borne out by the terminology of that text's preface, which refers to itself as a "device," an "instrument," and a "literarie Engine" that readers may manipulate "with speedie motion, and turning of a hand."[3]

Sixteenth-century uses of the word *technologia* (τεχνολογια), a Greek term imported into Latin by Cicero, carry similar connotations, referring not to mechanical practices but rather to rhetorical or philological methods. Guillaume Budé's 1554 *Lexicon Graeco-Latinum* defines *technologia* as an art (*ars*) or discipline, or as an artifice (*astutia, impostura, frauda*), reflecting the commonplace attitude that humanistic learning is the product of human contrivance, and not of nature. Peter Ramus frequently uses the term *technologia* in his work on dialectic to denote a rhetorical technique or a "systematic treatment of grammar."[4] Gabriel Harvey shows his debt to Ramus when he refers in his copy of Cicero's *Ad Atticum* to the "technologia Hopperi," Marcus Hopper's 1563 Greek–Latin dictionary or "artificiosa nomenclatura," as Harvey also calls it.[5] For Ramists, a *technologia* could denote a dictionary or reference text – as is the case with Caspari Streso's 1634 *Technologia Theologica Exemplo Illustrata*, a collation of commentaries on *1 Romans* – or it could denote the methodical ordering of any discipline of knowledge, including the systematic study of the relationship between different scholarly disciplines.[6]

This humanistic conception of *technologia* as polyvalent instrumentalism enables machinery to contribute to the shaping of Renaissance attitudes towards the efficacy and legitimacy of non-mechanical instrumentalities. Many writers seize upon the term *engin*, which denotes both wit and machinery, and the term *virtù*, which signifies political efficacy as well as the motive power of a machine, to foreground the etymologically latent connections between mechanical operations and intellectual or political strategies. The Elizabethan scholar Thomas Blundeville explains in his 1574 *True order and methode of wryting and reading hystories* that his work explores the "meanes and instrumentes" of historical actions, a formula he repeats in his 1594 *Exercises*, an anthology of practical scientific treatises that likewise instructs its readers in the use of "instruments" including quadrants and cross staffs.[7] Like many of his contemporaries, Blundeville recognizes the similarities between a historical method grounded in the close examination of "means and instruments," or the tangible causes of historical events, and the discipline of mechanics, grounded in the operation of mechanical instruments that effect tangible results in the physical world. According to the logic that yokes them together so frequently in the latter half of the sixteenth century, mechanics and politic history are allied in that both disciplines investigate the human manipulation of the material world.

Machinery also provides a conceptual and material framework for Renaissance culture to dissect and modify its vexed relationship to subtlety, a term whose diverse uses expose the culture's persistent triangulation of mechanical, intellectual, and political artifice. A number of late sixteenth-century authors of treatises on mechanics employ the term *manganaria* to describe mechanical artifice. In his 1593 *Institutionem Mathematicarum*, Conrad Dasypodius defines mechanics as an "ars Manganariorum instrumentorum," or the art of manipulating appearances by means of instruments.[8] Etymologically linked to the Greek terms *magus* and *magganon*, or deceit, the term *manganaria*, also used by Alessandro Giorgi and Bernardino Baldi in their translations of Hero of Alexandria and pseudo-Aristotle, reflects the degree to which machinery is recognized as a model for human artifice and contrivance.

Machinery mediates some of the most urgent political and intellectual problems vexing humanistic culture. Yet machines are also mediators in the most literal sense of the term insofar as they intercede between the external world and the subjective experience of the human intellect or the senses. Many of the machines analyzed in this book – speaking tubes, optical instruments, the printing press – are mediating devices that alter or interrogate our received experience of the external world. In doing so, these machines create a heightened awareness that the faculties of sense and intellect are themselves mediating instruments that perform their functions with varying degress of success. Galileo and Bacon both look to mechanical instruments as a way to transcend the errors and limitations of the senses, but they are also aware that machines, like the "uncertain light of the sense" and the imagination, distort the information they transmit. Bacon thus compares the mediating faculty of the human intellect to an enchanted glass or an "uneven mirror" in that it "distorts the rays of things" when it "treacherously implants and mixes its own nature into the nature of things" unless reduced by methods. That machinery mimics, rather than corrects, the errors and vanities of our sensual instruments is a central problem in Bacon's natural philosophy, one echoed by many Renaissance writers as they study mechanical objects as meditations upon the uncertainties of human experience, from the unreliability of the senses to the wayward nature of the passions.[9]

Renaissance treatises on natural magic, as well as works of literature and art, are replete with these "enchanted glasses," machines that imitate, supersede, or travesty the senses. Alternately viewed as agents of truth and as instruments of deception, these machines compound and transform Renaissance culture's concerns about mediation rather than eliminate them. Because they foreground the intermedial nature of human knowledge and interaction, machines provide a theoretical tool kit for Renaissance culture to analyze non-mechanical forms of mediation, from translation and rhetoric to diplomacy and the art of perspective. As metaphors in political and literary texts, machines redefine the moral and epistemological ramifications of instrumentality – the use of human, mechanical, or intellectual instruments to achieve a particular end. Not only do machines materially transform the mediatory capacity of our sensual faculties, but they also participate in refashioning relationships between human beings and their instruments, from readers and their texts to rulers and servants. Yet even as machinery promises to compensate for the defects of our natural instruments, these auxiliary sources of power upset confidence in the instrumentalities of Renaissance culture by threatening to arrogate or replace their natural counterparts.

The enthusiastic yet qualified interest in machinery during the sixteenth century is the product of a revolution in method taking place in natural philosophy but also in logic, law, and politics.[10] In the process of rebelling against traditional codifications of knowledge and replacing them with new intellectual methods, humanists look to machinery as both a master metaphor and a model for these new techniques. For Bacon, the correspondences between mechanical and intellectual techniques are all-pervasive, and Bacon is one of many Renaissance writers who assimilates machinery and mechanism to a corresponding group of intellectual and political strategies of subtlety or dissimulation. Yet the project of establishing correspondences between mechanical and intellectual methods proves perilous for Renaissance humanism, either because human beings do not behave like machines, or because – as Edmund Spenser ultimately admits – we should not behave like them. Humanism and its machines are thus engaged in a series of ongoing struggles, for as strenuously as Renaissance writers attempt to accommodate machinery to their habits of thought, machinery resists that accommodation, alternately exalting and annulling the culture's most cherished values and its most precarious beliefs.

This book is not a history of mechanics per se, but rather a study of the ideational role that machines play in sanctioning or condemning instrumentality and artifice. It evolved from the perception that, before the advent of a systematic mechanical philosophy in the middle of the seventeenth century, there was a fascination with mechanical devices in Renaissance culture that had not been adequately explained by historians of science. Perpetual motion machines, hydraulic garden machinery, and automata, while failures or oddities to the scientist's eye, assert their importance through their interplay with some of the period's most conventional discourses and practices, including theatrical spectacles, moral philosophy, and portraiture. The role played by machinery in courtly or humanistic settings, moreover, cannot be understood by tracing the scientifically sanctioned roles that some machines come to play towards the end of the seventeenth century. For several decades after their invention, telescopes remain earthbound, tools for reading letters surreptitiously. Hydraulic pumps supply not steam engines but rather the mechanisms generating the wetting sports of the Renaissance garden, items similar in design to their descendants but radically different in the cultural work they perform.

Historians have frequently characterized the intellectual climate of late sixteenth-century Europe as one preoccupied with technique. Exemplified by a passion for difficulty and by a penchant for artful display, the academic and courtly cultures of Elizabethan and Jacobean England nurture virtues including ingenuity, dexterity, and grace through the mastery of mechanical devices. Recent work by R. Malcolm Smuts, Steven Shapin, and Hélène Vérin has illustrated how scientific practices participate in the cultivation of intellectual virtuosity during the period. According to Smuts, John Dee, Salomon de Caus, and Prince Henry were all fascinated by "mechanical gadgetry," and each sought to forge a "philosophy of artificial works" in which mechanics contributes to a reformulation of the relationship between art and nature.[11]

Yet in spite of the era's obsession with technical skill, or with what sixteenth-century writers often call method or practice, there is no such thing as technology before around the middle of the seventeenth century. While there are many texts depicting mechanical devices, there is little if any categorical distinction between mechanics and other intellectual disciplines.

In an era preoccupied with the classification and arrangement of knowledge, objects which from our contemporary standpoint appear to belong to a discrete category cannot predictably be located in any particular place. Descriptions of mechanical objects often surface where a text's organization falters, under miscellaneous headings such as "Ludicra," "Extravagants," or even "Chaos" (in Guido Pancirolli's 1599 *De Rerum Inventoribus*, John Bate's 1634 *The Mysteryes of Nature and Art*, and Giambattista della Porta's 1589 *Magia Naturalis*, respectively). Furthermore, discussions of mechanics may seem trivial in context: Porta's descriptions of optical instruments and pneumatic machinery appear alongside recipes for hair dye and instructions for tattooing. Yet, as Patricia Fumerton has shown in her *Cultural Aesthetics*, the incidental and the peripheral are often deceptively central, foregrounding Renaissance culture's most acute anxieties and problems.[12] Some of the objects analyzed in this book may well be marginal in that they fall beneath the threshold of scientific legitimacy, but it is the very marginality of Renaissance machinery that allows it to infuse the culture's habits of thought.

When I do refer to *technologia* or technology, a term which first appears in English in around 1615 and in Romance languages slightly earlier, I use it in the capacious, sixteenth-century sense discussed above. The term "natural magic" more closely approximates the modern use of the term "technology" in that it signifies procedures that appear supernatural but are in fact produced by natural means. Yet even this latter term is unsatisfactory in that it fails to capture the mutual permeability between mechanics and other intellectual disciplines or the interplay between mechanical and non-mechanical objects as shown by Horst Bredekamp's study of the logic governing the arrangement of Renaissance *Kunstkammern*, in which machines, natural curiosities, and artifacts are placed side by side to demonstrate and alter the continuum between art and nature.[13] Both inside and outside the *Kunstkammer*, Renaissance culture correlates machinery to non-mechanical objects and practices rather than constitutes mechanics as a separate discipline. Instead, machinery lurks in the interstices of the Renaissance imagination: its meanings are formed out of an interplay with the culture's aesthetic and political sensibilities and its philosophical dilemmas.

Circumscribing a scope of study for a field that defies disciplinary boundaries has proven challenging. The sketches of engines made by artist-engineers such as Leonardo Da Vinci and Francesco Di Giorgio Martini certainly qualify as machinery, but what about the fantastic caricatures of Giuseppe Arcimboldo or François Desprez, human figures composed out of kitchen implements, compasses, and bellows? A treatise on an astronomical instrument such as Thomas Hood's 1590 *The Use of the Jacob's Staffe* surely constitutes a work of mechanics, but how might one categorize Thomas Blundeville's 1594 *Exercises*, an anthology of texts on cosmography and mechanics that asks its gentlemanly audience to view such "exercises" as the intellectual ornaments of the Elizabethan courtier?

It is thus difficult and even misleading to distinguish mechanical and non-mechanical treatises from each other on account of their shared idioms and their overlapping intellectual aims. The difficulty of carving out a disciplinary identity for machinery during the period is compounded by the manifold resonance of Renaissance culture's mechanical vocabulary. The use of terms such as "engine," "device," "motion," and "instrument," as well as "subtle" and "artificial," demonstrates that machinery belongs to a larger semantic network which includes in its purview any witty device from an emblem or an epigram to a morsel of political advice. A 1590 translation of Francesco Sansovino's *Quintessence of Wit*, a collection of "conceits," "maxims," and "poleticke [*sic*] devises" originally composed in 1578, offers the heading "artificiall devises" for Machiavellian adages such as "it is necessary to be a fox, to know how to discypher snares."[14] Authors of technical treatises provide different offerings in similar packages: Cyprian Lucar promises "profitable devises" such as "strange engines" to the artificer who reads his 1590 text, while a 1594 treatise written by Hugh Plat and dedicated to the Earl of Essex offers "artificiall conceipts" and "ingenious devices," including optical instruments and self-moving plows, to a patron expert in political devising.[15]

This network of terms and techniques affiliated with Renaissance machinery is indebted to the ancient Greek concept of *metis*, that "complex but very coherent body of mental attitudes and intellectual behaviour[s]" whose semantic and cultural range is traced by Marcel Detienne and Jean-Pierre Vernant in their *Cunning Intelligence in Greek Culture and Society*.[16] During the Renaissance, machines are commonly perceived to cultivate faculties of *metis* or cunning. Detienne and Vernant define *metis* adversarially: it is the "opposite" of force, consisting of any technique or method of a "different order" from strength that enables "the weaker party" to "reverse the natural outcome of [an] encounter and to allow victory to fall to the party whose defeat had appeared inevitable."[17]

Often, but not always, regarded by Renaissance writers as a species of *metis*, machines embody the cunning and subversive tactics of the weak. In his preface to Henry Billingsley's 1570 translation of Euclid's *Elements*, John Dee uses the term "Menadrie" to refer to the capacity of mechanics to produce effects "above Natures Vertue and power simple."[18] As the means by which "Vertue and Force may be multiplied," Dee's concept of "Menadrie" characterizes mechanical power as auxiliary and compensatory in that it enables the triumph of the weak over the strong. Like many of his contemporaries, Dee adopts the pseudo-Aristotelian *Mechanical Problems'* definition of a machine as the means by which "the less master the greater, and things possessing little weight move heavy weights."[19]

The political and social ramifications of this definition of machinery are recognized and exploited by a number of Renaissance writers including the fifteenth-century humanist Giovanni Tortelli. In his 1471 *De Orthographia dictionum e graecis tractarum*, the future Vatican librarian provides a commentary upon the term *horologium* that reveals the extent to which machines enact and reconstitute the classical concept of *metis*. Tortelli begins with a historical account of the clock but soon embarks upon a digression contrasting the arts of hunting and fowling, the latter of which involves the use of night owls (*noctua*) and screech-owls (*ulula*) in order to pursue other birds. Fowling differs from hunting, Tortelli writes, in that "one uses cunning, the other violence [hoc insidiosum: illud violentum]," and that "the one works secretly, the other in the open [hoc ex occulto: illud ex aperto]."[20]

By contrasting the different techniques required by hunting and fowling, the former employing open force and violence, and the latter cunning and secrecy, Tortelli's digression invokes a conflict between natural and artificial power of paramount concern to Renaissance culture, particularly with respect to the growing material and discursive presence of machinery. Tortelli's contrast between the two practices reflects his culture's more widespread ambivalence towards artifice which manifests itself in the continual and pervasive examination of whether it is better to hunt or to fowl – to do things openly and directly, or to do them covertly and indirectly. By providing new models of cunning, machinery shapes this diacritical preoccupation with instrumental means, often prompting a reappraisal of the aesthetic and moral doctrines according to which Renaissance writers either sanction or condemn artifice.

Like more classic expressions of guile such as fowling, which relies upon birds that only emerge at night, Tortelli argues, the clock "speaks to us even when the sun is hidden [sed et occultato sole sermo]," and is thus able to circumvent the limits of nature. But it is Tortelli's final distinction between hunting and fowling that underscores the entry's latent yet pervasive antithesis between force and subtlety and drives home its sociopolitical implications. While hunting is the preserve of the wealthy, fowling is practiced by commoners, confirming what "Aristotle and others have written, that it is the nature of the poor . . . to employ trickery, and of the rich to employ force: and so the former are compared to little foxes [*vulpeculae*], the latter to the lion." With little recourse to more direct expressions of power, the poor instead assume the slyness (*dolos*) of a fox, the creature whose brand of *metis*, according to Detienne and Vernant, exemplifies how "the cunning [*techné*] of the weaker" can take the stronger by surprise and bring about his downfall.[21]

Renaissance machines enact precisely such reversals of power. Drawing from the pseudo-Aristotelian *Mechanical Problems* and from Book 10, chapter 1 of Vitruvius' *De Architectura*, sixteenth-century natural philosophers define mechanics as an art beyond the power of nature that enables the lifting of heavy objects with minimum effort: "qua magna pondera, machinis adhibitis, praeter naturam, in altitudinem tolluntur: minori potentia."[22] In the engine-houses of Bacon's *New Atlantis*, instruments are made to perform tasks "more easily, and with small force, by wheels and other means," thus reinscribing ancient narratives of *metis* in which the weak master the strong with the help of *techne*.[23] Not all machinery, however, is understood during the period as a tool of *metis*: in the hands of monarchs or aristocrats, machines can reinforce absolutist political structures or exclusionary marks of social distinction. Yet even in the context of the Renaissance court, machinery can accrue meaning as a compensatory power insofar as it exemplifies the conquest of difficulty, or *sprezzatura*, cultivated by the Renaissance courtier as a means of hiding defects or outstripping rivals.

Renaissance dictionaries confirm the adversarial capacity of mechanical power by defining terms such as "machine," "engine," and "device" as synonymous with fraud, cunning, and other non-mechanical forms of power that work by deception or obfuscation rather than by force. Randle Cotgrave's 1611 French–English dictionary defines *engin* as a "toole" or "instrument" but also as "understanding, policie, reach of wit; also suttletie, fraud, craft, wilinesse, deceit." In the same year, the first edition of John Florio's Italian dictionary defines the Italian *ingegno* as wit, engine, art, skill, or cunning, and the 1659 edition, revised largely before Florio's death in 1625, refines the existing definition of the term by adding that *ingegno* also means "any kind of engine, machine, frame . . . or any water-works." Two of the earliest dictionary appearances of the term *technologia*, in Guillaume Budé's 1529 *Commentarii Linguae graecae* and in the *Lexicon Graecolatinum* of Jean Crespin, first printed in Geneva in 1562, define it as the art of verbal artifice: as "de arte dissero" and (in Crespin) as "sermo & ratiocinatio de arte, artificiosa ratio."[24] Linked semantically and morally to the realm of imposture inhabited by Spenser's Malengin, Jonson's Subtle, and the stage Machevill, mechanical devices participate in and alter the culture's understanding of conflicts between force and fraud. By cultivating this network of connections between cunning or wit (*engin*) and mechanical power (*engin*), Renaissance writers enlist machinery as both a metaphorical and an actual tool to negotiate the relationship between those forms of power that rely upon physical effort, and those that circumvent it through subtlety.

"Subtlety" is a key term in this book, a word whose complex and often contradictory spectrum of meanings unfolds Renaissance culture's manifold anxieties towards political, intellectual, and mechanical practices that complicate the act of defining and distinguishing between nature and artifice. At its best, subtlety denotes intellectual acuity, precision, or prudent machination. At its worst, subtlety is shorthand for intellectual nit-picking, rhetorical superfluity, excessive intricacy, or dishonesty. Jesuits, scholastic philosophers, and Satan are all frequently described as subtle, but so too are clean air, discriminating and acute intellects, and clever devices both literary and mechanical. In 1550, the neo-Stoic physician Girolamo Cardano produces a voluminous encomium on subtlety, *De Subtilitate*, that jumbles together political, intellectual, and mechanical artifice. Cardano praises clocks and automata for their subtlety, a quality that also describes the dissimulations of Tiberius, the game of chess, and the insidious passion of jealousy, or "subtle hate [haine subtile]." Cardano's rival Julius Caesar Scaliger responds with *De Exotericae*, an impassioned defense of the "exoteric" that repudiates all things subtle, praising directness and obviousness as an aesthetic and political principle.[25] Yet as Cardano is quick to point out on the opening page of *De Subtilitate*, subtlety is a complex term whose spectrum of definitions includes its own opposite, signifying obscurity but also the perspicuity necessary to elucidate obscure ideas and objects. If subtlety is "that which seems very open and easy, but which is very obscure [(ce que) peut sembler apert & facile, qui est tresobscur]," it is also, according to Cardano, the "means by which things difficult to discern are grasped by our senses [par laquelle les choses sensibles difficilement sont comprises par les sens]."[26]

Subtlety is also a central concept in the writings of Francis Bacon, whose persistent triangulation of mechanical, intellectual, and political instrumentality informs the central arguments of this book. In his scientific and political writings, Bacon is preoccupied with subtlety, as Graham Rees has noted. In using the term to describe both the faults and the ideals of various intellectual methods and techniques, Bacon's repeated invocation of subtlety demonstrates the close confederacy between his scientific methodologies and his moral and political convictions. In the *Phenomena Universi*, Bacon inveighs against "chemists and the whole pack of mechanics and empirics" for "being accustomed to meticulous subtlety [accuratae subtilitas] in a few things." He objects to the use of machinery since "all the subtlety of mechanics [mechanicorum subtilitas] stops short of what I am seeking," that is, to examine "nature's recesses." Yet despite his frequent rantings against the "preposterous subtlety of argument and thought [praeposteram illam argumentorum & meditationem subtilitatem]," Bacon resorts to the same term to describe his own proposed method.[27] In the *Phenomena Universi*, Bacon seeks the "subtlety and truth of the basic information or true induction [verae Inductionis subtilitate]," and in the *Descriptio Globi Intellectualis* he refers to the "great and accurate subtlety" of his own philosophical system.[28]

Bacon's articulation of his scientific method in these early drafts for the *Instauratio Magna* oscillates between two contradictory definitions of subtlety. Subtlety can denote an empirical, highly particularized mode of scientific investigation, but it can also signify an intellectual pitfall, a "vanity" akin to the "contentious learning" that Bacon defines as the posing of "subtile, idle, unholesome, and (as I may tearme them) vermiculate questions."[29] Directed one way, subtlety reveals truth; directed another way, it obfuscates that truth. Bacon is ultimately unable either to oppose or wholly to embrace the use of machinery in his scientific method precisely because machines embody both kinds of subtlety at once. While mechanical devices correct the errors of the naked understanding, they also limit our perspicuity by tricking the senses or enabling the perception of minute distinctions that distract us from more substantial knowledge. If "mechanics . . . take small light from natural philosophy," as Bacon writes in the *Filium Labyrinthi*, "and do but spin on their own little threads," it is because they fail to recognize that the subtlety made possible by machinery produces a selective blindness even as it clarifies the minutiae of the natural world. Describing the limitations of the microscope, Bacon laments that it is "only useful for looking at very small things," permitting the scrutiny of super-subtle details at the expense of a more comprehensive and thus accurate view of nature.[30]

Bacon's conflicted attitude towards mechanical subtlety emerges most clearly in his interpretation of Daedalus in his 1609 *De Sapientia Veterum*. In the fable entitled "Daedalus, or Mechanique," Bacon interprets the Cretan engineer as an allegorical embodiment of mechanical artifice, his labyrinth symbolizing the "subtilty and divers intricate passages" of mechanical objects and practices. Pointing out that "hee which invented the intricate nooks of the Labyrinth, did also shew the commodity of the clue," Bacon represents machinery as simultaneously obfuscatory and enlightening, concluding that "Mechanicall arts are of ambiguous use, serving as well for hurt as for remedy, and they have in a manner power both to loose and bind themselves."[31] Bacon's explication of the Daedalian duplicity of mechanics in the *De Sapientia Veterum* helps to explain his ambivalent depiction of the discipline in *The New Atlantis*, where mechanical devices alternate between elucidation and deception. In the perspective-houses of Salomon's House, various "glasses and means" make eyesight "so sharp as to discern small points and lines," but they also create "all delusions and deceits of the sight." The coexistence of these two competing aspects of machinery's "subtility" helps to explain why the Bensalemites, who "hate all impostures and lies," nonetheless delight in the "false apparitions, impostures, and illusions" created by the mechanical inventions whose workings they conceal from the outside world. Even as *The New Atlantis* proposes a Utopian vision of an honest mechanics, stripped of all its dangerous subtleties, Bacon undercuts that vision by recreating the political instrumentalism of his *Essayes*, in which "an Habit of Secrecy, is both Politick, and Morall."[32]

Bacon's concerns about the "ambiguous use" of machinery inform his wider interest in weighing the legitimacy of all sorts of subtle devices, political, rhetorical, or mechanical. Drawing from Tacitus, Lipsius, and Machiavelli, Bacon's 1597 *Essayes* unfold an early version of this project to determine what constitutes justifiable dissimulation: as he puts it in "Of Simulation and Dissimulation," the *Essayes* discern "what Things are to be laid open, and what to be secretted, and what to be shewed at Halfe lights, and to whom, and when."[33] Bacon turns to natural philosophy, and in particular to mechanics, in order to ponder the justifiability and efficacy of artifice in other arenas of human action, from statecraft to gardening to the masques that he writes throughout the 1590s but later dismisses as "toyes." For Bacon, the trouble with the masque in general, and with scenic machinery in particular, is that its tricks and slights are too easily divulged. The "alterations of Scenes," he writes in "Of Masques and Triumphs," are only pleasurable if effected "quietly, and without Noise." Moreover, scene changes must tantalize their audiences with their subtle motions, "draw[ing] the Eye strangely, and mak[ing] it with great pleasure, to desire to see that, it cannot perfectly discerne."[34] The comment reveals the underlying reciprocity between mechanical, political, and intellectual subtlety that informs Bacon's work: scenic machines, if properly functioning, reinforce that quality of subtlety which knows what to reveal and what to show "at half lights." While no single chapter of this book is devoted exclusively to Bacon's attitudes towards machinery, his mutually animating understanding of mechanical, political, and intellectual subtlety forms the backbone of my argument throughout. Chapter 3 examines the sympathies between mechanical and political mediation in Bacon's works, and chapter 5 explores his use of machinery as a model for the regulatory mechanisms of scientific method as well as for the potentially deregulating effects of intellectual subtlety.

Apart from chapter 1, whose primary focus antedates most of the texts analyzed in the remainder of the study, this book has largely forfeited chronological order for considerations of argument. There are nonetheless certain transformations taking place within the century and a half covered by this book – in particular, the emergence of new philosophical and political habits of thought, collectively termed the "new humanism" by Richard Tuck and others, whose repercussions are profoundly felt in the culture's attitudes towards machinery. Yet the principal narrative motivations of this study are thematic, and the treatment of individual motifs and arguments both sequential and cyclical, so that the latent themes of each chapter emerge as the dominant concerns of the subsequent one until the culminative chapter 6, which integrates and recasts certain problems addressed by each preceding chapter.

Chapter 1 ("Automatopoesis: machinery and courtliness in Renaissance Urbino") begins in early sixteenth-century Italy, where the court-centered revival of Archimedean mechanics, with its emphasis upon the concealment of power and its attendant valorization of *facilità*, accompanies the emergence of a courtesy theory that prescribes various dissimulatory techniques as social and intellectual tools. The most pressing conflicts of early sixteenth-century Urbino, in particular the contested status of artifice, are worked out simultaneously in treatises on mechanics and in courtly, humanistic texts such as Baldassar Castiglione's *Book of the Courtier*. By challenging the sharp distinction between mathematics and mechanics made by Plato, the revival of Archimedean mechanics assists in and refracts the culture's continual reappraisal of the relationship between art and nature. A methodological confederacy between courtly and mechanical practices in Castiglione's Urbino is evident in the culture's mutually supporting definitions of *virtù* and *sprezzatura*, terms understood across both disciplines as the conquest or eradication of difficulty by means of artifice.

Chapter 2 ("Artificial motions: machinery, courtliness, and discipline in Renaissance England") traces the interpenetration of courtliness and mechanics in sixteenth- and early seventeenth-century English culture, arguing that machinery becomes a vehicle for both the clarification and interrogation of prevailing courtly ideals. The chapter begins by tracking the anxious transmission of Italianate subtlety, in its political, intellectual, and mechanical dimensions, to Tudor England through the writings of John Dee, whose work on mechanics is shaped by his contact with the Urbino mechanician Federico Commandino. Particularly from the latter half of the sixteenth century onwards, the interrelated discourses of mechanics and courtesy theory work together to cultivate a prized group of intellectual and physical qualities. Technical treatises advertise their instruments as tools of *sprezzatura*, representing the practice of mechanics as a guarantor of the *virtù* and grace crucial to success at court. While authors of handbooks on gentlemanly comportment, including Blundeville and Henry Peacham, forge analogies between mechanical and courtly subtlety, other writers of the period recognize machinery as a tool with which to implement Stoic virtues such as fortitude and constancy. Others still, motivated by their disdain for courtly artifice or their unwillingness to embrace the twin paragons of reason and discipline, regard machines as fickle, deceitful, or otherwise complicit in the perversion of normative courtly or philosophical values.

Chapter 3 ("Inanimate ambassadors: the mechanics and politics of mediation") explores machinery's capacity to exemplify and transform Renaissance humanism's understanding of the mediatory quality of knowledge and experience. The chapter argues that mechanical objects and practices both aggravate and modify concerns about the political and epistemological problems posed by the use of instruments – human or mechanical – as mediating devices. By examining the functional and thematic correspondences between machines and ambassadors in paintings (Holbein's *Ambassadors*), literary texts (Shakespeare's *Hamlet*), and cryptographic texts, this chapter demonstrates how the mediatory role of machinery reproduces and sometimes exacerbates the problems posed by political instruments, such as ambassadors, as well as those posed by the mediatory interference of our sensory instruments. From Johannes Trithemius to John Wilkins, natural philosophers look to mechanical devices to refine rhetorical and physical techniques of obliquity and secrecy, inventing ambassadorial roles for machines such as telescopes, speaking heads, and cryptographic devices. These "inanimate ambassadors," to use the term coined by Francis Godwin, both rectify and threaten the inherently faulty mediatory capacity of the human intellect as well as the equally vexed process of mediation between a ruler and his instruments. The political implications of the *nuncius inanimatus* are teased out in the travel journal of an Elizabethan organmaker to the Ottoman Empire, which describes how the performance of an automatic organ interrogates the model of a political regime dependent upon a network of human instruments.

Chapter 4 ("The polymechany of Gabriel Harvey") examines the mediatory capacity of machinery as it inflects the reading practices of the Elizabethan writer and would-be courtier Gabriel Harvey. The first part of the chapter elaborates upon the arguments launched in chapters 1 and 2, examining how Harvey regards the discipline of mechanics as a tool of courtly *sprezzatura* and of political instrumentalism. Interpreted in the context of his consumption of Italian courtesy theory and political philosophy, Harvey's reading of technical treatises informs and at times frustrates his efforts to fashion himself into a Sidneian courtier or a Burghleian *politique*. Yet Harvey's readings in contemporary mechanics also help him flesh out a different kind of instrumentalism in the form of his "polypragmatical," anti-courtly, and Ramist pedagogical program. Through extended readings of Harvey's marginalia in John Blagrave's *Mathematicall Jewell*, Geoffrey Chaucer's *Treatise on the Astrolabe*, and other texts, this chapter demonstrates how the union of book and instrument achieved by such texts assists Harvey in his attempt to cultivate "polymechany," an almalgam of virtues including political prudence, grace, pragmatism, and technical skill.

Like chapter 4, chapter 5 ("Homer in a nutshell: George Chapman and the mechanics of perspicuity") demonstrates how machinery reshapes the interpretive strategies of Renaissance readers by inculcating intellectual virtues such as subtlety and perspicuity. Focusing on the Homeric translations of George Chapman, the first part of this chapter argues that Chapman's cultivation of a "deep-searching" reader is informed and rivaled by the mechanical devices designed by Thomas Hariot and Robert Hues, two early readers of Chapman's translation of the *Iliad*. Hariot's telescopes and Hues' globes provide Chapman with models to articulate and revise his own conception of the relationship between readers and texts, particularly those texts, such as Chapman's own, which are self-consciously and deliberately obscure. The second half of the chapter examines how the technical virtuosity required by minutiae such as the "Iliad in a Nutshell" reproduces and amplifies the challenges encountered by Chapman and by other Renaissance readers and translators of Homer's texts. Like Chapman's Homer, whose ideal reader is the "perfect eye" of Hariot's telescope, mechanical and rhetorical subtleties demand similarly Lyncean critical strategies, techniques alternately prized and mocked by the era's defenders and excoriators of subtlety.

Chapter 6 ("Inhumanism: Spenser's iron man") unites and reformulates the problems of earlier chapters by exploring the far-reaching implications of some of the cultural fantasies and anxieties attendant upon Renaissance automata and war machinery. The chapter argues that Talus, Artegall's iron groom in Book v of *The Faerie Queene*, is one of a number of devices employed by Spenser in order to articulate and (at times) challenge the militaristic ideals espoused by Essex and his circle in the 1590s, as well as the oft-accompanying Stoic fantasy of imperturbability. Talus' hard body and his insensibility externalize Spenser's apprehensions about the "stonie philosophie," concerns which also manifest themselves in Book v's insistent focus upon tactile experience and upon the mollifying effects of mercy and passion both in war and by law. While attractive to Spenser on account of his capacity for physical and emotional distantiation, Talus nonetheless challenges the moral legitimacy and the efficacy of mechanical warfare, and in his robotic fits of frenzied violence he wreaks havoc upon Renaissance humanism's central assumption that the human is a distinct and privileged ontological category. By incarnating the appeals and the dangers of Stoic imperturbability and of Essexian militarism in Talus' cyborg frame, Spenser offers a glimpse into the moral and spiritual consequences of eradicating the distinctions between humanity and its machinery.

Machinery's discursive and material intervention into the intellectual conflicts of Renaissance culture accompanies the emergence of the so-called "new humanism" of the sixteenth century, a composite of political and philosophical attitudes including (according to Glenn Burgess' formula) Machiavellianism, neo-Stoicism, Taciteanism, and what Smuts terms "court-centered politics." Interested primarily in "techniques of political manipulation," many new humanist writers seek to vindicate dissimulation and deceit as profitable political tools, placing a "disenchanted, even cynical, emphasis on political instrumentality."[35] Inasmuch as it provides a tangible model for that instrumentality and an imaginative framework for debating its efficacy, machinery often corroborates, and sometimes disturbs, the most cherished orthodoxies of the new humanism.

The majority of English writers studied in this book can be linked to one or more of the intellectual communities which grow up around Robert Dudley, Earl of Leicester, Robert Devereux, Earl of Essex, and Henry Percy, ninth Earl of Northumberland. The keen interest in machinery shared by all of these men, and by many of their followers, is as central an ingredient of their new humanist alignment as is their admiration for Tacitean historiography or for the Stoicism of Lipsius.[36] At least on the surface, the study of mechanics harmonizes with new humanism's emphasis upon discipline, action, materiality, and the harnesssing of natural forces by means of *virtù*.

Yet for those writers not fully committed to the canons of the new human-ism or its classical models (Tacitus, Seneca, Plutarch), machinery also offers a means to dispute the viability of Stoic philosophy or to critique the arts of political deception prescribed by some, if not all, of the neo-Taciteans.[37]

Despite the seemingly broad scope of the writers studied in this book, virtually every Elizabethan and Jacobean writer addressed in the ensuing chapters shares intellectual and political sympathies with the Leicester–Sidney circle, with Essex's secretariat, or with Percy's so-called "school of night." George Chapman, Francis Bacon, Ben Jonson, Henry Savile, and Robert Johnson are all followers, employees, or acquaintances of Essex. Gabriel Harvey, who is friendly with Sidney, also spends a brief time in Leicester's service, while Dee and Spenser are each acquainted with both Leicester and Essex. Christopher Marlowe, Walter Ralegh, and Thomas Hariot each revolve, at various times, in one of the diverse constellations of Henry Percy's circle, while Samuel Daniel, Chapman, and Bacon straddle the intellectual and political sympathies of both Essex and Percy.[38]

While each of these writers responds differently to the moral and political exigencies of mechanical artifice, many of them are immersed, to varying degrees, in an Essexian culture of subtlety which looks to mechanics as a means of harnessing and deploying the powers of *metis* to their greatest advantage. Like Leicester, who proves an important sponsor of technical texts and projects in England and Holland during the 1570s and 1580s, Essex studies mechanics with many of the most prominent Elizabethan mechani-cians, including John Dee, Thomas Digges, and Hariot. Both Leicester and Essex regard machinery as a guarantor of military might, moral discipline, and also, perhaps, of political artifice. Insofar as mechanics, unlike mathe-matics, is based upon the study of material causes and their tangible effects, the discipline offers a symbolic legitimation of political secrecy, thus sup-porting the Tacitean attitudes that inform late Elizabethan historiography as well as the notion of the *arcana imperii* central to Jacobean political philos-ophy. Technical and scholarly works composed by followers of Essex, from William Bourne's *Inventions or devises* to Bacon's 1597 *Essayes* and Savile's translations of Tacitus, foreground problems of political instrumentality by yoking their inquisition into secrets of state to the mechanical investigation of the secrets of nature.

Unlike his brother-in-law Essex, Henry Percy's interest in mechanics is closely tethered to his interest in the occult sciences, but it is also informed by his philosophical attitudes, particularly his adherence to a Lipsian neo-Stoicism that regards machinery as a symbol of right reason and as therapy for the Stoic sage. Discussed at the end of chapter 2, Percy's devotion to mechanics, particularly to Archimedes' work on equilibrium, is motivated by his belief in its applicability to Stoic values such as resistance to adversity and mitigating the deleterious effects of the passions. Writing to his son in around 1609, Percy urges him to study astronomy, geometry, and "the doctrine of the motion of optics" since these disciplines produce a "well-fashioned mind . . . free from perturbations and unseemly affections."[39] Mechanics can cultivate the *apatheia* necessary to combat adversity, and it can strengthen the internal regulatory mechanisms of the aspiring Stoic – so much so that, in around 1606, Percy recalls having overcome his desire for a mistress by "working through the optical demonstrations of Alhazen," an Arab physicist studied by his friend Hariot.[40]

The remainder of this introduction exposes the logic according to which sixteenth-century political writers, including Bacon, Jean Bodin, and Justus Lipsius, enlist mechanical objects or practices in their efforts to formulate attitudes towards artifice and instrumentality. Often by reworking familiar mechanical metaphors used by Aristotle and Plutarch, these and other writers ground political, moral, and epistemological instrumentalities in mechanical exempla or otherwise analogize the relationship between mechanical operations and political virtues such as prudence.

Lipsius and Bacon each look to machinery to ponder the validity and efficacy of their own political and moral philosophies. What Richard Tuck calls the "cool instrumentalism" of Bacon's 1597 *Essayes* is complemented by the young Bacon's belief in machinery's capacity to lay bare the secrets of nature and to correct the errors of our senses. In 1605, Bacon calls for men to abandon their books in favor of furnaces, "quitting and forsaking *Minerva*, and the Muses, as barreyne virgines, and relying upon *Vulcan*," whose underground laboratory epitomizes experimentation and practice. "Bookes be not onely the Instrumentals," Bacon continues, for there also exist "Sphaeres, Globes, Astrolabes, Mappes," and other "appurtenances . . . as well as bookes." According to *The Advancement of Learning*, the value of "instrumentals" in scientific inquiry is analogous to, and even dependent upon, a political instrumentalism reliant upon spies and similar mediatory instruments. Indeed, Bacon argues that no progress will be made by natural philosophy without undertaking "experiments appertaining to Vulcanus or *Dedalus*, Furnace or Engyne . . . therefore as Secretaries, and Spyalls of Princes and States bring in Bills for Intelligence; so you must allowe the Spyalls and Intelligencers of Nature, to bring in their Billes, or else you shall be ill advertised."[41]

Bacon's implicit analogy between mechanical and human instruments derives from Aristotle's discussion of the instrumental relationship between master and servant in Book 1 of his *Politics*: "of tools some are lifeless and others living; for example, for the helmsman [κυβερνoσ] the rudder is a lifeless tool and the look-out man a live tool . . . so also an instrument is a tool for the purpose of life . . . and a servant is a living instrument."[42] Using the term opγανον (organ, instrument) to denote both living and lifeless tools, Aristotle's analogy between political and mechanical instrumentality has far-reaching, conflictive implications for Renaissance culture. While the correlation between mechanical and human instruments can legitimate the one by means of the other, it can also interrogate the immediacy and the reliability of instrumental relationships. As Aristotle points out, automatic machinery both perfects and supersedes the master–servant relationship by eliminating the need for explicit command: "if every instrument could accomplish its own work, like the statues of Daedalus, or the tripods of Hephaestus . . . master craftsmen would not need servants, nor masters slaves."[43] The analogy between human and mechanical instruments is thus a precarious one: Daedalus' self-moving statues possess so unmediated a relationship to their creator's will that they threaten to erode the mutually constitutive relationship between Aristotle's κυβερνoσ, or governor, and his cybernetic assistants.

Plutarch also uses mechanical metaphors to articulate a qualified justi-fication of political instrumentalism. In an essay of the *Moralia* entitled "Precepts of Policie," Plutarch compares fawning courtiers, as they "winde and insinuate themselves into the favour of kings and princes," to the snares of cunning fowlers: "As for the flatterers that belong to Princes courts, they play by their lords and masters, as those fowlers do, who catch their birds by a pipe counterfeiting their voices."[44] Even as Plutarch uses a technical metaphor to denounce court flatterers, he also imagines good counselors as the "lively tooles, and sensible instruments of governors" and likens governors in turn to the "carpenter or mason" who must carefully use the "plumbs, levels, and rules" assembled around him. Like Daedalus' self-moving devices, which both epitomize and imperil instrumental means, Plutarch's analogy exposes the danger of relying upon instruments which might "make [one's] work rise crooked and out of square." As "sensible instruments" which may be used well or ill, counselors expose the fragile contingency of a political instrumentalism dependent upon unstable or subjective external measures.[45]

During the sixteenth century, Aristotle's and Plutarch's mechanical metaphors for government and self-government are actualized as princes and courtiers collect and study mechanical devices in the hope of hon-ing the instrumentalism upon which contemporary courtly and political practices are often predicated. Rulers widely divergent in their policies are united by their belief in the applicability of mechanics not only to military endeavors but also to the temper of political interactions and intellectual methods.[46] By sponsoring technical treatises, collecting instruments, and employing machinery in court spectacles, statesmen including Emperor Charles V, King James I, and Lord Burghley reveal their awareness that machinery clarifies and justifies political instrumentalism by reproducing and testing out its principles in palpable form.

At the same time, writers including Nashe, Chapman, and Spenser look to machinery in order to meditate upon the exigencies of court life or to question the viability of prevailing political ideals. Other writers come to regard machinery as a resource for self-government, enlisting mechanics as a metaphor or an actual tool for the discipline central to both the Platonic and Stoic impulses of sixteenth-century humanism. Ramus, Harvey, and Savile all stress the pedagogical utility of mechanics in privileging action and practice over the pursuit of theoretical knowledge. For each of these writers, engines and devices offer an encoded language of critique capable of probing, obliquely, humanism's most urgent political and intellectual concerns or of exposing the inadequacy of its most commonplace assumptions.

In his study of Justus Lipsius, Gerhard Oestreich argues that "technical and practical sciences" such as mechanics and navigation typify the methodological presuppositions of the new humanism embraced by Lipsius and his generation.[47] Nowhere is this better illustrated than on the title-page of Lipsius' 1637 *Opera Omnia*, engraved by Peter Rubens: on the viewer's right, a personification of Politics holds a rudder and spear and balances a globe upon her knee. Flanking her are Virtue and Prudence, and beneath the center arch are battering rams and other Roman war machinery, an allusion to Lipsius' *De Militia Romana* and his 1596 *Poliorceticon*. In the latter of these volumes, Lipsius anticipates the title-page of his posthumous *Opera Omnia* by promising his reader that the treatise on mechanics will draw his genius towards inspiration, making it sharper and more subtle ("ductu aetherii tui ingenii, acrioribus istis & subtilioribus").[48] The study of mechanical devices, which are "artificial, subtle, and tricky things [rem illepidam, subtilem, aut tricosam]," not only improves military strategy but also exercises political and intellectual subtlety, qualities prized by Lipsius and exemplified by his favorite Roman historian, the "subtilitate" Tacitus.[49]

Lipsius' correlation between political and mechanical subtlety reveals his recognition of the interdependence between physical and ethical theory. According to Jason Saunders, natural philosophy provides Lipsius with a "necessary foundation for valid moral theory." Like Percy, Lipsius regards mechanics as a guarantor of Stoic virtues in that it frees the mind from trivial concerns and grants us a moral discipline that arises out of our recognition of a rational and ordered universe.[50] In this respect, Lipsius' attitude towards mechanics anticipates the rise of the mechanical philosophy, which, according to Steven Shapin, "discipline[s] the production of knowledge . . . [by] managing or eliminating the effects of human passions and interests."[51]

Often perceived as possessing a "protoscientific" quality by many of their Renaissance readers, the writings of Tacitus are yoked to attitudes towards mechanics during the period. The Roman historian's rational investigation of the "causal mechanisms" lurking behind historical events inspires what Oestreich calls the "scientific treatment of practical politics" in the latter half of the sixteenth century, challenging the providentialist historiography of earlier writers.[52] Sixteenth-century responses to Tacitus regularly note the historian's disinterestedness and his objectivity, qualities which might alternately be construed as reliable or untrustworthy, since, as Guicciardini remarks, Tacitus' writings contain prudent advice for those living under tyranny but also teach "tyrants ways to secure their tyranny."[53] In his 1612 *I Ragguagli di Parnasso*, the Italian political satirist Traiano Boccalini imagines Tacitus' potentially hostile attitude towards the preservation of *arcana* in explicitly mechanical terms, presenting the historian as the inventor of a pair of "politick spectacles" that reveal to their users the "secret thoughts" of princes and their "tricks of government."[54] At the end of Boccalini's account, however, Apollo resolves to limit the use of these spectacles to "choice personages" such as secretaries and counselors, thus demonstrating the two-handed nature of a political instrumentalism capable of either unmasking or compounding the deceit and secrecy upon which political authority relies.

If Tacitus' writings possess a mechanistic quality, it is altogether different from the theoretical certainty offered by the Euclidean proof, with its appeal to abstract, universal truths, that later helps Grotius or Hobbes fabricate a "mathematics of politics" in which "all natural events obey the same invariable laws."[55] Instead, Tacitus' brand of scientific outlook stresses the close observation of material, circumstantial reality – a practical, experimental method whose strongest kinship is not with mathematics but with mechanics and other applied sciences. As a consequence, machinery becomes complicit, for some Renaissance readers, in Tacitus' complex legitimation of artifice by concretizing the justifiability of using instruments (political or mechanical) to enforce – or to counter – policy and deceit. In another episode, Boccalini's princes of Parnassus appeal to the legitimacy of the *arcana imperii* by means of a Plutarchian analogy between mechanical and political instruments, arguing that "if Tailors for the cutting out and making up of clothes, were allowed needle and sheers; and Smiths, hammers and pincers," then rulers should be allowed to "throw dust in their Subjects eyes, or cast a mist before them, which was . . . the most necessary instrument for the right Government of States."[56]

For many late sixteenth-century writers, the circumstantial nature of political knowledge strengthens its affinities with the discipline of mechanics. According to Plutarch's *Moralia*, politics must "intermedle with casualties" and is thus distinct from geometry with its unchanging rules. The geometrician knows that a triangle always has three sides, whereas the politician, like the mechanician, deals with "things that varie and alter . . . and never medleth with those that be firme, stable, and immutable." Whereas the geometer enlists his "contemplative facultie" to understand "first and principall things," politics demands the faculty of prudence, which "descendeth to things full of varietie, error, trouble, and confusion."[57]

Plutarch's understanding of prudence as the intellectual faculty that governs the contingent sphere of human events explains why so many sixteenth- and early seventeenth-century writers treat politics and mechanics as sister arts united by their shared resistance to the ethereal realm of theoretical knowledge. His world lacking in the certitude of Hobbes' later vision of a quasi-geometrical state of nature, the sixteenth-century *homo politicus* must be sensitive to continual fluctuation and nuance. With its ability to rationalize and to predict the variable responses of tangible matter in changing circumstances, the practice of mechanics assures a degree of certainty even in the most conditional of political environments. In his 1577 *General and Rare Memorials*, John Dee offers "(*almost*) a Mathematical demonstration . . . for a faesable Policy" – almost, because Dee recognizes that policy can never be as predictable as the certain world of geometry. While Dee calls the text a "Plat Politicall," he demonstrates the close coupling of prudence and technical skill in the late sixteenth-century imagination by referring to himself throughout the work as a "mechanician" and advertising on its opening page a new navigational instrument or "paradoxall compass."[58]

When Edward Dacres introduces his translation of Machiavelli's *Discourses Upon Livy* in 1641, he compares the author to an "approved and experienced Mariner" and his text to a "sea-card" that will "serve for your experience . . . whereby you may become able and expert, as well in the entrances and passages into all creeks and harbors of quiet, as in the discovery and avoidance of all rocks and shelves."[59] Dacres' sea-card, like the rudders, compasses, and other navigational instruments so frequently invoked by Lipsius and Bodin, symbolizes the *virtù* and prudence required to endure the mutable whims of a Machiavellian political world. Unlike the eternally three-sided triangle of Plutarch's geometer, the objects measured by mechanical and navigational instruments are in perpetual flux.

In particular, sixteenth-century Ramists and military humanists regard mechanics as a guarantor of prudence, intellectual pragmatism, and, above all, method. Thomas Digges writes to the Earl of Leicester in the dedication of his 1579 *Stratioticos* that his work aims at "reducing the Sciences mathematicall from Demonstrative Contemplations, to Experimental Actions."[60] Digges admits that he formerly took delight in "searching the most difficult and curious Demonstrations Mathematicall" but subsequently resolved to "reduce . . . those Imaginative contemplations, to sensible Practicall Conclusions" for the service of "my Prince and Countrie." For Digges, mathematical demonstrations only serve the real business of war and navigation insofar as they can be reduced, or converted, into practical knowledge. Digges models his pursuit of "practicall conclusions" after the tools of pilots and mariners, whose "Charts and Instruments true and infallible" expose Digges' once-cherished mathematical theories as "pretie devises" and "meere toyes," the product of "land mans reason" rather than the sailor's prudence and experience.[61]

As the intellectual faculty which governs the knowledge of "unstable and wavering things," prudence is often explicated through mechanical exempla. In his *Six Bookes of Politickes*, Lipsius compares the "guiding rule" of prudence to the carpenter's "plum[m]et & the square" and to the "needle that hath touched the Load-stone," or mariner's compass.[62] In a fluctuating political atmosphere where "limitted and certaine" precepts offer no help, mechanical instruments such as compasses promise to inculcate the Protean adaptability that is the cornerstone of prudence and Machiavellian *virtù*.[63] While Lipsius, Bodin, Dee, and Digges seize upon the capacity of mechanical devices to systematize and measure contingency, thus yoking the study of mechanics to Machiavellian political virtues such as adaptability and flexibility, other writers lump mechanics and "politicke Philosophie" together in order to launch a joint critique of what Fulke Greville scornfully terms the "instrumentall following arts." Complaining in his *Treatie of Humane Learning* that nothing "can be certaine" in political philosophy, Greville compares the fashionable political instrumentalism of the era to "things of Mechanicall condition" in that both disciplines "force their bodies out of native parts . . . / And not so perfect Nature, but delude." Though both disciplines deal in the "trafficke of humanity," mechanics and politics are nonetheless limited in their practical value. Greville concludes that he "who too long in their cobwebs lurks, / Doth like him that buys tooles, but never workes."[64] Mocking the widespread fetishizing of practice and experience, Boccalini likewise satirizes the commonplace analogy between political prudence and technical aptitude by hypothesizing the construction of a "sailing card" designed to help men avoid the "deplorable wracks, which [they] so often suffer in the Courts of great Princes." Incapable of gauging the "giddy humour of a selfe-conceited Prince" or the "irregular" and "voluble" movements of court flatterers and parasites, the device malfunctions because it is insufficiently sensitive to calibrate the "retrograde motions" of beings "perpetually turned and gired about" by passion and self-interest.[65]

Yet for most sixteenth- and early seventeenth-century writers, the discipline of mechanics cultivates political virtues such as prudence and flexibility by enforcing the conviction that the validity of any theory (political or mechanical) depends upon its ability to account for the ever-changing circumstances of the material world. For many such writers, prudence, or the ability to adapt to changing circumstances, is most effective if accompanied by the ability to maintain an internal equilibrium despite changing circumstances. With apparent disregard for the difficulty of reconciling Stoic resolve with protean flexibility, Renaissance writers often depict constancy and adaptability as complementary skills contingent upon one another. In *The Book of the Courtier*, elasticity is a key virtue, for the courtier must accommodate himself to the whims of his prince and shape himself to the ever-changing demands of decorum. Yet while the courtier must demonstrate a chameleon-like versatility, he must also preserve an internal consistency, a "steadfastnesse and pacyence, abidinge with a quiet and untroubled minde all the strokes of fortune."[66] These oxymoronic demands for a constancy-in-change and a versatile steadfastness are fulfilled by the machinery of Renaissance court spectacle – the stage machines, clocks, and perpetual motion machines that are both steady and responsive to change. When contemporary observers describe the movements of a perpetual motion presented to King James I by the Dutch engineer Cornelius Drebbel in 1612, they remark upon its constancy and also upon its "ebb and flow," the way in which it "waxes and wanes" and yet still "turn[s] without ceasing, as long as the world exist[s]."[67]

Constancy and flexibility are two of the many courtly virtues attributed to machinery by Renaissance writers. In his *Novum Organum*, Bacon imagines machinery as the apotheosis of *disinvoltura* in that it both mimics and assists in the effortless display crucial to success at court. Alluding, perhaps, to the 1585 competition instigated by Pope Sixtus V to design a machine capable of moving a large Egyptian obelisk, Bacon compares the intellectual method of his Instauration to a hoisting machine: "let us suppose some enormous obelisk for the decoration of a triumph or similar splendid occasion had to be moved from its place, and men tried to do this with their bare hands, would not any sober-minded spectator think this the height of folly?" Like the engineer who supplements his "bare hands" with the "powerful assistance of instruments," the "bare force of [the] mind" must also be supplemented by the intellectual instruments of method. Implicit in Bacon's analogy is the idea that both the hoisting device and his own *organon* rely upon the diligent nonchalance of the courtier in order to mitigate the appearance of human effort. In the process of defining intellectual method as a species of *sprezzatura*, Bacon offers a qualified approval of courtly dissimulation: by effacing its own traces of effort, machinery perfects the art of concealing art, banishing the affectation that is the result of "senseless effort."[68]

Bacon's stated goal in the *Novum Organum* is to transform the "whole operation of the mind" so that "the thing [is] accomplished as if by machinery."[69] Yet what, exactly, does it mean to perform something "as if by machinery" according to Bacon? Like Dee's concept of "Menadrie," which defines mechanical power as a species of courtly *facilità*, Bacon regards mechanical operations as models of intellectual method and grace. In "Of Fortune," Bacon defines *disinvoltura*, or disengagement, in terms of the well-oiled gears of a machine, explaining that it thrives "when there be not Stonds, nor Restivenesse in a Mans Nature; But that the wheeles of his Minde keepe way, with the wheeles of his *Fortune*."[70] Motivated by a courtly aesthetic that privileges kinematic grace and regularity, Renaissance descriptions of machinery often serve the function of praising – or caricaturing – court culture. In *The Unfortunate Traveller*, Thomas Nashe's Jack Wilton visits an Italian pleasure garden containing artificial stars "in their proper orbs [which] observed their circular wheelings and turnings," as well as counterfeit songbirds whose artificiality exaggerates and mocks Italianate courtliness.[71] Emerging alongside the etiquette dictating specific rules of comportment for the human body, Renaissance culture's discursive attention to the elegant motions of machinery grafts the kinematic and behavioral standards of the Renaissance courtesy treatise onto the machinery of court spectacle. Contrary to Christopher Hill's argument that there is an aristocratic disdain for mechanics before the middle of the seventeenth century, there is abundant evidence of a courtly enthusiasm for mechanical objects, at least those capable of being invested with fitting aesthetic and social values.[72]

In addition to providing working models for the rules of physical decorum set down by courtesy treatises, machines also provide symbolic and actual models for the moral and intellectual discipline prized both within and outside of the court. In Elizabethan and Jacobean England, a number of writers test out various ethical principles through their study of mechanics. Emphasizing an "indifference to and imperturbability in the face of the events of the unknowable external world," many neo-Stoic writers imagine machines as tangible prototypes for the proper control of the passions, for constancy, or for temperance.[73] Robert Johnson and Thomas Wright both turn to mechanical metaphors in order to legitimate – and to complicate – the moral validity of a strict, Stoic rule of reason. In an essay entitled "Of Discretion" in his 1607 *Essaies; or, Rather imperfect offers*, Johnson stresses the importance of an "inward moderation, by which al disordinate passions and irregular motions, are subjected to the rule of reason." At the end of the essay, Johnson concludes that "a man must rule his affections, and make reason like another Automedon to direct them" so that he may resist pride and "other such unjust rebellions of passion."[74] Yet while Johnson imagines an automaton as a model for the government of the affections by right reason, another machine supplies him with a powerful metaphor for the dangers of intellectual subtlety. In "Of Wit," Johnson cautions against "a witte too pregnant and sharpe" like the "working and craftie witte" of Tiberius, the master dissimulator of Tacitus' *Annals*. Such excessive subtlety, Johnson argues, demands "precise" discipline lest those who practice it "sort to no end, being like the clocke which most artificiously composed, is soonest disordered, and put out of frame."[75] One machine offers symbolic resistance against the upheavals of passion, exemplifying consummate self-discipline. The other provides an ominous warning about the dangers of dissimulation and the crafty, unreliable nature of human wit.

Thomas Wright expresses a similarly conflicted attitude towards the moral and epistemological integrity of machinery in his 1604 *The Passions of the Minde in General*. Wright begins by urging the "civil gentleman, and prudent politician" to "bridle" his passions and restrain the "inordinate motions" of his affections. Chastising those who are "over-ruled" by their passions, Wright observes that "a man had need of an astrolabe always to see in what height or elevation his affections are, lest, by casting forth a spark of his fire, his gun-powdered minde of a sudden bee inflamed."[76] Like Johnson's automaton, Wright's astrolabe represents the rational, self-sufficient restraint comprised by the Stoic ideal of *apatheia*, or by the tight

rein of reason over the passions demanded by Plato's *Phaedrus*.[77] Yet for
Wright, machinery exemplifies the deceptive sway of human affection even
as it also symbolizes right reason's capacity to temper our passions. He
compares the distorting effects of the affections upon our judgment to
as "when the eyes are troubled, we cannot perceive exactly the objects of
our sight," and then extends the comparison, likening the passions "to
greene spectacles, which make all things resemble the colour of greene."[78]
By invoking the mediatory intervention of spectacles in order to explain
how passions muddy our understanding, Wright diverges radically from
his own conviction concerning the intrinsic rationality of machinery, an
attitude that emerges out of his depiction of the astrolabe as a metaphor for
rational self-government. When invoked as agents of illusion, devices such
as spectacles are capable of confirming skeptical and Stoic concerns about
the mutiny of the passions or the deceitfulness of the senses. Yet spectacles
also foster fantasies about the elimination of sensory deception, as they do –
sort of – in Jan van der Straet's "Conspicilla," an engraving depicting the
invention of eyeglasses from his 1580 *Nova Reperta*, a series of engravings
celebrating recent technological discoveries. Invoking a Pauline opposition
between the dark glass of mortal vision and the acute (in)sight afforded by
eternal life, the engraving boasts that lenses have wiped the illusions from
people's eyes: "eyeglasses were invented, which remove dark veils from
the eyes [inventa conspicilla sunt, quae luminum obscuriores detegunt
caligines]." Yet despite their ubiquitous spectacles, van der Straet's figures
struggle to see: in the right foreground, a man holds a book only inches
from his face, while in the background, another man stumbles along with
a cane. Even as spectacles strip away falsehoods, making man see clearly
and impartially, they also compound the illusions to which man is already
subject, perpetuating the very epistemological concerns they promise to
eradicate. In an apt malapropism, a character in Ben Jonson's *News from
the New World Discovered in the Moon* refers to telescopes as "perplexive
glasses," instruments that distort and confuse as well as clarify. As Bacon
also recognizes, machines are of "ambiguous use" to Renaissance culture,
serving alternately as "hurt" and as "remedy" in resolving the culture's most
urgent conflicts and questions.[79]

CHAPTER I

Automatopoesis: machinery and courtliness in Renaissance Urbino

> Method and practice . . . are entirely within our control. We see every
> day how engineering skill and machinery can raise weights which oth-
> erwise could not have been moved by any force; this feat demonstrates
> the power of method.
>
> Desiderius Erasmus, *De pueris instituendis*[1]

In the late fifteenth- and early sixteenth-century Urbino courts of Federico
and Guidobaldo da Montefeltro, the emergence of a new and powerful discourse of court etiquette accompanies the revival of Archimedean mechanics, a discipline whose methodologies and intellectual concerns are closely
allied with some of the aesthetic and philosophical principles endorsed by
The Book of the Courtier. By examining Castiglione's courtesy theory within
the intellectual context of the court culture which produced it, this chapter
explores how Renaissance machinery privileges a courtly etiquette predicated upon the concealment of difficulty, helping to define the seductive
ideals of grace and *sprezzatura*.

In his *Nova Iconologia*, Cesare Ripa depicts *Artifitio*, or Artifice, as an ele-
gantly dressed courtier whose right hand rests upon an *Argano*, or winch,
while his left hand gestures towards a hive of bees (figure 1.1). According to the emblem, Artifice is sustained by a precarious balance between
effort, represented by the beehive, and ingenuity or ease, represented by
the winch. Ripa explains that the mechanical device, which consists of a
horizontal axle around which a chain passes in order to hoist large objects,
symbolizes the courtier's ability to do very difficult things with little effort
("le faccende difficillissime con poco sforzo mandate a fine").[2] Since the
winch "vanquishes . . . nature [vince . . . la natura]," Ripa argues that it
illustrates the principles set down by the pseudo-Aristotelian *Mechanical
Problems*, which "teaches us that we may by way of art triumph over those
things in which we are opposed by nature [che noi per via dell'arte superi-
amo quelle cose alle quali par che repugni la natura stessa della cosa]."[3]

Iconologia di Cef. Ripā
A R T I F I T I O.

1.1 Cesare Ripa, *Nova Iconologia*, "Artifitio"

While a hoisting device might seem an unlikely symbol for courtly artifice, Renaissance courtesy texts often define qualities such as *facilità* and
sprezzatura in the same terms as the *Mechanical Problems*: as the effortless
resolution of difficulty. The *Mechanical Problems* defines a machine as anything which "assists difficulties to produce an effect contrary to nature," a
definition which privileges the same art of concealment prescribed by *The
Book of the Courtier's* demand that the courtier "use in every thyng a certain
Reckelesness [*sprezzatura*], to cover art withall, and seeme whatsoever he
doth and sayeth to do it wythout pain, and (as it were) not myndyng it."
Only complete facility, or the appearance thereof, yields grace: any trace of
laboriousness results in affectation (*affetazione*), that "daungerous rock" of
studied display avoided only by executing every gesture with the confident
indifference of a machine.[4]

Operating with "little force," Ripa's mechanical *Artifitio* provides a working model for courtly dissimulation, unfolding an alliance between courtiership and mechanics based upon their mutual repudiation of effort: "to use
force," Castiglione observes of the ideal courtier, "geveth a great disgrace,
and maketh every thing how great so ever it be, to be litle estemed."[5] By
representing artifice as the mitigation of difficulty by mechanical means,
Ripa's *Artifice* redefines grace and *sprezzatura* as techniques exemplified by
the machinery of Renaissance court spectacle – the hoisting machines and
other instruments of theatrical illusion that permit the easy resolution of difficulties. In its recreations as well as in more intellectually serious endeavors
to cultivate technical virtuosity, Renaissance court culture employs various
machines, from astronomical instruments to hydraulic garden machinery,
to inculcate a group of intellectual and physical strategies crucial to the
"civil engineering" of its subjects.[6] The practice of mechanics cultivates
the *actuezza*, or sharpness of wit, privileged by courtesy literature, while
mechanical devices themselves are perceived as infused with *ingegno* (wit;
engine), an inventive spirit which grants them their motive power.

Henri de Monantheuil, court mathematician to Henri IV of France,
writes in the preface to his 1599 translation of the pseudo-Aristotelian
Mechanical Problems that the universe is "a machine . . . the most powerful,
practical, and elegant contrivance of all time."[7] That machines offer idealized, if not slightly absurd, models of graceful contrivance for the princes
and courtiers who view and collect them does not escape keener spectators
such as Johannes Kepler, who upon visiting Rudolf II's Prague *Kunstkammer*
in 1598 is struck by an automaton in the form of a "drummer who beat his
drum with greater self-assurance than a live one."[8] Kepler's reaction demonstrates how perfectly a machine might realize the "not regarded agylitie and

slighte conveyaunce" demanded of Castiglione's ideal courtier.[9] The spring-driven limbs of Rudolf II's automata inspire Kepler to build mechanical models of the cosmos and to conclude that the "machine of the universe is not similar to a divine animated being, but similar to a clock" which moves by gears and wheels rather than by a soul.[10]

Renaissance machinery supplies its courtly audience with kinematic and moral fantasies of the consummate control of "motions" – a complicated term in the sixteenth century that denotes puppets and automata but also human gestures and emotions, the former easily regulated and the latter not so easily. In an effort to control human motions, both corporeal and affective, Renaissance courtesy theory draws upon Platonic and Stoic philosophies of self-discipline, as well as Ciceronian ideals of decorum. It also turns to machinery as both a metaphor for and a literal realization of this self-discipline – an emblem, albeit a strange, problematic one, for what Erasmus, in the above epigraph, calls the "power of method." As Wayne Rebhorn has observed, to manifest *sprezzatura* "is to imply scorn for normal, human limitations [and] physical necessities," and for many Renaissance writers, machinery epitomizes the discipline necessary to transcend the physical limitations that hinder one's opportunities at court. In his pedagogical writings, which emphasize the regulatory process of civility in limiting natural impulses, Erasmus looks to trained animals and to machines in order to assert how easily one can accomplish seemingly difficult and unnatural tasks: just as "an Elephant maye be taught to walke upon corde, [or] a beare to daunce . . . we see daylye, burdens to be lyft up by engins and arte, which otherwyse could bee moved by no strength."[11] Machines and trained animals are popular features of Renaissance court spectacle for precisely this reason: they corroborate the ultimate courtly fantasy in which artifice vanquishes and conceals the defects of nature.

While hoisting machines supply Erasmus and Ripa with models of effortless display and corporeal restraint, machinery does not represent the "power of method" cultivated by texts such as the *De Pueris Instituendis* in a monolithic or unconflicted way. While machines provide models for self-control, this chapter and the one that follows argue that mechanical devices also warn against the perils of too much self-control, cautionary emblems for the hyper-artificiality repudiated by sixteenth-century courtesy literature. In their actual use and in their imagined status, machinery and mechanics arbitrate Urbino's conflictive attitudes towards the political and intellectual instrumentalism of court culture. Some of the most cynical moments in *The Book of the Courtier* directly liken the courtier to an instrument, as when Lord Octavian compares the courtier to a "whettstone," a tool "which cutteth not a whitt" yet can "make a toole sharpe." The comparison suggests that the ideal courtier should act not according to his own will but rather according to that of his "toole," or prince, thus making the "ende of this Courtier . . . harde and somtime unpossible."[12] Even as machines exemplify courtly *sprezzatura*, they likewise convey anxieties about the instrumental nature of those courtly practices which demand the regulation of natural impulses by artificial means. Courtesy theory and mechanics work together to reconfigure cultural attitudes towards the political and corporeal instrumentalism upon which courtiership is predicated, as well as towards the "instrumentalities [παρασκευν]" scorned by Plato – the means, methods, and machines that the intellectual and scientific culture of Castiglione's Urbino labors to accommodate to its flexibly constituted Platonism.[13] In other words, the Archimedean revival of mechanics is a project that aims to make the courtly, Platonic humanism of early sixteenth-century Urbino comfortable with its own instrumentality.

Interpreted by some readers as "escapist," "idyllic," or a "kind of Utopia," and by others as a "pragmatic – even cynical – manual for survival in a treacherous age," *The Book of the Courtier* alternately effaces and underscores the political and physical instrumentalism of the ideal courtier as well as the instrumental quality of its own aims and methods as a didactic text.[14] Combining a Platonic hostility to method with the pragmatism of a how-to guide to court etiquette, *The Book of the Courtier* oscillates between idealism and instrumentalism and between pedagogical opacity and transparency, as Lauro Martines and Eduardo Saccone have pointed out.[15] Even as it playfully syncretizes these disparate tempers, *The Book of the Courtier* is uncomfortable with both, for no sooner does one interlocutor delineate a systematic method for cultivating courtliness, but another undermines or mocks it. As Pietro Bembo finishes his idealized discourse on love, his listeners declare his route to transcendence impassable: Lord Gonzaga maintains that the ladder by which one ascends to purely spiritual love is "so stiepe . . . that it will be much a do to gete to it," and Gaspar agrees that it would be "harde to gete up for men," and "unpossible for women."[16]

The earliest readers of Castiglione's dialogue are puzzled by the text's apparent resistance to its own didacticism, alternately viewing the text as a hands-on guide to courtly manners or a *Cyropaedia Redivivus* whose fictional courtier, according to Thomas Hoby, has "no more imperfection . . . then in Cirus himself." In a commendatory sonnet in Hoby's 1561 translation, Thomas Sackville praises Castiglione for his adherence to philosophical idealism: "Ne proud ne golden Court doth he set furth / But what in Court a Courtier ought to be."[17] Idealistic and pragmatic readers alike desire to systematize Castiglione's work and convert it into a pedagogically transparent, easily digestible set of precepts, thus diluting the didactic ambivalence of the original text. Lodovico Dolce's 1552 edition of *The Book of the Courtier* reduces Castiglione's advice into abstracts and marginal summaries. So too does Hoby's translation when it repackages the text as a book of maxims by adding an appendix entitled "A Breef Rehersall of the Chiefe Conditions and Qualities in a Courtier." Even though Hoby admits that "Castilio [professes not to] folowe not any certayne appointed order of preceptes or rules," the translator cannot resist reinventing the text as a "storehouse of most necessary implements for the conversacion, use, and training up of mans life with Courtly demeaners" – hardly a view occasioned by Count Lodovico's assertion that grace cannot be taught.[18]

The Book of the Courtier's reluctance to teach the courtly precepts it sanctions reveals a discomfort with pedagogical instrumentality common amongst late fifteenth- and early sixteenth-century Italian neo-Platonists. Despite the fact that one recent historian describes *The Book of the Courtier* as a "technical treatise for the self," Castiglione strives to maximize the moral efficacy of his text without reducing it to a mere instrument or primer which, like Aristotle as viewed by Renaissance proponents of Plato, is "plodding" and "suitable chiefly for schoolboys" rather than for an elite initiate.[19] Plato's didactic obscurity invites praise from late fifteenth-century Italian humanists such as Cardinal Bessarion, who defends the Athenian philosopher against George of Trebizond by acknowledging that while Plato does "not, to be sure, lay down any definite rules like a schoolmaster – how one should orate, or dispute, or do things of that sort," he nonetheless does "sow in his dialogues (which were artfully and learnedly written) many very useful precepts."[20] For scholars such as Bessarion, one of Plato's principal appeals is his repudiation of the overt didacticism and utilitarianism associated with Aristotle as well as with the study of instrumental or serving sciences such as mechanics.

According to a commonplace of humanist logic, Plato is superior to Aristotle not despite but rather because his teachings are obscure and unmethodical and because his dialogic style "made it difficult to find out what his positive doctrine was."[21] Castiglione's dialogue cultivates this difficulty, for while it does at times read like a textbook on courtly behavior, certain of Castiglione's interlocutors, particularly Count Lodovico, ensure that it never becomes one. As early as the dedicatory epistle, Castiglione complicates the didactic instrumentality of his text by defending his project of creating a perfect courtier against those who claim that "it is a vaine thing to teach that can not be learned."[22] Echoing the common defense of Plato against accusations of pedagogical opacity, Castiglione argues that his dialogue is didactically useful, despite its failure to offer attainable models of courtly behavior, in that it prompts "Courtiers . . . to drawe nigh in effect to the ende and marke that I in writing have set beefore them."[23] In the same breath, however, Castiglione distances his text from the larger philosophical conflicts concerning "the intelligible world and of the Ideas or imagined Fourmes," or the debates and quarrels over Plato undertaken by many of Castiglione's contemporaries.

After dismissing the larger philosophical substructure that informs his work, Castiglione abruptly departs from his chosen models – Cicero's *De Oratore*, Xenophon's *Cyropaedia*, and Plato's *Republic* – by admitting the practical impossibility of his project on account of the limitations of actual (as opposed to ideal) courtiers: "and if with all this they [courtiers] can not compasse that perfection . . . he that cummeth nighest shall be the most perfect: as emong many Archers that shute at one marke, where none of them hitteth the pinn, he that is nighest is out of doubt better than the rest."[24] At this instant, Castiglione's stated project of creating an ideal courtier falls flat as he admits that the efficacy of his text is ultimately contingent upon the extent to which actual courtiers might approximate the unattainable perfection to which they should all aspire. As Count Lodovico points out, "it is so harde a matter to knowe the true perfeccion, that it is almoste unpossible," his aptly placed "almost" exemplifying the vexed, self-mocking idealism of Castiglione's text.[25]

In this manner, *The Book of the Courtier* generates conflict over its own, often contradictory, pedagogical techniques, revealing its profound discomfort with both the Scylla of pragmatism and the Charybdis of idealism. In a famous passage, Count Lodovico describes perfect grace as attainable, yet in the same breath refuses to explain how the courtier might attain it through particular precepts: "Bound I am not," he protests to the other interlocutors, "to teache you to have a good grace, nor anye thing els, saving only to shew you what a perfect Courtyer ought to be." Like the soldier who knows what kind of armor he wants but cannot explain how to "hammer or temper it," Lodovico proclaims that "I am able to tel you what a perfect Courtyer ought to be, but not to teach you how ye should doe to be one."[26] The Count's explanation of grace is both systematic and totally elusive: while grace defies definition, it is paradoxically acquired through imitation, and while it is "not to be learned," the courtier may nonetheless "steale thys grace from them that to hys seming have it." To complicate matters, even if Lodovico's grace can indeed be taught, it must never appear as if it is learned, since grace is, *ipso facto*, a quality that must appear "stolen," or surreptitiously acquired, rather than deliberately copied.[27]

The definitions of grace and *sprezzatura* which accumulate throughout Books I and II of *The Book of the Courtier* foster some tense interactions between the text's idealizing and its pragmatic strains and create a friction also provoked by the text's ongoing debate over the relative merits of arms and letters, a cultural shorthand for the larger conflict between action and contemplation that Hoby translates as "doing" and "beholding."[28] The problem with the active life, and especially with the military profession, is that it requires effort – effort which might undermine the crucial illusion of *sprezzatura*. The problem with the *vita contemplativa*, on the other hand, is that it threatens to amplify the recreative *otium* of the courtier into an effeminate indolence. Oscillating between the view that "vertue consisteth in doing and practise" and that courtiers should give themselves "somewhat more to the beehouldinge," or contemplative, life, *The Book of the Courtier* scrutinizes the competing claims for the superiority of each, but concludes that both the life of the mind and the life of the body are noble only to the extent that they comprise and support the other.[29]

Pietro Bembo's diatribe on love in Book IV pursues a similar rapprochement between mind and body, for while indebted to the Platonism of Marsilio Ficino, Bembo nonetheless prompts the reader to "consider [that] Platonism in a worldly context" by emphasizing the interdependence between earthly and heavenly desires.[30] According to Bembo, worldly love and physical beauty provide access to the divine, a thesis that aims to bridge the tangible and intangible realms in a manner which anticipates the arguments of sixteenth-century Urbino mechanicians, men such as Guido Ubaldo del Monte and Bernardino Baldi who defend the practice of mechanics on account of its unique capacity to reconcile and even "intertwine" physical and mathematical being. Yet the extent to which physical experience might provide a means for transcendence is left unresolved by Bembo's speech, which leaves open the possibility that the realm of the spirit is primarily, or even solely, accessible by means of the body, thus exposing the core of his Platonic idealism to the unsettling paradox that the flesh can serve as an instrument of its own transcendence.[31] By refusing to articulate a fixed relationship between the rival scopes of action and contemplation or of body and spirit, Castiglione's text participates in its culture's broader intellectual project to harmonize the ideal and the instrumental and to reconstitute the relationship between the mathematical and the physical realms, an undertaking nowhere more apparent than in Urbino's enthusiasm for the discipline of mechanics.

The Urbino courts of Federico da Montefeltro (d. 1482) and his son Guidobaldo (d. 1508) were among the most prominent centers of scientific learning around the turn of the sixteenth century. Duke Federico was an avid practitioner of mathematics, mechanics, and military engineering, and throughout the 1460s and 1470s he employed a team of engineers, led after 1472 by Francesco di Giorgio Martini, to construct his Ducal Palace, a structure which boasted the most advanced fortifications of its day as well as *trompe l'œil* features and elaborate *intarsie* of scientific instruments.[32] Both father and son were enthusiastic scientific patrons, sponsoring numerous Latin editions of ancient scientific texts as well as original mathematical works by Piero della Francesca (*De Quinque Corporibus, c.* 1485–90) and his student Luca Pacioli (*Summa Arithmetica,* 1494), both dedicated to Duke Guidobaldo.[33] Upon founding the *Collegio dei Dottori* in Urbino in 1506, Guidobaldo established what was eventually to become the *Officina degli strumenti scientifici,* an important center for practical scientific learning through Galileo's time.[34] Guidobaldo even posed alongside Pacioli for a 1495 painting by Jacopo de' Barbari that depicts the mathematician illustrating a theorem from Euclid. A rhombicuboctahedron made of glass and filled halfway with water hovers over Pacioli's shoulder, a complex geometrical solid similar in its intricacy to those decorating the inlaid walls of the Montefeltro *studioli* in Urbino and in Gubbio, ornate examples of the technical virtuosity that characterizes both the architecture of the Montefeltro court and its intellectual climate.

The Montefeltro court attracted scholars and mechanicians with a wide range of scientific interests, from the military engineer Roberto Valturio, whose *De Re Militari* was one of the most popular treatises on military tactics during the sixteenth century, to more theoretically minded figures such as Giorgio Valla, Pietro Bembo (of *Book of the Courtier* fame), and Alessandro Piccolomini, all of whom collected Greek scientific manuscripts and disseminated them throughout Europe. Northern European scientists such as Georg Peurbach and his colleague Regiomontanus (Johannes Müller) traveled to Venice and Urbino in the 1470s to study ancient scientific manuscripts, to learn Greek, and to secure the patronage of Duke Federico or of his friend Cardinal Bessarion, founder of Venice's Marciana library and himself an avid collector of scientific texts and instruments.

Attracted to the Marciana collection and to Federico's equally impressive library, which contained some 1,100 volumes by his death in 1482 including manuscripts of Hero, Archimedes, Pappus, Euclid, Ptolemy, and Vitruvius, this loosely affiliated group of Italian and German scholars helped to make these and other ancient scientific texts available to a wider audience.[35] From their research in the collections at Venice and at Urbino, Peurbach produced an important epitome of Ptolemy's *Almagest*, and Regiomontanus an edition of Archimedes, printed posthumously in 1544. Giorgio Valla's 1501 *De Rebus Expetendis*, an encyclopedia of scientific problems in the style of Seneca's *Quaestiones Naturae*, was (in addition to Valla's 1498 compilation of Greek scientific texts dedicated to Guidobaldo) one of only a few printed sources of its time for the work of ancient mechanicians such as Hero, Archimedes, Apollonius, and Pappus. Stressing the importance of using instruments to demonstrate mechanical problems, Valla's compilation continued to prove useful well into the sixteenth century for scientists including Leonardo Da Vinci and Copernicus.[36] Valla also lectured on Euclid, and one of his students, Bartolomeo Zamberti, produced the first printed Latin edition of Euclid's *Elements* in 1505, dedicating it to Guidobaldo. Three years later, in 1508, Luca Pacioli lectured on Euclid in the church of St. Bartholomew in Venice from Zamberti's edition of the text to an audience which included Bembo and a number of other humanists associated with the Montefeltro court.

The scientific undertakings of the scholars and natural philosophers affiliated with the Montefeltro court are often difficult to reconcile with their non-scientific inclinations, their interest in mechanics sitting ill at ease with the Platonic leanings of scholars such as Bembo and Bessarion. While known to posterity as Castiglione's impassioned *portavoce* of Platonic love, Bembo studied with Angelo Poliziano and with Niccolò Leonico Tomeo, both of whom were deeply interested in mechanics.[37] In his *Panepistemon*, a brief treatise first printed in 1497 which classifies the various disciplines of knowledge, Poliziano offers a tripartite definition of mechanics – it is partly a rational science ("pars rationalis est quae numerorum mensurarum"), partly a manual art ("altera chirurgice"), and partly an art of magnifying strength, or the appearance thereof, by means of which heavy weights are easily lifted up high ("autem partes manganaria: per quam pondera immania minima vi tolluntur in altum"). Tomeo, who lectured at the University of Padua between around 1497 and 1509, was an editor and translator of various Greek texts on mechanics including a 1525 Latin translation of the pseudo-Aristotelian *Mechanical Problems*, a work which attempts to elevate the status of mechanics relative to the discipline of mathematics.[38]

Like Tomeo, Cardinal Bessarion helped to disseminate Greek texts on mechanics. Better known for his attempt to find a common ground between Plato and Aristotle in the *Adversus Calumniatorem Platonis*, Bessarion was apparently unconcerned that Plato had denigrated the mechanical arts in his *Republic*, and he commissioned manuscript copies of works on mechanics by Archimedes, Hero, and Pappus.[39] One of these manuscripts, a volume of Ptolemy's *Geography* copied by Bessarion's friend Giovanni Rhosos, contains a miniature depicting the astronomer seated amid various cosmographical instruments: an astrolabe hangs on the wall, a quadrant lies in the corner, and two *torqueta* sit on the table next to him.[40] That Bessarion, Bembo, Tomeo, and Poliziano all shared an appreciation for both Platonic philosophy and ancient mechanics is easier to comprehend in light of James Hankins' assessment of the Platonic revival in late fifteenth-century Italy, which he argues was not a " 'retreat into metaphysics' or a 'flight from the city of men,' " but rather a "profound integration of the active and contemplative life whereby the latter could give health and wisdom to the former."[41] Bessarion, for one, felt that Plato and Aristotle differed primarily in form and method, and not in content; rather than establish Plato as an exclusive authority, Bessarion instead sought to accommodate Plato's ideas to more instrumental systems of thought, from Aristotelianism to mechanics. The accommodating nature of Bessarion's Platonism is articulated clearly by the astrolabe designed for him by Regiomontanus in 1462: on the face of the instrument is engraved the figure of a man with angel's wings, suggesting that the pragmatic, worldly discipline of mechanics dignifies its practitioners, exalting their spirits and giving rise to lofty contemplation as well as producing material effects in the tangible world.[42]

The commentaries and prefaces of Greek texts on mechanics produced by the scholars and scientists affiliated with the Dukes of Montefeltro reveal that one of the discipline's profoundest appeals resides in its implicitly courtly artifice. The first two Latin editions of the pseudo-Aristotelian *Mechanical Problems*, Vittore Fausto's 1517 edition and Tomeo's 1525 text, were both edited by friends of Bembo, and at the beginning of his commentary, Tomeo notes that Aristotle calls what is done by mechanics "beyond nature [praeter naturam]" as it circumvents the laws of nature in order to effect things for the benefit of humankind.[43] Tomeo aptly translates Aristotle's παρα as *praeter*, meaning beside or next to as well as beyond or against, and he also appropriates a quotation from Antiphon, cited in the first paragraph of the *Mechanical Problems*, for the motto on his title-page: "For we overcome in art those things by which we are conquered in nature [Arte enim superamus ea a quibus natura vincimur]." This is precisely what Castiglione's Federico Fregoso demands of the courtier: he must use all his wiles to "frame himselfe" to whatever his prince desires, "though by nature he were not enclined to it." Moreover, he must do so without using "force [*sforza*]," a term which for Castiglione is virtually synonymous with the *affetazione* or "precisenesse" that destroys the courtier's all-important illusion of effortlessness. Fregoso's prescription to circumvent or surpass nature without using force echoes the pseudo-Aristotelian thesis that machinery compensates us when "nature produces effects against our advantage." "When, then, we have to produce an effect contrary to nature, we are at a loss, because of the difficulty, and require skill," pseudo-Aristotle writes. "Therefore we call that part of skill which assists such difficulties, a device [*techne*]."[44]

This circumvention of "difficulties" without physical force links the prevailing cultural aesthetic of the Montelfeltro court, as represented by *The Book of the Courtier*, with that court's far-reaching interest in mechanics, a discipline commonly defined during the period as "the moving of very great weights with small force by means of instruments and devices."[45] Machine and courtier both rely upon a power contrary to force, one which eliminates or conceals the need for strenuous effort and fosters an illusion of negligent diligence by concealing its own mode of working. *The Book of the Courtier* even describes the courtier's behaviors and gestures as *operazioni*, or "operations," a term used principally by engineers such as Da Vinci, for whom it carries a palpably mechanical meaning.[46] That Castiglione's idiom coincides with the vocabulary of Renaissance mechanics further cements the semantic and intellectual connections between courtly machination and the motive powers or *operazioni* of machinery. One of the spokesmen of courtly dissimulation in Castiglione's text turns out to be Bembo's friend Leonico Tomeo, who gives an example of the "honest and comelie kinde of jesting that consisteth in a certein dissimulacion, whan a man speaketh one thinge and privilie meaneth another."[47] Tomeo's contribution to the analysis of courtly wit in Book II of Castiglione's text suggests that like mechanical *virtù*, courtly *virtù* is an adversarial and dissimulatory power, one that relies upon trickery rather than force to overturn the natural course of things.

In its effort to eulogize, if not to define, the courtly *sprezzatura* from which grace springs, Castiglione's text explores some of the political, aesthetic, and moral implications of Urbino's mechanical renascence. In its complex configuration of the relationship between nature and artifice and between action and contemplation, *The Book of the Courtier* is embroiled in some of the principal methodological conflicts besetting the scientific culture of its day. Taking their cue from the psuedo-Aristotelian *Mechanical Problems*, which argues that "mechanical problems . . . have a share in both mathematical and physical speculations," Tomeo and his colleagues at Padua develop a view of mechanics as an intermediary science, capable of reconciling mathematical and physical methods of scientific inquiry. "While machines are natural," writes Tomeo, since they are made of natural materials, their "mode and power of working [modum operandique vim] are mathematical, for weights and measures are abstracted from the natural material in which they are found in order to reveal their principles of design."[48] In other words, mechanics works both within and outside of the phenomenal world, and machines, while they produce effects in the physical world, are nonetheless capable of abstraction into the world of ideals or forms.

Like the Alexandrian school of mechanics, represented by Hero and Pappus, the pseudo-Aristotelian *Mechanical Problems* differs from Platonic, Pythagorean, and Euclidean texts in its reluctance to distinguish mathematical from physical demonstration or to privilege the former over the latter. For the author of the *Mechanical Problems*, questions of mechanics are neither "identical with physical problems, nor . . . entirely separate from them," a thesis which collapses the Platonic and Pythagorean distinction between the abstractions of mathematics and the world of physical objects, whose behavior is determined by instruments and by the senses.[49] This impulse to mediate between the material and the immaterial, or the active and the contemplative realms, permeates Urbino's intellectual and scientific culture, from Bembo's "stayre" of love to the geometrical solid that dangles next to Guidobaldo in Barbari's painting of the Duke, a mathematical concept granted physical presence by virtue of its capacity to contain water.

The popularity of the Neoplatonic philosopher Proclus, whose commentary on Euclid's *Elements* is first printed by Valla's student Zamberti in 1505 and whose works are read avidly by Bessarion and Bembo, testifies to the prevailing reluctance to make overly tidy distinctions between mathematical and physical being. At times, Proclus echoes the *Timaeus* in his view of mathematics as fundamentally different from, and superior to, mechanics, since it is immaterial and "makes ready our understanding and our mental vision for turning towards that upper world."[50] Yet Proclus defines "mathematical being" as itself intermediate, since while it is not subject to physical change, it inevitably touches upon and affects the world of objects. While Proclus still privileges theoretical over practical science, arguing that "we must posit mathematical knowledge and the vision that results from it as being worthy of choice for their own sakes, and not because they satisfy human needs," he is willing to admit, unlike Plato, that the applied sciences, including the "art of making useful engines of war" and the "art of wonder-working [*automatopoeien*]," possess utility and dignity.[51]

Proclus' concession to the nobility of the mechanical arts thus compromises Plato's strict distinction between phenomenal and ideal nature. Inflected by Proclus' argument that mechanics is neither separate from nor inferior to the realm of mathematical inquiry, debates over the relative status of mechanics and mathematics rage throughout sixteenth-century Italy. The two generations of mechanicians working in Urbino after the death of Duke Guidobaldo, a group which includes Federico Commandino and his students Guido Ubaldo del Monte and Bernardino Baldi, pursue the project of reconciling mathematical and physical reality through the recovery and study of the *Mechanical Questions* as well as works by Archimedes, Hero, and Pappus.

Among the chief adversaries of the Urbino school is Niccolò Tartaglia, whose 1546 *Quesiti e Inventioni Diverse* faults the pseudo-Aristotelian text for "prov[ing] each of [its] problems partly by physical reasons and arguments and partly by mathematical." Throughout the *Quesiti*, which takes the form of a dialogue between the author and Diego de Mendoza, Charles V's ambassador to Venice, Tartaglia contrasts the methods of the mechanician, who "considers, judges, and determines things according to the senses and material appearances," with that of mathematicians such as Euclid, who reach their conclusions "according to reason, all matter being abstracted." Tartaglia concludes that the method used by the author of the *Mechanical Problems* will never yield certain conclusions, since "things constructed or fabricated [of matter] can never be made as perfectly as they can be imagined apart from matter." It is for this reason that the mathematician only trusts "demonstrations and arguments abstracted from all matter," since only these possess "the highest degree of certainty."[52]

In his 1577 *Mechanicorum Liber*, Guido Ubaldo complicates Tartaglia's distinction between mathematical certainty and the unverifiable world of "things constructed," mocking those "keen mathematicians of our time who assert that mechanics may be considered either mathematically, removed [from physical considerations], or else physically. As if, at any time, mechanics could be considered apart from either geometrical demonstrations or actual motion!"[53] In the preface to his 1581 Italian translation of Guido Ubaldo's work, Filippo Pigafetta echoes the author's conviction that mechanics is "intertwined," a hybrid of several disciplines including "natural philosophy, mathematics, and the practical arts." Rather than approach mechanical questions through only one of these disciplines, Pigafetta argues that "it is necessary to consider [mechanics] in two manners: one that regards theory and the application of reason to things that must be done . . . the other that is carried out in practice."[54] It is this mediatory capacity of mechanics which ensures the discipline's great appeal within the intellectual culture of the sixteenth-century Italian court, a culture marked by its playful yet ambivalent application of artifice and its dialogic approach to philosophical questions.

The late sixteenth-century courtly natural philosopher Bernardino Baldi views mechanics as a discipline capable of mediating between theoretical and practical knowledge. His *Cronica de matematici overo epitome dell'istoria delle vite loro* (c. 1580), a biographical dictionary of ancient and modern scientists influenced by scientific encyclopedias such as Diogenes Laertius' *Lives of the Philosophers* and Peter Ramus' *Scholae Mathematicae*, stages a *paragone* between theory and practice by rewriting the history of science as an ongoing rivalry between the two, one best resolved by the Alexandrian engineers, by Archimedes, and by Baldi's own teacher Commandino. While Pythagoras treats geometry "separate from material things [separolla de la materia]," and Plato writes "not to dabble in material things but rather to raise them to the highest contemplations of Theology [non per servisene in cose materiali, ma . . . per alzarsi col mezzo loro all'altissime contemplationi della Teologia]," Baldi praises the proponents of the Peripatetic and Alexandrian schools for the useful application of their mechanical inventions. Archytas, a Greek mechanician often mentioned by Renaissance writers for his construction of an automatic bird, proves "eccellente non meno nelle attioni, che nelle speculationsi," excelling in both action and speculation, while Archimedes, "Prince of Mathematics" and also of "mechanical invention [Principe de Matematici [e] degl'Inventori di machine]," perfectly integrates the discipline of practical mechanics with that of theoretical geometry.[55]

Baldi goes one step further towards privileging practical over theoretical science in his translation of Hero of Alexandria's *Automata*, printed in 1589, and in his commentary on pseudo-Aristotle's *Mechanical Problems*, printed posthumously in 1621. In the latter work, Baldi is careful in his preface to distinguish between *theoricam* and what he calls *Chirurgicam* or *manu operatricem*, the manual operations and practical sciences that "treat real matter [vero materiam tractant]" rather than imaginary problems. In his preface to Hero's *De Gli Automati*, Baldi argues that the science of "machine semoventi," or self-moving machinery, is nobler than mathematics: despite the fact that mathematics deals with "quantità separate della materia" while mechanics does not, the latter discipline ultimately penetrates the spirit of the universe more deeply in that it reveals "i più secreti, & occulti misterii della Filosofia" – the most secret and hidden mysteries of Philosophy.[56] True automata, Baldi argues, possess "il contrapeso occulto," or hidden counterweights, that make their movements appear miraculous (*thauma*): such objects include the self-moving machines designed by Regiomontanus, "cosi mirabile queste, e passano quasi i termini della Fede [such wonders, and almost surpassing the limits of Faith]."[57]

Yet automata do not surpass those limits, and in both the *Automata* and the *Mechanical Problems*, Baldi is careful to point out that mechanics observes "tutti le leggi" of nature and that it is a discipline "honesto" and "virtuoso."[58] In his translation of pseudo-Aristotle, Baldi takes further steps to legitimate mechanics by defining *machinatoriae*, or machine-making, as a a subset of *magnanaria*, or the discipline of improving appearances through art. The courtly theories of *cosmesis* and the Aristotelian principles of mechanics thus intersect in Baldi's work as he confirms and expands upon the courtly ethos laid down by Castiglione.

For Guido Ubaldo and Baldi, the practice of mechanics is capable of mediating between competing disciplines of knowledge, competing metaphysical realms, and competing conceptions of nature and artifice. Defenders of mechanics look to machinery's uniquely natural artifice, praising the discipline in the same paradoxical terms as Castiglione's definition of *sprezzatura*. In his 1543 *Cosmographia*, Francesco Maurolico writes in his dedicatory letter to Bembo that while "mechanics operates outside the laws of natural philosophy" and produces "effects against nature with the aid of machines," its causes are nonetheless natural. Yet on the same page, Maurolico complicates this already perplexing relationship between art and nature, arguing that mechanics surpasses other disciplines of natural philosophy precisely because it works "by power or by art."[59] Moreover, Maurolico argues, geometry achieves its fulfillment in mechanics, rather than the other way around, since only mechanics can achieve mastery over the physical world. Maurolico thus dedicates much of his work to the study of mechanical instruments: the fourth and final section of the *Cosmographia* contains chapters on the construction of quadrants, astrolabes, and *trochilia*, or windlasses. Yet the ultimate effect is nonetheless a text alternately celebratory and anxious about the capacity of art, or *techne*, to master natural forces.[60] The twists and turns by which mechanics, according to Maurolico, can be both wholly natural and wholly artificial evoke Count Lodovico's equally elusive description of grace, a quality he alternately attributes to "skill" and "diligence" or to a "naturall disposition of person."[61] The extent to which the courtier's art can or should produce effects contrary to nature is left as unresolved by Lodovico's discussion as by Maurolico's treatment of *techne*, in which the *naturalezza* of machinery confounds simple distinctions between nature and artifice.

The Urbino unwillingness to privilege mathematics over mechanics is encouraged by the fact that *automatopoeien*, or the "wonder-working" machines of ancient engineers such as Hero and Pappus, are commonly viewed as aesthetic models for the concealment of effort. In the Urbino court, self-moving machinery mystifies the relationship between nature and art in a manner similar to the courtly grace which, while outwardly the "gift of nature and of the heavens," is more often the result of "studye and diligence."[62] Even as they go beyond or against nature, machines are subject to courtly etiquette in that they, too, depend upon a masterful illusion of *naturalezza*. Guido Ubaldo's *Mechanicorum Liber* imagines mechanics as a noble artifice precisely because it operates "against nature or rather in rivalry with the laws of nature."[63] In the Italian translation of Guido Ubaldo's text, Pigafetta translates the passage as "quasi sopra naturale," a crucial modification of the Latin phrase *praeter naturam* used in contemporary editions of the pseudo-Aristotelian text. Do machines rival (and thus approximate) nature, do they act contrary to nature, or do they (almost) surpass nature? With its surplus of definitions for the discipline of mechanics, Guido Ubaldo's text endorses a complex, composite view of the relationship between nature and art.

According to Guido Ubaldo, the engineer whose mechanical inventions best rival nature is Archimedes. "So does his hand imitate nature," he writes, "that nature herself is thought to have imitated his hand."[64] Even Nature appears artificial by contrast to Archimedes' "natural" artifice, which overturns the priority between nature and art in a manner similar to the courtly art of *sprezzatura*. Both Guido Ubaldo and Castiglione are indebted to Cicero and Quintilian for their understanding of natural artifice as "diligent negligence [negligentia diligens]," as Cicero terms the orator's meticulous attention to the concealment of effort and affectation.[65] For Cicero, as for Castiglione, facility and *naturalezza* are key principles of decorum, but they are also, as Cicero admits, illusions sustained through continual practice: "subtlety of style [orationis subtilitas] seems easy to imitate at first glance, but when attempted nothing is less difficult [nihil est experienti minus]."[66] Castiglione adopts Cicero's example of cosmetics to demonstrate how feigned negligence can offset the intrusion of artifice: Count Lodovico remarks that a woman appears more beautiful when she adorns herself "so scarcely . . . that whoso behouldeth her, standeth in doubt whether she be trimmed or no," while the woman "so bedawbed, that a man woulde wene she had a viser on her face" looks as synthetic and inert as an "image of woodde without movinge."[67]

The results of affectation in *The Book of the Courtier* are often described in terms of a wooden, inflexible inhumanity like the inanimate rigidity of the awkward Mr. Peterpaul, the mascot of *affetazione* who dances "on tipto without moving his head, as though he were all of wood, so heedfullie, that truely a man would weene he counted his paces."[68] While the regular, stiff motions of machinery might appear apt for supplying metaphors for courtly affectation, many writers affiliated with the Urbino court instead look to machines as a model for *sprezzatura*, *facilità*, and *leggiadria*.

In this, too, sixteenth-century Italian court culture follows the cue of Cicero and Quintilian, both of whom look to machinery to demonstrate that the highest expression of art is the "concealment of its existence [ne ars esse videatur]," a precept which for Quintilian is exemplified by Archimedes, who with his machines "singlehandedly succeeded in appreciably prolonging the resistance of Syracuse when it was besieged."[69] Mechanical objects help to elucidate Cicero's understanding of the relationship between art and nature, a relationship which for the Roman lawyer, as for Castiglione's Urbino, is subject to continual revision and complication. In his *De Natura Deorum*, Cicero uses the example of a sundial to argue that art, like nature, is infused with reason and divine providence: he writes that "when you look at a sun-dial or a water-clock, you infer that it tells time by art and not by chance," thus proving that the world is not "devoid of reason."[70] Yet in the subsequent passage Cicero scolds those philosophers who "think more highly of the achievement of Archimedes in making a model [sphaerae] of the revolutions of the firmament than of that of nature in creating them," since the "perfection of the original shows a craftsmanship many times as great as does the counterfeit [simulacra sollertius]." For Cicero, mechanical devices alternately exalt and debase rational nature, and Archimedes' sphere lies at the axis of his conflicted attitude towards artifice. While Archimedes built his globe "just like Plato's God who built the world in the *Timaeus*," human artifice in no way resembles divine creation according to Cicero: "if in this world phenomena cannot take place without the act of God, neither could Archimedes have reproduced the same movements upon a globe without divine genius [divino ingenio]."[71] Two competing notions of the relationship between nature and artifice coexist in his description of Archimedes' sphere: in the former, as in Plato's *Ion*, art is a pale imitation of the natural world, while in the latter, as in the

Timaeus, human artifice offers proof that God himself is a "mechanikos," the traces of his divine work evident to us in the form of mechanical models of the heavenly spheres.

Sixteenth-century Urbino shapes both its courtiers and its mechanical objects according to the Ciceronian principles of negligent diligence, fashioning human and mechanical instruments alike into exemplars of grace and *facilità*. Technical treatises by Duke Federico's engineers, including Francesco Di Giorgio Martini and Roberto Valturio, use a revolutionary style of scientific illustration to juxtapose the apparent facility to the actual complexity of their designs for military and civic machinery. This cut-away or transparent view, which Di Giorgio Martini may have adapted from the Sienese engineer Mariano di Jacopo, better known as Taccola, is the first effective means for showing the interior and the exterior of a machine simultaneously.[72] By both obscuring and revealing the hidden workings of machinery, Martini's and Valturio's illustrations foster the same interplay between *facilità* and *difficultà* cultivated by the subtle knot of courtly decorum, which demands that its adherents perform (or seem to perform) difficult tasks easily. Di Giorgio Martini's notebooks, many of which date from his stay in the Montefeltro court, are filled with designs for hoisting machinery to move heavy obelisks with ease, thus actualizing Count Lodovico's definition of *sprezzatura* in physically concrete terms.

It is Baldi whose work best articulates the alliance between mechanical artifice and courtly dissimulation that develops in the Montefeltro court. Better known as the author of the *Cronica de matematici* and as the translator of Hero and pseudo-Aristotle, Baldi was also commissioned by Francesco Maria delle Rovere II, the Duke of Urbino during the 1590s, to write several historical works about the Duchy: these include biographies of Dukes Federico and Guidobaldo (*Federici Urbini Ducis Vita* and *Guidi Ubaldi Urbini Ducis Vita*), a treatise on courtiership (*De Aula Libri Sex*), an encomium to Urbino (*Urbini Encomium*), and a description of the Ducal Palace constructed by Di Giorgio Martini under Federico's reign, the *Descriptio Palatii Ducum Urbinatum*.[73] Baldi's primary interest in these works, particularly in the description of the Ducal Palace, is in documenting the nature of the *artifizi*, the various decorations and feats of technical and artistic virtuosity which adorned the Montefeltro palace. Baldi is full of praise for the rooms and *loggie* designed by Martini and "made with almost miraculous art [fatte con artificio così mirabile]." Baldi describes in detail reliefs of antique war machinery attributed to Martini, the "battering rams, tortoise-shaped tanks, ballistic devices, and catapults [arieti, testuggini, baliste, e catapulte]" which serve to "move great weights . . . or perform other things in the service of art [muovere grandissimi pesi . . . [o] far altre cose per servizio dell'arte]."⁷⁴

A room decorated with depictions of military engines showcases Urbino's military strength as well as the culture's active effort to recuperate classical works of military tactics by Frontinus, Vegetius, or Aelianus Tacticus to evoke the moral and architectural grandeur of ancient Rome. Yet Baldi's description of the reliefs and the rest of the palace also demonstrates how, for Duke Federico's court, technical virtuosity is one of the principal expressions of courtly artifice. Baldi's account of the construction of the Ducal Palace shows a keen interest in the dissimulatory techniques used by Federico's artists and engineers – the *trompe l'œil* paintings, the faux marble columns, and the clever disguising of lead pipes in order to make them appear like alabaster.⁷⁵ The "honest and comelie kind of . . . dissimulation" advocated by Castiglione's Tomeo, which demands that courtiers conceal their defects, is legitimated by the very edifice in which *The Book of the Courtier* is set.⁷⁶

In his *Cronica de matematici*, as well as in his description of Federico's palace, Baldi reconciles mechanical artifice to the aesthetic and intellectual sensibilities of the Urbino court. The sharpness of wit or *acutezza* privileged so insistently by Castiglione's text in its emphasis upon eloquence and verbal sparring resurfaces in Baldi's encyclopedia in a strange marriage of courtly wit and mechanical dexterity. The German scientist Regiomontanus, who visited Urbino at the turn of the sixteenth century, is praised for the "marvelous sharpness of his divine wit [mervigliosa acutezza di suo divino ingenio]," while Luca Pacioli, court mathematician to Duke Guidobaldo, is commended for "the acuity of his wit [l'acutezza del suo ingegno]," and Peter Ramus for his "suegliatissimo ingegno," a wit both "impetuous and audacious [impetuoso, & audace]."⁷⁷

Echoing Castiglione's celebration of wit, Baldi's text drives home a distinction common to sixteenth-century pedagogical treatises and works of ethical psychology: between slow wit and quick wit, the latter often referred to as *ingegno* and associated with scientific skill but also with the crafting of subtle devices in the political or rhetorical sphere. Across sixteenth-century Europe, writers invested in anatomizing and classifying the intellectual faculty of *ingegno* assimilate it to other instrumentalities, both political and mechanical. Elaborating upon a distinction made by Juan Luis Vives in 1531, Roger Ascham explains the difference between slow and quick wits in his 1570 *Schoolmaster* by describing the latter as "more quick to enter speedily than able to pierce far, even like over-sharp tools, whose edges be very soon turned."⁷⁸ Ascham is one of a number of sixteenth-century writers who associates ingenuity with the acuity of a sharp instrument. In his 1575 *Examen de Ingenios*, the Spanish writer Juan Huarte categorizes disciplines of knowledge (and their attendant virtues) which are dependent upon *ingenio*: these include the literary skills of poets and orators, qualities befitting politicians and courtiers (polish, agility, scheming), and the skills required by "all the wits and engineers who make artificial motions [todos los ingenios y máquinamientos que fingen los artífices]."[79] This correlation between ingenuity and mechanical devising is taken to its extreme by Antonio Persio's 1576 *Trattato dell'Ingegno dell'Huomo*, which defines *ingegno* (mental power; genius; wit) in terms of the animation of an inanimate object, thus implicitly comparing it to the operation of machinery. Describing the nature of human wit, Persio points to Archimedes' sphere and to the self-moving statues invented by Archytas, who "composed a dove of lead, which having been given the spirit, and the breath, flew in the guise of a living dove [compose una colomba di legno, che havendole dato lo spirito, & il fiato, volava alla guisa d'una viva colomba]."[80] Like *ingegnería*, or marvels of engineering, human *ingegno* operates like a self-moving device, its elaborate mechanism motivated by *pneuma* or spirit.

For many sixteenth-century writers, it is the instrumental quality of human wit that makes it so readily comparable to machinery. In *Of Wisdome*, Pierre Charron imagines *ingenium* as a "sharp, subtile, [and] piercing" tool, an instrument with which man may "save and shield himself . . . from deceits and subtilities."[81] Yet while the instrument of human wit is a "taste of the immortal substance" given to us by God, it must be bridled by piety and method lest it impel us "to search, ferret, contrive without intermission," turning us into "a perpetuall motion machine without rest" or a "wandring instrument, mooveable, diversely turning."[82] The complex and fluctuating motions of machinery thus reflect the excessive subtlety and inconstancy to which, from Charron's skeptical perspective, the human intellect (and particularly the faculty of invention) is subject. One of the warning signs of an over-subtle mind according to Charron is the fabrication of what his close contemporary Montaigne calls "subtill devices," a category which includes machines noted for their "rarenesse or noveltie, or for their difficultie."[83] Charron, too, compares the extravagant subtlety of human wit to mechanical "works that shew rather finenesse of wit than bring profit with them [les ouvrages . . . qui ont esté en subtilité seule sans utilité]" such as the "wooden pigeon of Architas [la colombe de bois d'Architas]," the "flie and eagle of Montroyall [Regiomontanus] [la mouche et l'aigle de Montroyal]," and the "sphear of Sapro King of the Persians, and that of Archimedes with his other engins [la sphere de Sapor Roy des Perses, celle d'Archimedes et ses autres engins]." These machines may surpass nature, but they also reveal "how rash and dangerous the spirit of man is, especially if it be quicke and vigorous [combien l'esprit humain est temeraire et dangereux, mesmement s'il est vif et vigoureux]." For Charron, then, machinery epitomizes the menacing autonomy of human wit, a sovereign *ingenium* comparable to a perpetual motion machine impelled by a mysterious force.[84]

The potentially disturbing metaphysical implications of this commonplace analogy between human and mechanical *ingenium* are not lost on sixteenth-century writers such as Timothy Bright, who insists that human faculties do not function like "ingens, by a force voyd of skil and cunning in it selfe, & by a motion given by devise of the Mechenist." Rather than abandon the mechanical analogy, Bright reworks it, arguing that the faculties function like machines coupled to, and governed by, their engineers, "as if Architas had bin him selfe within his flying doves, & Vulcanne within his walking stooles, and the moving engine as it were animated with the minde of the worker." Held together by a subtle knot, our faculties respond to the promptings of reason like Daedalus' loyal statues, yet both sets of instruments "require direction, and also foreine impulsion," to use Bright's words, to perform their appointed tasks.[85]

The mutually supportive capacities for courtly machination and mechanical invention are exploited by mechanicians of the Archimedean revival in order to legitimate the discipline of mechanics according to the intellectual and social norms of court culture. Baldi does this by teasing out the semantic connections between *ingegno* and *ingegnería* in his portrait of fellow Urbino scientist Federico Commandino. Commandino exemplifies *sprezzatura*, for while he is "assiduous in his studies" he is also "able with only a little work to penetrate the greatest mysteries [negli studii fu egli assiduo . . . con un poco di studio penetrava le cose più scure]." Not one to suffer from the self-neglect or the misanthropy typical of the scholar, Commandino is in fact "judicious and conversant in the manners of the court [giuditioso e conversato in corte]," and "agile [nelle cose agilibi di molta bontà]."[86]

Federico Commandino is one of the foremost proponents of Archimedean mechanics in sixteenth-century Urbino, a movement which reinvents the Siracusan engineeer in order to legitimate courtly artifice as well as to champion the larger humanist thesis that, in the words of W. R. Laird, "contemplation is valuable only to the extent that . . . it ends in action."[87] Urbino's scientists look to ancient accounts of Archimedes by Plutarch, Athenaeus, and Polybius in order to integrate his particular brand of technical virtuosity and resourcefulness into prevailing courtly sensibilities. Archimedes' *facilità* is a focal point for scientists and humanists alike, who look to the *sprezzatura* of Archimedean mechanics, and of Archimedes himself, as a model for their own courtly performances. In his *Cronica de matematici*, Baldi calls Archimedes an "ingegno più divino que humano," noting the "marvelous ship [nave mirabile]" he built for King Hieron of Siracusa "with such facility that it could not but stupefy Hiero [con tanta facilità, che ne fece stupire Hierone]." Guido Ubaldo shares Baldi's interest in those inventions that highlight Archimedes' *facilità*: he describes how, "with the help of a block and tackle," the engineer "pulled a load of 5000 pecks with one hand" and how "alone with his machines he pulled a heavily loaded ship onto the shore and then pulled it toward himself as if it were being moved in the sea by oars or sails."[88] For both Baldi and Guido Ubaldo, mechanical power can redress the problem of affectation by mitigating the awkwardness of physical effort. "Without machines," Vitruvius observes in his *De Architectura*, "every kind of work is difficult," an attitude that helps to consummate the marriage of courtly and mechanical artifice during the sixteenth century.[89]

Guido Ubaldo, Commandino, and Baldi each reveal the influence of Plutarch's description of the engineer in his *Life of Marcellus*, where Archimedes and his machines lead Siracuse's heroic but unsuccessful resistance against Marcellus' Roman legions. Plutarch identifies Archimedes as both a practical artificer and a theoretical mathematician: he is able to take his "geometrical speculation [and] apply it to things corporall and sensible," thus harnessing theory in the service of practice. Insofar as Archimedes reconciles the "handy craft" of mechanics with the loftier science of mathematical speculation, he recuperates the practical, experimental sciences devalued by Plato, thus providing Plutarch with the opportunity to refute Plato's condemnation of mechanics. Plutarch praises two of Archimedes' predecessors, Archytas and Eudoxus, for using mechanics "to prove and confirme by materiall examples and sencible instruments, certeine Geometrical conclusions, whereof a man can not finde out the conceiveable demonstrations, by enforced reasons and proofes." When Archytas and Eudoxus invent geometrical instruments called mesolabes, Plutarch recounts how "Plato was offended with them, and maintained against them, that they did utterly corrupt and disgrace, the worthines and excellency of Geometry, making it to discende from things not comprehensible, and without body, unto things sencible and materiall, and to bringe it to a palpable substance," after which time mechanics came to be deemed less noble than geometry and other abstract sciences.[90]

Yet Plutarch also describes Archimedes as a figure who regarded his own engines and devices as nothing but "vyle, beggerly, and mercenary drosse," thus reinscribing Plato's derogatory attitude towards mechanics into his account of the engineer's life. Despite Archimedes' military activity as an engineer for his besieged Siracuse, he is celebrated by Plutarch for employing "his witte and study onely to write thinges, the beawty and subtilitie whereof, were not mingled any thinge at all with necessitie."[91] Archimedes emerges from Plutarch's account not as a "rude mechanical" but rather as the elite practitioner of an esoteric, contemplative science who scorns the "common commodity," or practical application, of his inventions. Reluctant to pursue the "fame and glory" that attends human knowledge, Plutarch's Archimedes instead pursues a "divine wisdome," keeping the "treasure and secrets" of his devices to himself.[92]

Plutarch imagines Archimedean mechanics as an occult science whose practitioners can be "brought into an extasy or traunse" by their investigations. Several of Plutarch's anecdotes highlight the excessively contemplative, hermetic nature of Archimedes' genius: in one, Archimedes cannot bear to put down his work in order to take a bath, so that while he is anointed with "oyles and swete savors, with his finger he did draw lines apon his naked body." In another, Archimedes is "so earnestly occupied" with a mathematical proposition that, when surprised by a Roman soldier, he refuses to depart before "he had done his conclusion" and is murdered.[93] By transforming Archimedes from an engineer into a high priest rapt in contemplation, Plutarch betrays his own discomfort with the technical ingenuity, the active engagement with public life, and the pragmatic experimentalism that distinguish Archimedean science from its Platonic and Pythagorean counterparts. Metamorphosed into a solitary magus, Plutarch's Archimedes upholds the priority of speculation over action and of spirit over matter.

Renaissance writers manipulate the conflicting aspects of Archimedes' biography to valorize – or to deprecate – both pragmatism and idealism and both the active and the contemplative life. Throughout sixteenth-century Europe, Archimedes comes to represent the highest pinnacle of mechanical ingenuity as he graces the frontispieces of works such as Tycho Brahe's *Astronomiae Instaurate Mechanica* (1598) and Salomon De Caus' *Les Raisons des Forces Mouvantes* (1616). Archimedes is the ideal to which Renaissance mechanicians aspired: Jacques Besson, master engineer to Charles IX of France, is described by a contemporary as the reincarnation of Archimedes, while Thomas Tymme calls the Dutch inventor Cornelius Drebbel "another Archimedes," and William Oughtred praises the mathematician Henry Briggs as the "English Archimedes."[94] Yet Archimedes also comes to epitomize courtly, as well as technical, virtuosity, qualities certainly linked in the mind of Giorgio Vasari, who describes the Archimedean engineer Da Vinci as able to "raise and draw great weights . . . by means of levers, windlasses, and screws," and as a man of great "grace" and "dexterity." As much the model courtier as the model scientist, Archimedes possesses an indifference towards his own technical acuity noted several times by Plutarch, who describes the engineer as "mak[ing] light account of all his devices . . . [they] were but his recreations of geometry, and things done to pass the time with."[95] Given the effortless resolution of difficulty achieved by both the inventor and his machines, Archimedean mechanics provides a means for sixteenth-century writers to accommodate a palpably uncourtly activity – designing and operating machinery – to a courtly sensibility. In a milieu where "indirection is so prized" and "obviousness so unseemly," according to Daniel Javitch's account of the Montefeltro court, Plutarch's account of Archimedes provides an exemplary model for the courtly *facilità* that makes artifice seem natural and studied effort spontaneous.[96]

In his official capacity as military engineer for King Hieron of Siracuse, Archimedes creates war machinery so powerful that, according to Plutarch, "it appeared the goddes fought against the Romaines." His cunning inventions, including "handes of Iron" and "hookes made like cranes billes," lift the Roman galleys clean out of the water, resisting the force of Marcellus' huge legion until the Roman army matches cunning with cunning and uses a tower "secretly [to] convey" their soldiers into the besieged city of Siracuse. Throughout his account, Plutarch emphasizes the ease with which the engineer and his machines are able to perform tasks of great difficulty. He solves arcane mathematical and physical problems with "grace," proving his demonstrations "so exquisitely, with wonderfull reason and facilitie" as he translates "profounde and difficult matters" into "plaine and simple tearmes." Yet Archimedes' successes are not the result of a "naturall gift in him," but rather due to the "extreme paines he tooke, which made these things come so easily from him, that they seemed as if they had been no trouble to him at all."[97] Like Ripa's *Artifitio*, Archimedes makes difficult problems appear easy through the careful negligence prescribed by Cicero and Quintilian and incorporated into Castiglione's ideal of *sprezzatura*, that quality of "not regarded agylitie and slighte conveyaunce" which demands that one "minde anye other thinge more than [what one is doing], to make him beleve that loketh on that he can not do amisse."[98]

Central to Archimedes' bravura performances of indifferent facility are his machines themselves, devices designed to perform enormously difficult tasks with ease. One such machine results from Archimedes' boast to King

Hieron "that it was possible to remove as great a weight as he would, with as little strength as he listed to put to it." To prove his point, Archimedes designs an "engine with many wheels and pulleys" that enables him, "sitting alone at his ease far off, without any straining at all" to pull the boat out of the water "fair and softly with his hand, [coming] as gently and smoothly to him as if it had floated."[99] By distributing the weight of the ship across a network of pulleys and wheels, the engine amplifies the virtual power of its user without requiring the application of physical force. Often referred to as the "Charistion" during the Renaissance, the very name of Archimedes' device associates it with *Charis*, the classical antecedent to the Renaissance concept of grace that, according to Anthony Blunt's definition, "will vanish if a man takes too much pains to attain it, or if he shows any effort in his actions."[100]

The easy, fluid motions of Archimedes' "grace machine" help to explain the engineer's singular appeal among the scientists and scholars of the Montefeltro court, where the Archimedean revival gains its initial momentum. Renaissance machines conceived and designed according to the principles of the Charistion serve as emblematic and literal instruments for the *sprezzatura* and the *virtù* anatomized and celebrated by *The Book of the Courtier*. Like Machiavelli, Castiglione defines *virtù* as an active and practical power; according to Lord Octavian, it "consisteth in doing and practise."[101] Alternately defined as ingenuity, strategy, or resourcefulness, *virtù* is a combination of "aptness and skill with inventive power and cleverness in originating and contriving," a dynamic, practical power that, according to Victoria Kahn, approaches what Aristotle calls *techne*.[102] Drawing from Plutarch's descriptions of prudence in the *Moralia*, Castiglione's Lord Octavian compares the *virtù* of the Prince to a "Carpenters square, that is not only straight and just it self, but also maketh straight and just whatsoever it is occupied about."[103] Defined as the effectual use of prudent knowledge, *virtù* functions like a machine in that it can gauge the fluctuating circumstances of the political world. In the Renaissance vocabulary, after all, *virtù* signifies human power or ingenuity, but it also signifies the motive power of a machine.[104]

The next chapter demonstrates how some of the key intellectual, social, and aesthetic values of Castiglione's *Book of the Courtier* find a conduit within the discourse and practice of mechanics in Elizabethan and Jacobean England. Through their shared investment in grace and nonchalance, mechanics and courtiership become mutually supporting disciplines that privilege a set of social and aesthetic styles based upon the concealment of effort or the conquest of difficulty. The chapter begins with John Dee, whose contact with Urbino mechanicians such as Federico Commandino influences his understanding – and defense – of mechanics in his 1570 *Preface* to Henry Billingsley's English translation of Euclid's *Elements*. In this work, Dee accommodates mechanical power to courtly *facilità* and political skill, offering an Archimedean definition of mechanical art consonant with both *sprezzatura* and Machiavellian *virtù*. Rather than seek to reconcile mechanics with Platonic philosophy, Dee and his contemporaries guarantee the legitimacy of mechanics by means of new intellectual and moral values, ones more at ease with the instrumentalism of their age.

CHAPTER 2

Artificial motions: machinery, courtliness, and discipline in Renaissance England

In Elizabethan and Jacobean England, the discipline of mechanics is reconstituted as an instrument of civility and of intellectual and moral discipline by humanists and scientists alike. Particularly after 1570, when John Dee publishes his *Mathematicall Preface* to Henry Billingsley's English translation of Euclid's *Elements*, the discipline of mechanics shapes and is in turn shaped by the contours of England's eager yet anxious importation of Italianate subtlety in its political, intellectual, and scientific forms. Yoked together by their mutual enthusiasm for a paradoxically "natural" artifice, Dee's *Preface* and Castiglione's *Book of the Courtier* both promote the art of "Menadrie" by providing their readers with the necessary implements to perform tasks "above Natures vertue and power simple."[1] By tracing the collateral, mutually legitimating discourses of courtliness and mechanics, this chapter demonstrates how courtly practitioners of the mechanical arts and "rude mechanicals" alike strive to identify mechanical objects and practices as instruments of civility, discipline, and self-government.

Dee's *Preface* is one of a number of Elizabethan treatises on mechanics which answers the Platonic suspicion of mechanics by locating new guarantors for machinery in courtly and political instrumentality. As the dichotomous and unyielding idealism of Renaissance Platonism gives way, at least in part, to more contingent, new humanist values such as prudence and expediency, mechanics is redeemed by virtue of its methodological affinities to the pragmatic and relativistic philosophical outlooks that dominate late sixteenth-century thought. At the same time, scholars, poets, and natural philosophers integrate machinery into the aesthetics of courtly *sprezzatura* canonized by Castiglione, allying the operation of mechanical devices with the cultivation of a new order of virtues and values – equipoise, grace, prudence, and resolve. While such qualities are regarded as instrumental to success at court, thus explaining how and why machinery intervenes so persistently in court recreation and spectacle, they are also prized by neo-Stoic writers and others hostile to the court as tools to implement philosophical strategies of resistance. In the case of Henry Percy, an avid student of both Archimedean mechanics and Stoic ethics, the former discipline serves the latter in supplying tangible models and equations for the internal equilibrium of the Stoic sage.

It is during the brief but pedagogically revolutionary reign of Edward VI (1547–53) that the first generation of English scientists – among them Dee, Robert Recorde, and Leonard Digges – defend mechanics as a legitimate discipline. In the decades that follow, scholars and scientists of varying social ranks struggle to strip mechanics of its associations with rudeness and to yoke the discipline to the canons of a courtly aesthetic. Technical treatises by Elizabethan mechanicians including Thomas Digges, William Bourne, and John Blagrave work to integrate mechanical objects and practices into courtly sensibilities, while Thomas Blundeville, Henry Percy, and Henry Peacham all endorse mechanics as a suitable exercise for the Elizabethan and Jacobean gentleman. These authors of books of conduct view mechanics as an inculcator of intellectual and moral discipline, and (to use the titular term of Blundeville's 1594 work) of "exercise" for correct physical deportment.

Far from being relegated to the province of the rude mechanical, the study of mechanics is reinvented in the latter half of the sixteenth century as an instrument of courtly grace, so much so that the regular, even movements of machines come to epitomize physical control, elegance, and emotional tranquility. Mechanical "motions," a term which denotes physical movement but also the violent force of human passions, become powerful symbolic and dramatic vehicles for regulating physical and ethical conduct. Yet even as mechanical objects and practices cultivate physical and moral rectitude in their Renaissance practitioners, they can also exemplify contrary qualities such as fickleness, affectation, or immoderate passion.

The introduction of Italian courtesy theory to Tudor England is part of a more widespread importation of Italianate subtlety – an amalgam of artistic skill, political cunning, and mechanical ingenuity perfected by the culture which, at least from the English perspective, had mastered craftiness in all its possible forms. Sixteenth-century English writers look to the art of mechanics to mold the stereotype of the subtle Italian and his English impersonator. Thomas Nashe dreams up a banqueting house, complete with mechanical birds, in order to satirize Italianate artifice in *The Unfortunate Traveller*, while Robert Dallington looks to the "rare invention of water-workes," automatic organs, and "infinite sort of such devise[s]" in the gardens of Pratolino and Tivoli as tangible expressions of the "subtill conceit" and "perilous wit" epitomized by Machiavelli.[2] The climactic

theories of behavior fashionable during the period strengthen the intertwined stereotypes of the machinating Italian and the subtle mechanician.
Thomas Wright finds Italians and other southerners more prone to "crafti-
nesse and warinesse," while a 1591 treatise entitled *A Discovery of the great
subtilitie and wonderful wisdome of the Italians* observes that the Italians surpass all other nations in "invention, craft, and worldly pollicie" because they
are "wittie and subtill headed," masters of all "cunning slights, craftie con-
veyances, and deceitfull cozenages."[3] Italianate sublety certainly manifests
itself in Papal intrigues and in Florentine political philosophy, but it also
surfaces in the hydraulic garden devices and the feats of civil engineering
at which the Italians supposedly excel.

   While many English writers of the period are suspicious of Italian machination, political and mechanical, English scholars nonetheless travel to Italy,
particularly to Padua, Venice, and Urbino, to reap the advantages of Italian
ingenuity. From around 1500 onwards, there is a considerable amount of
intellectual traffic between England and Italy, much of it scientifically ori-
ented. Thomas Linacre and Reginald Pole both travel to Padua to study
with Tomeo; while in Italy, Linacre contributes to Tomeo's translation of
Proclus' *Sphaera*, printed by Aldus in 1499.[4] William Grocyn, John Colet,
William Lily, Richard Pace, Cuthbert Tunstall, William Latimer, Thomas
Lupset, and Thomas Starkey all travel to northern Italy between 1488 and
1523, where several of them help to edit Greek scientific texts with Tomeo
and his colleagues in Padua, Venice, and Urbino. This scholarly commerce
is surely strengthened by the strong political alliance between the Duchy
of Urbino and the Tudor monarchy during the period: Duke Guidobaldo
was made a Knight of the Garter by Henry VII, and in return, Henry was
given Raphael's painting of Saint George – with Castiglione acting as the
ambassador of the Italian court on the 1506 journey.[5]

   The political and intellectual alliances between early Tudor England and
Urbino provide fertile ground for the reception of Castiglione's writings
as well as for a growing English enthusiasm for Archimedean mechanics. In 1563, John Dee travels to Urbino to meet Federico Commandino,
then serving as court mathematician to Francesco Maria della Rovere. In
1570, the same year that Henry Billingsley's English translation of Euclid's
Elements is first printed, Dee and Commandino collaborate on an edition
of *De Superficierum Divisionibus* by the Arabic mathematician Mahomet
Bagdedini.[6] Influenced by the Archimedean mechanics of Commandino
and his Urbino school, Dee's *Preface* approaches its subject "both Mathematically and Mechanically," celebrating the speculative art of the mathematician but also the "commodious," practical work of the mechanician.[7]

With a hermeticism grounded in experimentation and in useful, even commercial, ends, Dee's scientific writings, particularly those written in the wake of his encounter with Commandino, grant the discipline of mechanics a twofold legitimacy in both the contemplative and the active spheres. The study of mechanics elucidates the divinely ordained motions of the cosmos, but it is also a practical, worldly pursuit whose principal end is the manipulation of the natural world.

In his *Preface*, John Dee uses the term "Menadrie" to refer to the subdiscipline of mechanics that "demonstrateth, how, above Natures Vertue and power simple: Vertue and force may be multiplied."[8] According to Dee, Menadrie includes "all cranes, Gybbettes, & Ingines to lift up, or to force any thing, any maner way," but in particular the "pollicies, devises, and engines" of Archimedes, machines which counteract all the "Force, courage, and pollicie of the Romaines." From the Greek μενοσ (strength or force) and αδρανοσ (powerless, weak) Menadrie is a species of *metis* that amplifies the power of the weak. Insofar as it countermands Roman "pollicie" with the "pollicie" of a mechanical device, Dee's Menadrie is also analogous to political *virtù*, that adversarial power defined in contradistinction to force which combats the effects of fortune or nature. Working against nature, Dee's Menadrian mechanics is consonant with Machiavelli's explanation of *virtù* in *The Prince*, in which political efficacy is likened to the mechanical ingenuity required to hold back the violent current of a river with "floodgates and embankments."[9]

Dee's *Preface* exploits the affinities between mechanical and political artifice already latent in sixteenth-century Italian political and scientific discourse. As the work of William Sherman has shown, Dee is hardly an eccentric magus shut off from the world, and his interest in mechanics is primarily worldly and thus at odds with the Platonic strains evident in works such as the *Monas Hieroglyphica* and the *Heptarchia Mysteria*. For Dee, mechanics is ultimately an art of political manipulation, a means to "finde out, and devise, new workes, straunge Engines, and Instruments: for sundry purposes in the Common Wealth."[10]

Perhaps in an effort to make the study of mechanics more congenial to his royal and aristocratic patrons, Dee's *Preface* accommodates mechanics to courtly *facilità* as well as to political *virtù*, using the figure of Archimedes to do so. Noting Archimedes' "wonderful reason and facilitie," Dee follows Plutarch and Athenaeus in describing how "he alone, with his devises and engynes" could accomplish feats beyond human power. In the section on "Trochilike," or the "strange works and incredible" made possible by wheels and pulleys, Dee once again uses an Archimedean device as an example of *facilità*, describing how when Hiero of Siracuse "was not hable to move a certaine Ship (being on ground) mightie *Archimedes*, setting to, his Skruish Engine, caused *Hiero* the King, by him self, at ease, to remove her, as he would."[11]

All of Dee's examples of Archimedean *sprezzatura* lead up to his defense of "Thaumaturgike," or mechanical "Wonder-worke" that is "naturally, mathematically, and mechanically, wrought" even though its effects appear "mervaylous, above the power of Nature."[12] Praising Archimedes alongside Archytas, Daedalus, and Regiomontanus, Dee launches a tirade against his "disdainfull countreymen" who consider marvelous machines to be the product of unlawful conjuring: against nature, as well as above it. By the time Dee reaches the end of his diatribe, the *Preface* has completely departed from the overtly Platonic, occult justification offered by the opening pages of the text, where mathematics is celebrated as a divine language full of "wonderfull mysteries, by numbers, to be atteyned unto."[13]

In earlier works such as his 1564 *Monas Hieroglyphica*, Dee looks not to self-moving machines but rather to his Monad, a subtle knot of mathematical and metaphysical theories, as a key to unlock the secrets of nature. Dee imagines the Monad as a tool that enables the "astronomer [to] be able to observe heavenly bodies under one roof without any mechanical instruments made of wood or brass [sine mechanicis ullis, ex ligno vel Orichalco confectis]." While Dee's Monad "proves the wonders [miranda] . . . of various devices," it does so without the help of machinery, thus transcending the physical nature of mechanical demonstration and alleviating the typically Platonic discomfort with instrumentality that characterizes the *Monas Hieroglyphica*.[14]

In the six years that elapse between the *Monas Hieroglyphica* and the *Preface*, Dee's natural philosophy is profoundly reshaped by Commandino and by Peter Ramus, who presents a copy of his *Prooemium Mathematicum* to Dee in 1567. By 1570, Dee no longer appeals to a mystical Platonic theology as the sole guarantor of either mathematics or mechanics, nor does he represent mechanics merely as a worldly (and thus inferior) application of mathematical principles. By contrast, Dee's *Preface* defines mechanics as an "artificiall method" through which "Number . . . a thyng so Immaterial, so divine, and aeternall" is accommodated to our "grosse" understanding. By grounding the immaterial truths of mathematics in the experience of "corporall thynges seen, or felt," mechanics helps us "learn a certaine Image, or likenes of numbers," bringing us closer to the ineffable by grounding the abstractions of mathematics in material form. While the speculative study of mathematics still enables humankind to "Mount above the cloudes and sterres," mechanics provides a contrary but equally valuable means by which we may "descend, to frame Naturall thinges, to wonderfull uses." Dee invokes the Neoplatonic ladder made famous by Castiglione's Bembo but transforms the image so as to emphasize the equal importance of mathematics and mechanics, respectively, as the "Meanes, to Ascend or Descend by." By virtue of its capacity to help us move down, as well as up, this ladder, mechanics counterbalances mathematics such that we may, "when [we] list, retire home into [our] owne Centre."[15]

More accommodating to the mechanical arts than Plato, who argues that mathematics "plainly compels the soul to employ pure thought," the Platonism of Dee's *Preface* more closely resembles that of Proclus in that it denies the metaphysical purity of mathematics and instead acknowledges its "middle nature." Like Proclus, Dee refuses wholly to privilege spirit over matter or to dissociate the one from the other, and he praises mathematics for its capacity to mediate between earth and heaven, "beyng (in a maner) middle, betweene thinges supernaturall and naturall . . . not so absolute and excellent, as thinges supernatural: Nor yet so base and grosse, as things naturall."[16] Like Guido Ubaldo, who regards mechanics as noble because it derives "from the union of two noblest arts, geometry and physics," Dee imagines mechanics as a blend of purer disciplines whose hybridity, like Donne's violet, grants it greater strength.[17] This is particularly clear in Dee's manuscript notes on Book XII of Euclid's *Elements*, dated December 10, 1569, in which he neglects the purely mathematical consequences of Euclidian geometry and focuses instead on its practical ramifications in the field of mechanics. "The great mechanicall use (besides mathematicall considerations)," Dee writes of two of Euclid's corollaries, "may have in wheeles of mylles, clockes, cranes, and other Engines for waterworkes, and for warres, and many other purposes [which] the earnest & witty mechanician will soone boult out, and gladly practise." While Euclid's theorems might parenthetically be a means to attain "certayne knowledge demonstrative," Dee's stated "intent" in this draft version of his *Preface* is to give his reader "some ready aide . . . to invent and practise things mechanically."[18] In other words, Euclid's *Elements* is only valuable for Dee to the extent that its theories yield practical, tangible uses, a sentiment that echoes Ramus' assessment of Archimedean mechanics as a "a science whose final aim is use, not contemplation [artium fine esse usum, non contemplationem]."[19] Dee ends his *Preface* with an impassioned defense of "Archemastrie," the art of bringing mathematical knowledge "to actuall experience sensible" in order to achieve the "performance of complet Experie[n]ces." Grounded in sense experience, mechanical artifice is natural in a way that mathematics, untethered to any concrete experience, is not. Influenced by a hermeticism grounded in "actual experience," Dee's defense of machinery as both natural and practical is what makes the work, according to Roy Strong, a "revolutionary manifesto" of Renaissance science.[20]

The Elizabethan investment in mechanics is fueled by a diverse set of philosophical and political convictions, and the disparate uses to which rulers, aristocrats, and scholars put their study and collection of mechanical objects reveal the ideological malleability of the discipline. Capable of upholding the dominant values and beliefs of the Tudor court, mechanical devices are equally capable of challenging normative values or mocking political authority. Tutored by Dee as a child, Robert Devereux, Earl of Essex had a "preoccupation with astronomical instruments" according to Mordechai Feingold, and he commissioned designs from instrument-makers including Thomas Hariot and Edward Wright. One of these is a pocket-dial which Devereux carried with him during his uprising, histrionically handing the timepiece over to his chaplain on the morning of his execution.[21] Robert Dudley, Earl of Leicester, who was instrumental in encouraging English advancements in military tactics during the 1570s and 1580s, had a fondness for clocks, installing several at Kenilworth Castle. Queen Elizabeth shared Dudley's interest: one contemporary inventory of her belongings lists no fewer than twenty-four different timepieces.[22] Elizabethan and Jacobean palaces attracted contemporary visitors with their array of mechanical curiosities: at Whitehall, contemporary visitors describe a clock in the shape of an "Ethiop" riding a rhinoceros, while Hampton Court boasts an "ingenious waterwork."[23]

For William Cecil, Lord Burghley, an ardent supporter of practical scientific learning, the advancement of the discipline of mechanics promises to fashion England into the technically sophisticated empire imagined by contemporary texts such as Humphrey Gilbert's *Academy* (*c.* 1572) and W. S.'s 1581 *Discourse of the Common Weal of this Realm of England*.[24] In his *Scholarum Mathematicum*, Ramus singles out "Guilielmus Caecilus," along with Dee, as a principal supporter of the mathematical sciences in England.[25] Mechanicians from England and abroad write numerous letters to Cecil demanding protection for their new inventions under his emergent patent system. Richard Eden writes to Cecil with the offer of an "automaton" comparable to those purportedly crafted by Poliziano and Roger Bacon, while Emery Molyneux writes to him in 1596 with the promise of an "Ingyn never before seen or hearde of."[26] Thomas Hood writes to Cecil in the hopes of establishing a "mathematicall lecture," subsequently given in 1588 at a ceremony for the foundation of Gresham College, a London technical university catering to the new generation of explorers and experimenters.[27] As a shareholder of the Mines Royal company and an advocate of Sir Thomas Smith's Society for the New Art, a short-lived attempt at the establishment of a mechanical and metallurgical academy, Cecil keenly understood the political applications of the inventions presented to him, as did the mechanicians who wrote to him.[28] Like Cecil's collection of maps, which were tools "for the business of political administration," the machines he sponsored and helped to patent, including surveying instruments, military engines, and navigational devices, were instrumental in legitimating, rationalizing, and increasing sovereign power.[29] Yet even the most impractical mechanical devices – technical curiosa such as clocks or fountains – also held a fascination for Cecil, as attested to by accounts of the hydraulic garden machinery and other mechanical gadgets constructed for his house at Theobalds, a palace so rich in its ingenious devices that King James would persuade Robert Cecil to exchange it for Hatfield House in 1605. The younger Cecil capitulated but subsequently hired Salomon de Caus to build new and more spectacular machinery at the residence.[30]

The dedications of scientific treatises addressed to Cecil make frequent appeals to the political value of the mechanical "secrets" they contain. While they do not attribute occult or mystical qualities to machinery, these texts instead endow their inventions with arcane characteristics intended to appeal to Cecil's official involvement in the preservation and manipulation of secrets of state. William Bourne, who dedicated several of his treatises to Cecil and produced a manuscript on optical glasses especially for the Lord Treasurer, writes in his 1578 *Inventions or devises* that like the "brasen head" of Roger Bacon, or other "strange workes that the world hath marvayled at," his automata and speaking heads might appear to operate "by Inchantment" but in fact are "done by wheeles, as you may see by clockes." In offering to Cecil the guardianship of his mechanical secrets, Bourne's devices enact and justify the *arcana imperii* – the political techniques of manipulating the wonder, the error, or the ignorance of beholders to cultivate an aura of techno-political mystery. In revealing to Cecil the secret operation of his automata, which seem to work "by Inchantment" but which are set into motion "by no other Meanes, but by good Artes and lawfull," Bourne legitimates the preservation of political *arcana*, even boasting that his devices will keep the "common people" in awe.[31]

Eden likewise couches his inventions as models of political manipulation when he writes to Cecil to offer him an automaton, a device Eden describes rather obliquely by citing Roger Bacon's *Discovery of the Miracles of Art*,

Nature, and Magick, now commonly known as *Letter on the Nullity of Magic*: "multa sunt archana admiranda in operibus artis & naturae [there are many arcane wonders in the works of art and nature]." Given Eden's desire that the design of his device be revealed to Cecil's eyes alone, the allusion to Bacon is an apt one, for in this treatise, a work edited by John Dee and printed in Hamburg in 1618, the medieval philosopher repeatedly warns that "the divulging of Mysteries is the diminution of their Majesty, nor indeed continues that to be a Secret, of which the whole fry of men is conscious," yet at the same time promises his readers to reveal the designs of "Engines for flying," instruments for breathing under water, and "infinite such like inventions."[32]

Edward Worsop also dedicates his 1582 *Discoverie of Sundrie Errors and Faults Daily Committed by Landemeaters* to Cecil, insisting that his work differs from those "learned books" which "can not bee understoode of the common sorte" even as the full title of the work also promises "manifest proofe that none ought to be admitted to that function, but the learned practisioners of those Sciences."[33] Throughout, Worsop is torn between assuring the lay mechanician that the "demonstrations, and proofes herein [are] verie easie to the Readers" and championing the difficulty and obscurity of his text, particularly its use of scientific jargon or "peculiar termes." Alternately sanctioning and condemning the secretive nature of scientific discourse, Worsop creates the illusion of an exclusive text whose promised secrets are revealed only to an elite audience. In doing so, he appeals to his dedicatee, Cecil, as a purveyor of arcana, and then appeals to his common readers as a purveyor of counter-arcana, offering them a glimpse of the privy knowledge which rightfully belongs to Cecil and the Elizabethan state. Even his use of the vernacular, a convention often misconstrued as a sign of the increased "openness" of scientific discourse during the Renaissance, becomes a tool of secrecy in Worsop's hands.[34] Justifying the text's coining of new English terms for surveying, one of the interlocutors of the *Discoverie* explains that he has abandoned the more familiar Latin terms because "you would not have your cunnings in land measuring knowen to any but your selves." Unglamorous surveying instruments though they may be, Worsop's devices accrue value as political secrets. Learned by "studies, and practises" rather than by "naturall witte," his instruments also accrue an aura of courtly mystery, since their mastery depends upon art and yet still promise to be "easie" to operate according to the dedication.[35]

Clocks and other mechanical devices serve royal users and patrons as working models of the *arcana imperii* by symbolically enforcing the aura of mystery upon which royal prerogative relies. In court spectacles, in collections, and in paintings and texts, machines are harnessed to the emergent absolutist state as instruments of rule. As one seventeenth-century epigrammatist points out, in an observation he attributes to Justus Lipsius, the inscrutable inner workings of machines legitimate political secrecy by analogy: "Just as we see the hand of the clock and read the hours from its turning without having insight into the ingenious workings of its complex gears," he writes, "the actions of princes and lords lie open before our eyes, but their purposes and motives are hidden from our eyes."[36]

The analogy is a persuasive one for early seventeenth-century political philosophers including Tommaso Campanella, Gabriel Naudé, and Arnold Clapmar, each of whom recognize that politics, like the illusions effected by spectacular machinery, relies upon "private or hidden procedures or counsels [intimas et occultas rationes, sive consilia] in order to work."[37] When Campanella observes that "clockmaking and other mechanical arts...easily lose their reverence when their workings become obvious to ordinary people," he is tacitly endorsing the conviction that political authority is enhanced by the instruments of secrecy and mystery.[38] No more marvelous than carefully orchestrated political fictions, mechanical marvels are only magical, according to Campanella, until they are understood: "the invention of gunpowder, the printing press and the use of the magnet were once regarded as magic, but now that everyone understands the art, it is common knowledge [l'invenzione della polvere dell'archibugo e delle stampe fu cosa magica, e così l'uso della calamità; ma oggi che tutti sanno l'arte è cosa volgare]."[39] In his 1625 *Apologie pour tous les grands personnages qui ont esté faussement soupçonnez de magie* Naudé extends the analogy between political and mechanical illusions, arguing that mechanics *is* politics inasmuch as both disciplines manipulate appearances to their best advantage. Defending Roger Bacon and John Dee from accusations of necromancy, Naudé protests that though these men are "esteemed magicians," they are "nothing but Politicians [ont esté estimer Magiciens qui n'estoient que Politiques]," and he goes on to exonerate from similar charges all "those who design and construct artificial machines [ceux qui dresse & compose ses machines artificielles]."[40]

The analogical habits of mind which yoke the illusions of natural magic to the deceptions of the Renaissance *politique* ensure the participation of machinery in negotiations concerning the moral or political circumstances under which secrecy and dissimulation are legitimate instruments of rule. Nowhere are these negotiations more complex and strained than in the case of Cornelius Drebbel's perpetual motion machine, first presented to King James in 1607 and then demonstrated by Drebbel at court upon his

return to London in 1612. Contemporary accounts of Drebbel's device reveal
how James comprehends and attempts to command spectacular machinery
to legitimate his reliance upon the *arcana imperii*, even as the machine's
performance arrogates and threatens the mystification of political power
upon which Jacobean kingship is predicated.[41]

In a 1607 dedicatory letter addressed to King James, Drebbel promises
that his perpetual motion machine offers a "working model [levendige
instrumentum]" of "that pleasing sweetness which is perceived from the
hidden causes of things."[42] In his written presentation of the device to James,
as well as in eyewitness accounts of the engineer's public performance of the
machine at James' court in 1612, Drebbel cannily manipulates the device as
a working model of Jacobean political mystery, one that both appropriates
and transforms its key concept of the *arcana imperii*, or mysteries of state.
An account of Drebbel's 1612 demonstration of the machine by Thomas
Tymme enshrouds the device in both hermetic and political secrecy: while
the full title of Tymme's work promises to open "Nature's Secret Closet"
by revealing the operation of the machine, one of the interlocutors admits
at the beginning of the dialogue that Drebbel's device is "in the custody
of King James." Tymme's character complains that while "I did at sundry
times pry into the practice of [Drebbel]," he has gleaned nothing about
the machine's design, since Drebbel has divulged its secret to the King
alone: "this cunning Bezaleel, in secret manner disclosed to his Maiestie the
secret, whereupon he applauded the rare invention." By dubbing Drebbel
"Bezaleel," the craftsman appointed by God to make the tabernacle and the
ark of the covenant for the Israelites, Tymme not only implies that Drebbel
has been "specially chosen" by God, but also that, like the "forbidden arke"
to which King James compares his "absolute and indisputable prerogative"
in a 1622 speech to Parliament, the secrecy of the machine is guaranteed by
a divinely ordained authority.[43]

It is the 1607 account of a Bohemian traveler, Heinrich Hiesserle Von
Chodaw, which best reveals how King James views the machine as a potential confederate of his royal prerogative by virtue of its capacity to conceal
both the origins and the perpetuity of its own motive power. Von Chodaw's
account begins when Drebbel, arriving at court, announces that God has
revealed to him, and only to him, the secret of perpetual motion. The King
laughs, expressing surprise that "this great secret which had remained hidden
to all learned men from the beginning of the world, should be revealed to
him alone."[44] The subsequent exchange between the engineer and his royal
patron reveals Drebbel to be a master of equivocation and evasion. When
James asks how the machine remains in motion, Drebbel responds only

that it is moved by "the perpetual motion, which lay inside" and advises James to invite philosophers to his court to "study this and speculate on it, and say whence the motive power comes, and what the perpetual motion is." When pressed once again to reveal the secret of perpetual motion, Drebbel instructs James to "seal [the machine] up and lock it away as long as you like," promising wryly that it will continue to function "as long as the world exists, or as long as it was not broken." In this brief exchange, Drebbel manages to relocate inside the inner workings of the machine the most pressing political questions vexing James' reign while at the same time presenting the perpetual motion as capable of enacting some of the most potent fantasies of the Jacobean court. As sole proprietor of the machine, James is made the exclusive guardian of a piece of politico-scientific *arcana*, one which ensures his status as a philosopher-king whose court invites intellectuals to come and "speculate."

In order to demonstrate its symbolic power as an emblem of royal prerogative, Drebbel persists in withholding the secret of the machine from King James, who according to Von Chodaw "would not stop asking the man [Drebbel] whence [the perpetual motion] came." After several months, Drebbel finally relents, and his "secret was revealed to the King under the condition that he should reveal it no further."[45] The private revelation invites the King to preserve secrets of nature and, by analogy, secrets of state, from the public eye. Controlled by Drebbel, the perpetual motion also enacts the dialectical interplay between revelation and concealment which, according to James' *Basilikon Doron*, is a key attribute of the adept ruler, who should "not be so facile of accesse-giving at all times . . . and yet not altogether retired or locked up, like the Kings of Persia."[46] Writing about the performance of a similar machine at an eighteenth-century German court, Simon Schaffer has argued that perpetual motion machines uphold the ideologies of "baroque absolutism" by virtue of the fact that their "inner workings remained privy to the calculations of the eminent and the skillful."[47] Yet by frustrating James' repeated attempts to penetrate into the "secret closet" of the device, Drebbel's device unites and places on a level the esoteric machines of the mechanician with the mysteries of state that are the instruments of absolute monarchy.

As the symbolic arbiter of stability and continuity, Drebbel's "wonderful Sphere" legitimates the idea of monarchy for early seventeenth-century writers such as John Johnston by offering proof of the "constant and most apparent motions and law of the Heavens."[48] On the eve of the English Civil War, the inventor and staunch Royalist Edward Somerset, Marquis of Worcester, designs a perpetual motion machine for Charles I, presumably as a guarantor of the essential permanence of the Stuart monarchy. While imprisoned during the Interregnum, Somerset confirms the political value of the machine constructed for Charles by building himself an "engine so contrived [that] the pretended Operation continueth" eternally; the perpetual motion of his "semi-omnipotent engine" is so certain that Somerset "intend[s] that a Model thereof be buried with me," as if to ensure eternal life.[49] Imagine King James' horror when, after running smoothly for several years at Eltham Palace, Drebbel's device grinds to a halt when, Pandora-like, the Queen "touched it with her curious hand, with the result that all actions ceased [postquam ei curiosam manum admovisset Regina, ita ut omnes actiones cessarent]."[50] Political authority is both created and overthrown by mechanical artifice, by the perpetual motion machines and the scenic devices which, according to Roy Strong, are intended as expressions of "the Renaissance exaltation of wonder."[51] Yet machines designed to leave their audiences *stupiti*, or amazed, only sustain the sovereign mystery they enact so long as their inner workings remain both obscure and in good repair.

Machines can thus legitimate or complicate secrets of state when their makers and spectators forge analogies between political mystery and the subtlety of machinery. Often Archimedean in both their designs and effects, machines can also exemplify the *facilità* of the ideal ruler or courtier. Across late sixteenth-century Europe, machines designed for heads of state act as symbolic and physical vehicles for enacting unconstrained displays of power. In his 1575 translation of Taisnier's work on navigation, Richard Eden recalls having heard "credible reporte, that the Earle of Rocumdolse, an Almaine, made an engin, wherewith the sayde king Charles [IX of France] when he was but xvi yeeres of age, lyfted from the grounde a weyght, whiche the strongest man in the courte was not able to remoove." By distributing the weight of a heavy object across a network of pulleys and ropes, Charles IX's hoisting device, an "engin not unlyke that whiche in auncient tyme Archimedes invented for the Syracusians" according to Eden, reduces the need for physical force, thus reinforcing the King's agility and grace as well as the fulcrum-like nature of his sovereign power.[52]

The Elizabethan and Jacobean court relies upon machinery to justify monarchical power, to elucidate its conflictive relationship to political secrecy, and to weigh some of its key moral and intellectual conflicts. By circumventing the need for physical effort and supplying an intellectual recreation that sharpens wit and dexterity, machines readily harmonize with certain courtly sensibilities. Yet purged of its practical applications and reclaimed by the court as a speculative, even frivolous, recreation, machinery can also epitomize the artifice and the indolence at odds with the active *virtù* of the ideal courtier. As they become assimilated to courtly culture, machines are abstracted into multiple and competing moral emblems which are capable of symbolizing autonomy and servitude, constancy and flux, grace and affectation. Whether held up as a manifestation of courtly ideals or used to denounce excessive artifice, frivolity, or lassitude, mechanics is understood not as a discrete intellectual discipline but rather as a vehicle for contemplating the moral and intellectual legitimacy of instrumental means.

Renaissance technical treatises frequently stress the "facilitie" of the mechanical devices they advertise. Judging from the prefaces and dedications of numerous treatises written between around 1550 and 1630, the crucial role of objects such as surveying or astronomical instruments lies not in what they do but in how they do it. Thomas Fale's 1627 *Horologiographia* provides an "easie and perfect way to make all kinds of Dials," while John Blagrave's 1585 *Mathematicall Jewell* offers "a reduction of the Arts Mathematicke . . . unto an easie, methodious, plaine, and practique discipline."[53] By emphasizing the effortlessness with which technical activities can be executed, these texts rhetorically situate the operation of mechanical instruments within the repertoire of ornamental tactics which assure the grace and social distinction of the Renaissance gentleman. Blagrave's *Jewell* advertises its multi-purpose measuring device as a "singuler Instrument . . . that performeth with wonderfull dexteritie" the operations of compass, globe, and quadrant. Addressing itself to "Gentleman and others desirous of speculative knowledge," Blagrave's *Jewell* appeals to aspiring courtiers such as Gabriel Harvey, whose annotated copy of Blagrave's text is analyzed in chapter 4 of this book, by equating technical aptitude with the deftness of Castiglione's courtier as he performs "easye and pleasaunt exercyses." Readily manipulated with "incredible speed, plainenesse, facilitie, and pleasure," the *Jewell* reinforces the dexterity central to what Castiglione's Elizabethan translator terms a "ready aptnesse."[54]

Blagrave's *Jewell* upholds the courtly ideal of doing difficult things easily, thus confirming Steven Shapin's claim that scientific practice is a "species of *sprezzatura*."[55] Enabling their users to perform tasks without moving from a given location, surveying and measuring devices simulate the *facilità* crucial to aristocratic self-fashioning. Henri de Suberville's 1598 *Henry-metre*, a treatise on a new kind of surveying instrument, makes a titular promise to take "all Geometric and Astronomical measurements without moving it from its place [toutes mésures Geometriques & Astronomiques . . . sans le bouger de sa place]," while a 1617 French treatise on mills whose title-page boasts a portrait of Archimedes and his lever provides numerous ways "to make water mount up on high, without too much pain and effort [pour faire monter l'eau au hault, sans beaucoup de peine & despens]."[56] Robert Tanner's 1587 *Mirror for Mathematiques* promises "playne and most easie instruction," while the title-page of Aaron Rathborne's 1616 *Surveyor* depicts the figure of *Artifex*, surrounded by instruments, above an inscription that reads "inertia strenua." Like Ripa's *Argano* (from the Greek *argos*, meaning inactive), Rathborne's surveying instrument occasions the paradoxical state of "strenuous inertia," a quality comparable to Cicero's *negligentia diligens* in that it fosters an illusion of effortlessness. If, according to Castiglione's Count Lodovico, the courtier's artifice lies in not "put[ting] more diligence in any thing than in covering it," the deceptions of machinery likewise aim to produce an "art that appeareth not to be art" by eliminating the need for strenuous effort.[57]

Despite their potential affiliation with courtly *sprezzatura*, mechanical devices do need to be defended against and imaginatively refashioned for those who regard mechanics as a discipline unfit for gentlemen. As Patricia Parker has pointed out, sixteenth-century writers use the term "mechanical" to disparage any artisanal, base activity, denigrating the "constructed or artefactual" by distinguishing it from the "spontaneous or natural."[58] The laboriousness of certain mechanical activities is seen by some as antipathetic to courtly *facilità*: King James I expresses a common concern when he warns his son not to be "a player upon instruments . . . nor yet to be fine of any mechanicke craft." Yet in the *Basilikon Doron*, James is principally concerned that Henry not engage in activities "such as men commonly winne their living with," and his use of the term "mechanicke" refers not to a specific discipline or skill, but rather to the style or spirit in which it is performed. James concedes that any mental or physical activity could run the risk of becoming "mechanical" if performed improperly, and likewise all "exercises" are potentially decorous so long as they are performed gracefully, effortlessly, and "moderately, not making a craft of them."[59] As James' enthusiastic patronage of Drebbel and Salomon de Caus suggests, mechanics can be, and frequently is, reclaimed by and for a courtly audience.

Aware of the nebulous character of their collective epithet, Renaissance mechanicians are quick to reinvent the stereotype of the "rude mechanical." The Italian mechanician Niccolò Tartaglia apologizes in a dedication to Henry VIII for "inventions which are mecanicall and common things tolde and declared in a blunt and barbarous style," and Elizabethan mechanicians frequently make similar – and similarly feigned – protestations of rudeness in their dedications and prefaces.[60] Bourne and Leonard Digges demure respectively that they are "utterly unlearned" and lacking in the "pithie eloquence" of a gentleman. These claims of rudeness constitute an attempt to cultivate the insouciant dilettantism of the gentleman scholar and to supply a textbook example of the undercutting of expectation that Frank Whigham has identified as one of the master tropes of Elizabethan courtesy theory.[61]

One need look no further than the conventions of Renaissance pastoral to recognize how rudeness and simplicity are capable of being refashioned into markers of aristocratic nonchalance. The feigned humility of Bourne and Digges is best understood in the context of a courtly culture which, according to Javitch, demands that its participants "veil sophisticated and complex meanings under [a] cloak of simplicity" and "pretend to be very rustic when, in fact, [one] is most civilized."[62] Bourne and Digges disparage their works as "rude and base inventions" and as a "rude and homely tale," epithets meant to deflect attention away from their efforts and to evoke that peculiar brand of artlessness and rusticity which is the exclusive domain of the courtly elite. Like Castiglione's image of a prince dressed up as a wild shepherd "but with an excellent horse and wel trimmed for the purpose," the rhetoric of the Elizabethan mechanician diminishes expectation in order to exceed it. No rude mechanical, Digges is an educated and landed gentleman who boasts a lack of refinement in order to camouflage any hint of excessive effort and to distinguish himself from the professional instrument-maker. His very motto, "Mediocrità Firma," testifies to Digges' efforts to integrate mechanics into a moralized, courtly ethos by punning on the correspondence between the arithmetical and the golden mean.[63]

The persistent claims of ease and facility made by technical treatises underscore the recreative dimension of Renaissance mechanics. Machinery forms part of the landscape of aristocratic *otium*, contributing to the "fetish of recreation" that Whigham and Rosalie Colie have detected throughout the intellectual culture of the period. Adapting the rhetoric of the courtesy manual and the pastoral poet, Renaissance technical treatises emphasize the trifling and playful quality of their work even when their inventions might possess some practical application. Bourne dismisses his *Inventions or devises* as "trifles or toyes," while Thomas Hill's 1581 *Naturall and Artificiall Conclusions* offers its readers material "for the recreation of wittes at vacant tymes."[64]

As with Robert Burton and Thomas Browne, however, both of whom use the term "recreation" to denote a serious, productive kind of intellectual exercise, the recreations of machinery are not wholly bereft of intellectual merit. The mechanical operations and feats of legerdemain taught by technical treatises are, to use the sixteenth-century phrase, "serious jokes" – tricks and puzzles that conceal metaphysical and epistemological questions.[65] Rather than master a particular procedure or concept, the "recreative" mechanical practitioner learns to master himself, the precise control of his instruments acting as a metaphorical and an actual tool for intellectual and moral discipline. Alternately serving for adornment, distraction, and the cultivation of *virtù*, the optical tricks and automata explained in works by Bourne and Hill possess the same kind of cultural currency as the verbal and physical pastimes practiced by Castiglione's courtiers. Even the most mundanely useful device is profitable for its recreative value: Worsop advertises his surveying instrument as a device to help the reader perform "pretie feates, and fine sleightes . . . knackes, and jigges," displays of wit and subtlety described with a conventional courtly vocabulary.[66]

The recreative dimensions of mechanics reach a pinnacle in the first third of the seventeenth century with the appearance of texts such as Denis Henrion's *Collection, ou Recueil de Divers Traictez Mathematiques* (Paris, 1621), Nicolas Hunt's *Newe Recreations of the Mindes Release and Solacing* (London, 1631), and Henry Van Etten's *Mathematicall Recreations* (London, 1633). Less concerned with disseminating a body of scientific knowledge than they are with cultivating technico-literary virtuosity, these texts represent the recreative aspects of machinery as a *gioco serio*, a serious game that distracts, perplexes, or consoles its practitioners. Henrion's treatise, dedicated to the brother of the French King, offers "witty and recreative questions [questions ingenieuses et recreatives]" to "delight and sharpen the intellect [delecter et aguiser l'entendement]" and to "cultivate your gentle spirit [cultivez vostre bel esprit]."[67] Likewise, Hunt's 1631 *Newe Recreations of the Minde* calls itself "a rare and exquisite invention for the exercising of acute Wits."[68] Yet only some of its "Mysteries" and "Rarities" are of a scientific nature: while Book 2 is devoted to mechanical and mathematical tricks, Book 1 contains a who's who list of prominent men and the college, Inn of Court, or profession to which they belong, revealing a body of knowledge as esoteric to the common reader as the world of scientific novelties. The secrets of nature and the *arcana* of polite society converge in Hunt's *Recreations*, ensuring the cultivation of scientific virtuosity by aligning mechanical wonders with the revealed secrets of a social elite.

Van Etten's *Mathematicall Recreations* presents its material with a similar topos of recreation, and it unabashedly aestheticizes the machinery it describes, delighting in the "diverse pretty Dyalls" whose intricacies "recreate the Spirits" rather than perform precision measurements. While the pasteboard fire-breathing dragons and other mechanical "spectacles of pleasure" described by Van Etten serve little scientific purpose, they do play a diacritical role in the simultaneous eschewing of work and idleness that characterizes the ethos of the Jacobean aristocracy. Van Etten acknowledges that while "sundry fine wits . . . have sported and delighted themselves upon severall things of small consequence," these scientific *nugae* nonetheless serve to "recreate the Spirites," thus embodying the intellectual subtlety and the frivolity both prized and denigrated by aristocratic culture.[69]

Allied with a nonchalance that verges upon idleness and intellectual laxity, machinery is a malleable marker of social and intellectual distinction which easily sheds its association with *facilità* and comes instead to exemplify the facile cleverness and the affectation repugnant to true gentlemanliness. The Elizabethan scientist Henry Savile voices a commonplace concern when, according to John Aubrey, he identifies the mathematician Edmund Gunter's reliance upon mechanical devices as a sign of intellectual trickery and of lazy, sham scholarship. Whilst under consideration as a candidate for the Savilian Chair of Geometry, Gunter begins using "his sector and his quadrant and fell to reading triangles," according to Aubrey, at which point Savile scornfully remarks, "This is showing of tricks, man," and dismisses him, a reaction to be expected from a man who "could not abide witts" and preferred the "plodding student" to his cleverer companions: "If I would look for witts," Savile once commented, "I would goe to Newgate: there be the Witts."[70]

When one of Savile's students, William Oughtred, attacks the "preposterous" use of mechanical instruments in a 1630 debate with William Forster, his distinction between the proper and the improper "mechanicall wayes of Instruments" functions as an intellectual and social exclusionary tool by keeping flexible the boundaries between the artifactual and the natural. Responding to Richard Delamain's 1630 *Grammelogia*, which defends mechanics by arguing that "to begin with instrument is not to juggle, nor to do tricks," Oughtred protests that "the true way of Art is not by Instruments but by Demonstration." "It is a preposterous course of vulgar Teachers," Oughtred continues," to begin with the instruments, and not with the Sciences."[71] Using a mechanical device is only acceptable if it "serves and ancillates to the highest contemplations," and when instruments supplant rather than supplement "sound learning," their practitioners become "doers of tricks" and "juglers," terms that evoke the menial servility of a court jester.[72] "Corrupted with doting upon Instruments," Delamain is "quite lost from ever being made an Artist" by Oughtred's account, for he is guilty of an excessive diligence, a slavish adherence to technique, and above all a lack of originality that produces the affectation condemned by Renaissance courtesy literature. Addressing himself to the "English Gentrie," Oughtred insults Delamain's modest upbringing, calling him a "vulgar Teacher" while boasting of his own genteel status and Cambridge education. Yet Oughtred also accuses Delamain of having stolen his design for a horizontal dial, which Oughtred claims to have invented and shown to Henry Briggs in 1618, well before the instrument appears in Delamain's *Grammelogia*. According to Forster, whose dedication to his 1633 translation of Oughtred's *Circles of Proportion* recounts the latter's dispute with Delamain, Oughtred justifies his own mechanical ways as socially and intellectually acceptable, while condemning those of the plebeian and imitative Delamain, by asserting that "the use of instruments is indeed excellent, if a man be an Artist: but contemptible, being set and opposed to Art."[73] It is a statement whose Count Lodovico-like vagueness subjects the practice of mechanics to the ever-changing rules of courtly decorum so as to leave indeterminate the extent to which, and the means by which, mechanics might serve as an ornament for an intellectual or social elite even as it helps to divide the base from the noble and the artifactual from the seemingly natural.

The recreative dimension of machinery helps to voice the court's discomfort with the triviality and even the impropriety of its spectacles and recreations. Visiting the pleasure gardens in Augsburg in 1580, Montaigne describes fountains which "spurt out thin, hard streams of water to the height of a man's head, and fill the petticoats and thighs of the ladies with this coolness [elancent de l'eau menue et roide jusques à la teste d'un home, et ramplissent les cotillons des dames et leurs cuisses de cette frecheur]."[74] The erotic playfulness of these so-called wetting sports, hydraulic machines designed to spray unwitting visitors, foreground and mock the aristocratic fetish of recreation, for an inscription on the fountain chastises the reader, "You were looking for trifling amusements; here they are; enjoy them [Quaesisti nugas, nugis gaudeto repertis]."[75] Complicit in the spectator's own frivolity, hydraulic garden machinery chides but also smirks at the vain subtleties which entertain its noble audience. Although similar machines are found in aristocratic settings such as Prince Henry's Richmond Palace and Sir Henry Fanshawe's Ware House, the trifling quality of garden machinery means that it always runs the risk of becoming vulgar. This is certainly Henry Peacham's complaint when he describes the rude throngs clamoring to see Drebbel's perpetual motion machine installed for a time at Eltham Palace. In his "Sights and Exhibitions of England," prefaced to the 1611 edition of Thomas Coryate's *Crudities*, he asks, "Why do the rude vulgar so hastily post in a madnesse / To gaze at trifles?," comparing Drebbel's "heavenly motion" to unicorns' horns and other "toyes not worth the viewing."[76] Given Peacham's conviction in the nobility of mechanics as expressed in *The Compleat Gentleman*, his contempt for the triviality of Drebbel's device and for the vulgarity of its audience demonstrates that machines are unreliable markers of civility and grace.

Both in spite and because of its potential associations with vulgarity and affectation, machinery contributes to the articulation of courtly values by exemplifying the physical and intellectual instrumentalism of the ideal courtier. The corporeal discipline prized by Renaissance court culture takes as its model the self-regulated motions of machinery, confirming Poliziano's conviction that we should "use our body not as some part of us, joined to the soul, but rather as an instrument."[77] Automata, in particular, embody the grace and *facilità* stipulated by courtesy theory: according to one early sixteenth-century Spanish observer, these machines move with "such order and precision that a living man could not do it with greater perfection [tanta orden y compás que un hombre bivo [vivo] no la pueda hazer con más perfectión]."[78] Often praised by their Renaissance audiences for being "subtle" and "graceful" in their gestures, automata possess certain kinematic correspondences to the motions of the ideal courtly body, correspondences strengthened by the fact that the term "motion" describes mechanical movements but also the physical and emotional gestures of human beings.

Nascent theories of biological mechanism are evident in the sixteenth-century use of the term "motion." In his *Trattato dell'Arte*, Giovan Paolo Lomazzo defines the painter's task as capturing "the vertue and efficacie of motion," a skill mastered by Da Vinci both on the canvas and in his "artificiall motions," or designs for machines.[79] The vivid, dynamic realism of the art of painting is surpassed by mechanics: as Da Vinci himself explains, it is by "la scientia strumentale over[o] machinale," by instrumental or mechanical means, "that all animated bodies that have movement perform their actions, and these movements are based on . . . lever and counterlever [cociosiache mediante quella tutti li corpi animati, che anno moto, fanno tutte loro operationi, i quali moti nascono dal[la] lieva e contralieva]."[80] Even before the body comes to be conceived of as a machine, the rules of composition and control concerning the motions of the human body are revealed through mechanics, a conviction borne out by John Wilkins' 1648 *Mathematicall Magick*, which undertakes to prove that "the naturall motion of living creatures is conformable to [the] artificiall rules" of machinery.[81]

The machinery of court spectacle appeals to a similarly mechanistic aesthetic, one that regards machinery as a kinematic model of decorum. In a poem legitimating the art of dance according to mechanical and cosmic principles, John Davies compares "Comeliness," or decorum, to the self-regulating motions of machinery in that both are impelled by reason to dispose "things and actions in fit time and place":

> Who sees a clock mooving in every part,
> A sayling Pinesse, or a wheeling Cart,
> But thinks that reason ere it came to passe
> The first impulsive cause and mover was?[82]

The clock, cart, and pinesse, the rotating plates at the ends of an astrolabe or quadrant, all move in graceful circles in the same way that the dancer is impelled by decorum to reproduce the graceful motions of the cosmos. Impressed upon by intrinsic rather than extrinsic forces, Davies' ideal dancer functions like those "intrinsicall self-movers," such as clocks and perpetual motion machines, which (according to John Wilkins) "receive their motion from something that does belong to the frame it self."[83] The dancer's *primum mobile* is not the *virtus impressa* but rather courtly *virtù*, that internalized, self-regulating mechanism which governs human motions both corporeal and affective.

Set into motion during spectacles and processions, machines can also quite literally embody the grace of the courtly body in motion. The Spanish chronicler Christobál de Villalón describes an automaton made by Juanelo Turriano, one of Emperor Charles V's engineers, that dances with "order and precision [ordén y compas]," and a similar automaton (if not the same one) is praised as "graceful [*agraciada*]" by another Spanish chronicler in 1575. Like the "ancient statues which moved," this mechanical lady "dances . . . to the sound of a drum which she meanwhile beats and goes round in circles."[84] Making circular, unconstrained movements, this automaton presents ideal courtliness as the ability to deploy one's body as an instrument, to possess an automated responsiveness that evokes courtly discipline but also the fawning servility of the perfect princely instrument. The kinesthetic correspondences between bodies and machines can disrupt as well as uphold the idea of a divinely appointed hierarchy which locates human beings high up on the chain of creation. An automaton might exemplify the instrumentalized body governed by right reason, or it might symbolize a non-sentient being, devoid of reason and ruled by sheer impulse or by powers extrinsic to it, thus lacking in the essential qualities which promise to reserve for humanity a discrete and privileged place in the universe.

Machinery also supplies Renaissance writers with an idiom to define and modify their attitudes towards intellectual and moral discipline. As the work of Lynn White and Otto Mayr has shown, conduct books and treatises on the art of government from the late fourteenth century onwards enlist images of clocks to symbolize temperance and order.[85] Geometrical and astronomical tools in particular are common emblems for moral and physical rectitude, in part by virtue of Aristotle's comparison between the stability of the happy man and the "four-square [τετραγωνοσ]" and of Plutarch's analogy between a prince's servants and the "lively tooles and sensible instruments of governors."[86] Castiglione adopts Plutarch's analogy to describe the moral exemplarity "of the prince, who like the Carpenters Square" ought to "maketh straight and just whatsoever it is occupied about."[87] The idea that geometrical and astronomical instruments "square" or justify their users, enforcing virtue symbolically through technical precision, holds a particular appeal for neo-Stoic writers, whose emphasis upon constancy and self-sufficiency finds a conduit in the operation of mechanical devices. In his *Relox de Principes*, Antonio de Guevara describes his popular neo-Stoic work as a "diall," or clock, that dictates "how we oughte to occupye our mindes, and how to order our lyfe." The temperance and self-discipline associated with clocks is not simply metaphorical: Richard Delamain presents King Charles I with an equinoctial dial in 1630 not as a timepiece but as a tool for "commanding the ebb and fluxe of our uncertaine world."[88]

Practical yet recreative, mechanical devices offer a space for mental exercise and moral forbearance. Frequently likened by their authors to whetstones, files, and other honing tools, treatises on mechanics promise to sharpen that "dextrous habit and faculty," as Sturtevant defines it, "necessary for Artisans and gentlemen alike."[89] Cesare Ripa thus represents "Esercitio" (exercise) as a young man with a clock on his head ("in capo terrà un horologio"), and diverse instruments at his feet, in order to signify the efficacy of his mental operations: all the devices are "shiny and resplendent, showing they are exercised in their operations [che sieno lustri, & resplendenti, & mostrino d'essere esercitati nell'operationi loro]."[90]

More far-reaching correspondences between mechanical cunning and intellectual agility are evident in Thomas Blundeville's *Exercises*, an anthology of treatises on cosmology and mechanics first printed in 1594, and in Peacham's *Compleat Gentleman*, a manual of gentlemanly advice first printed in 1622 that includes mechanics and cosmography among the "conceits of wit and pleasant invention" which "fashion [the gentleman] absolut in the most necessary and commendable Qualities concerning

Minde or Body." Treated alongside conventional aristocratic diversions such
as heraldry and horsemanship, Peacham's promotion of mechanical skills
is grounded in the conviction that, like "ingenious epigrams" and exercises
of verbal wit, the operation of machinery nurtures intellectual dexterity
in noble men such as the late Prince Henry, who as Peacham notes was
expertly trained in mechanics by Peacham's "loving friend Master Edward
Wright."[91]

Although not published until a decade after Henry's death, Peacham's
Compleat Gentleman is a product of the cooperation between courtly and
mechanical artifice that characterizes the intellectual climate of Henry's
court.[92] Prince Henry was indeed the perfect pattern of technical ingenuity:
he was an avid collector of mechanical devices, particularly the automated
model ships made for him by Wright, and he attracted prominent mechanicians to his court including Thomas Hariot, William Barlow, and William
Gilbert.[93] In an earlier work entitled *Graphice*, a treatise on painting and
drawing first published in 1606, and revised in 1612, Peacham reflects the
valorization of technical ingenuity typical of Prince Henry's court. Aban-
doning the opposition between intellectual and manual activities voiced
by James I, Peacham instead urges young men to "exercise your pen in
drawing and imitating cards and maps . . . for the practice of the hand doth
speedily instruct the mind."[94] It is for similar reasons that *The Compleat
Gentleman* recommends the "cunning working of all tools with all artificial
instruments whatsoever," the paintbrushes, compasses, and astrolabes that
exercise the intellect while also improving corporeal control, particularly
the "evenness of carriage" distinctive to the absolute gentleman.[95]

The "engines of war," "clocks and curious watches," and other machines
described by Peacham in his chapter on geometry are models of *sprezzatura*
that perform their operations "with no great labor." Possessing an "infinite subtlety," machines imbue their users with a spirit of ingenuity and
even, according to Peacham, generate *ingenium*, "infusing life as it were
into the senseless bodies of wood, stone, or metal. Witness the wooden
dove of Archytas," which flies by reason of "weights equally peised" within
its body.[96] His alliance between machinery and composure, equipoise, and
gentlemanly grace is borne out by Peacham's description of Archimedes,
who "with his left hand only . . . could by his skill draw after him the weight
of five thousand bushels of grain," an account echoed in the prescriptions
he lays down in a later chapter entitled "Of Reputation and Carriage."
In the latter chapter, Peacham compares temperance, the virtue which
helps us curb our "unruly Passions," to the equilibrium maintained by "the
Caspian Sea," which remains "ever at one heigth without ebb or refluxe,"

its capacity for self-regulation aspiring to the motions of self-moving machines.[97]

In Thomas Blundeville's *Exercises*, a popular anthology of technical treatises first published in 1594 and recommended by Peacham, the operation of machinery is part of the corpus of strategic exercises and gestures required of the Renaissance gentleman. Blundeville's text reprints several sixteenth-century treatises on the operation of instruments including Blagrave's *Mathematicall Jewell*, a work by Thomas Hood on the use of a cross-staff, Gemma Frisius' instructions on the use of a quadrant, and several works by Blundeville himself. Accompanying the texts, paper compasses and other astronomical instruments are provided for the reader to assemble, thus providing an added dimension of physical "exercise" which helps to explain Blundeville's own comparison between the *Exercises* and "my horse booke," a treatise on the arts of horsemanship written several years earlier. Compiled for Elizabeth Bacon, the daughter of Sir Nicholas Bacon and sister of Francis, Blundeville's anthology accommodates the active, militaristic aspects of mechanics to a sphere of feminine gentility, promising "grace" and "comeliness" to male and female readers alike.[98] Writing a half-century later, John Aubrey confirms the enduring social applications of the technical skills taught by Blundeville's text, noting of Francis Bacon that "his sisters were ingeniose and well-bred; they well understood the use of the globes, as you may find in the preface of Mr. Blundevill[e's] *Of the Sphaere*."[99]

Part conduct book and part technical treatise, Peacham's *Compleat Gentleman* and Blundeville's *Exercises* each reveal an interdisciplinary preoccupation with practice or technique typical of certain intellectual communities during the Elizabethan and Jacobean period. Blundeville was an influential figure amongst a group of scholars, including Bacon, Henry Savile, John Hayward, and Samuel Daniel, who were all affiliated to some degree with the Earl of Essex in the 1590s and whose historiographical techniques are grounded in an attention to particulars, to discontinuity and conflict, and to the identification of the rational, material agents of historical events. Blundeville's 1574 *The true order and methode of wryting and reading hystories* marks the rise of what John Salmon has called the "exemplar" theory of history, a discipline dedicated to the study of what Blundeville, in his preface to the work, calls the "meanes and instrumentes" of historical actions.[100] The *Exercises* reflects Blundeville's dedication to the search for causal mechanisms, albeit by means of a different discipline. Like the methods of the "politic" history popular during the last two and a half decades of Elizabeth's reign, mechanics focuses attention upon what Henry

Savile, in his annotations to Book 1 of Tacitus' *Histories*, calls the "counsels and causes" of history.[101]

For this younger generation of Elizabethan scholars, both their enthusiasm and their distaste for mechanics is mediated by their engagement with the methods and concerns of Tacitean history. The translator of Tacitus' *Histories*, editor of Xenophon and Bradwardine, lecturer on Euclid, and founder of the Savilian Chairs of Geometry and Astronomy, Savile regards the practice of mechanics as capable of upholding Essexian values such as pragmatism, militarism, and resolve, but the discipline also arouses the Oxford polymath's concerns about political instrumentality, so much so that in *The Ende of Nero and the Beginning of Galba*, the bridge composed by Savile to replace the missing portions of Tacitus' *Histories*, he depicts Nero, in response to Vindex's revolt, calling his counselors at an "unseasonable houre of the night" to show them "certaine conceits, and new strange devises of musicke by water instruments."[102]

In addition to exemplifying the demonic theatricality of Neronian politics and the erosion of scholarly rigor in favor of vacuous cleverness, machinery helps Savile to mediate the attractions and the limitations of both the active and the contemplative life. Two decades after Dee's visit to Urbino, Savile set out for Northern Italy in order to collect scientific manuscripts. At the Paduan library of Gian Vincenzo Pinelli, he made copies of texts by Pappus, Geminus, and Hero, leaving behind a collection of notes on ancient mathematicians as well as some jottings on Roman historians such as Tacitus, whose *Histories* he would later translate.[103] Savile was accompanied on a portion of his Italian tour by Robert Sidney, the younger brother of the poet Philip. In 1580, shortly after Robert Sidney departed Savile's company, Philip wrote to his brother to urge him to persevere in the studies encouraged by his Oxford mentor. "I wish you kept still together," Philip begins, and then entreats his brother to master the art of horsemanship and to continue his study of classical history in order to master "stratagems" and the art of "defensive militarie." According to Sidney, the writings of Tacitus are particularly useful for "searching the secrets of Government," but so too are "the mathematicalls," in which "Mr Savell is excellent." Lastly, Sidney urges his brother to "beare the mechanical instruments wherin the Dutch . . ."[104] Although the remainder of the passage is missing, Sidney clearly presents mechanics as the indispensable third angle of a pragmatic and militaristic education triangulated by gentlemanly exercises such as horsemanship and by the study of politic history.

Savile endorses a similar view of mechanics in a 1592 oration to Queen Elizabeth delivered at Oxford, asserting that scholars and soldiers must be trained in applied sciences including the "making of warlike engines." The study of mechanics offers a corrective to the "exquisite superfluity" of "needless sciences," vain practices such as "painting, carving, & curious cookery" that inflict "great damage" by making "our wittes, over-witty."[105] In his attempt to demonstrate that "Armes & Learning may both Flourish together in One State," Savile looks to mechanics to heal a perceived rift between arms and letters and refute those who argue that learning "withdrawes ye minde from outward matters, & gives it over wholly to contemplation . . . whereof ye minde being allured, and az it were wth Circes cup enchaunted, growes utterly both unwilling, & unfitt either for affaires of state, or warlike actions." Yet while the skillful mechanician may "wth little adoo frustrate ye assaultes of whole Armies, & Armades," the discipline of mechanics does not produce the "temper of maners, & calmenes of passions" afforded by the traditional spheres of humanist learning.[106]

Savile's interest in mechanics is largely philological and historical, and his sole printed work on the discipline is a discourse on Roman military engineering appended to his 1591 edition of Tacitus. In unpublished notes and works including his lecture notes on Euclid and his *Prooemium Mathematicum*, he does demonstrate an enduring if qualified interest in mechanics. In the notes to his Latin manuscript version of Ptolemy's *Almagest*, written in October 1568 for the completion of his M.A., Savile discusses an astrolabe and a torquetum designed by Regiomontanus, a sphere invented by Johannes Stöffler, and treatises by Regiomontanus and Giorgio Valla on the use and construction of astrolabes.[107] He owned a manuscript copy of one of Galileo's earliest works on mechanics, a treatise entitled *Dell'Utilità che si traggono della Mechanica & de suoi Instromenti*, and he owned and annotated Henri de Monantheuil's 1599 edition of Aristotle's *Mechanical Problems*, which calls mechanics the "sapientissimus [wisest]" and "potentissimus [most powerful]" science.[108] When Thomas Bodley begins construction on the Oxford library that bears his name, Savile recommends that special cases be designed for mathematical and mechanical instruments; upon the subsequent foundation of the two Savilian chairs, Savile specifies in the official documents that the chosen professors must instruct their students in the use of mechanical instruments and that they must construct their own instruments, depositing them, along with their lecture notes, in the Bodleian Library for general perusal.

Yet Savile's conviction that mechanics is suited to the active life of the Sidneian courtier-soldier – or, for that matter, to the meditative existence of the Oxford scholar – is tempered by his limited confidence in the spiritual rewards of the active life as well as by his circumspect attitude towards the facile and "over-witty" kind of intellect he associates with mechanical ingenuity. Despite Savile's ongoing efforts to enhance the dignity of the mechanical sciences at Oxford, he labors to keep mechanics subservient to "purer" or more contemplative scholarly pursuits, namely mathematics and theology, thus inverting the priority of practice over theory espoused in the oration to Elizabeth. In his unpublished *Prooemium Mathematicum*, Savile traces the discipline of mathematics back to the Chaldeans, the Druids, the "Magi Zoroastres," and finally to Seth and Abraham, a narrative that emphasizes the mystical nature of a science originally used both for "obser-vation of the stars [stellarum observationibus]" and also for "ceremonies of the gods [ceremoniis deorum]."[109] Savile praises the mathematical investi-gations of Abraham and the ancient Phoenicians as "perfectissimo" because they were "so incorrupt . . . not connected to physical things [tanta incor-rupta . . . non physicis connecticiis]." Amongst the Egyptians, where Sibyls and prophets numbered among the mathematicians, the study of number and ratio was a "sacerdotis misteria," a sacred mystery shared only amongst a priestly, hermetic elite. By contrast, Savile refers to an ancient practi-tioner of mechanics such as Daedalus as an "artifex," or craftsman, skilled in his art but in no way privy to any divine revelation of the inmost mysteries of nature. While relegating the Cretan engineer to the status of *artifex*, Savile also relegates his inventions to the status of myth, suggest-ing later on in the *Prooemium* that Daedalus' automata are the product of poetic fancy, and not scientific fact ("fabulis poeticiis similia, ac artificio facta no[n]").[110]

Savile's preference for the contemplative abstractions of mathematics over the materiality of mechanics is voiced again in his lecture notes on Euclid, published in 1621 but first delivered several decades earlier. Here, Savile regards mathematics as a recondite and subtle art that is pure because unsullied by the corrupting influence of matter. The overly contemplative disengagement from "outward matters" for which Savile faults certain dis-ciplines of learning in his 1592 oration reemerges in the lectures on Euclid as one of the principal assets of mathematics, while mechanics, in turn, is denigrated as an impure discipline mixed with material things ("non simplicis & purae, sed cum materia quodamodo mixtae").[111] Ultimately incapable of regarding mechanics as a contemplative and moral science, Savile differs from many of the neo-Stoic writers of his age who look to ancient mechanicians such as Archimedes and Daedalus as models of the tranquility advocated by philosophers including Seneca and Boethius, both of whom regard the study of natural philosophy as a means to achieve Stoic *apatheia*.

The writings and scientific activities of Henry Percy, Earl of Northumberland reveal his profound belief in the mutually supportive goals and methods of Stoic ethics and the study of mechanics. In a letter of advice addressed to his eldest son, begun around the time of his birth in 1596 and revised during Percy's imprisonment, he stresses the importance of studying mechanics, optics, and astronomy since they produce a "well-fashioned mind . . . free from perturbations and unseemly affections." Friend or patron of Thomas Hariot, Robert Hues, Nathaniel Torporley, and other mechanicians, Percy views mechanics, much like he views Stoicism, as a strategy for maintaining aristocratic dignity "in the face of public disgrace and political invalidity," and he turned to both disciplines during his fifteen-year imprisonment in the Tower of London.[112] Mechanics provides a safer guide than nature for the Stoic sage: according to Percy's *Advice*, the "deeper contemplations" required by the study of mechanical processes serve a meditative and regulatory function, helping us to "quit ourselves of these ugly perturbations." The manipulation of the world by mechanical means assists in consummating Stoic *apatheia*, thus confirming Cicero's argument in the *De Finibus* that the study of natural philosophy "bestows a power of self-control that arises from the perception of the consummate restraint and order [of the universe]."[113] Renaissance neo-Stoics even go so far as to compare the Stoic sage to a machine: in his *Paradoxes*, John Hall compares the resolute man to a "Cylinder . . . perpetually rowled on his owne Axis," his self-sufficiency and constancy turning him into a self-regulating piston or engine.[114]

Percy does not restrict his studies to a single subdiscipline of mechanics but rather advocates the study of all "organical engines artificial, whether they be by weight, springs, fire, air, wind, water, vacuity, variety, density, upon what grounds soever they be caused."[115] Yet he is particularly interested in Archimedean mechanics, and specifically in questions of statics and hydraulics, fields whose key concerns – balance and equilibrium – translate Stoicism's moral principles into a tangible science. According to Stephen Clucas, Percy considered himself a "promotor Archimedis," and many of the natural philosophers who enjoyed his support undertook projects and experiments based upon postulates from Archimedes' work on hydraulics and statics.[116] Percy owned, and heavily annotated, Guido Ubaldo's 1588 *In Duos Archimedis Aequaeponderantum Libros Paraphrasis*, and he applied Archimedes' principles of leverage to the construction of conduits for a plumbing system at Syon House between 1600 and 1602. Percy was not hindered in his study of Archimedean mechanics after his imprisonment in 1606. Both Hariot and Torporley corresponded with the imprisoned

Percy about various applications of Archimedean mechanics: the former wrote with some observations on the Archimedean investigations of Simon Stevin, while the latter wrote to answer some questions posed by Percy regarding the use of siphons to raise water.[117]

Two portraits of Henry Percy, a miniature executed by Nicholas Hilliard in the 1590s and a posthumous portrait of the earl by Anthony Van Dyck, both invoke and moralize principles of Archimedean statics, specifically the equipoise produced by unequal weights balancing across either end of a fulcrum. In the Van Dyck portrait, Percy is seated next to a table upon which lies a paper representing a diagram and seven lines of a Latin inscription, partially obscured by his elbow: "Dis . . . / Quid . . . / Vero Ad . . . / Ratio Gravior . . . / Eadem Sit Dista . . . / Grave Appenditiur Addistantia / In Qua Gravius Fiet Aequilibrium." The diagram and the accompanying text both refer to two postulates from Book 1 of Archimedes' *De Aequaeponderantibus*: Proposition 3, which states that unequal weights balance at unequal distances, the heavier weight at the lesser distance from the center, and its corollary, Proposition 6, which states that commensurate magnitudes balance at distances reciprocally proportional to the magnitudes. These propositions form the bedrock of Archimedean statics, so much so that Guido Ubaldo adopts a similar diagram, accompanied by the motto "Mechanicorum Machina," for the title-page of his Latin paraphrase of Archimedes, and it is Guido Ubaldo's text upon which the inscription in the Van Dyck portrait is probably based.[118]

The diagram and the text contain a moral lesson by demonstrating how equilibrium can be achieved through imbalance, and stasis through flux. The paradoxical nature of these Archimedean propositions would have appealed to Percy's Stoic search for tranquility and resolution in a world governed by fickle opinion and turbulent passion. Translated into the moral sphere, equilibrium denotes the temperance and composure that counterbalance the vicissitudes of fortune, opinion, and passion. In a letter defending the Stoicism of Epictetus, Poliziano describes both the "well-adjusted body" and healthy emotional disposition as the result of an "equilibrium" which is "destroyed when the balance is tipped in the direction of either excess or deficiency."[119] On the see-saw of human passions, the happy man struggles to maintain an even keel, a task that Archimedean statics reduces to a reliable set of formulae.

The philosophical implications of Archimedes' theories of equilibrium are even more apparent in Hilliard's miniature, the painting upon which Van Dyck likely based his posthumous portrait of Percy. In Hilliard's picture, which dates from around 1594, Percy reclines in a pastoral landscape;

above him, hanging from the branch of a tree, a heavy sphere balances a feather across a lever, demonstrating Archimedes' third proposition, that unequal weights balance at unequal distances, the greater weight at the lesser distance. According to John Peacock, the sphere and the feather also contain a rebus that plays upon the Northumberland family motto as well as upon Percy's own Stoic predilections: the word sphere resembles the French *espère*, or hope, while the feather, or *penne*, resembles *peine*, French for pain or effort.[120] Hope thus counterbalances affliction, a sentiment borne out by the Northumberland motto, *Esperance en Dieu*. These Archimedean postulates become Percy's covert emblem – so much so that a seventeenth-century English scientific manuscript refers to Archimedes' sixth proposition from the *De Aequaeponderantibus* as "Percy's theorem."[121]

Percy's scientific activities reveal a multi-faceted interest in the mechanics of counterbalance: in addition to his work on hydraulics and statics, Percy read deeply in horology, which would have taught him that the mechanics of clocks is based upon principles of counterweight. Redressing imbalance with their internal mechanisms, clocks create the material preconditions for temperance, that virtue which most closely approximates the Aristotelian definition of virtue as counterbalancing opposing vices. Percy's Archimedean emblem possesses additional moral weight since it demonstrates how resistance to an oppositional force is more effective at a greater, rather than a lesser, distance from the fulcrum. Taken symbolically, such a postulate empowers withdrawal and rewards emotional or moral distance from an imagined center, a deeply Stoicized ramification of Archimedean mechanics further strengthened by the commonplace perception that mechanics is essentially a defensive or adversarial science of resistance. In his 1551 *Pathway to Knowledge*, Robert Recorde explains that Archimedes' machines are not offensive weapons but rather "counter engines," devices intended solely to resist Marcellus and "withstande his wonderfull force."[122] Archimedean mechanics thereby supplies an even more fitting metaphor for Stoic resistance to the Herculean powers of the state, and Percy's emblem becomes a working model for rational detachment and for the resistance to adversity sought by the Stoic sage.

One of the key virtues which Percy seeks through his study of mechanics is a morally fortifying self-absorption. In an essay written around 1604, Percy explains how his study of Alhazen, an eleventh-century Arabic writer on optics, helps him to tame his "lethargious passions" and his "giddie . . . thinckinge" while struggling to overcome his desire for a mistress.[123] Tempering his ardor with the study of Alhazen's proofs, and "leapinge from the demonstration to my Mistris, and returning from my

Mistris to the demonstration," Percy achieves an Archimedean equipoise out of his "great strife of humours . . . both beinge yt in equal ballance . . . neither masteringe the one the other."[124] Percy's conviction that the study of natural philosophy counterbalances the immoderate pleasures of the flesh is indebted to Book IV of Seneca's *Natural Questions* and to Plutarch's *Moralia*. In "No Pleasant Life According to Epicurus," Plutarch counters the Epicurean argument that scientists including Archimedes and Euclid were governed by passion when they were "charmed and enchanted" by the "fine invention of the Mathematicall sciences." By contrast, Plutarch contends that natural philosophy is a "heavenly and divine delight," a true pleasure distinguishable from lust or gluttony in that it prevents us from becoming "subject to all passions and perturbations."[125]

In other essays of the *Moralia*, Archimedes and Euclid exemplify Stoic *apatheia*, a quality which Plutarch himself alternately admires and attacks. In both the *Moralia* and the *Lives*, Plutarch describes Archimedes as possessing a self-absorption so intense as to seem parodic. In one description, Archimedes is "so bent & intentive unto the table before him, in which he drew his figures geometricall, that his servitours were faine to plucke him from it by force, for to wash and annoint him," and when they washed him, "he would be drawing and describing of new figures upon his owne bodie." In the *Life of Marcellus*, Archimedes' preoccupation costs him his life. The engineer is so "earnestly occupied . . . [in] the demonstration of some Geometricall proposition" that he is surprised by a soldier, to whom Archimedes begs not for his life but for enough time to finish his mathematical demonstration.[126]

Archimedes' extreme inattention to anything but his scientific endeavors lies at the foundation of Renaissance culture's complex understanding of the moral and intellectual authority of mechanics. William Cornwallis is one of a number of Renaissance writers who praises Archimedes' masterful self-absorption, invoking the "calmnesse and contentment" of the Syracusan engineer, "so busie about knowledge as not hearing the clamors and noyses" of war, as a model of Stoic *apatheia*: at his death, Cornwallis recounts, Archimedes wished only for "a little time to finish his intendment. What a tranquilitie [*sic*] minde was heere."[127] The same discipline defended in the 1560s and 1570s by Dee and Ramus as worldly and practical can likewise serve as an instrument of retirement, a tool of contemplative self-absorption, a flight from materiality. In a 1614 work entitled *The Golden Meane* and dedicated to the imprisoned Percy, John Ford imagines the mechanical inventions of the mythical engineer Daedalus as instruments of retreat and transcendence, explaining that in unlucky times men "must imitate that

Daedalus" who "conquers adversity by flying from it" with his mechanical wings.[128] Yet such self-absorption has its liabilities, as Geoffrey Whitney points out in a 1586 emblem that warns against inattention to pressing dangers by depicting two men engrossed in a chess game while a fire rages in a building next to them: "Awake from sleepe secure, when perrill doth appeare," the poem begins, "Still Archimedes wroughte, when foes had wonne the towne, / And woulde not leave his worke in hande, till he was beaten downe."[129]

Even as they exemplify grace, decorum, self-government, or instrumental means, mechanical devices are not reliable purveyors of method or discipline. That clocks often break or prove otherwise untrustworthy does not escape many Renaissance writers, for whom clocks are artificial, fickle, or dishonest. Nashe compares the factionalism amongst the English clergy during the Marprelate Controversy to the "Clocks of England, that never meete iumpe on a point together," while in Jonson's *Cynthia's Revels*, Mercury describes the "affected" courtier Asotus as someone who "will lie cheaper than any beggar, and louder than most clocks."[130]

Serving alternately as symbols of order and as icons of intellectual, moral, or political disorder, machines could exemplify the perpetual flux of the human mind or the violent alterations wrought upon it by the passions. In Chapman's *Bussy d'Ambois*, Tamyra compares our failure to "keep our constant course in virtue" to a "false clock," remarking that we need to be "sometimes one, sometimes another," and every thought "differs from [every] other: every hour and minute."[131] Images of machines out of control are common metaphors for immoderate passion or inconstancy: Guillaume Du Vair compares the "violent or vehement motions of our soul" to an accelerating wheel, while Robert Johnson compares the "affected" movements of our "disordinate passions" to the "irregular motions" of a machine, even as he also advises us to rely upon our "automedon" of reason to control those passions.[132] Even as machines guide their collectors and users towards acquiring discipline through right reason, they are, like courtesy treatises, ambiguous givers-out of the decorum they prescribe: imitate them imperfectly, and the result is affectation, not grace, inconstancy, not resolve, and mechanical insensibility, not humanity.

CHAPTER 3

Inanimate ambassadors: the mechanics and politics of mediation

The frontispiece of the first volume of Jean-Jacques Boissard's *Icones Quinquaginta Virorum illustrium* (Frankfurt, 1597), a biographical compendium of prominent scientific and political figures, depicts four engravings illustrating its subjects at work. Clockwise, from the top, it illustrates (1.) three men with astronomical instruments observing a comet outside the window; (2.) a man at a lectern, reading; (3.) two advisors speaking with a figure seated in a chair of state; (4.) a man with a globe, a quadrant, and a mathematical text, performing a calculation.[1] Three of the engravings depict the use of instruments, at least if one considers the lectern and book to be species of instruments, the inanimate tools of scholarship. The engraving depicting the scene of counsel might at first appear to be out of place, yet what it depicts is a ruler's use of men *as* instruments. The counselors represent the "lively tooles and sensible instruments" whose proper deployment, according to Plutarch, is integral to successful rule. As instruments of state, the advisors occupy a similar structural position to the mechanical devices in the other three engravings. Political advisors are the "plumbs, levels, and rules" of governors, and like their inanimate counterparts, they are only as effective as the skill of their operator permits.[2]

The implicit correspondence between human and mechanical instruments in Boissard's frontispiece demonstrates the mutually constitutive relationship between political and mechanical instrumentality that informs moral, political, and epistemological concerns about mediation in Renaissance culture. Both mechanical and human instruments are potential guarantors of instrumental means, or any morally indifferent technique whose legitimacy is calibrated by measuring its use-value against its moral rectitude. In this capacity, mechanical instruments help to plot the calculus between expediency and morality, thus altering attitudes towards instrumentalism in the political sphere. As mediating devices, mechanical instruments concretize, and sometimes exacerbate, the moral and intellectual dilemmas which inhere in the mediated nature of political interactions, from a ruler's reliance upon ambassadors to the rhetorical strategies of indirection that pervade the Renaissance court. At the same time, mechanical instruments draw attention to and often intensify the epistemological dilemmas produced by the senses – the natural instruments through which the understanding receives its mediated knowledge of the outside world.

This chapter argues that Renaissance culture works out its intellectual, moral, and political anxieties surrounding instrumentality through the complementary problems posed by ambassadors and mechanical devices, the living and lifeless instruments that preside over the mediation of information from one place to another. Albeit in different ways, ambassadors and machines both threaten to erode human agency, so much so that one late medieval writer compares the cipher-like identity of the messenger to an "organ" or instrument: "A nuncio is he who takes the place of a letter: and he is just like a magpie, and an organ, and the voice of the principal sending him, and he recites the words of the principal."[3] The *nuncio* resembles an "organ" in his capacity to reproduce the will of his "principal," a role repudiated by Hamlet in a play obsessively concerned with the deleterious effects of mediation upon the human subject: "Call me what instrument you will, though you can fret me, you cannot play upon me."[4] The instrumentality of animate and inanimate organs alike arouses ontological, moral, and political concerns in *Hamlet* as well as in Renaissance culture at large. Either they fail to transmit their messages properly, eroding a ruler's confidence in his instruments, or they convey information too accurately, duplicating their principal with eerie precision and thus effacing the precious distinction between a ruler and his instruments.

Renaissance courtesy and political treatises urge courtiers and statesmen to act as "the Commanders instrument," a fulcrum of power between the Prince and his will so effective "that we can not distinguish the *end* of the instrument, from that of the *agent* which mooves the same."[5] This intimate, unmediated relationship between ruler and servant, in which servitude is defined as performing "but the actions of an instrument," is indebted to Aristotle's concept of "conjoined" instrumentality: ideally, according to *The Politics*, a servant is so completely ruled by the will of his master that even outside the presence of his authority, that authority exerts itself upon the servant as seamlessly as an impressed force passes across a lever. Insofar as it moves independently once impelled to do so from an outside source, self-moving machinery provides an apt metaphor for the proper execution of "separate" (as opposed to "conjoined") instrumentality as it is conceived by Aristotle and cultivated by the diplomatic and courtly etiquette of the

Renaissance. A seventeenth-century Spanish writer contrasts the nature of "joyned Instruments," such as the saw that remains still until it receives "guidance to motion and cutting from the Sawyer," to the nature of a "separate instrument" as exemplified by the authority that a king or potentate possesses when he "operates in far distant places as if he were present." The instrumentality that exists between the absent monarch and his servants resembles "those examples of artificial Engines . . . in which the motive faculty it self . . . is communicated by Art to those engines," such as the "watches, clocks, and Engines wherein many wheeles are orderly moved in the absence of the workman, yet by a vertue imprinted upon them by the first direction of the Artist."[6] Inasmuch as they exemplify instrumental means, clocks and other self-regulating engines, such as organs and automata, are complicit in instrumental political attitudes even as they also transform and challenge those attitudes.

Changes in diplomatic practice are both cause and symptom of the instrumental political culture of the sixteenth century. Particularly under the direction of rival office-holders William Cecil and Sir Francis Walsingham, the Tudor state effects profound changes in the structure and aim of its intelligence service and its diplomatic corps, growing more bureaucratically complex and more comfortable with morally dubious techniques.[7] One of the results of this increasingly sophisticated intelligence network is the proliferation of ambassadors and other emissaries, intermediaries upon whom the monarch relies in order to relay messages, negotiate alliances, and procure information. As these new methods of diplomacy evolve, the concerns they provoke are themselves shaped by a variety of machines and devices, including cryptographic wheels, speaking tubes, and optical devices, each of which promises to solve problems inherent in conventional diplomatic practices. At least in theory, mechanical devices convey information with greater accuracy and security than their human counterparts, yet they also threaten to dismantle the very foundation of the political structures they purportedly serve by transforming and undermining the instrumentality they appear to exemplify. Able to betray secrets or to perplex the senses, these mechanical ambassadors accentuate, rather than palliate, the mediated nature of political interaction in particular and of human knowledge in general.

The culture's concerns about the ambassador's capacity to double for his ruler are borne out by the common, if erroneous, etymology of the term "ambassador" traced by many Renaissance dictionaries. The word "ambassador," a relatively new word in contrast to its older near-synonyms ("legate," "nuncius, "proxenos"), is derived from the Latin *ambire* (to go about), and its roots *ambo-*, or *ambi-*, which signify going around, or going two (or both) ways. Bernard Du Rosier's 1436 *Ambaxiator Brevilogus* explains that the origin of the term arose from the habit of sending two or more envoys, in two different directions, on a single embassy, presumably to double one's chances of delivering a message successfully.[8] While this custom does not appear to have persisted throughout the Renaissance, the ambassador is often imagined as figuratively, if not literally, double, from the twofold idiom of his secret codes to his potential for deceit.

Du Rosier's duplicate and divided ambassador, heading simultaneously in two divergent directions, enacts *in extremis* the kind of schismatic identity created by the techniques of indirection prized by Renaisssance political culture. Particularly from the latter half of the sixteenth century onwards, political philosophers including Guicciardini, Bodin, Lipsius, and Bacon urge princes and courtiers to communicate their aims obliquely and indirectly. In "Of Cunning," Bacon outlines the various ways in which men may "insinuate" their desires, and in "Of Negociating," he argues that "it is generally better to *deale* . . . by the Mediation of a Third, then by a Mans selfe."[9] Pierre Charron recommends that princes achieve their ends "by close and covert meanes, by equivocations and subtilities, to circumvent by faire speeches and promises, letters, ambassages, working and obtaining by subtile meanes [par moiens couverts, par equivoques, et subtilités affiner par belles paroles et promesses, lettres, ambassades, faisant et obtenant par subtils moiens]."[10] The figure of the ambassador supplies a rhetorical model for these strategies of obfuscation, yet as Lipsius points out, he is more of a pawn than an agent of deception, since princes are wont "to deceave by speech, by letters, by Ambassadors, and even [deceive] the Ambassadors themselves, and do abuse them by whom they imagine to deceave others."[11] The ambassador is the object, and not the subject, of falsification: he is merely a fulcrum across which deception travels, prompting numerous Renaissance writers to observe that "a Prince that desireth, by means of his ambassador, to deceive another Prince, must first abuse his own Ambassador."[12]

Courtesy literature reinforces these strategies of indirection by demanding that princes and courtiers divert their actions and requests through a variety of rhetorical and physical techniques. According to Castiglione's Fregoso, the courtier ought to "frame hys suite" to his prince delicately and indirectly, either by altering the tone of his delivery or by getting another courtier to petition for him.[13] A century later, Joseph Hall teases out the implicitly mechanical nature of Castiglione's courtly instrumentalism by describing the "good and faithful courtier" as one whose "brest is not a cisterne to retaine," but rather acts as "a conduit-pipe, to vent the reasonable and honest petitions of his friend."[14]

These ambassadorial strategies of indirection and obliquity are comprised by the term "ambage," a word which first appears in Chaucer's *Troilus and Criseyde*, a text deeply concerned with the flawed nature of mediation. Chaucer's master of ambage is the double-agent Calchas, who employs "double wordes slye, / Swiche as men clepen a word with two visages." Three centuries later, George Puttenham uses the term "ambage" as a synonym for *periphrasis*, a rhetorical device which, like enigma, irony, and the "courtly figure *Allegoria*," operates by means of "darkenes and duplicitie."[15] A fairly common term in the sixteenth century, ambage describes any circuitous verbal or physical technique used for deceit or delay, as well as natural intricacies and bureaucratic entanglements. In its applicability to the art of political negotiation, ambage is a favorite subject of Francis Bacon, who outlines various techniques of mediation and indirection in his *Essayes* and in *The Advancement of Learning*. In "Of Cunning," Bacon recommends that "when you have any thing to obtaine of present dispatch," it is best not to ask directly but rather to "entertaine, and amuse the party, with whom you deale, with some other Discourse." He recounts the story of one "*Counsellor* and *Secretary*," probably Walsingham, who "never came to *Queene Elizabeth* of *England*, with Bills to signe, but he would alwaies first put her into some discourse of Estate, that she mought the lesse minde the Bills." For Bacon, calculated obliquity and the art of digression are crucial political skills: in "Of Cunning," he remarks admiringly "how long some Men will lie in wait, to speake somewhat, they desire to say; And how farre about they will fetch . . . It is a Thing of great Patience, but yet of much Use."[16]

Many Renaissance writers and artists grant ambage a mythographic pedigree in the figure of Hermes, whose multiple role as *nuncio* to the gods, arbiter of technical and rhetorical skill, and master of "cunning trickery [dolie techne]" corroborates the commonalty between animate and inanimate instrumentality.[17] In the *Homeric Hymns*, Hermes reverses the hoofprints of the cattle he has stolen, dumbfounding his adversaries by leaving a duplicitous, untraceable trail.[18] Creating the ambagious illusion that he has traveled in two divergent directions simultaneously, Hermes is the first ambassador in the Renaissance sense of the term. Artists and engineers often render Mercury emblematically in mechanical form, alongside organs and *sufflators*, or pneumatically-driven speaking heads, whose whispers suggest an affiliation with the eavesdropping god. King James I procures a "revolving statue of Mercury" from Tycho Brahe, while Benvenuto Cellini's statue of

Mercury contains a hydraulic pump designed to spout water, an apt medium to represent the god who, according to Renaissance accounts, was himself a maker of speaking heads and similar automata.[19]

Mercury is an apt mascot for this chapter, which evolved out of the observation that mechanical devices surface in a number of Renaissance texts and cultural practices relating to ambassadors or to methods for the conveyance of messages. The desire for a swifter and more surreptitious means to transmit messages is evident in technical treatises of the period, which envision machines including telescopes and speaking tubes as solutions to the problems posed by human instruments unable to convey messages accurately or securely. These machines act as "inanimate ambassadors," as one treatise refers to them, standing in for human eyes and ears to relay political intelligence. Yet even as these devices promise to solve the problems of living ambassadors, they often distort their messages or otherwise fall short of their idealized status as perfect mediators.

Mechanical devices are also used literally as ambassadors, sent by monarchs as objects of diplomatic exchange. When deployed in this manner, as in the case of an English organ-maker sent to the Ottoman court in 1599 to demonstrate his instrument, and whose journal figures prominently in this chapter, machines disclose the political risks of instrumentalism. Their capacity for reiteration or duplication, accompanied by their apparent autonomy, threatens to upset the relationship between principal and organ. Like Daedalus' statues, these inanimate ambassadors vex the Aristotelian distinction between separate and conjoined instruments, exalting and annulling instrumentality by turns.

In a pair of letters written by the mathematician and bishop Cuthbert Tunstal while serving as an ambassador in Antwerp in 1520, he identifies a Bavarian instrument-maker named Nicholas Kratzer as a possible candidate for English intelligence work. Two letters, one written to Henry VIII and another, almost identical, letter written to Cardinal Wolsey on the same day, both recommend Kratzer, referred to by Tunstal as "deviser of the King's horologes," as a useful instrument to "find out the mind of the Electors touching the affairs of the empire."[20] Tunstal's rationale behind recommending Kratzer lies both in his nationality and in his capacity as a "deviser," characteristics in turn related to each other, since Germans, especially those, like Kratzer, from the Nuremberg area, were commonly imputed to possess great mechanical acuity.

Whether or not it was ultimately successful, the attempt to enlist Kratzer as a spy reveals the affiliation between political and technical skill in

Henrician England. The corpus of texts on the art of diplomacy, which emerges alongside the courtesy manual in late fifteenth-century Italy, advocates the importance of technical skills for would-be ambassadors, in part to cultivate qualities such as dexterity of intellect ("ingenii dexteritas") and quickness of mind ("argute & elegantor respondet").[21] Eloquence is equally important: Angel Day writes that legates should possess "a ripe and quicke conceit" and must master the "exercise of the Pen [and] the Wit."[22] The diplomatic benefits of rhetorical virtuosity explain why so many writers, including Chaucer, More, Wyatt, and Sidney, are called upon to perform embassies. Yet monarchs also ask engineers, jugglers, and barbers to deliver messages, suggesting that anyone able to handle an instrument, from a pen to a scalpel, is equipped to relay political intelligence.[23]

Like Boissard's frontispiece, the logic underpinning these diplomatic practices conflates the ability to *use* an instrument with the ability to *be* an instrument. So too do Tunstal's letters, whose double and oblique way of conveying information demonstrates the mutually constitutive strategies of political, rhetorical, and mechanical ambage. The content of each letter, one addressed to the King and another to his secretary, Cardinal Wolsey, is essentially the same: Tunstal has met with Kratzer, and he has asked the instrument-maker to "find out the minds of the Electors."[24] Yet only to Wolsey does Tunstal write that he "wishes to know the King's pleasure" about whether to keep Kratzer in Antwerp, a question he does not pose directly to the King. Just as Kratzer might serve to "find out the mind" of the Electors, Wolsey (acting in his Skeltonic capacity as crafty conveyance) might find out Henry VIII's mind for Tunstal. Tunstal's reliance upon indirection is reinforced in his own acts of writing, for in both letters he refers to himself as "Tunstal." In all likelihood, this use of the third person suggests that the letters were written by Tunstal's secretary, yet it might testify to Tunstal's rhetorical positioning of himself as an instrument – as the object, rather than the subject, of his letter. In either case, the letters reveal just how circuitous a network of intermediaries is potentially involved in a given request: a secretary, writing for Tunstal, addresses Wolsey in order to ask the King whether he desires Kratzer to find something out from the German Electors.

Upon Kratzer's arrival in England in 1517, he was introduced by Erasmus to Thomas More, who employed him as a tutor for several years in his household school. By 1520, when Tunstal wrote his two letters, Kratzer had established himself as one of Henry VIII's official instrument-makers, and in the following year, Wolsey appointed him to the first Chair of Astronomy and Mathematics at his newly founded Corpus Christi College.[25] Kratzer designed instruments for both the King and Wolsey, including an extant polyhedral sundial for the Cardinal, and he wrote two treatises on clocks and dialing, both adressed to Henry VIII. One of these, the *Canones Horopti*, offers training in technical skills which in turn possess explicit political applications by dint of their semantic and intellectual affiliation with a Skeltonic atmosphere of counterfeit countenance. In it, Kratzer promises his readers that by mastering the art of dialing, they will cultivate *calliditas, astutia, sollertia,* and *dexteritas.*[26] Largely purged of their negative connotations, this related set of attributes signals a new way of conceptualizing virtue for Tudor humanists and *politiques* as more traditional political virtues, including honesty and loyalty, are expended or made obsolete.

The political and intellectual lessons offered by Kratzer's *Canones Horopti* are echoed by early Tudor interludes such as John Redford's *Wit and Science* and John Rastell's *Interlude of the Nature of the Four Elements* (c. 1519), which stages a rivalry between Studious Desire and Sensual Appetite for the attention of the protagonist, Humanyte. While Sensual Appetite woos Humanyte with revels and wenches, Studious Desire joins forces with Experience to lure Humanyte away from his sensual stirrings with demonstrations of mechanical instruments and maps, teaching him "points of cosmography" through the use of "figures," and dazzling him with optical devices.[27] Experience's learned demonstrations of navigational and cosmographical devices, lessons influenced by contemporary scientific texts including Waldseemüller's 1507 *Cosmographiae* and the 1512 *Margarita Philosophica*, force Humanyte to rethink his relationship towards his senses – natural instruments which prove less reliable than their mechanical counterparts.[28] Early on in the play, Studious Desire argues that nothing, not even sense experience, is surer and more obvious than the experience afforded by mechanical "instruments," devices which reveal truths "so certain, / That every rude carter should them perceive plain." When Experience struggles to explain a scientific precept to Humanyte, he resorts to the rooted demonstration of his mechanical devices: "For here, lo, by mine instruments, / I can show the plain experiments."[29] Inasmuch as they are pitted against the frivolous "disports" offered by Sensual Appetite and his cohort Ignorance, including dancing, singing, eating, and the "touching of soft and hard," Experience's maps and devices are depicted as honest, morally purifying recreations.[30] Yet since the end of *The Four Elements* is lost, we do not know if machinery triumphs over the distortions of passion and appetite, or if the play ultimately abandons its apparent faith in mechanical instruments as trustworthy mediators of human experience.

As tangible representations of intellectual and political machination, machines possess direct applications for cosmocratic displays of power in Henrician England. Both Kratzer and Rastell belong to a community of playwrights, artists, and engineers responsible for designing spectacles such as the 1527 royal entertainment at Greenwich in honor of the arrival of two French ambassadors.[31] Kratzer also serves as a courier, aiding in the circulation of texts and instruments for his more prominent acquaintances. In 1517, he is sent to Antwerp by Peter Gillis in order to sell "several astrolabes and sphaeres" and to bring back a book for Erasmus.[32] The instrument-maker appears to have periodically served a similar function for More and Cromwell, importing books from Germany and the Low Countries into England. A letter written from Kratzer to Cromwell in 1538 reports that the clockmaker has received the latest writings of the Lutheran humanist Spalatinus by sea, and that "these I gave to Hans Holbein in order that he might give them to you."[33] Kratzer's activities suggest that humanistic scholarship depends upon intermediaries, and that the ambassadors of humanism, living instruments such as Kratzer and Holbein, are also bound up in the realm of machinery. The role played by Kratzer and Holbein as conveyors of books and instruments is pivotal for understanding Holbein's *The Ambassadors*, a painting which teases out the correspondences between ambassadors and machines, the living and non-living mediators of political interactions and of human knowledge.

Hans Holbein's *The Ambassadors* is a virtuoso rendition of both the appeals and the dangers of mediation as performed by ambassadors, by mechanical instruments, and by the conventions of illusionistic perspective. *The Ambassadors* has become a cliché for our understanding of how a painting's objects can, as Norman Bryson puts it, launch an "assault on the prestige of the human subject."[34] Frequently regarded as a still-life or an emblem of *Vanitas*, its human figures are more "artificially crafted" than the inanimate objects around them, as Greenblatt argues in his interpretation of the painting.[35] Interpretations of Holbein's painting often speculate about the nature of the relationship between its objects and its subjects: Jean de Dinteville, the French ambassador to England in 1532–33, and his friend Georges de Selve, an ambassador-at-large who came to visit Dinteville in England that year. Thanks to Mary Hervey, many of the objects represented in the painting, including geometrical instruments, globes, and books, are identifiable as the specific products of individual artists – a hymnal of Luther's, a mathematical text and a torquetum designed by Peter Apian, and instruments which resemble those made by Kratzer and which feature in his own portrait by Holbein, executed several years earlier.[36]

While the provenance of many of these objects is known, the presence of the scientific texts and instruments remains unclear, in part because these items are not suited to the subjects of *The Ambassadors* in the way that objects are suited to their subjects in Holbein's other portraits. Holbein habitually represents his sitters alongside the tools of their trade: the Hanseatic merchant George Gizse is represented with scales and other merchants' tools, and Kratzer is depicted with his mechanical instruments. That Dinteville and Selve are not depicted alongside instruments reflecting their occupation has prompted Lisa Jardine to remark that the objects are "mere curiosities and ornaments (suggesting the urbanity of the sitters)," in contrast to Kratzer's portrait, where the objects are "part of the painting's subject."[37]

The objects in *The Ambassadors* are indeed worldly goods inasmuch as they are virtually all foreign. The German books and globes, as well as the mosaic floor, a copy of the floor from the Sanctuary of Westminster Abbey which was made with materials brought from Italy during the reign of Henry III, reveal that the world inhabited by these two ambassadors is subject to continual dislocation on account of the conveyance of both material goods and human instruments. The anamorphic skull is by no means the only alien presence in the painting, and if the various objects in the painting do not seem to belong it is because the painting is about objects removed from their proper place – about French diplomats, German books, and Italian *tesserae* which have been relocated to England.

The mosaic floor is the symbolic foundation of the painting in that the process of mosaic, like its perceived etymological relative *museum* and the related concept of *emblematura*, involves a technique of bricolage, a fitting together of disparate items to make them look as though they belong together.[38] *The Ambassadors* employs *emblematura* pervasively, from the mosaic floor to the emblem of a death's head sported by Dinteville, an image mirrored in the anamorphic emblem of the skull. The collection of objects surrounding the two ambassadors can be seen to denote the collected or artifactual nature of human identity, since as Findlen and others have argued, the collection of objects in Renaissance culture is part and parcel of the larger "task of constituting the self as an object of display."[39] *The Ambassadors* both enacts and questions such a task, inviting its viewers to look for connections between the subjects and the objects on the canvas, yet refusing to make those connections explicit or undercutting them through contorted, almost parodic, repetition. The medallion around Dinteville's neck, a medal of the order of Saint Michael depicting a death's head, is reproduced twice more on the canvas, in the death's head beside him and in the anamorphic skull, a *copia* that both strengthens and complicates the status of these objects as emblems of *Vanitas*.

Dinteville in particular was a "container for the deposit and display of objects," as Jay Tribby has described the aristocratic collectors of the Renaissance. According to his brother François, Dinteville is a "connoisseur in mechanics," and he may well have met Holbein through their mutual acquaintance, Kratzer.[40] Dinteville's interest in mechanics is borne out by a letter written to his brother in May 1533, while he was sitting for Holbein's portrait, in which he requests "the portrait of the oval compass which you wrote to me about; for I am very eager to understand how it is made [le portraict du compas auvale duquel (vous) m'avez escript; car je suis bien empesché à comprendre la façon de laquelle il est fait]."[41] Dinteville's implication that an image of a compass might constitute a "pourtraict" suggests that the distinction between portrait and still-life, or between paintings of subjects and paintings of objects, is tenuous at best. Indeed, many sixteenth-century engineers refer to their mechanical inventions as portraits: Suberville refers to his "Henry-metre," a surveying device, as the "pourtraict" of Henri IV insofar as it symbolically reproduces and enacts royal power. François Beroald describes his illustrations of mechanical instruments, executed for the 1579 edition of Jacques Besson's *Théâtre des Instrumens*, as "pourtraicts" insofar as they are original designs ("nouvelles compositions") rather than copies. Accordingly, "portraits" of machinery are afforded the same protection under developing patent laws as are images of human subjects. Besson received a royal privilege in 1569 for the first edition of the work, prohibiting readers from constructing or representing his inventions "either in painting or by constructing them [tant à la peinture qu'en la fabrique]."[42] Insofar as originality exists as a legal or aesthetic category in the sixteenth century, machines are accorded the same prestige of uniqueness as human subjects, and both are equally subject to the threat of reproduction.

The Ambassadors elides the distinction between still-life and portrait as it teases out the correlation between its subjects and its objects, both of which are involved in the mediation or conveyance of information. Holbein's painting reveals an even deeper preoccupation with the exigencies of mediation in that its very canvas necessitates a mechanical device in order to mediate between two conflicting perspectives. In order to have an undistorted view of the painting's anamorphic image, the beholder must use an optical device to correct the obliquity of the skull, realigning the image

3.1 Albrecht Dürer, *Institutionum geometricarum libris*, drawing a lute in perspective

with the rest of the painting. Such perspective devices are used to rectify the deliberate perspectival error created by an anamorphic image, but they also assist the painter in creating an illusionistic, correct perspective. Albrecht Dürer's 1525 *Unterweysung der Messung* (*Institutionum geometricarum*), a treatise on the art of perspective, demonstrates the use of perspective devices by depicting the painter in the act of representing his subject (here, a lute) through an optical device across a table fitted with a perspectival grid (figure 3.1). The optical device and the grid help the painter to convert a three-dimensional subject onto the two-dimensional medium of the canvas. While it generally aims at reproducing an image with the greatest possible verisimilitude, the art of perspective transposes and distorts its subject in order to render it realistically on the canvas.

The perspectival duplicity of the painter's canvas is mirrored in *The Ambassadors* by the presence of its two subjects, men whose mediatory capacity is analogous to that of a perspective device. In the Dürer illustration, the lute and the grid are placed on a table between the figures like the geometrical and astronomical instruments in Holbein's portrait, as if to remind us that painting requires the mediation of its subjects through mechanical devices. Since the subjects of Holbein's painting, Dinteville and Selve, are themselves mediating instruments, the presence of the instruments between them reinforces their occupation as instruments of state, a vocation which involves the conveyance, and often the distortion, of information.

Holbein's painting employs not one but rather two perspectival grids: one represents the anamorphic skull, and the other represents the rest of the painting from a conflicting perspective, thus dividing the viewer's eye, at least if unaided by an optical device, between two contrasting points of view. The perspectival discontinuity of the painting is echoed by numerous compositional and emblematic clues that hint at the difficulty or failure of union in the political and aesthetic spheres. On the table between the two ambassadors lies a lute, a conventional symbol of harmony or concord and the object used by Dürer in his *Unterweysung der Messung* to represent the intrinsic yet flexible fidelity of perspective, an art which ideally ensures a harmony between the material world and the painter's canvas. In *The Ambassadors*, however, one of the lute's strings is broken, a reminder that neither the art of perspective nor, perhaps, the ambassadors themselves can sustain the fidelity which they are designed to preserve. As Hervey points out, Andrea Alciati's 1531 *Emblemata* uses the symbol of the broken lute to symbolize the impossibility of maintaining political alliances, a probable allusion to the 1526 League of Cognac, breached before the publication of Alciati's work. The emblem's motto laments how politicians fail to "tune the chords [tendere chordas]" of international diplomacy and observes the ease with which one ill-tuned or broken string ruptures the precarious balance of power in the age of Emperor Charles V – a ruler to whom both Dinteville and Selve were sent on embassies.[43]

If its two competing perspectival fields symbolize the inherently disharmonious relationship between actual and representational space, *The Ambassadors*' broken lute represents the difficulties of ambassadorial communication – the myriad ways in which messages are bungled or treaties broken. Both formally and thematically, Holbein's canvas attunes us to the inevitability of discord. The distended skull merely accentuates the disunity and distortion that is the subtle yet pervasive theme of the painting as a whole.

Despite repeated critical attempts to analyze the painting allegorically, *The Ambassadors* is, simply put, about ambassadors. Not only do its books and instruments reflect upon the instrumental nature of the painting's subjects, but a number of the objects and techniques used by Holbein are also ambassadorial. There is actually an overdetermined quality to the painting's ambassadorial theme, but the details of this theme emerge only obliquely, as if to underscore the obliquity of the ambassador's rhetorical and political techniques. The terrestrial globe identifies sites important to European foreign relations, but it also marks the kingdom of Prester John, the fictional ambassador to the Pope, whose purported account, *The Legacy or embassate of prester John unto Emanuell, Kynge of Portyngale*, is translated into English by John More and printed by William Rastell in 1533, the same year in which Holbein paints the French ambassadors.[44] The broken lute is a symbol of diplomatic discord, while the skull reflects the chimeric nonentity of the ambassador, its perspectival obliquity symbolizing the potential distortions to which verbal and visual representations are subject when mediated through instruments.

True to the occupation of its subjects, *The Ambassadors* is also explicitly involved in the conveying of secrets. Curiously, it provides the only official record of Selve's otherwise secret visit to England to see Dinteville.[45] Several of the painting's objects are also involved in the purveyance of secrets. The terrestrial globe is, as Jardine points out, "a substantial piece of commercial and industrial espionage" whose construction is enabled by the cartographer's access to secret documents concerning explorations. The perspective device needed to rectify the painting's anamorphic image may also allude to the ambassadors' role as conveyers of secrets: in his *Polygraphia*, first printed in 1518, the German cryptographer Johannes Trithemius points out that "catoptrique," or the science of reflective mirrors, is (along with lemons and armagnac) a useful medium for transmitting messages in secret.[46] Lastly, the German books embody secrecy in a different manner: German was almost universally unknown to foreigners in the 1530s, and it was thus a useful medium for the transmission of secret information. Wolsey hired native German speakers, including acquaintances of Holbein and Kratzer employed in London steelyards and printing shops, to translate "encoded" German messages into English.[47]

The Ambassadors betrays a profound cynicism about the instrumentality of its subjects. It asks us to contemplate the intercessory role played by its human subjects in light of the mediatory role of the mechanical devices represented on the table between Dinteville and Selve, as well as that of the anamorphosis, which enables the viewer to mediate between conflicting perspectival positions. Greenblatt regards the skull as a *memento mori* that reminds us that the hermetic legacy of the ambassador is to mediate between earth and Hades. If the skull indeed alludes to Thomas More, as Greenblatt has argued, it is the perfect expression of a man who, as all three of his sixteenth-century biographers note, utterly disliked being the

King's instrument. Nicholas Harpsfield writes that "of his owne selfe and of nature [More] neither desired nor well lyked to be intricated with Princes affaires, and of all other offices he had little minde and fancie to be any ambassadour," a sentiment echoed by *Utopia*'s Raphael Hythloday, who protests that service (*servias*) is only one syllable removed from servitude (*inservias*) and is a "way of life . . . absolutely repellent to me."[48]

The painting's various twistings and turnings force the viewer to be "intricated" in precisely the ways which More and Hythloday disdain. The shadows cast by the scientific instruments fall ambagiously, or in divergent directions, while Apian's torquetum turns as it measures the eccentric motions of planetary bodies. The manual on double-entry bookkeeping, an accounting practice regarded as crafty and ambagious when introduced during the fifteenth century, also evokes twists and turns by virtue of the intricacy of its methods. Tunstal writes to More in the dedication of his 1522 *De Arte Supputandi* that his motive in learning double-entry bookkeeping is to "avoid the trickery" of moneylenders and to "free myself of annoyance from crafty men."[49]

If *The Ambassadors* is about the exigencies of being an instrument, then it is also about the exigencies of using one. Given how scrupulously some of Holbein's other sitters dictated the composition of their portraits, one might wonder why Dinteville and Selve chose to be represented alongside a grotesquely distorted skull.[50] Accounts of anamorphic portraits are quite common, but they typically toy with human faces, not skulls, playing upon the similarity or difference between one person and another. Defined by one Renaissance writer as the art of making "one picture to represent several faces," anamorphosis usually operates by superimposing one face onto another, either to legitimate a genealogy by means of the overlapping strata of royal faces, or to force a resemblance for comic effect.[51] In his 1661 catalogue of mechanical inventions and other artifices, Thomas Powell gives examples of each. One anamorphosis depicts a chancellor of France from one angle, and a "multitude of little faces" representing his various ancestors from the other. Others are caricatures, yoking together physically disparate creatures to demonstrate their moral or intellectual affinity: the image of a Spaniard turns into an ass when examined askew, and an ornately dressed courtier becomes a fox.

The anamorphic image in *The Ambassadors* is fundamentally different in that there is no face or subject of which it is a distortion except the ambassador himself, a figure subject to the superimposition of another identity through the will of his principal. The painting represents the relationship between ambassador and monarch as bound up in an anamorphic play of resemblance and distortion. Yet the principal of *The Ambassadors* is conspicuously absent; instead, Holbein depicts only organs and instruments, devices for the mediation of human voices, faces, and letters – all of them oblique, displaced, or broken. Whether or not the painting alludes directly to More, it ultimately recapitulates both Hythloday's and his own concerns about the exigencies of political involvement and the potentially self-annihilating effects of serving as an instrument of state.

Holbein's painting refracts many of the anxieties surrounding ambassadorial mediation in Renaissance culture. When they appear in sixteenth-century texts, ambassadors often bungle messages or deliver them – to borrow Puttenham's phrase – with "tedious ambage." Shakespeare's mediators, figures such as Pandarus, Juliet's Nurse, and Pompey Bum, possess what one critic has called "a natural genius for retardation," and their verbosity or incompetence invariably obstructs the action of the play.[52] Montaigne devotes an entire essay to legatory incompetence, while Puttenham describes a series of ambassadorial gaffs to illustrate the myriad ways in which rules of decorum are breached. Some ambassadors suffer from "too much finesse and curiositie" in their speeches, and others "laugh . . . dissolutely" at strange customs, misconstrue foreign words, or speak "undecently," which "maketh a whole matter many times miscarrie."[53]

Ambassadors are also, of course, perceived as liars, but they occupy a peculiarly oblique relationship to both truth and falsehood since they are often the unwitting medium for lies that originate with their sovereign principals. Voicing a common observation, a 1590 miscellany of political maxims recommends that an ambassador must "not imagine himself to be a dissembler," but rather must honestly believe the lies he tells, so that consequently, "A Prince that by the means of his embassadour would deceive an other Prince, must first deceive the Ambasadour."[54] The object of deception rather than its subject, the ambassador is the consummate master of the truthful dissimulation or "honest and laudable deceipt" that is the cornerstone of *prudentia mixta* in Renaissance political thought.[55]

Sixteenth- and early seventeenth-century technical treatises explore the possibility that mechanical devices might solve some of the moral and epistemological problems posed by using human instruments to deliver messages. In addition to the widespread use of ciphers and secret languages in order to make written messages unintelligible if intercepted, mechanical instruments promise to eliminate a ruler's dependence upon human intermediaries. The problem with the new mediating devices is that they are, in Bacon's words, of "ambiguous use." While telescopes arouse fantasies about the possibility of an unmediated, perfectly accurate means of surveillance, they also threaten to distort the secrets they transmit, and they awaken the disturbing realization that one might be spied on undetected.

In Thomas Tomkis' 1615 *Albumazar*, an adaptation of a play entitled *L'Astrologo* written by the Neapolitan cryptographer and natural philosopher Giambattista Della Porta, an enthusiastic purveyor of mechanical messengers dreams up various optical and pneumatic instruments that perform ambassadorial tasks, from a "wind instrument" that "breathe[s] ten languages" to a device that "multiplies objects of hearing" so that the user "may know each whisper from Prester John . . . as fresh as 'twere deliver'd / Through a trunke." The recommendation of far-fetched devices that "have the power / T'unlock the hidden'st closets of whole states"[56] or to function as ambassadors is common enough by the turn of the seventeenth century for Ben Jonson to travesty the machinations of modern espionage in *Volpone*. *Volpone*'s Sir Politic-Would-Be, an aspiring intelligencer who prides himself on knowing the "ebbs and flows of state," regales Peregrine with the exploits of a master spy who sends out "weekly intelligences . . . in cabbages," dispensing them to ambassadors "in oranges, musk-melons, apricocks," and even "Colchester oysters."[57] Able to procure information from a "conceal'd statesman" in a "trencher of meat," this fellow can then "convey an answer in a tooth-pick," a mockery of the more improbable vehicles, including nuts and ladies' fans, through which Renaissance cryptographers recommend the conveyance of secrets. Sir Politic-Would-Be's greatest instrument of espionage, a water-works that powers a bellows in order to waft the scent of onions onto a ship, surpasses even the most ridiculous cryptographic devices of Jonson's day.[58]

In his epigram "The New Cry," Jonson derides the elaborate codes used by those "ripe statesmen" who "all get Porta, for the sundry ways / To write in cipher," and who have "found the sleight / With juice of lemons, onions, piss to write."[59] Referring to Porta's two works on cryptography, the 1563 *De Furtivis Literarum Notis Vulgo* and the 1589 *Magia Naturalis*, Jonson mocks the outlandish "tacitis ambagibus [ambagious tactics]" advocated by the Neapolitan natural philosopher for transmitting furtive letters.[60] One of the most common devices described in sixteenth-century cryptographic texts is the Alberti Ring, an instrument designed by Leon Battista Alberti in his 1466 *De Cifris*. In its simplest form, the device consists of two concentric metal discs that move independently like an astrolabe or planispheric instrument: one disc is engraved with a normal alphabet, and the other disc with a scrambled alphabet or code, so that the user can translate from plain text to code, and back to plain text, by moving the concentric rings. These instruments increase in intricacy throughout the Renaissance as cryptographers design codes to be more difficult to solve: Giovanbattista Palatino proposes triple and quadruple rings in his 1540 *Dalle Cifre*, and he also recommends introducing spurious symbols onto the ring that serve no function except to confound would-be decoders.[61]

Renaissance cryptographers including Palatino, Porta, and Trithemius perceive a number of different technical and temperamental affinities among the disciplines of cryptography, mechanics, and the occult sciences. In his *Polygraphia*, Trithemius persistently compares the art of secret writing, with its "great and difficult occult and secret mysteries [grands & arduz mysteries occultes & couvertes]," to mechanics and the occult sciences.[62] Cryptography's occult legacy is secured by his assertion that Pythagoras, Zoroaster, and Hermes Trismegistus all practiced secret writing, as did "certain alchemists who wished to hide and lay out the rules and secrets of their science [certains Alchimistes (qui) ont voulu secrettement couvrir & descrire les reigles, & secrets de leur science]."[63] Many of Trithemius' encoding techniques involve the use of astronomical symbols and tables, so that coded messages might be mistaken for astronomical charts.[64] Like contemporary cosmographical texts, sixteenth-century editions of the *Polygraphia* contain fully functional, paper encoding rings, or volvelles, which Trithemius aptly terms "figures Planispheriques," devices which resemble, both in form and function, ready-to-assemble paper astrolabes. For Trithemius, however, the kinship between mechanics and steganography, or secret writing, is predicated as much upon the mutual condemnation of both disciplines as it is upon the techniques and tools employed by them. Protesting that cryptography is "sincere, pur, [et] naturel," Trithemius compares his work to that of Albertus Magnus, the medieval "perscrutateur" of nature's secrets who was accused of being a necromancer on account of his construction of "admirables merveilles & experiments."[65]

Other Renaissance writers are more inventive still in their pursuit to perfect the encoding and secret transmission of information by mechanical means. Two early seventeenth-century manuscripts composed by Henry Reginald, both in the British Library, contain proposals for the mechanical conveyance of privy communiqués. In one manuscript, Reginald imagines two instruments, which he terms *Macrolexis* (large writing) and *Stenolexis* (secret writing), capable of dispatching "briefe speedie and Secrete Intelligence, without messenger or letter."[66] In addition to developing systems of mathematical notation in order to scramble and descramble alphabets, as Trithemius does with his "algarithmes," Reginald proposes a device called the "Nuncius Volucris," an airborne automaton in the shape of a bird or a fly.[67] In another manuscript, composed in 1603 and dedicated to King James, Reginald elaborates upon his "Nuncius volatilibus," a mechanical carrier pigeon which he boasts will deliver messages "in a more speedie maner, then by the flying of any feathered fowle."[68] Reginald's inspiration for the device is probably the avian automaton or "volatile blanc" designed by Archimedes to transmit messages, though he also compares his invention to Archimedes' sphere, a mechanical model of the cosmos constructed with "sane sol[l]ertia," or judicious cleverness.[69]

The instruments commonly employed to transmit political intelligence during the Renaissance are often less fantastical than the intermediaries imagined by Jonson's *Volpone* or by projectors like Reginald, yet they are equally fraught with moral problems and practical difficulties. The search for a perfect mechanical mediator reveals a lack of trust in human instruments, either on account of their potential disloyalty or their incapacity to reproduce messages accurately. By promising to correct the faults of human intercessors, machines also allay the culture's discomfort with its political instrumentalism even while it reproduces that instrumentalism in a new medium.

Sixteenth-century descriptions of telescopes or "perspective trunkes" illustrate that machines which have since come to serve very different functions were originally conceived as solutions to the procurement and transmission of secret information. Numerous accounts circulate about Roger Bacon's purported invention of glasses which could "make things at hand . . . appear at distance, and things at distance, as hard at hand . . . yea so farre may the designe be driven, as the least letters may be read, and things reckoned at an incredible distance."[70] The first makers of perspective glasses, including Thomas Digges and the Dutch inventor Hans Lippersley, imagine their devices as tools of espionage. In the preface to the 1571 *Pantometria*, which contains three treatises written by his father Leonard, Thomas Digges describes what may be the first account of a functional telescope, though its primary functions are surveillance: "my father," the younger Digges recounts, "was able, and sundrie times hath by proportionall Glasses duely situate in convenient angles, not onely discovered things farre off, read letters . . . but also seven myles of[f] declared what hath been doon at that instante in private places."[71] Useful for reading private letters or peeking into neighbors' windows, Digges' telescope magnifies personal, rather than sidereal, dispatches.

Even as the scientific applications of the telescope are explored with the simultaneous efforts of Hariot, Galileo, and various Dutch spectacle-makers, the idea persists into the seventeenth century that optical devices are political, and not astronomical, instruments. Mario Biagioli attributes the success of Galileo's telescope to the astronomer's ability to translate his device into a cogent political symbol of Medici power in which Cosimo II is imagined as exercising his authority over his subjects by means of the instrument.[72] Appropriate to Cosimo's essentially political understanding of telescopic power, Galileo fashions himself into a "sidereal messenger," a trustworthy emissary of Medici power who relays his lunar dispatches with speed and accuracy.

The use of telescopes and other optical devices as tools of surveillance involves a politicization of the art of perspective similar to that at work in the court masque, where the central position of the sovereign is "determined by the laws of optics." Suberville's *L'Henry-metre*, dedicated to Henri IV, describes its "Royal and Universal" suveying instrument as able to take measurements "from one sole place, without moving from that place [Instrument Royal, et Universel . . . lequel prend toutes mesures Geometriques & Astronomiques . . . sur une seule station . . . (sans) bouger de sa place]."[73] Making tangible the omniscience that characterizes sovereign power, the Henry-metre turns its user into the king of all he surveys, offering him the best seat in his theater of power, one from which he need not move in order to see and be seen by his subjects. The Elizabethan inventor Edmund Jentill fashions a similar device for William Cecil, writing the Lord Treasurer in 1594 in order to offer him "an instrument, wherby the distance to anything . . . shal bee obtayned without moving." Previously convicted of counterfeiting, Jentill writes to Cecil from prison, his inventions offered as favors "to be performed . . . in redemption of my great amisse and fault committed."[74] By offering Cecil an instrument that augments the Lord Treasurer's capacity for surveillance, Jentill's invention capitulates to the awareness that he is woefully subject to the scrutiny of a polity able to overcome any distance or obstacle in its detection of crime.

The glassmaking techniques which yield telescopes and microscopes also aid in the fabrication of convex and concave distorting glasses that produce what Dee's 1659 translation of Roger Bacon's *Discovery of the Miracles of Art, Nature, and Magick* calls "Perspective Artificial Experiences."[75] As *lusus scientiae*, these optical devices throw sensual experience into disarray, revealing it to be subjective and capricious. Teasing out the intrinsic falsifications of human vision by externalizing and intensifying them, these "artificiall experiences" heighten the skeptical recognition that our senses are the inescapable and untrustworthy ambassadors of human knowledge.

In spite of – or perhaps because of – their capacity to exacerbate a skeptical distrust of the senses, mechanical devices slip easily into the role of ambassador or spy. The fantasies shaped by Renaissance optical devices are often voyeuristic in nature, involving the surreptitious discovery of secrets. With a perspective device, anyone can become an intelligencer: one early seventeenth-century treatise on perspective devices illustrates "how to shew to one that is suspitious, what is done in another chamber or roome, notwithstanding the interposition of the wall," and how to "see those that passe to and fro in the streets, without being seene of any."[76] Optical devices also service auto-voyeuristic fantasies, enabling their users to see themselves in an estranged or distorted way by offering an unfamiliar vantage point from which to view a familiar image. Numerous treatises describe glasses that multiply or fracture the human face, such as the one made by Cornelius Drebbel "in which one could see one's face seven times."[77] While devices such as Drebbel's act as rehearsal spaces for a protean identity, others foster autoscopic moments by enabling their users to see themselves as others see them. One particularly common trick illustrated in technical treatises is "how to see the back of one's head" with the use of two glasses, a task which, however mundane to anyone who has visited a hairdresser, exemplifies what Heidegger has called the "enframing" effect of technologies that alter the viewer's perspective by allowing that viewer to see himself from a new or distant angle.[78] Like Heidegger's example of the first photographs taken of the earth from the moon, the images produced by the first telescopes prompt the recognition that the earth is neither as large nor as central as it appears from our subjective perspective.

By altering the perspective from which familiar objects are viewed, telescopes and optical devices attest to our inescapably subjective view of ourselves and the world we inhabit. For some, these devices confirm the arguments put forth by sixteenth-century skeptics such as Montaigne, who asserts that knowledge obtained through the senses is unreliable because it lacks a higher guarantor: there is "nothing beyond" the senses, Montaigne writes, "that may stead us to discover them."[79] While optical devices can "stead" or regulate the senses, they can also arouse an anxious delight as they reveal the senses to be fallible mediators of the world around them. In his *Apology for Raymond Sebond*, Montaigne describes the senses as if they were incompetent ambassadors, since by the "meane and intermission [of the senses] all knowledge comes unto us, if they chaunce to miss in the report they make unto us, if either they corrupt or alter that, which from abroad they bring unto us . . . we have nothing else to hold by."[80] Like Holbein, who situates human mediators in a visual field rife with illusion and distortion, Montaigne's *Apology* looks to the ambassador as a master trope for the inherent, and inherently feeble, mediation of the senses. Distorting mirrors and optical tricks refract this skeptical crisis of confidence, for they mimic and expose the subjective nature of sight in particular and of the passions and senses in general. Robert Burton compares the delusions of melancholics to the experience of a man who "looketh through a peece of red glasse [and] judgeth every thing he sees to be red," while Thomas Wright compares the distorting prism of human passion to "green spectacles" which discolor reality in a similarly totalizing manner.[81] For Wright, the metaphor of colored spectacles discloses an even more intractable skeptical dilemma: namely, the cognitive confusion between subject and object that makes it impossible to perceive the mediating lenses – jealousy, melancholy, hatred – through which human experience is constituted.

In treatises concerned with correcting the flaws of ambassadorial communication, such as Francis Godwin's *Nuncius Inanimatus, or the Mysterious Messenger*, the perceived fallibility of the senses prompts the exploration of artificial methods, including perspective devices and speaking tubes, to convey political intelligence. Godwin begins his treatise by stating that "nothing can be perceived by human understanding without the help of the exterior Senses." The inescapably mediatory role of sense experience shapes Godwin's analysis of the related exigencies of political mediation, since "he that intends to communicate the secrets of his minde to one either absent or present, it is altogether necessary that he have an accesse by this way [of the senses]."[82] Unfolding his analogy between the untrustworthiness of the senses and the unfaithfulness of messengers and ambassadors, Godwin suggests that while the mediated nature of our interactions is to some degree unavoidable, the "intermission" or gap between principal and organ can be narrowed by the use of mechanical devices, the titular "inanimate messengers" of his work. Godwin prescribes a variety of techniques for those who "will not trust to the fidelity of the Messenger" in order to circumvent the problems that arise due to the "treachery or negligence of those that carry [letters]."[83] In addition to using smoke-signals, carrier pigeons, and other "inter-nuncios," Godwin describes how the ancient Picts constructed a "brazen pipe" inside Hadrian's Wall in order to communicate secretly "through each Tower and Castell" built along the wall. Through this "rare artifice," the Picts were able to speak to each other from far away "without any interruption, to signify where about they feared the assault of the enemy."[84] The concealed speaking tubes employed by the ancient Picts preserve the secrets they ambagiously convey more securely than direct, immediate speech, for according to Godwin, speech "doth disclose one mans minde unto another, and as it were joyn them both together." Since the voice and the ears are "not safe" as modes of communication, speaking tubes "faithfully perform" what our senses cannot, overcoming the "impediments" of distance as well as the less tangible obstacles which prevent messages from arriving at "the place in which they are destinated."

While Godwin's speaking tube is designed to mitigate the errors of the senses, it manages to do just the opposite, both by supporting the skeptical conviction that the senses do "deceive and enforce the understanding [il trompent . . . et en eschange sont trompez par elle]," and by transmitting knowledge even more circuitously than their human counterparts.[85] Renaissance skeptics often observe that the human senses transmit knowledge ambagiously: the canals of our ears, Charron writes, are "oblique and crooked [obliques et tortueuses]," so that air and sound do not enter immediately but rather mediately or collaterally.[86] By increasing the distance over which sound must travel in order to reach its object, the speaking tube extends the already labyrinthine paths of the human ear, entangling and imperiling the information it is supposed to transmit.

Its stated purpose as "unlocking the secrets of mens hearts," Godwin's text reveals its speaking tube to be of ambiguous use, since it teaches readers to intercept messages as well as encrypt them. The two-handedness of ambassadorial machinery is also revealed by an early account of a telescope contained in a 1608 "intelligencer," or newsletter, which recounts the reception of several ambassadors by Prince Maurice of Nassau in the Hague. After describing the visit of emissaries from the King of Siam, the text relates an exchange between Maurice and the spectacle-maker Hans Lippersley, who has come to demonstrate a new telescopic device "through which one could discover and view distinctly things far away from us [moyennant lesquelles on peut decouvrir & voir distinctement les choses esloignées de nous]." The correspondences between the conventional scene of diplomacy with which the newsletter begins and the unconventional diplomatic function served by Lippersley's perspective glasses are teased out by one of the audience at court, a Spanish general named Spinola who recognizes the instrument to be a tool of espionage. Spinola comments to Maurice's brother that "I will no longer know if I am secure, since you will see me from far away [ie ne scaurois plus estre en seurté, car vous me verrez de loing]," since "by these glasses they will see the enemy's tricks [par ces lunettes ils verroyent les tromperies de l'ennemi]." From Spinola's standpoint, the telescope threatens to strip away any sense of security and privacy, yet Maurice's brother suggests quite the opposite: by virtue of its capacity to observe the enemy from a great distance, the device preserves the security of both sides by enabling the Dutch to "defend our people without firing at all against you [nous defendrons à nos gens de ne tirer point à vous]." In its dual capacity to lock and unlock secrets of state, Lippersley's instrument nullifies the efficacy of secrecy as a political weapon and ultimately alters the aims and methods of diplomacy itself.[87]

With the exception of the telescope, the majority of devices capable of serving ambassadorial functions are not new inventions but rather variations on techniques outlined in Roman military treatises by Frontinus, Vegetius, and others.[88] What is novel, however, is the extent to which Renaissance writers perceive such devices as capable of radically altering the temper of political interactions as well as the integrity of sense experience. The epistemological ramifications of ambassadorial machinery are explored at disturbing length by John Wilkins' 1641 *Mercury: or the Secret and Swift Messenger*. The text teaches the use of alternative means of communication, including gestures, smoke signals, and sound-carrying devices such as pipes "to discourse with a Friend, though he were in a close Dungeon, in a besieged City, or a hundred miles off." Though some of the media recommended by Wilkins, such as birds, are in fact animate creatures, many others aspire to transcend the materiality of communication in the animate realm. Wilkins promises that his inanimate messengers, including arrows, bullets, and "inchaunted glasses" can reveal "what was done in any part of the world" and are "far swifter than the natural Motion of any corporeall Messenger," many of them aspiring to transcend the materiality of human communication.[89]

Yet the fantasy of a disembodied voice sundered from its point of origin in a speaking tube, or the silent idiom of hand gestures, quickly turns into a nightmarish phantasmagoria. Explaining how the ancient Picts used speaking tubes to communicate when "barred out with Walls, or deterred by Enemies," Wilkins points out that because there is a "certain Space of Intermission, for the Passage of the Voice, betwixt its going into these Cavities, and its coming out," it is possible for a speaking tube to detach the voice from its source: "if both ends were seasonably stopped, whilst the Sound was in the midst, it would continue there till it had some vent."[90] By isolating speech from its agent, speaking tubes dissociate us from our faculty of speech just as the telescope detaches our instruments of sight, allowing for vision where no eye is present. Both kinds of devices are "separate" rather than "conjoined" instruments, potentially autonomous from the entity governing them.

Wilkins does, however, envision speaking tubes and other mechanical messengers as a means to correct human, and specifically ambassadorial, inadequacies. One of the introductory epistles to Wilkins' *Mercury* laments

that "Our Legates are but Men, and often may / Great State-Affairs unwill-
ingly betray," either because they have drunk too much "tell-tale Wine"
or because they blurt out their secrets "like Fire pent in."[91] The corrective
instruments and codes envisioned by Wilkins guard secrets of state, but
they also promise to encode all forms of interaction by means of "mystick
Nods" and "feet [which] are made to speak, as well as walk." Like his 1638
Discovery of a World in the Moone, in which lunar inhabitants communicate
via "such inarticulate sounds, as no Letters can express," Wilkins' *Mercury*
dreams of resuscitating an Edenic language untarnished by ambiguity, a
language so perfect that it eliminates the need for language altogether by
"Making our Knowledge, too, intuitive."

Both Wilkins and Godwin envision the mechanization of communication and the eradication of speech as possible solutions to the miscommuni-
cations that inhere in the medium of language. Wilkins was very indebted to
Godwin: his *Discovery* reworks portions of Godwin's *Man in the Moone*, an
account of the sidereal embassy of Domenico Gonzalez, while *Mercury* was,
as Wilkins admits, "occasion'd by the writing of a little thing, call'd *Nuncius
Inanimatus*," the treatise by Godwin published in Latin in 1629. Above the
date of publication on Godwin's title-page are the words *In Utopia*, which
are crossed out, and the phrase *Londini Anglia* written in their place. Both
Godwin's *Nuncius Inanimatus* and Wilkins' *Mercury* are indeed utopian
texts under erasure, since the nature of their utopian vision is so paradoxical: they imagine complete legibility and unmediated knowledge to be the
result of encoded and "mystick" forms of communication.[92]

The speaking tubes described by Renaissance writers are two-handed
instruments capable of being used as conduits for secret messages but also
as tools of surveillance to intercept private conversations. In the *Anatomy
of Melancholy*, Burton describes "artificiall devices" for overhearing confessions, perhaps designed in the manner of the listening tubes depicted
by Athanasius Kircher in his treatise on acoustics, circuits of hollow pipes
aurally linking one room to another.[93] In a dedicatory epistle to *Mercury*,
Richard West eloquently teases out the contradictions which inhere in
the speaking tube and in Wilkins' text: "But Secrecy's now publish'd; You
reveal / By Demonstration how we may conceal."[94] Renaissance cryptographers and scientists likewise appreciate the dilemma that their inanimate
nuncios serve two contradictory functions: secrecy and universality. In his
Characterie, Timothy Bright argues that the selfsame codes used to transmit
secrets are also a *lingua franca* that enables strangers to "communicate their
meaning together in writing, though of sundrie tongues." For Trithemius,
too, the art of steganography can serve the inverse purpose, enabling its

users to "communicate to all men [communiquer à tout homme]" and thus "make understood all the mysteries and secrets of the whole world [faire entendre tous mysteres & secrets de tout le monde]."[95]

The observation that cryptographic texts and instruments "publish" the secrecy they preserve unfolds the dialectical relationship between concealment and revelation exemplified by Renaissance culture's mediatory instrument *par excellence* – the printing press. The act of printing paradoxically protects a writer's secrets by divulging them, for only through reproduction and dissemination are the unique features of a text protected – either directly, by copyright or privilege, or indirectly, by virtue of their existence in the public sphere. Like speaking tubes and telescopes, the printing press both conceals and exposes, a twofold capacity recognized by Miguel de Cervantes as he narrates his hero's two successive encounters with machinery in Part 2 of *Don Quixote*. In the first, Quixote is tricked by Don Antonio when he arranges for a young man to disguise himself inside a speaking head and reveal secrets about Quixote to a group of amused onlookers.[96] Directly after his encounter with the speaking head, Quixote suffers further exposure at the hand of a printing press when he witnesses the printing of his own, unfinished text – a work he had assumed to be "burnt by now and reduced to ashes for its presumption." At the very moment that Quixote sees himself duplicated in printed form, he is indexed, his identity expunged by the same mechanical process that produced that identity in the first place.[97] Like Wilkins' speaking tube and Lippersley's telescope, Cervantes' speaking head and his printing press eradicate the possibility of sanctuary in an individuated, unreproducible, and private self.

Like sufflators and fire-blowing war machines, speaking heads are pneumatic machines, structurally analogous to the pipes which counterfeit voices and birdsongs as well as the automatic organs such as those depicted in Book III of Salomon de Caus' 1615 *Raisons des Forces Mouvantes*.[98] In Agostino Ramelli's 1588 *Diverse e Artificiose Macchine*, a statue topped with mechanical birds, similar to those in the Roman banqueting house described in Nashe's *Unfortunate Traveller*, conceals a hollow tube through which a man, hidden from sight, may blow to create an artificial chirping sound. These pneumatic machines are hermetic in several senses of the term: concealed from view, and powered by air, they are iconographically linked to the messenger god. Mercury is often depicted in Renaissance engravings with organs or bellows, pneumatic devices operated by *pneuma*, or breath, which produces a faint whisper. This whispering sound not only evokes Mercury's capacity to transmit (or betray) secrets, but it also counterfeits the human voice. In organs and sufflators, this creates an uncannily anthropomorphic

effect, traces of which are evident in the range of contradictory meanings for
the term "organ" during the Renaissance. "Organ" can denote the instrument of the human voice, as in the "shrill pipes" of Shakespeare's Viola,
but it can also denote the mechanical imitation of natural human speech.
As Raymond Williams has illustrated, the terms "organic" and "organicall" carry a spectrum of meanings during the Renaissance which includes
their own opposites: "organicall" can signify a natural sound or physical
structure, but it can alternatively signify the reproduction of that sound or
structure by means of mechanical artifice.[99]

That organs blur the precarious distinction between human and mechanical instrumentality is demonstrated by the travel journal of an Elizabethan
organ-maker named Thomas Dallam, whose description of his instrument,
a gift from Queen Elizabeth to be performed for the Ottoman Sultan, provides an extended examination of the anxious and conflictive relationship
between rulers and instruments, or principals and organs, at the end of
the sixteenth century. As a self-moving and autonomous "separate" instrument, Dallam's organ exposes the political hazards inherent in the constitution of sovereignty through instruments – that is, the way in which
power is delegated to instruments (either human or mechanical) that in
turn modulate the dynamics of political interaction. An organ-maker who
made instruments for King's College, Cambridge and Worcester Cathedral,
Dallam traveled to Constantinople in 1599 where he joined the company of
Henry Lello, the English ambassador to the Levant, with instructions from
Elizabeth I to deliver his "marvelous organ" to the Sultan Mahomed III.
Gifts of mechanical devices are common features of sixteenth-century
embassies, a practice whose motivations are clarified by a 1596 letter in the
Calendar of State Papers stating that a "great and curious present is going
to the Grand Turk" which will "scandalize other nations, especially the
Germans."[100] Dallam's embassy, like the attempt to enlist Nicolas Kratzer
as a spy some eighty years earlier, attests to the political and diplomatic
value of technical ingenuity. Yet Dallam's organ proves an untrustworthy
ambassador, for it intermittently interrogates the political instrumentality
upon which both the Ottoman court and Tudor diplomacy rely. The two
performances of his organ, an automatic concert followed by one given by
Dallam's own hands, shuffle back and forth between separate and conjoined
instrumentality, ultimately calling into doubt the delegation of sovereign
power through instruments.

   Throughout his diary, Dallam is acutely aware of his own status
as an instrument of the Tudor polity, and he is also attuned to the

instrumentalism of the Turkish Sultan, whose every action and gesture is mediated through his instruments. Upon Dallam's arrival, he is told by the Sultan's secretary, or "Coppagaw," to "make the instrument as perfitt as possibly I could, for that daye, before noune, the Grand Sinyor [Mahomed III] would see it, and he [the English ambassador] was to deliver his imbassage to the Grand Sinyor."[101] The ambassador's speech and the performance of the organ are analogous displays: both "take the place of a letter" and are equally dependent upon the flawless reproduction of a message initiated by Elizabeth's prompting. As Dallam prepares to assemble the organ, Lello reminds him of the responsibilities of his charge, and Dallam reassures him that the organ will perform "better than it was when Her Maiestie sawe it in the banketinge house at Whyte Hale."[102] Like Lello's own embassy to the Sultan, Dallam's organ must repeat – verbatim – a score set down by the Queen. As Walter Ong has noted, rhetorical and mechanical composition both rely upon a process of "assembling . . . previously readied material," precisely what Lello and Dallam do to prepare for their audience with the Sultan.[103]

On the day of the organ's performance, Dallam and his assistants bring the instrument to the Sultan's palace. As the organ is ushered in through the door, the Englishmen are locked out, so that much of Dallam's account of the performance is based upon what he manages to eavesdrop from behind the locked door. After the Sultan enters, he is "seated in his Chaire of Estate, [and] command[s] silence." As Lello waits to deliver his "imbassage and his Letteres," the organ begins its address: "All being quiett, and no noyes at all, the presente began to salute the Grand Sinyor," having been preset by Dallam to wait "a quarter of an hour for his cominge thether."[104]

The seemingly autonomous performance of Dallam's organ provides an exemplary model of political instrumentality, yet its very autonomy threatens the status of the human emissaries who populate the Ottoman court, disturbing the principle of conjoined instrumentality upon which the Sultan's power relies. While the organ clearly appeals to the Sultan in that it performs with only the most tacit prompting from its master, it also upsets him because he cannot discern any tangible authority exerted by the instrument-maker, still locked behind the door, over his machine. Although the organ is programmed to play of its own accord four times per day, Dallam (still behind the door) shows one of the Sultan's servants how the performance can be repeated if he "tuche a little pin with his finger," which his servant does to the Sultan's great satisfaction.[105] Clearly delighted by the discovery that he can control the organ through his servant's hand, the Sultan commands the Coppagaw to repeat the performance, thereby affirming the efficacy and justifiability of the network of instruments upon which his political power is predicated. Operated by proxy with a hidden pin, the organ's performance legitimates the Sultan's spectacle of power by analogy: both are apparently immediate and spontaneous yet meticulously choreographed by concealed instruments.

The analogy falls apart when the Sultan, seated "ryght before the Keaes, wheare a man shoulde playe on [the organ] by hande," is unsettled by the fact that "those keaes did move when the orgon wente and nothinge did tuche them." For the Sultan, an organ which plays automatically is a mechanical rendition of his worst political fear, a *Fantasia*-like nightmare of unruly instruments, unchecked by their master, running amok. The Sultan demands to see the organ be played, rather than play itself. Dallam is brought into the midst of the spectacle by the Coppagaw, who tells him that it is the "Grand Sinyore's pleasur that I should lett him se me playe on the orgon." As he enters, Dallam quickly discovers how the Ottoman court relies upon what Norbert Elias has called a "lustre of aloofness," an etiquette of *disinvoltura* and physical detachment.[106] Though he passes right by the Sultan, Dallam observes that the ruler "woulde not turne his head to louke upon me," and the organ-maker momentarily refuses to approach the organ "because the Grand Sinyor satt so neare the place wheare I should playe that I could not com at it, but I muste needes turn my back towards him, and touche his Kne with my britchis, which no man in paine of death myght doe savinge only the Coppagaw."[107] To touch the Sultan would disturb a political edifice founded upon the network of auxiliaries at the Sultan's disposal, instruments who mediate their ruler's every command. Dallam is thus intricated in the circuitous tactics and in what Puttenham calls the "backward or sideling" motions prescribed by "Orientall" courts: the Sultan gives several gold pieces to his servant, who in turn places the money in the pocket of Dallam's coat while it lies on the ground.[108]

The Sultan's reaction to the organ's self-moving keys reveals how mechanical devices can either exemplify or undermine the instrumentalism informing political decorum in Ottoman and European courts alike. His desire to see a manual performance of the organ, as well as his persistent efforts in exercising his commands through his servants, underscores the Sultan's desire to keep organs conjoined to their principals. Thus, as Dallam begins to play, the Sultan seats himself very close to the organ, "wher he myghte se my handes." The visible connection between Dallam's hand and his organ restores the conjoined instrumentality needed to uphold a political structure threatened by the earlier, automatic performance of the organ.

The autonomous motions of machinery interrogate the political authority that rests upon the visible presence of living instruments, or slaves. In this respect, the Sultan espouses Aristotle's argument in the *Politics* that "lifeless instruments," or machines, correct the flaws of "living instruments" but also threaten to upset the political order by "anticipating the will of others" and precluding the need for a master.[109] Self-moving devices like the "statues of Daedalus" described by Aristotle epitomize the master–servant relationship even as they render that relationship obsolete, their perfect servitude making rulers and their instruments indistinguishable from each other.

When Dallam enters the court, he is struck by the Sultan's impressive train, which includes 400 dwarfs and around 300 "dum men, that could neither heare nor speake." Dallam is particularly intrigued by the presence of the deaf-mutes, court entertainers and servants whose inability to speak assures an ideal audience as well as a flawless diplomatic corps. Yet as the Jacobean essayist William Cornwallis observes, while the Turks "have certaine Mutes to perform their executions" and to deliver messages, they also punish tattle-tales and spies by removing their "babling instruments," thus making it difficult to discern whether a given deaf-mute is a loyal emissary or a traitor.[110] No longer able to convey secrets with their organic instruments of speech, the deaf-mutes employed by the Sultan instead rely upon a gestural language like those imagined by Wilkins and Godwin. Attempting to converse with them after the performance of the organ, Dallam describes in amazement how "those dumb men . . . lett me understande by theire perfett sins [signs] all thinges that they had sene the presente dow by its motions." Like Wilkins' fantasy of "mystick nods," the Sultan's deaf-mutes speak an "intuitive" yet utterly foreign and incomprehensible language that both consummates and erodes the networks of communication radiating out from the Sultan himself.[111]

The etiquette of detachment and circumlocution evident in Dallam's account of the Ottoman court belongs to a more widespread set of rules of decorum enthusiastically embraced by Renaissance political philosophy and courtesy literature, which prize obliquity and ambage as social tools and rhetorical styles. Puttenham defines periphrasis, which he aptly nicknames the "figure of ambage," as "when we go about the bush, and will not in one or a few words express that thing which we desire to have knowen, but do chose rather to do it by many words."[112] Ambage obfuscates the speaker's purpose by concealing it within a labyrinthine network of digressions: in his 1614 *The Dove and the Serpent*, Daniel Tuvill terms this rhetorical device "winding and oblique speech" since it functions by "bouts and circuits" to confound the listener.[113]

Another courtly technique of ambage involves the use of a mediator to ventriloquize demands. Tuvill and Bacon both regard the use of intermediaries as akin to the rhetorical technique of periphrasis, since by both means a man may "(by little and little) winde, and as it were scrue himselfe" into another man's thoughts.[114] Bacon advocates several "sinister or crooked" techniques of ambage in "Of Cunning," "Of Negociation," and other *Essayes*. One might voice one's opinions as if they were common knowledge: "it is a Point of *Cunning*, to borrow the Name of the World; As to say; *The World sayes*, Or, *There is a speech abroad*."[115] Or one might speak ambagiously, either by "amus[ing] the party, with whom you deale, with some other Discourse," or by "insinuat[ing]" their message by "wrap[ping] it into a Tale; which serveth both to keepe themselves more in Guard, and to make others carry it, with more Pleasure." Each of these methods relies upon a pretense of disinterestedness, or *disinvoltura*, in which the speaker obfuscates his demands by feigning indifference to them. Perhaps reflecting on Walsingham's method of soliciting Elizabeth, Bacon recalls having known a man who, "when he wrote a Letter, he would put that which was most Materiall, in the *Post-script*, as if it had been a By-matter."[116]

Bacon's painstaking anatomy of political and rhetorical techniques of mediation in his *Essayes* helps to enlighten his complex set of attitudes towards the use of mediating instruments in his natural philosophy. Viewed concurrently, Bacon's political and scientific writings are complementary investigations of the ethical and intellectual limits of instrumentalism that explore both the benefits and the drawbacks of the mediating devices employed by both disciplines. As a natural philosopher, Bacon recognizes the limited efficacy of instruments to regulate the human intellect and mediate scientific knowledge, and his treatment of these issues is inseparable from his moral concerns regarding the political instruments available to rulers and *politiques*. In spite of Bacon's limited endorsement of dissimulation in essays such as "Of Negociating," "Of Counsell," and "Of Simulation and Dissimulation," other writings are less optimistic about the prudence and efficacy of mediating instruments, from telescopes to ambassadors and counselors. He is careful to alert his readers to both the necessity and the unreliability of the instruments that arbitrate our interactions and our knowledge of the external world. In "Of Counsell," Bacon considers both the expediency and the danger of political instrumentality: while the "Incorporation, and inseparable Conjunction of *Counsel* with *Kings*" is an ancient and prudent political custom, trustworthy or "inward" counselors are a rarity, so that it is a "Prudent King, such as is able to Grinde with a *Hand-Mill*."[117] The mechanical metaphor demonstrates the synchronicity of Bacon's political and scientific instrumentalism: the king who scorns the assistance of his instruments and uses a "hand-mill" approaches the same "height of folly" as the engineer who attempts "mechanical tasks, using [his] bare hands alone," even as the assistance provided by those instruments is limited.[118]

Bacon's qualified advocacy of political instrumentality informs the central argument of the *Novum Organum*: that the intellect must be "not left to itself, but . . . always subject to rule; and the thing accomplished as if by machinery."[119] Bacon's natural philosophy is governed by a master analogy between mechanical instruments and the intellectual "instruments" of method, both of which promise to improve the "natural unassisted working of the mind." In one incarnation of this analogy, Bacon argues that just as the invention of the "mariner's compass" proves essential to the discovery of new and remote lands, so too is it "essential to introduce a better and more perfect method of using the human mind and understanding . . . before we can reach the more remote and hidden parts of Nature."[120] A commonplace metaphor for political prudence in the sixteenth century, the mariner's compass symbolizes Bacon's "new instrument [novum organum]" in that it guarantees an "altogether better and surer intellectual operation."[121] Yet just as counselors and other instruments of state might be "full of cracks [plenus rimarum]," proving unfit for secret affairs or incompetent rulers, mechanical instruments cannot always correct the errors of the mind, for "the sense in itself is a weak thing and prone to aberration, nor are instruments for magnifying or sharpening the senses of much use."[122] Ultimately, the *Novum Organum* concludes, the mediation of knowledge through mechanical devices yields errors similar to those created by the inescapably mediatory nature of sense experience, and at times even exacerbates those errors. Bacon thus classifies mechanical instruments as "instances of the door or gate" in that they aid our senses by mediating our experience of the outside world, and they help us "maintain a closer commerce" with things at a remove from us.[123] Yet like the portals of our senses, mechanical devices only open the door to truth halfway. Two-handed engines, mechanical devices demonstrate to Bacon the potential for moral and intellectual rectitude, and also for depravity and error, in all instrumentalities.

Renaissance dramatists recognize the poignancy of failed mediation as well as the potentially tragic consequences of a political instrumentalism that strips its practitioners of their agency, individuality, or integrity. Two plays in particular – Marlowe's *Jew of Malta* and Shakespeare's *Hamlet* – stand out as quintessential tragedies of mediation, plays whose protagonists resist but ultimately succumb to the pervasive instrumentality of each play's political culture. Both plays depict the tragic consequences of living in a mediated world by staging the moral, political, and epistemological dilemmas which result from the ambagious nature of human interaction and, in the case of *Hamlet*, the mediated nature of human knowledge.

The chief characteristic of *The Jew of Malta*'s political temper is the *de facto* legitimation of any effective method or policy, a sanctioning of instrumental means which the play persistently equates with machinery. Narrating his history of shifting loyalties and forsaken allegiances, Barabas boasts to Ithamore that he once disguised himself as an "engineer" while serving as a spy "in the wars 'twixt France and Germany," and "Under pretense of helping Charles the Fifth, / Slew friend and enemy with my stratagems."[124] Truthful or not, the confession nonetheless exemplifies Barabas' condition in the play: a double agent whose lack of fidelity is expressed through his capacity for mechanical contriving and whose gusto for artifice and deception operates simultaneously in the rhetorical, political, and technical spheres.

Barabas' frequent justifications of his "policy," a key term throughout the play, are steeped in the conventional idiom of Machiavellian instrumentality:

> Thus, loving neither, will I live with both,
> Making a profit of my policy;
> And he from whom my most advantage comes
> Shall be my friend.[125]

Yet in his fantasy of making friends out of his enemies, Marlowe's hero fails to implement the radical neutrality essential to the authentic Machiavellian spirit of policy. In this respect, Barabas' capacity for unalloyed instrumentalism falls short of the "praegnant pollicy" given by the Machiavellian character of Revenge in Anthony Copley's 1596 *A Fig for Fortune*: "Use Friend and Foe, and Neuter all alike, / Onlie as Instrumentall implements / To thy designe." Copley's Revenge does not wish to make friends of his enemies, but instead recommends that one should "Destroy them all" once one's aims are effected.[126] As the debacle of Marlowe's final scene illustrates with grim literality, Barabas fails to use his "Instrumentall implements" to his best advantage: rather, he *becomes* an instrument, exploited as a tool of Christian policy. At numerous points in the play, Barabas is acutely aware of his status as an instrument and relies upon this fact in order to justify his morally abhorrent actions. "Christians do the like," Barabas protests as he unveils his final stratagem, thus fashioning himself into an unwitting accessory to the "malice, falsehood, and excessive pride" of Christian society.[127] He legitimates his actions as automated responses to the culture around him, depicting himself as a reluctant medium or a passive lever through which violence and deception pass from Christian to Turk and back again. His disavowals of responsibility are, of course, the typical defense of the messenger, the Renaissance dramatic character most frequently scapegoated for uttering words he has simply been commanded to repeat. Whipped for bringing the unhappy news of Anthony's marriage in *Anthony and Cleopatra*, one of Cleopatra's messengers complains that "To punish me for what you make me do / Seems much unequal."[128] Barabas adopts a similar line of defense, arguing that he is persecuted by Christians for crimes they coerce him to commit and beliefs they compel him to embrace. Defensively exonerating itself from the immorality of the play, Thomas Heywood's 1633 epilogue mimics and perhaps also mocks Barabas' reliance upon the conventional defense of the messenger: "We only act, and speak, what others write."[129]

Barabas' disavowals of agency manifest themselves in a very particular group of speech acts – the misquotation and parodic reiteration of those around him. Greenblatt has argued that Barabas' persistent reliance on maxims has a de-individuating effect, turning him into a stock Machiavel character who spouts hackneyed commonplaces. Yet if Barabas quotes and misquotes obsessively, it is because he perceives his own words as belonging to someone else, his utterances estranged from their point of origin like a voice trapped in a speaking tube. Misquoting a line from Terence's *Andria*, Barabas observes, "Ego mihimet sum semper proximus" – I am always next to myself – a hint of a bifurcated, ambassadorial identity subject to displacement by the words and decrees of others.[130]

What Greenblatt and Katherine Maus respectively refer to as Barabas' "self-estrangement" and his protean "polymorphousness" in turn helps to elucidate his involvement in the world of machinery.[131] *The Jew of Malta* explores the political and moral exigencies of instrumental means through mechanical instruments, and the most demonic manifestations of Barabas' means-based political strategy are his machines, culminating in the elaborate mechanical device that hoists him on his own petard at the end of the play.[132] To an Elizabethan audience, Barabas' training as an engineer would have intensified his association with the devious polymorphousness of the stage Machiavel. Engineers are commonly depicted during the Renaissance as chameleon-like and cunning by virtue of the intricate, flexible machines they design as well as their tendency to shift patrons, countries, or political loyalties. An emblem for the dreaded importation of morally dubious, alien values, the Renaissance engineer often arouses a fear of Italianate subtlety which conflates technical skill with Machiavellian ruse. Ben Jonson rolls all these qualities of the engineer – protean theatricality, technical subtlety, and Machiavellianism – into his description of Inigo Jones, who in "shifting of its faces doth play more / Parts, than the Italian could do."[133] The fear that engineers are mutable is partly based upon the transformative capacity of their machines, machines such as Jones' *machina versatilis* or the portable war machines described by Da Vinci in a letter to Lodovico il Moro as "easy to raise and take down."[134] This mutability is easily refracted back onto the protean identity of the engineer himself: Jonson allows Inigo Jones' quick-change theatrical machines to shape his depiction of the *machinatore's* inconstant and unreliable character so that he becomes a "puppet" and a "motion," an actor who plays every part except a "real Inigo."[135]

The transformative capacity of stage machinery thus symbolizes the theatrical, fluid identity typified by Marlowe's Barabas, whose virtuoso performances are brought to an end by his own, excessively intricate, theatrical device. Swallowed up by his *Diabolus ex machina*, Barabas meets a fate appropriate to his double-dealing nature when the secret trap-door beneath him "fall[s] asunder" so that he "doth sink / Into a deep pit past recovery."[136] The machine he has built to "bring confusion" to Christians and Turks alike is a *machina versatilis* in the most literal sense of the term, a machine of ambiguous use whose double-hinged design reflects Barabas' impossibly divided role as a mediator and his failure effectively to manipulate his enemies as "instrumentall implements."

A tragedy of ambage, *Hamlet* explores the epistemological exigencies of mediation as well as the difficulties which arise in a culture permeated by rhetorical and physical techniques of indirection and obfuscation. The play is filled with characters who serve, professionally or incidentally, as messengers, ambassadors, or spies: Cornelius and Voltimand, Claudius' ambassadors to Norway; Rosencrantz and Guildenstern, the household spies sent to "glean" something about Hamlet's behavior; and the eaves-dropping Polonius, whom Claudius acknowledges as his most valuable instrument, commenting to Laertes that "The head is not more native to the heart, / The hand more instrumental to the mouth, / Than is the throne of Denmark to thy father."[137] Their instrumental status proves the undoing of more than one character: Polonius, Rosencrantz, and Guildenstern all die in the process of carrying out embassies, while Ophelia becomes the unwitting instrument of her father's attempts to apprise himself of Hamlet's purpose, and Laertes capitulates to "be the organ" of Claudius' schemes, an all-too-willing instrument ultimately done in by his own "treacherous instrument."[138] And then there is Hamlet himself, a man profoundly aware of his status as a "pipe" and an "organ," and yet defiant of his instrumental status. "You would play upon me," Hamlet teasingly accuses Guildenstern, "you would seem to know my stops," comparing himself to a challenging musical instrument: "'Sblood, do you think I am easier to be played upon than a pipe? Call me what instrument you will, though you can fret me, you cannot play upon me."[139]

Virtually every verbal and physical act in the play is accomplished through proxy or ambage, from Hamlet's "ambiguous giving out" and Polonius' periphrases to the letters, commands, and commissions mediated through Claudius and Old Hamlet alike. Polonius both exemplifies and travesties Bacon's recommendation to use a "bait of falsehood" to take a "carp of truth," advising Reynaldo "with windlasses and assays of bias, / By indirections find directions out."[140] A windlass is a circuitous path in hunting, but it is also a familiar term in the idiom of Renaissance stage machinery, signifying a winch or other mechanical contrivance that operates by hoisting weight through the roundabout path of a pulley. Predicated upon the mechanical principle that heavy weights are easier to lift if distributed over a wider and more circuitous course, the windlass becomes a master trope for *Hamlet's* rhetorical and political reliance upon indirection – an indirection that fails as a rhetorical technique (for Polonius), as a revenge tactic (for Hamlet), and as a principle of political authority (for Claudius).

Motivated in part by a disdain for political and courtly instrumentalism, and in part by the skeptical attitude that human knowledge is always already mediated by the senses, mediation is demonstrated in *Hamlet* to be both inescapable and inescapably corrupt. Claudius is anxiously aware from the outset of the play of his dependence upon his emissaries, dispatching Cornelius and Voltimand to Norway with the direction that the two messengers possess "no further personal power / To business with the King more than the scope / Of these dilated articles allow."[141] Claudius' instructions to his potentially wayward messengers clearly foreshadow Hamlet's dilation of the embassy commissioned to him by his father. Old Hamlet's ghost enlists his son as an instrument of revenge, but also as an emissary to rectify the "forgèd process" of his death that has been "given out" through rumor, a poison symbolically akin to the one poured into the "natural gates and alleys" of Old Hamlet's ears.[142] The "porches" of the ears, the instrumental implements of the play's numerous acts of eavesdropping, are revealed to be unreliable mediators of the voices they absorb. Polonius' plan to "be plac'd . . . in the ear" of Gertrude and Hamlet's "conference" costs him his life, while Hamlet's attempt to "hear the process" of Claudius' prayer also proves unsuccessful, thus testifying to the ease with which the "faculties of ears and eyes" can, as Hamlet points out, distort the intelligence they transmit.[143]

Hamlet scorns the instrumentalism of Claudius' court even as he both participates in and transforms it into a set of epistemological and ontological precepts that underscores the mediated nature of human knowledge and identity. He scorns the ambassadorial office assumed by Rosencrantz, a role that strips his friend of agency by demanding that he absorb and replicate his sovereign's will at the expense of his own. Rosencrantz "soaks up the king's countenance, his rewards, his authorities," but when the King "needs what you have gleaned, it is but squeezing you, and, sponge, you shall be dry again."[144] Hamlet repudiates this ambassadorial expunging of the self, even devising a "new commission" to save himself from the fate that awaits him in England, but in so doing, he replicates, organ-like, the identity of Old Hamlet, using his "father's signet" to forge the papers and deliver Rosencrantz and Guildenstern in his place.[145] Profiting from the surrogacy and the essential replicability of messengers, seals, signets, and other instruments of diplomacy, Hamlet slips into the role of messenger and deploys ambage as a countermine, thus playing Claudius' reliance upon ambassadors against itself according to the plan he has already unraveled to Gertrude by means of a mechanical metaphor: "Let it work; / For 'tis the sport to have the engineer / Hoist with his own petard."[146] Yet the "engineer" is Hamlet himself, who like Laertes falls prey to his own machinations like a "woodcock to my own springe." Acutely aware of his instrumental status, Hamlet recognizes that the tragically mediatory nature of human knowledge and political interaction turns him, as he depicts himself to Ophelia, into a "machine."[147]

CHAPTER 4

The polymechany of Gabriel Harvey

"the less strength; the more cunning, practis, & agilitie necessarie . . ."
Gabriel Harvey

Responding in *Pierces Supererogation* to Nashe's dismissal of him as a
"nobody," Gabriel Harvey cautions him that "Polyphemus was a mightie
fellow . . . but poore Outis was even with him, and No-boddy coniured
his goggle eye, as well." While Harvey protests that "I am neither Ulysses,
nor Outis," he clearly allies himself with "Noman," the alias assumed by
Ulysses to deceive Polyphemus in the *Odyssey*.[1] Embodying wily intelligence, Homer's Ulysses serves as Harvey's guide in his own odyssey through
Cambridge and the Elizabethan court. "How wool Ulisses discourse, or,
dispatch this matter," Harvey asks himself, "What course of proceed-
ing, or conveiance, wool ye cunningest, & deepest witt in ye world,
take?"[2]

Harvey's celebration of Odyssean cunning epitomizes his political attitudes, his literary tastes, and above all his enthusiastic study of mechanics.
In their study of classical *metis*, Detienne and Vernant unfold the discrete "mental category" of resourcefulness, dexterity, and deceit that plays
a central role in ancient Greek habits of thought. In texts ranging from
Xenophon's *Cyropaedia* and *The Odyssey* to Aelian's *Tactics*, *metis* and its
related terms (*dolos, techne, mechane*) comprise a cunning intelligence which
upsets relations of power and ensures that the "defeat of the weak and the
frail is not a foregone conclusion."[3] The pseudo-Aristotelian *Mechanical
Problems* also offers a narrative of *metis* in that it conceives of mechanical power as enabling the triumph of the weak over the strong. Involving
the exploitation of hostile forces through devious means, *metis* is implicitly affiliated with mechanics in that both aim to surpass or vanquish the
limitations imposed by nature. *Metis* often relies upon mental acuity and
rhetorical skill, but it also demands expertise in instruments, the "nets,

wheels, traps, snares" and similar contrivances devised by clever and inventive minds.[4]

Gabriel Harvey is obsessed with narratives of *metis*. His writings are filled with anecdotes and adages promoting the wily intelligence and the adversarial powers of deception he associates with certain favorite texts, including Homer's *Iliad*, the poetry of Chaucer, the courtesy literature of Castiglione and Guazzo, and treatises on mechanics. This preoccupation with *metis* inflects Harvey's proto-Machiavellian political convictions, guides his courtly ambitions, dictates his tastes in poetry, and informs his interest in mechanics both as a discipline unto itself and as a set of techniques applicable in the social and political sphere. Harvey views mechanics as a species of "Tuscanisme," a discipline able to harness the powers of subtlety that permit the triumph of the weak over the strong. His perception of the affinities between mechanical and political artifice often emerges out of his digressive tendencies as a writer. In his *Commonplace Book*, he offers a snippet of prudent political advice next to a mention of "Rogeros flying horse," an automaton purportedly fashioned by Friar Bacon. "Chi la dura, la vince," Harvey writes, "whoever endures it, prevails over it," suggesting that the *virtù* of the resolute man is akin to mechanical power.[5]

The most poignant aspect of Harvey's fascination with *metis* is his wholehearted inability to comprehend and implement the intellectual and political strategies which he believes will aid him in his social and literary aspirations. In his *Commonplace Book*, Harvey exhorts himself to make Machiavelli his principal political authority; on the next page, however, he praises the "constant resolution and invincible importunity of Dandalo," a Venetian ambassador who, in order to prevail upon a stubborn ruler, "cast himself prostrate at ye feete of ye prynce, and crept under his Table lyke a Dogg: lying there in most base and abject manner, untill at last . . . he bredd compassion in A hart of flynte, & wunne the inexorable Tyrant to his purpose." Harvey appears to view Dandalo's canine servility as an example of *The Prince*'s injunction to "know how to make good use of the beast and the man," for he praises it as a "very notable Doggtrick," useful in a world where "the wiser man . . . cherisheth, & tenderith his animal powers."[6] Crawling around on the floor like a dog is not, of course, what Machiavelli has in mind when he advises the prince to employ the nature of the fox and the lion. Harvey recognizes this elsewhere, remarking that "unworthy subjugation or contemptible need are not due to anyone else. To be sufficient unto oneself is magnificent; to beg for the help of another is abject (ne cuique servias vilis: aut cuiusque indigeas contemptibilis. Sibi ipsi sufficere, magnificum est: alterius opem implorare, abiectum est.)"[7] Searching for a more dignified, and less bestial, political etiquette, Harvey hangs his hopes for advancement both at Cambridge and at court upon the precept that "a little pollicy prævaileth, when A great deale of strength fayleth." Yet for all his earnest study of "right artificiality," Harvey is nonetheless puzzled about how best to deploy the policy and artifice advocated by his favorite courtesy treatises and works of political philosophy, a confusion compounded by his study of mechanics.[8]

Readers of Harvey's marginalia have been mystified by his creation of fictional personae such as Eutrapelus, Eudromos, and Chrysotechnus, each of whom embodies a different facet of Harvey's aspirations.[9] Harvey's marginal personae, like many of his neologisms, are created out of terms indebted to the classical vocabulary of *metis*, forged from his reading of Homer and other ancient purveyors of cunning. The creation of epithets is, of course, a distinctive feature of Homeric epic, where Odysseus is referred to as *polymetis*, *polymechanos*, and *poikilometis*: polymorphously cunning, expert in diverse wily tricks, and full of inventive ploys.[10] With names like "easily or dextrously turning" (Eutrapelus), "swift-footed" (Eudromos), and "golden technical excellence" (Chrysotechnus), each formed out of compound Greek words, Harvey's personae resemble Homeric epithets in their grammatical structure as well as in their spectrum of meanings.[11] Moreover, some of Harvey's neologisms are near-literal translations of the Odyssean epithets cited above: terms such as *polytechnia* and *polypraxia*, best translated as "polymechanical" and "polypragmatical," suggest that his distinct, perplexing idiom is firmly situated within the network of skills and attitudes comprised by *metis*.

Harvey's approach towards mechanics as a tool of *metis* and a guide to the variable rules of court life is stimulated in part by his amicable, if angst-ridden, relationships with several prominent men. Harvey was acquainted with Philip Sidney, Robert Dudley, Thomas Smith, and (to a lesser extent) Robert Devereux and William Cecil, each of whom was keenly interested in the political and social applications of machinery. Harvey solicits help from these men in the hopes of improving his social status, and he follows their cue in intellectual matters, studying the texts and disciplines deemed most suitable by his aristocratic friends and patrons. Sidney and Essex, in particular, sway Harvey's reading habits through gifts and recommendations of books. Harvey writes in his copy of Sacrobosco, dated by him in 1580, that the text was "Sidneis two bookes for the Sphaere. Bie him specially commended to the Earle of Essex, Sir Edward Dennie, & divers gentlemen of the Court."[12] Around the same time, Harvey jots in his copy of Livy that he had some "private discussions [ego intime contuleramus]" about the Roman historian with "Philippus Sidneius aulicus," and two decades later, Harvey is still soliciting recommendations, writing in his volume of Chaucer that "the Earle of Essex much commends Albions England."[13]

Harvey's vaulting ambition to be a "megalander," or a great statesman, provokes the disdain of his contemporaries and continues to elicit derision from modern readers. Yet his careful reading and rereading of Castiglione, Guicciardini, and Machiavelli teaches Harvey that, with enough cunning and careful emulation, even the son of a rope-maker might achieve political greatness. Among his favorite "megalandri" are statesmen such as "Wulsey, Crumwell, Gardiner, & Cicill," men so adept at political machination that all others look like "noovices, & pupills in pollicy."[14] When he speaks admiringly of these *politiques* and their "desines & practices" in the laboratory of the Tudor court, Harvey enlists an explicitly mechanical vocabulary. Stephen Gardiner's attempt to assassinate Queen Elizabeth elicits Harvey's praise for its technical skill: "that wily Winchester [i.e. Gardiner] was the only Daedalus, & framer of that ingin." Whether consciously or no, Harvey clearly associates political cunning with technical ingenuity, for in the midst of his encomium to Gardiner, Harvey turns abruptly to applaud Elizabethan England's "arch-discoverers at sea," adventurers including Cavendish, Frobisher, and Drake.[15] In Gassarus' *Historiarum et Chronicorum Totius Mundi Epitome*, which Harvey acquired in 1576 and inscribed with the phrase "Bishop Gardiners Text," his marginal comments demonstrate a palpably politicized interest in the history of mechanical inventions and other "gallant devyses." Next to a passage recounting the "first invention of Gunnes in Germany," Harvey comments, "A brave devyse for a Moonke No kyng, or Captayn cood ever devyse the lyke ingin."[16] Invented by a lowly monk rather than a king, firearms strengthen the power of the weak, confirming the efficacy of *metis* in a manner similar to the story of Tamburlaine, discussed a few pages later in Gassarus' text and glossed by Harvey as the rise of "a lusty stowt Heardman" into "A most valiant & invincible Prynce." The invention of the gun and the story of Tamburlaine's meteoric rise to power both confirm Harvey's suspicion that he inhabits an iron age in which cunning artifice overpowers direct force, and in which one may "atcheive [*sic*] more with the little finger of Pollicy, than you can possibly compasse with the mighty arm of Prowesse."[17]

Upon his dismissal from the Earl of Leicester's service in 1578, Harvey is famously diagnosed by Nashe as "fitter for the Universitie then for the Court," though in truth he proves fit for neither community.[18] Particularly after 1580, when he is "peltingly defeated" by Andrew Perne for the post of public orator at Cambridge, Harvey expresses an intermittent disgust with scholarship, exhorting himself to waste no further time "scribbling" in his margins.[19] Yet this anti-intellectualism – the combined product of his Ramism, his admiration of the active life of the courtier-soldier, and his proto-Baconian empiricism – is shadowed by an equal and opposing hyper-intellectualism, so much so that Harvey's most scathing censures of scholarship appear directed, at least obliquely, at himself. In *Foure Letters*, Harvey laments that sincere erudition has been abandoned in favor of "Castilioes fine Cortegiano . . . Guatzoes newe Discourses of curteous behaviour . . . Plutarche in Frenche, Frontines Stratagemmes, Polyenes Stratagemmes . . . or sum other like Frenche or Italian Politique Discourses."[20] The list virtually duplicates Harvey's own library catalogue, an irony compounded by his frequent marginal promptings to put down his books or to "read for lyfe," rather than for reading's sake. Though it does not necessarily do so, his study of mechanics promises to ease Harvey's strained and conflictive relationship to the court and the university, and to both the active and the meditative life.

His courtly aspirations prompt Harvey to pore through numerous texts on the art of gentlemanly manners, including Guazzo's *La Civil Conversatione* and Castiglione's *Book of the Courtier*, each of which he owns in Italian as well as in English editions. His marginal notes to Hoby's English translation of the *The Book of the Courtier* illustrate how dutifully he attempts to put Castiglione's precepts into practice. Filled with abridgements and reviews of the text's key ideas, these notes betray the industrious eagerness with which Harvey seeks to fashion himself into an ideal courtier.[21] Harvey is particularly devoted to mastering the "negligent diligence" or *sprezzatura* discussed in Book I of *The Courtier*, and he reminds himself in the margins of Hoby's translation that "A Courtier must do, & speak everie thing as well, as possibly he can: yet with such a dexteritie, & such a negligent diligence, that all may think, he might do much better, if he woold."[22] Harvey's distaste for the *affetazione* shunned by Castiglione's Count Lodovico is also apparent throughout his copy of Quintilian, in which he underlines the terms *odiosus affectatione* and *odiosa affectatio*, offering his own understanding of the term in a marginal description of the stilted Demosthenes, whose "jestes cam hardly, and heavily from him; not with any naturall facility, but artificially inforcid."[23]

The man who best approximates Harvey's courtly ideals is Philip Sidney. In addition to his panegyric to Sidney in Book IV of the *Gratulationes Valdinenses*, Harvey's recognition of Sidney's exemplary courtliness is most evident in his ardent study of the art of horsemanship. Harvey owned and

annotated John Astley's 1584 *The art of riding* and Thomas Blundeville's
1580 *The foure chiefest Offices belonging to Horsemanship*, clearly stating his
motivation in reading both works in a note at the beginning of Blundeville's text: "it importeth a Courtier, to be a perfect Horseman."[24] In *The
Book of the Courtier*, horsemanship is one of the principal litmus tests for
sprezzatura: Count Lodovico remarks that those riders who "goe so bolt
upright setled in saddle" have an "yll grace," while the graceful rider disre-
gards the discomfort of his seat: he "appeareth not to mind it, and sitteth
on horseback so nimbly and close as though . . . on fote."[25] Harvey may
have had this passage in mind while annotating Blundeville's text, for at
the beginning of a chapter describing the rider's proper posture, he writes,
"How the rider ought to sitt in his Saddle." He also collates Blundeville's
and Castiglione's observations on equestrian decorum: next to a list of
appropriately gentlemanly sports in his copy of *The Book of the Courtier*,
Harvey writes "Ars Blundevili," commenting that "all such exercises, [are]
honorable for a Gentleman: necessary for every right active man."[26]

Harvey is assiduous – perhaps even too assiduous – in following
Castiglione's and Blundeville's recommendations. Adopting a severe reg-
imen of "ingenious diet, and daily exercises of agility [dieta ingenii, et
exercitium agilitatis, quotidianus]," he urges himself in his notes to *The
Book of the Courtier* "to leape wel, to renn wel, to vaulte wel, to wrastle wel,
to cast the stone, to cast the bar."[27] Yet in his copy of Blundeville, Harvey
misconstrues courtliness as a "profession" to be learned like the practice of
law or medicine. Calling Blundeville's text a "very pregnant method / for
every brave man on horseback," Harvey counsels himself to adopt "Chivalrie, & Armes, [as] his principal and singular / Profession, above all other
qualities . . . / . . . One principal proprietie: other accessarie / & perfunctorie
qualities."[28] Yet courtliness, at least as defined by Castiglione and Sidney, is
wholly inimical to Harvey's notion of a "principal proprietie": instead, true
chivalry fosters and demands a dilettantism in which every skill appears
"accessarie & perfunctorie" rather than learned. Sidney's specter haunts
Harvey's running marginal commentary on the arts and exercises proper to
the courtier, yet the courtly ideal he embodies is distorted and exaggerated
by Harvey in his over-eager attempt to instill in himself the qualities he
admires in his friend.

Sidney's *Apology for Poetry*, which Harvey might have seen in manuscript
before its publication in 1595, opens with an anecdote about Sidney's visit
to the court of Rudolf II, where he and Edward Wotton "gave our selves to
learne horsemanship of Iohn Pietro Pugliano." A reputed horseman who
also proves a fool, Pugliano asserts to Sidney "that no earthly thing bred

such wonder to a Prince as to be a good horseman. Skill of government was but a *Pedanteria* in comparison."[29] Sidney's anecdote is intended to introduce the argument that no art, not even poetry, is so superior to all other gentlemanly activities that it can compensate for that perfect synthesis between action and contemplation embraced by the *Apology*. Yet Harvey's own hyperbolic praise of the art of horsemanship, largely written during the mid-1580s just after Sidney composed his *Apology*, reveals the extent to which he misconstrues the Sidneian precepts he attempts to cultivate. In *Pierces Supererogation*, Harvey sounds like Pugliano, applauding Astley as the "perfect patterne of Castilios Courtier," ranking Blundeville's text in the "Catalogue of Xenophontian woorkes," and lauding those "two brave Knightes, Musidorus and Pyrocles, combined in one excellent knight, Sir Philip Sidney." Suffering from Pugliano's excessive "fertilnes of the Italian wit," Harvey's frantic pursuit of the "perfect Patterne" of courtiership runs counter to the basic aesthetic and social doctrines of both Castiglione's *Courtier* and Sidney's *Apology*.[30] Sidney warns his readers against slavish imitation and excessive adherence to precepts: "neyther artificiall rules nor imitative patterns, we much cumber our selves withall." Both poet and courtier should imitate only by "borrow[ing] nothing of what is, hath been, or shall be," exercising a "learned discretion" in adhering selectively to the "artificiall rules" of decorum.[31] At the end of the *Apology*, Sidney distinguishes between the courtier and the "professor of learning" in that while the courtier performs actions "*according to Art*, though *not by Art*," the excessively rule-bound professor errs in using "Art to shew Art, and not to hide Art" such that he "flyeth from nature, and indeede abuseth Art."[32]

In its rejection of doing things "by art," if not "according to art," Sidney's *Apology* is hostile to the dependence upon technique manifested by Harvey, who is too wedded to what Sidney refers to as the "imitative patternes" of courtiership. From Harvey's perspective, courtly grace is achieved through the disciplined application of rules: wishing to cultivate "eloquentia, et urbanitas" in the margins of his Quintilian, Harvey resolves to pursue these qualities through "exercitatio."[33] This faith in "exercise" manifests itself in an assiduous attention to technical skills and methods: in his copy of Blundeville's treatise on horsemanship, Harvey takes great pains to mark what he terms the "extraordinarie instruments" of the discipline, equipment such as "*The parts of the bit*."[34] Harvey's wish to acquire and master the accouterments of the courtly "profession" belies a subtle but crucial misunderstanding of the nature of courtiership, particularly since the ethos of the court demands a knowledge different from, and even opposed to, the purely technical skill of the artisan. Castiglione's Count Lodovico opposes courtly grace to artisanal skill by comparing himself (in his refusal to define grace) to the soldier who knows what good armor is, but cannot "hammer or temper it."[35] Sidney likewise defines *Arkitecktonike*, or the highest end of knowledge, in contradistinction to the *techne* of the "serving sciences," by contrasting the saddler's skill to the "nobler" knowledge that prompts the soldier-horseman to "vertuous action."[36] Harvey's devotion to the perfection of specific techniques at the expense of pursuing what Sidney's *Apology* calls the "ending end" of knowledge characterizes his intellectual disposition towards a number of different scholarly disciplines. While both writers have been classified as Ramist thinkers, Sidney repudiates the use of "dictionarys method" and "artificiall rules" while Harvey embraces method and precept. "I love Method," Harvey proclaims in *Foure Letters*, and while he begins the passage by voicing the Sidneian sentiment that "pregnant rules avail much; but visible Examples amount incredibly," even alluding to Sidney's beloved Cyrus, he ends by insisting that "Nature without Arte" and "Arte without Exercise" are both "sory creatures," a conclusion antithetical to the very essence of Sidney's *Apology*.[37]

In a further attempt to cultivate courtliness, Harvey invents "Eutrapelus," a marginal persona who represents the consummate execution of the Italianate courtly ideals popularized by Castiglione and Guazzo. His name is drawn from the Greek ευτραπελια (turning well), a term used by Aristotle to denote verbal wit and "pleasantness in social amusement." Eutrapelus is clever and ingenious in conversation, an *eiron* whose principal weapon is his cunning use of words. In his volume of Guicciardini, Harvey describes how Eutrapelus uses language in order to effect a "pragmatic metamorphosis" by changing "great matters into small ones, small into great ones [magna in parva mutat Eutrapelus: parva in magna]."[38] By converting serious matters into jests and jests into serious discussions [aliorum seria, in iocos convertenda: tui ipsius Ioci in seria], Eutrapelus fulfills one of the key requisites of courtly *sprezzatura*; namely, the perfect tempering of the extremes of *gravitas* and *leggiadria* and of diligence and facility. By a "secret [*arcana*] metamorphosis," Eutrapelus does and says everything with an air of playful indifference, turning serious matters into trifles and vice versa in the manner of Erasmus' Folly.

Through Eutrapelus, Harvey welcomes the arrival of Italianate subtlety to England with open arms. In *Pierces Supererogation*, he celebrates how, at long last, "Tiberis flowed into the Thames" as the Italian "Civility in manners arrived in these remote parts." For Harvey, the introduction of "finest Tuscanisme" into England is simultaneously a revolution of manners, intellectual habits, political techniques, and the "cunningest experiments" of scientists.[39] He often turns to images and concepts drawn from mechanics in order to describe the attributes of Eutrapelus – the levity, the ironic wit, and the "entelechy" which are his chiefest instruments. In his *Commonplace Book*, Harvey defines rhetoric as an instrument, invoking "eloquence" as "ye mightiest engin of ye world."[40] Entelechy, usually defined as accomplishment or consummation, is a key attribute of Eutrapelus, and it, too, is an instrumental power, defined in the margins of his copy of Domenichi's *Facetie* as "the instrument at hand [praesans machina]" for all unexpected events and (in *Pierces Supererogation*) as a "noble Magnes" capable of drawing iron.[41] A composite of Machiavellian and mechanical *virtù*, entelechy is defined as "the saile of the ship, the flight of the bowe, the shott of the gunne, the wing of the Eagle, the quintessence of the Minde."[42] Harvey regards entelechy as synonymous with instrumental means: it comprises any effective method of harnessing the powerful, often hostile, forces of nature to one's best advantage.

Harvey imagines the ideal courtier and statesman as thoroughly instrumentalized beings, equipped with the weapons of wit and grace like the accouterments of a soldier armed for battle. "A swift chariot, drawn with slow horses, will never ridd way apace," Harvey observes in his *Commonplace Book*, "A man is commonly, as his cumpany, and Instruments ar."[43] In his copy of Foorth's *Synopsis Politica*, Harvey writes that the wise man's best weapon is a "twohandid dubbleedgid sword . . . Resolute audacity, and absolute Eloquence," and he describes the "stringes of yor Tongue" as if they were tautly strung bows poised to discharge their arrows: "The instruments, & powers of your witt & speech, ever most reddy with facility."[44] Comparisons between rhetorical and mechanical instrumentality are commonplace in Renaissance courtesy literature: Castiglione frequently compares the courtier's *acutezza recondita*, or sharp wit, to weapons including swords, poniards, and an "Adamant stone."[45] Yet when Harvey imagines the puissant weapons of courtly wit, the violence they effect is excessively brutal, jarring harshly with the courtly ideals he seeks to cultivate.

One of the principal ways in which Harvey seeks to cultivate his courtly *facilità* is through the study and practice of mechanics. In addition to several treatises on the use of the astrolabe, discussed at further length below, Harvey owned and annotated more than twenty-five classical and contemporary texts devoted to the applied sciences, and if one includes the numerous scientific texts to which Harvey alludes in his marginal comments, his readings in the field number in excess of one hundred texts.[46]

Amongst his annotated scientific texts still extant is a copy of John Blagrave's *Mathematicall Jewell,* acquired by Harvey in 1585, the same year the volume first appeared in print. Dedicated to Lord Burghley, Blagrave's text advertises its newly improved astronomical instrument as a tool of courtly *sprezzatura* that according to its title "performeth with wonderfull dexteritie, whatsoever is to be done, either by Quadrant, Ship, Circle, Cylinder, Ring, Dyall, Horoscope, Astrolabe, Sphere, Globe, or any such like heretofore devised." Forever aspiring to hone his negligent diligence, Harvey pores through Blagrave's text with its titular promise to help its readers perform mechanical exercises with "great and incredible speede, plainenesse, facilitie, and pleasure." His scribblings in the volume are unusually copious, the result of two separate readings, one in 1585 and another shortly after 1590, when Harvey's hand reappears, in a different quill, to remind himself of a new publication by Blagrave, his "familiar staff, newly published this 1590"[47] (figure 4.1).

Harvey absorbs the titular promise of Blagrave's text that the operation of mechanical devices fosters courtly dexterity. His attention to the social applications of mechanics is evident throughout his marginal notes in Blagrave's text as well as in texts such as Thomas Hill's *The Schoole of Skil* (1599), a text praised by Harvey for the facility of its "astronomical notes, easily reducible to the Spherical method of Scribonius [Scholia astronomica, ad methodum Scribonii Sphaericam facile redigenda]."[48] Harvey's conviction that the study of mechanics nurtures courtly *facilità* once again reveals the influence of Sidney. Writing in the margins of his volume of Sacrobosco, Harvey reminds himself that the study of cosmography is subject to Sidney's dictates of decorum: "Sacrobosco & Valerius, Sir Philip Sidneis two bookes for the Sphaere . . . To be read with diligent studie, but sportingly, as he termed it."[49]

Reminding himself to read "sportingly," or without too much rigor or diligence, Harvey emulates the scientific virtuosity of the Sidneian courtier-soldier. Writing to Edward Denny in 1580, shortly before Denny's departure to Ireland, Sidney advises him to spend his time studying works of military tactics, "as in descriptions of battaillons, camps, and marches," but he should temper this study "with some practise of Arithmetike, which *sportingly* you may exercise." Sidney continues by outlining a plan for scientific study congenial to courtly *facilità*, telling Denny to "reed a little of Sacroboscus Sphaere, & the Geography of some moderne writer, wherof there are many & is a *very easy and delightful studdy*."[50] Later that same year, Sidney writes to his younger brother Robert while the latter is traveling with Henry Savile to urge a similarly dilettantish familiarity with

O .

GH.

THE
MATHEMATICAL IEWEL,
Shewing the making, and moſt excellent vſe of a ſinguler
Inſtrument ſo called : *in that it performeth with wonderfull*
dexteritie, whatſoeuer is to be done,either by Quadrant, Ship, Circle, Cylinder,
Ring, Dyall, Horoſcope, Aſtrolabe, Sphere, Globe, or any ſuch like heretofore
ſſ.   deuiſed : yea or by moſt Tables commonly extant : and that generally
to all places from Pole to Pole.

The vſe of which Iewel, is ſo aboundant and ample, that it lea-
deth any man practiſing thereon, the direct pathway (from the firſt ſteppe to the laſt)
through the whole Artes of Aſtronomy , Coſmogtaphy, Geography, Topography,
Nauigation, Longitudes of Regions; Dyalling, Sphericall triangles , Setting figures; and
ſ.   briefly of whatſoeuer concerneth the Globe or Sphere: with great and incredible
ſpeede, plaineneſſe, facillitie, and pleaſure :

The moſt part newly founde out by the Author ; Compiled and publiſhed for the furtherance , as well of
Gentlemen and others deſirous of ſpeculatiue knowledge, and priuate practiſe : as alſo for the furni-
ſhing of ſuch worthy mindes, Nauigators, and trauellers, that pretend long voyages or new diſcoueries:
By *Iohn Blagrane* of *Reading* Gentleman and well willer to the Mathematickes; who hath cut all the printes
or pictures of the whole worke with his owne hands. 1585.

gabriel haruey. 1585.

Imprinted at London by Walter Venge, dwelling in
Fleetelane ouer againſt the Maiden head.

4.1 John Blagrave, *The Mathematical Jewel*, second title-page with MS. notes of
Gabriel Harvey

the rudiments of mechanics: "I think yow understand the sphere, if yow doe, I care little for any more astronomie in yow." Harvey may well have seen one or both of these letters; according to Grafton and Jardine, he may even have written the letter to Denny.[51] In either case, he digests Sidney's advice fully and reproduces it for private consultation in the margins of *The Mathematicall Jewell*.

Harvey's pen dwells upon Blagrave's preface, doubly underlining as well as marking with excited squiggles the phrases "ingenious practiser" and "practique discipline" as well as terms describing the facility of the device such as "*easie*" and "*methodious*."[52] On the first page of the text proper, Harvey is especially attentive to terms that yoke the operation of Blagrave's multi-purpose instrument to courtly virtues including dexterity and facility. In a passage describing how those interested in "the *making* of this Jewell, as also in dyalling, and all other *mechanicall working of mathematical devises*, [ought] to have a *handiness, & dexteritie in the use of the rule* and *compasse*," Harvey's underlinings and scrawls grow more abundant and frantic, and he places an X above the term "dexteritie," presumably to mark with greater emphasis this key aspect of courtly grace.

Harvey's marginal notes in *The Mathematicall Jewell* reveal a strong conviction in the courtly applications of mechanics. Taking his cue from *The Mathematicall Jewell*'s titular promise of "facilitie and pleasure," Harvey writes on page eleven of Blagrave's text that there is "nothing difficult in Mathematics, or Mechanical Instruments, or Experiments [nihil difficile in Mathematicis, aut Mechanicis instrumentis, aut Experimentis]." Asserting that the study of mechanics is "by no means tedious, or laborious [nullo taedio, aut labore]" but is instead "very easy and delightful [facilli[ssi]ma, et jucundissima]," Harvey distances himself from the artisanal workers and the professional instrument-makers for whom the practice of mechanics is an arduous manual skill.[53]

Yet in Blagrave's text and elsewhere, Harvey also demonstrates an attraction to the pragmatic and uncourtly side of mechanics. Indeed, Harvey is drawn to *The Mathematicall Jewell* for two contradictory reasons. While he aspires to the "sporting" dexterity of the gentlemanly scientific virtuoso, he simultaneously undercuts that aspiration with frequent and ardent encomia to the unlearned and ungentlemanly rude mechanical. Attracted to the *facilità* of the courtier and to his intellectual and social rival, the "sensible industrious practitioner," Harvey's divided loyalty is reconciled in Eutrapelus, who presides over practical, scientific skill and Essexian political prudence as well as courtly wit. Eutrapelus triumphs socially and intellectually without succumbing either to the frivolity of the courtier or to the vain subtleties of the scholar. Culling his knowledge from chemistry, politics, and similarly pragmatic disciplines, Eutrapelus digs up "the most powerful secrets of the world or new practices [potentissimis arcanis, aut neopracticis]." Yet Eutrapelus has little patience for knowledge which cannot be deployed in the active world: "He examines all the commonplaces and plucks out only those especially useful in terms of his target [Omnes executi texcellentissimos Locos Comm[unes] et sola decerpit suo scopo maxime conducentia]," relegating "bookish vanities [auctorum nugas]" to professors and rhetoricians.[54] Not only is Eutrapelus a codification of Harvey's ideals of courtly performance, but he is also a model *machinatore* in all senses of the term. With one foot in the enchanted glass of the court and another in the disenchanted, techno-political realm of a Ramist-inflected new humanism, Eutrapelus helps Harvey to negotiate his conflicting ambitions with respect to both the university and the court.

Despite Eutrapelus' intellectual skill, he is allied more closely with the recreative dabbling of the court than the sober erudition of Cambridge, and he consequently serves as a vehicle for Harvey to voice his contempt for the orthodoxies of university scholarship. Harvey's disdain for book-learning is a dominant theme throughout his notes to Blagrave's *Mathematicall Jewell*, where his sympathies oscillate between the text's "sporting" readers and the instrument-makers who construct the mechanical devices intended to accompany Blagrave's treatise and similar works. On the title-page, Harvey alludes to James Kynvin, the craftsman who designed the instruments intended to accompany Blagrave's text, praising him as a "fine workman, & mie kinde frend." His esteem for Kynvin prompts Harvey to launch into an encomium for "mie mathematical mechanicians," a group which includes Humphray Cole, John Read, John Reynolds, and assorted other "meaner artificers" responsible for the fabrication of clocks, compasses, and staffs.[55] These "artificial workmen" are among the first native-born generation of English instrument-makers, many of them trained by German and Flemish religious refugees such as Thomas Gemini, who came to London in 1552 and opened the first known mathematical instrument shop.[56] Many of these instrument-makers worked as engravers and mechanics for London printers, but they also took commissions from aristocratic patrons: Kynvin constructed a dial for the Earl of Essex, Cole designed a pocket compendium and other nautical equipment for Francis Drake to use on the first Frobisher expedition, and Blagrave found steady employment constructing and repairing sundials for churches, mansions, and colleges.[57]

Harvey delivers another encomium to the rude mechanical a few years later in *Pierces Supererogation* as proof that "he that will diligently seeke, may

assuredly finde treasure in merle, corne in straw, gold in drosse." Those who
best conceal "rich jewels of learning, and wisedome, in some poore boxes"
are lowly practical scientists such as "Humphray Cole, a mathematical
Mechanicia[n], Matthew Baker, a ship-wright, John Shute, an Architect,
Robert Norman, a Navigator, William Bourne, a Gunner," and a number
of other "cunning, and subtle Empirique[s]."[58] In both passages, Harvey
articulates a thorough disdain for the abstract learning of the "professor"
in contradistinction to the useful knowledge of the "sensible industrious
practitioner." He mythologizes this opposition between scholarship and
mechanics in terms of the strife between Minerva and Vulcan after the
smith god "tooke the repulse at the handes of [her] whom he would in
ardent loove have taken to wife":

> Yet what witt, or Pollicy honoreth not Vulcan? and what profounde Mathematician,
> like Digges, Hariot, or Dee, esteemeth not the pregnant Mechanician? Let every
> man in his degree enjoy his due: and let the brave enginer, fine Daedalist, skillful
> Neptunist, marvelous Vulcanist, and every Mercuriall occupationer . . . be respected
> according to the uttermost extent of his publique service, or private industry.[59]

Arguing in favor of a meritocracy that allows every "Mercuriall occupa-
tioner" his due respect, Harvey turns his back upon the university culture
that passed him over in spite of his great "industry" and "service." Harvey's
valorization of Vulcan as a practical artificer reveals the probable influence
of Ramus, who contrasts bookish study with practical learning by way of
comparison between Mars and Vulcan.[60] Working at his furnace, the crude
but industrious Vulcan triumphs over the learned disputations of the *schola*,
a victory whose ramifications must have appealed a great deal to Harvey
after his 1578 failure to be reelected as a fellow of Pembroke College and
his subsequent defeat to Perne for the post of public orator.

Harvey regards the discipline of mechanics as a subset of the habits
of mind which Grafton and Jardine have termed his "pragmatic Humanism," and which Harvey himself refers to in a letter to Robert Cecil as
"effectual practical knowledge." Comprising "historie, pollicy, lawe," a
Ramist emphasis on method, and the study of applied sciences including "cosmographie," the "art of navigation," the "art of warr," and the "tru
Chymique," Harvey assembles for himself a curriculum designed to reinforce his conviction that learning is only useful to the exent that it can be
deployed in practice.[61]

The writings of Ramus supply the glue that binds Harvey's interest
in mechanics to his technique-centered approach towards courtiership,
politics, and rhetorical practice. Harvey owned Ramus' *Ciceronianus* as well

as Omer Talon's *Academica*, both of which he purchased between 1568 and 1570, and his Ramist realignment of learning towards practice is apparent in his own *Ciceronianus*, a lecture given to his Cambridge rhetoric class in 1576 and printed the following year.[62] Method, that cornerstone of Ramist logic which aims to systematize learning and make it congenial to practical demands by providing a set of rules for the orderly and clear explanation and arrangement of knowledge, is a guideline for scientific inquiry for Ramus as much as it is a governing principle for the arts of dialectic and rhetoric. In later mathematical works such as the *Scholarum Mathematicum*, the lineaments of Ramist method translate into a preference for the humble but serviceable art of mechanics over the paper art of theoretical mathematics. "Mathematum non solum scholastica veritas & e libris demonstratio," Ramus urges, "sed popularis usus atque utilitas aestimatur," an unbookish, utilitarian attitude towards mathematics exemplified, according to Ramus, by Archimedes.[63]

Ramus' radical reorganization of intellectual disciplines, which elevates applied over theoretical mathematics and logic over rhetoric, is an aspect of method known to sixteenth-century Ramists as *technologia*. Literally meaning to bring under rules of art or to methodize, *technologia* comes to signify the Ramist project to create a "systematic philosophy of the inter-connections of the arts" or a science of "arranging the contents of the curriculum properly."[64] While Ramus never uses *technologia* to denote a machine or instrument, instead using the terms *mechanica* and *organica*, the modern usage of the term lurks within the Ramist notion of *technologia*, at least insofar as seventeenth-century Ramists make frequent analogies between method on the one hand and manual or technical activities such as architecture and engineering on the other. From the Ramist viewpoint, technical activities duplicate the way in which units of thought and disciplines of knowledge, like material objects, ought to be joined and assembled according to rule and mechanical precision: this is precisely why Walter Ong asserts that Ramist notions of dialectic are "proto-mechanistic."[65] Harvey adopts this Ramist attitude and its attendant idiom, even comparing the Greek–Latin glossary at the back of his heavily annotated copy of Cicero's *Ad Atticum* to the "artificiosa nomenclatura, vel technologia Hopperi," presumably a reference to Marcus Hopper's 1563 Greek–Latin dictionary.[66] Harvey praises Hopper's text for its "technologia et technopraxis," and he appears to have benefitted from its usefulness: in the voluminous notes made by Harvey in the glossary of Cicero's text, he has used Hopper's *organon* to cross-reference certain terms used in the *Ad Atticum*.

The qualities of *technologia* and *technopraxis* are presided over in Harvey's marginalia by the character of Eudromos, the pragmatic, "swift-footed" man who has at his disposal a variety of devious techniques in order to surprise his adversaries. In the margins of his Domenichi's *Facetie*, Harvey characterizes Eudromos' outlook as "polytechnical and polypragmatical [polytechnia et polypraxia]," quasi-Odyssean, quasi-Ramist neologisms also used to characterize sly Tudor politiques such as Gardiner and Wolsey. Eudromos is a discerning reader, "search[ing] out" and "unravel[ing]" the deepest studies and skimming through "all books for his worthwhile passages . . . with facility [Faciles omnes libros pervolutat Eudromos pro suis unius axiozelis locis]."[67] Eudromos shuns vanities and cobwebs of learning such as "grammar, philology, imaginary and superfluous things [grammatica, philologica, phantastica, ociosa omnia]," instead applying himself "only to energetic, extraordinary, and very powerful matters [sola curat energetica, egregia, praepotentia]." Anticipating Bacon's 1605 call to forsake Minerva in favor of Vulcan because "Bookes be not onely the Instrumentals," Eudromos exhorts Harvey to make the world his library, preferring "to be a critic of the world rather than a critic of words [malo esse Cosmocriticus quam Logocriticus]."[68]

Unlike Eutrapelus, who culls his courtly and oratorical precepts from written texts, Eudromos treats books like instruments and only reads as a means to an end. Eudromos' ancestors are men such as the "polypragmatica Crom[w]elli" and the "polytechnicam Gardineri," statesmen whose Machiavellian prudence regards the inflexible precepts contained in written texts as of limited use in worldly affairs.[69] Eudromos is also the product of Harvey's reading of Guicciardini, and it is in the margins of his copy of the Italian historian's *Detti et Fatti* that Harvey most vehemently expresses his contempt for the abstract, theoretical knowledge contained in books, railing against "bookwormes" and "scriblers" as "paperbook men, men in their bookes or papers: not in their heds, or harts."[70]

Harvey's invention of virtues such as "polytechny" and "polypragmatism" helps him to mediate between his competing intellectual impulses, reflecting his admiration for the active cunning of the Tudor *politique*, the wit and grace of the courtier, and the uneducated, raw skill of the mean mechanician all at once. In the margins of Luca Gaurico's *Tractatus Astrologicus*, Harvey praises Blagrave, Thomas Digges, and Cyprian Lucar as "notable mathematicall practitioners, & polymechanists."[71] Unlike "paperbook men" who rely too heavily on the authority of written texts, "cunning men" and "Artsmen" such as Digges and Hariot achieve results with only a few books at their disposal: "Theise be theire great masters," Harvey states admiringly, "theire whole librarie: with sum old parchment-roules, tables, & instruments."[72]

In spite of his gentle birth, Blagrave is a testimony to Harvey's belief that wisdom is often found in "poore boxes," particularly since, as Blagrave himself admits in the prefatory matter of *The Mathematicall Jewell*, he never attended university. Next to "The Author in his Owne Defence," a poem defending Blagrave's lack of education, Harvey scribbles that he was "an Youth: & no university man. the more shame for sum Doctors of Universities, that may learn of him."[73] Harvey finds further confirmation of the author's lack of scholarly training on page 19 of *The Mathematicall Jewell*, where Blagrave provides a brief list of books useful to him in the composition of his treatise. Glossing the passage with the comment, "his sole, or principal Authors," Harvey remarks, "Schollars have the bookes: & practitioners the Learning." Yet at the end of Blagrave's volume, Harvey appears to have forgotten his own lesson that knowledge is best acquired through practice rather than through books, for he provides his own, much more lengthy, catalogue of mathematical and astronomical works useful to him in his own scientific investigations.[74]

Harvey's elevation of "meaner mechanicians" such as Blagrave over university-educated natural philosophers is disingenuous, however, since many of the men he praises are fellow Cambridge graduates: Thomas Digges (B.A., Queens, 1551), William Buckley (B.A., King's, 1542), Thomas Hill (B.A., Christ's, 1553), and Thomas Hood (B.A., Trinity, 1578), to name but a few.[75] Harvey's contempt for the nugatory quality of Cambridge scholarship is certainly an expression of his "polypragmatical" Ramism, but it also reflects the bitter perversity of a man who, in Nashe's words, was deemed "fitter for the Universitie then for the Court." A few years after he was excused from Leicester's service in 1578, Harvey rails against the devaluation of scholarship in the margins of Joannes Ramus' *Oikonomia*:

Common Lerning, and the name of a good schollar was never so much contemned, and abjected of princes, pragmaticals, & common Gallants, as nowadays: in so much that it necessarily concernith, & importith the lernid, either praesantly to hate their bookes; or actually to onsinuate, & enforce themselves, by very special, & singular propertyes of emploiable, & necessary use, in all affaires.[76]

Harvey emerges here as a champion of true scholarship, defending it from the scorn and depreciation it has suffered at the hands of "common Gallants," or superficial courtiers. It is one of several comments from the period that reveal how, at least around 1580, Harvey is by no means ready to abandon his books in favor of the furnace. Throughout his comments in the *Oikonomia*, he repeatedly emphasizes the importance of careful and thorough reading, arguing that there is "no sufficient, or hable furniture, gotten by unperfect posting, or superficial overrunning, or halfelearning." Furthermore, he rejects the sporting, dilettantish knowledge of the "common Gallant" in favor of the plodding drudgery of the scholar, asserting that "In a serious, & practicable Studdy, better any on[e] chapter, perfectly, & thorowghly digested, for praesant practis, as occasion shall requier: than A whole volume, greedily devourid, & rawly concoctid."[77] There is no hint of courtly *sprezzatura* in Harvey's prescription for true erudition, a slow digestive process that cannot be achieved through natural alacrity of wit but only through graceless, indefatigable toil.

Written around the time that he embarks upon the study of the law at Trinity Hall, Harvey's notes in the *Oikonomia* reveal an industrious pedantry antithetical to the amateurish dabbling of the courtier: "lay down the law, lay down the law [legem pone, legem pone]," Harvey scribbles, for "Mulcasters College of Lawiers, must studdy, confer, & practis only Law."[78] Harvey's attention to disciplinarity and his emphatic insistence upon intellectual specialization once again reflects the influence of Ramus, who according to the margins of Harvey's Quintilian "discriminates acutely and rightly between the arts."[79] In keeping with Ramus' effort to distinguish among different scholarly methods, Harvey asserts that doctors must learn "only physique" and divines "only Divinity," since intellectual progress is best achieved by sustaining a professionalized focus upon one sole activity: "Archimedes, however great, was wholly and completely a Geometer [Archimedes, quantus quantus erat, totus totus erat Geometra]."[80] While it reveals Harvey's disillusionment with the dilettantish intellectual culture of the Elizabethan court, his enthusiastic pursuit of a "peculiar profession" contradicts Ramus' (and his own) view of the "perfit Orator," whom Harvey describes in the margins of his Quintilian not as "A bare Professor of any one certain faculty, or a simple Artist in any one kynde," but rather as "an Artist's Artist, equipped and armed at all points with most of the Arts [Artificum Artificem esse volvere; plurimis, maximisque Artibus . . . undiquaquae instructum, et armatum]."[81]

In his *Oikonomia* and other marginalia from around 1580, we find Harvey caught between competing pedagogical convictions and competing ways of understanding the social applications of his learning as he alternately praises and condemns the "sporting" knowledge of the courtier, the laborious discipline of the scholar, and the unbookish technical acuity of the mechanician. Whether or not he was dismissed by Leicester because his scholarly training was not sufficiently "emploiable" in the political and military arena, Harvey grows palpably more insistent after around 1580 that books are of no further use to him, even as he voices these objections in the margins of those books. He recognizes the inconsistency between his obsession with practice and his enthusiasm for reading and writing, urging himself to "evermore post on to practis" in his *Commonplace Book*: "Avoyde all writing, but necessary: which consumeth unreasonable much tyme, before you ar aware: you have already plaguid yourselfe this way: Two Arts lernid, whilest two sheetes in writing."[82] Harvey's skepticism concerning the value of study reaches a fever pitch in the margins of his Guicciardini, an author who questions the purpose of reading by describing books as locked treasure chests, the knowledge contained within them useless because inaccessible to the outside world. Thus, after inveighing against "scriblers," Harvey reminds himself later in the same volume to "leave scribbling," reinscribing ineffectual knowledge in his margins even as he condemns it.[83]

In Blagrave's text, annotated in 1585 and again in 1590, Harvey's distaste for book-learning is given renewed vigor by the study of mechanics. In one comment, Harvey urges himself to embrace the "irrefutable criterion" of mechanical devices and experiments in lieu of the vain, unreliable knowledge contained in written texts: "All sciences are founded upon perception and reason . . . Experience is the firmest demonstration and an irrefutable criteron. Give me ocular and rooted demonstration of every principle, experiment, geometric instrument, astronomical, cosmographic, horologiographic, geographic, hydrographic, or mathematical in any way."[84] *The Mathematicall Jewell* provides Harvey with his irrefutable criterion. Moreover, it resolves the tensions between Harvey the "scribbler" and Harvey the polymechanist because it is simultaneously a book and an instrument. On one of the endpapers at the beginning of Blagrave's text, there is a fully working astrolabe which either Harvey or a subsequent reader has cut out, assembled with string, and mounted onto the page (figure 4.2). A book which was (and still is) a fully functional astronomical device, Blagrave's *Mathematicall Jewell* promises to reconcile Harvey's attraction to written texts on the one hand, and to the "rooted demonstration" of machinery on the other.

In their study of Gabriel Harvey's habits as a reader and annotater of Livy, Grafton and Jardine argue that Harvey's approach to reading is "always goal-oriented – an active, rather than a passive pursuit." Given Harvey's tendency to read and annotate multiple volumes simultaneously, Grafton and Jardine propose that Agostino Ramelli's 1588 illustration of a book-wheel, a series of revolving lecterns mounted onto a cogwheel, is an apt "emblem" for

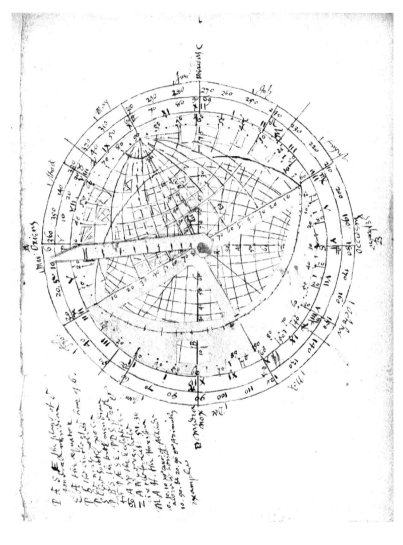

4.2 John Blagrave, *The Mathematical Jewel*, working paper astrolabe

Harvey's habits of collation and parallel citation.[85] By comparing Harvey's scholarly proclivities to a book-wheel, Grafton and Jardine tease out the congruence between *technologia* and technology, concepts united by the paper astrolabe assembled in Harvey's copy of *The Mathematicall Jewell*.

Harvey's aggrandizement of the mechanician over the scholar, and of instruments over books, does not indicate a wholesale rejection of book-learning in favor of greater demonstrative certitude so much as signal the apotheosis of an instrumentalized set of reading techniques which includes the assembly and operation of mechanical instruments but also the "goal-oriented" and "adversarial" reading strategies analyzed by Grafton and Jardine and by William Sherman.[86] By studying Renaissance reading practices in light of the material technologies which shape them, these and other scholars have illustrated how the interpretation of written texts is produced out of the interplay between books, book-related objects such as book-wheels and other machinery, and social and organizational institutions such as libraries and library catalogues.[87] Rather than view the book as a discrete entity that holds the key to its interpretation inside itself, these scholars instead regard the book as the focal point of a wide network of social interactions, material objects, and intellectual techniques exerted by and upon Renaissance readers.

The most tangible example of the interplay between books and instruments in the sixteenth century is the production of texts containing volvelles, astrolabes, or other working instruments that actively nurture pragmatic and instrumental reading practices. Such texts are quite common, ranging from the deluxe copy of Peter Apian's *Astronomicum Caesareum* presented to Henry VIII to the do-it-yourself paper astrolabe contained in the back of technical treatises such as *The Mathematicall Jewell*. The instruments in these volumes are designed to be used: they can be assembled without damaging the surrounding pages, and in the case of Apian's text, whose instruments yield extremely precise results, at least one quarter of the extant copies contain devices assembled by early readers.[88]

Those texts which do not include a working instrument often provide the necessary information for the reader to construct or procure one. Tanner's *Mirror for Mathematiques*, which Harvey mentions in the margins of his copy of Jerome Turler's *The Travailer*, contains instructions on assembling several astrolabes, and technical treatises of the period routinely refer readers to the workshops of instrument-makers.[89] The first such advertisement appears in Leonard Digges' 1556 *Tectonicon*, whose title-page informs its readers that Thomas Gemini awaits them at his shop in Blackfriars, "ready . . . to make all the instruments apperteyning to this booke."[90] By the 1580s, such advertisements are increasingly common, appearing in texts by Cyprian Lucar, William Barlow, and Edward Worsop, the last of whom refers his readers to Humphray Cole for "scales, compasses, and sundry sorts of Geometricall instruments in metall," and to John Read and John Reynolds for similar instruments in wood.[91]

Instruments are indispensable tools for Renaissance readers of treatises on surveying, cosmography, and navigation. The mutually interdependent relationship between books and instruments is borne out by the lack of categorical distinction between the two sets of objects in sixteenth-century library catalogues. A 1589 inventory of books belonging to Abraham Tilman while he was attending Cambridge records "twoe globes," a compass, "one deske," and "one looking glasse" alongside bibles and volumes of ancient history.[92] In 1629, shortly after his death, Henry Percy's library at Petworth is documented to contain "one cupboard with mathematical instruments, one large globe and two small ones," while Andrew Perne, whose thirty-five-year reign as Master of Peterhouse, Cambridge prevented Harvey from obtaining the post, bequeathed to Peterhouse his globes and all his astronomical instruments, catalogued alongside his books, in a will dated February 1589.[93]

Elizabethan readers recognize reading and writing as activities which demand a high level of technical skill and require the use of specific instruments. As Jonathan Goldberg argues in his study of scribal discipline in Renaissance culture, writing depends upon the careful manipulation of instruments and devices, as revealed by texts such as Palatino's 1540 *Instruments of Writing*, a treatise on penmanship which asserts that "it is practically impossible to perform well & perfectly whatsoever task without the necessary and appropriate tools."[94] The recognition that reading and writing require the correct deployment of instruments possesses a twofold significance, for while certain readers, Harvey included, supplement their booklearning with the actual use of instruments, many more readers, Harvey included, also develop reading methods that approximate the use of instruments. In this manner, the practice of reading is subjected to the same analogical thinking that governs a text such as the *Novum Organum*, in which Bacon repeatedly compares the "instruments [which] improve or regulate the movement of our hands" to the "instruments of the mind" that "provide suggestions or cautions to the understanding."[95]

The fashionable anti-Ciceronianism of the latter half of the sixteenth century, to which Harvey subscribes, privileges a group of intellectual strategies that construct an active, discriminating reader. Characterized by a "striving for terse precision," the anti-Ciceronian or "aculeate" style shuns clarity in favor of a style both more obscure and, according to its advocates, simpler than the additive *copia* of Ciceronian prose.[96] In part the product of changing tastes in historiographical method, this change in rhetorical style places a greater responsibility upon the reader as it tests his perspicuity and wit. Forever seeking to penetrate into the subtle and obscure meanings of a text and to "enter rowndly into ye bowels of ye matter" so as to "Reade, & Repeate for lyfe," Harvey imagines this aculeate reader as "praegnant" and "curious," the latter term meaning not peculiar but rather clever and attentive. The *Commentaries* of Aeneas Silvius, which contain "examples of skillful pleading," are "worthy of curious Reading" according to Harvey's *Commonplace Book*, while in the *Oikonomia*, Harvey refers to the acuity of a good reader as a "praegnant & curious reddines."[97]

The skills of the "curious" or aculeate reader are cultivated by specific literary genres including political maxims, technical treatises, epigrams, adages, and miscellanies. Harvey reads avidly in all these genres: his library contains Demosthenes' *Gnomologiae*, a collection of sayings; Martial's *Epigrams*; Domenichi's *Facetie, motti, et burle*, an anthology of witticisms; Erasmus' *Parabolae*; Foorth's *Synopsis Politica*, a collection of political maxims; Guicciardini's *Detti et Fatti*; an edition of Heywood's epigrams; and Oldendorpius' collection of "aphorismi pragmatici."[98] Many of these texts refer to their contents as "devices" or "conceits," terms which, in addition to their mechanical overtones, also alert the aculeate reader that his acuity will be deployed as he distills and digests the text's most useful morsels of knowledge.[99] An instrument such as Blagrave's astrolabe is methodologically akin to the textual "devices" contained in Elizabethan miscellanies and books of maxims such as *The Paradise of Dainty Devices* (1576), *A Gorgeous Gallery of Gallant Inventions* (1578), and *The Theater of Fine Devices* (a 1576 translation of Guillaume de la Perrière's *Théâtre des Bons Engins*), all of which describe their contents as "artificial," "witty," and "subtle." Emphasizing the exercise of the reader's wit, the language of literary miscellanies and collections of political maxims overlaps with that of contemporary technical treatises such as Robert Recorde's 1542 *Grounde of Artes*, which its author terms a "witty device," and Hugh Plat's 1594 *The jewell house of art and nature*, which contains "ingenious devices" and "artificiall conceipts."[100] Both kinds of texts employ a similar idiom in order to foreground the technical skills they demand, from the assembly of a paper astrolabe to the process of epitomizing and abridging knowledge into collections of "witty devices."

The spectacular range of meanings for the term "device" in sixteenth-century England reveals how the process of assembling and collating disparate materials in order to compose thesauri, storehouses, and books of maxims is implicitly mechanical in its character. Harvey was one of a number of Elizabethan writers who kept a commonplace book, a notebook organized according to topics or "commonplaces [loci communes]" and designed to keep easily accessible a wide repertoire of textual knowledge. Their contents arranged so as to be poised for use at a moment's notice, commonplace books bridge the gap between study and action by turning reading into a more active and instrumental activity.[101]

The intellectual affinity among different kinds of "books of devices," from commonplace books and epitomes to technical treatises, helps to explain a puzzling text entitled *The Storehouse of Industrious Devices, Benefitiall to all that delite in the mathematical sciences*, written by one E. G., possibly the mathematician Edmund Gunter, in around 1620. It consists of a series of sixteen illustrations of scientific devices, including an armillary sphere, a pair of compasses, a man demonstrating the use of a grid for drawing in perspective, and a double lectern equipped with what appears to be a magnifying glass (figure 4.3). No written explanations attend the illustrations, and no preface is provided to give us any sense of why the text depicts the objects it does, although since the illustrations are numbered, and many of them keyed, some text was perhaps intended to accompany them.

Unlike Blagrave's *Mathematicall Jewell* or other technical treatises which make explicit their didactic aims, *The Storehouse of Industrious Devices* never makes clear what it proposes for its readers to do with its images of machines and devices. Yet while its readers are given no explicit instruction in fabricating devices similar to the ones in the illustrations, this "storehouse" of "devices" nurtures the reader's critical faculties as he or she studies and mentally assembles the component parts of each device as if they were maxims in a commonplace book. By cultivating what Castiglione calls *acutezza recondita*, that quality of a text which makes acute readers "more hedefull to pause at it, and to ponder it better," the devices in E. G.'s treatise call upon the "covered subtility" and wit of the reader.[102] This is precisely how Harvey's polymechanical Eudromos reads: he "runs through all commonplaces and selects only the most powerful [percurrit omnes loci communes Eudromos: et sola selegit potentissima]."[103] Despite its noticeable lack of text, *The Storehouse of Industrious Devices* is an exercise in how to read acutely, and the text is predicated upon the notion that mechanical devices stimulate the reader's wit and perspicuity in a manner similar to rhetorical devices, conceits, or emblems.

Many sixteenth-century texts contain the kind of keyed illustrations used by E. G., even when their subject matter is not scientific in nature. Samuel

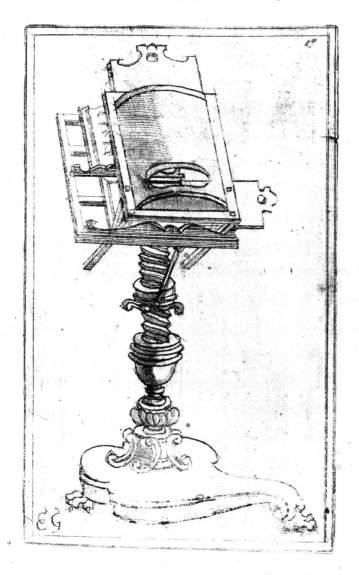

4.3 E. G., *The Storehouse of Industrious Devices*, lectern

Edgerton discusses a 1593 text depicting the Passion with the keyed illustrations common to mechanical and anatomical illustrations of the period in order to "recapitulate the life of Christ with scientific objectivity."[104] The use of this representational convention outside of its usual setting helps to explain E. G.'s inclusion of the lectern, puzzling if only because it is the least obviously mechanical object in the group. What does a book-stand, an item which encourages the study of written texts, have in common with instruments used by surveyors and astronomers to perform calculations? The product of a culture enamored of drawing sharp distinctions between textual and experiential knowledge and between contemplation and action, E. G.'s lectern offers a symbolic comment upon the mutually constitutive relationship between the knowledge attained from books and the knowledge gained from instruments. The lectern effectively collapses the distinction between book-learning and practical knowledge by portraying reading and writing as activities requiring instruments of the mind as well as of the hand. Moreover, its presence reminds us, as Roger Chartier puts it, that "there is no text apart from the physical support that offers it for reading . . . no comprehension of any written piece that does not at least in part depend upon the forms in which it reaches its reader."[105] As a literal support for written texts, the lectern underscores the way in which instruments and devices, from the printing press to the microscopes and globes discussed in the next chapter of this book, mediate the physical and the hermeneutic relationship between readers and their books.

Harvey's reading of Blagrave's *Mathematicall Jewell* and his assembly of its mechanical device illustrate how machinery can profoundly reshape the experience of reading, turning the reader into an "ingenious practiser" by virtue of the text's instrumentality. Harvey's divided allegiance between book-learning and practical knowledge is reconciled, at least in part, by the dual nature of Blagrave's text/instrument, an object that encourages the continual renegotiation of the tensions and fissures between theory and praxis. Renaissance readers and scientific practitioners delight in objects that conflate the distinction between text and instrument, from scientific texts which can be assembled into instruments to texts designed to contain instruments, such as MS Bodley 607, a collection of scientific treatises, including Sacrobosco's *De Sphaera* and several alchemical and calendrical works, whose inside cover reveals a hole, covered by a flap, designed to store a ring dial. If Renaissance texts can contain the potential to produce the "rooted demonstration" of a scientific instrument, then instruments can also contain text: witness globes, dials, and astrological compendia such as the one constructed by the late fifteenth-century Austrian instrument-maker Hans Dorn, which is fashioned in the shape of a book.

Harvey's interpretations of the works of Geoffrey Chaucer, particularly his *Treatise on the Astrolabe*, reveal a similarly complex reformulation of the relationship between books and instruments. In addition to Blagrave's treatise on his polypragmatical "singuler instrument," Harvey owned several treatises on the construction and use of astrolabes, instruments used to calculate the altitude of stars. His copy of Thomas Hood's *The Marriners Guide* (London, 1592), bound with Hood's revised edition of William Bourne's *A Regiment for the Sea*, provides basic instructions on the use of the instrument, as does his copy of Jerome Turler's *Travailer*, a gift to him from Edmund Spenser in 1578 along with several volumes of poetry.[106] Bound with Harvey's copy of Sacrobosco's *De Sphaera*, which he acquired in 1580, is a short treatise on the use of an *annulus*, a miniature astrolabe fashioned into a finger ring. Harvey was almost certainly the owner and annotator of the copy of Gemma Frisius' 1556 *De Astrolabio Catholico* now in the British Library, an instrument of "multiplex" uses, according to its full title, which Harvey mentions in his Sacrobosco volume.[107]

Harvey's interest in mastering the astrolabe is bound up with his pedagogical convictions, his political attitudes, and his literary tastes. On the title-page of his copy of *The Mathematicall Jewell*, across from the paper astrolabe to be assembled by the reader, Harvey reminds himself of the enduring value of Chaucer's brief work on this astronomical instrument: "Chaucer's conclusions of the Astrolabie, still in esse. Pregnant rules to manie worthie purposes."[108] Harvey was an avid reader of the medieval poet both before and after he acquired the 1598 folio of Chaucer's works edited by Thomas Speght.[109] Heavily annotated in contrast with the rather sporadic notes in the rest of the volume, Chaucer's *Treatise on the Astrolabe* holds a particular appeal for the playful yet pragmatic Harvey since, like *The Mathematicall Jewell*, it promises to bridge the methodological gap between book and instrument and to inculcate both the dexterity and the discipline prized by Harvey.

Spanning a period of more than twenty years, Harvey's copious marginal comments concerning Chaucer reveal the literary ramifications of his multifaceted instrumentalism. Harvey is the first to admit that his partiality for Chaucer is dictated in large measure by scientific, rather than aesthetic, standards: while "others commend Chawcer & Lidgate for their witt" or their "varietie of poetical discourse," he writes, "I specially note their Astronomie, philosophie, & other parts of profound or cunning art."[110] Transcending the "superficiall sheets" of literary texts that lack practical application, Chaucer's work unites the brazen and golden worlds of fact and fancy between which Sidney distinguishes so definitively in his *Apology*. Writing in the margins of Dionysius Periegetes' *Surveye of the world* (1572), Harvey insists that the poet be "exactly learned" and in possession of a "mathematicall witt." "It is not sufficient for poets to be superficiall humanists," he continues, "but they must be exquisite artists, & curious universal schollers."[111]

Two and a half decades later, Harvey's demand that the poet be well versed in the applied and theoretical sciences resurfaces in the margins of his Speght Chaucer. Harvey articulates his ideal of the hybrid poet-scientist through the two personae who appear in his annotations to Chaucer's works: Axiophilus, or the "lover of worthy poetry," and his rival Chrysotechnus, a man in possession of "golden technical skill."[112] Axiophilus drifts in and out of Harvey's margins from 1572 onwards, a reflection of his ambitions as a poet. A master of eloquence and (unlike Harvey himself) of foreign languages, Axiophilus also personifies the inspired poet, his "flowing fitts" bringing forth "so manie rhapsodies."[113] Unlike Axiophilus, Chrysotech-nus has no interest in inspiration: instead, he is a stickler for method who, as his name suggests, judges poetry by virtue of its technical excellence. Before Chrysotechnus makes his appearance in the Speght Chaucer as a consummate verse technician who "accounts a mean versifier a cipher in the algorisme of the first philosopher," he crops up in several of Harvey's obser-vations on jurisprudence, where a similar preoccupation with technique makes him "easily the most skilled of all the canon lawyers at all practices, tables, and instruments (of the law) [Chrysotechnus, practicorum omnium Canonum, tabularum, et instrumentorum facile peritissimus]."[114]

Chrysotechnus' valorization of technical skill reflects Harvey's more widespread tendency to privilege technical excellence over broader con-cerns of literary merit in his appraisals of medieval and contemporary poets. In his copy of Dionysius Periegetes, probably annotated around 1574, Harvey begins to formulate his literary theories according to scientific stan-dards, often isolating the mastery of practical mechanics and cosmography, such as the "notable Astronomical descriptions in Chawcer, & Lidgate," as the mark of superior poets. Chaucer in particular transcends the lim-itations of the "superficial humanist," and Harvey names him a "curious universal scholler" whose "conclusions of the Astrolabie" are "still excellent; unempeachable."[115]

Harvey's attraction to didactic scientific poetry is frequently motivated by his pursuit of "effectual practical knowledge" at the expense of more rarified, less useful, learning. He repeatedly praises texts such as George Buchanan's

De Sphaera, Maurice Scève's *Microcosme*, Du Bartas' *Sepmaines*, and other sixteenth-century works of versified natural philosophy.[116] Harvey is particularly enamored of Du Bartas, whose name appears more than a dozen times in his margins, always favorably. In *Pierces Supererogation*, Harvey describes the author of the *Sepmaines* and the *Urania* as a "right inspired and enravished Poet" and as the "onely Poet, whom Urany hath vouchsafed to Laureate with her owne heavenly hand." In other words, Du Bartas satisfies the competing poetic demands of Axiophilus and Chrysotechnus: he is divinely inspired and at the same time guided by the muse of astronomy. "Divine, & heroicall works," Axiophilus comments about Du Bartas' poetry in the margins of *The surveye of the world*, but also "excellent Cantiques for a mathematicall witt."[117]

Harvey's admiration for scientific didacticism distinguishes him from contemporaries such as Sidney and William Webbe, whose strict Aristotelianism prevents them from embracing the utilitarian genre of the scientific poem. Paraphrasing Aristotle's rejection of scientific didacticism in his 1586 *Discourse of English Poetrie*, Webbe compares Empedocles unfavorably to Homer, and while Sidney is willing to acknowledge that ancient natural philosophers "sang their naturall Phylosophie in verses," he makes a sharp distinction between the didactic poet and the "true" poet, the latter of whom creates fictions out of the "zodiack of his own wit" rather than from the province of Urania.[118] For Sidney and Webbe, poetic invention need not, and perhaps should not, adhere to strict scientific accuracy, in part because the study of natural philosophy may lead us astray through excessive abstraction or a misplaced sense of moral rectitude: "the Astronomer looking to the starres might fall into a ditch . . . and the Mathematician might draw foorth a straight line with a crooked hart."[119]

Throughout the *Apology*, Sidney repeatedly enforces disciplinary boundaries between poetry and the "serving sciences," boundaries that Harvey breaches in his marginalia. According to Harvey's logic, not only can a natural philosopher be a true poet, but a lowly mechanician can achieve the status of a great poet on the sole basis of superior technical skill. In his copy of Dionysius Periegetes, Harvey bemoans the relative ignorance of contemporary poets in matters of astronomy, and he weighs the poetry of Philip Sidney, or "Astrophilium," against the work of mechanicians including Blagrave and William Buckley, all three of whom are finally dubbed "Uraniae filios."[120] Sidney is in odd company with Harvey's other "sons of Urania," particularly since Blagrave's and Buckley's brief forays into the world of poetry are singularly undistinguished. Blagrave did write a few prefatory verses to *The Mathematicall Jewell*, and according to Richard

Mulcaster, "Master Bu[c]kley had drawne the rules of Arithmeticke into verses" while at Cambridge, but neither of these men distinguished themselves as poets any more than Sidney's use of an astronomical conceit in *Astrophel and Stella* earns him the title of astronomer.[121]

Harvey goes on to indict Edmund Spenser for his scanty knowledge of astronomical matters, recommending that the poet might learn the use of the sphere, the globe, and the astrolabe from Du Bartas, from Buchanan, or from mechanicians including Blagrave, Digges, Hariot, and Dee. Like the "Doctors of Universities" disgraced by the uneducated yet erudite Blagrave, Spenser's scandalous ignorance ("pudet . . . imperitiae") of astronomical matters prevents him from earning the approval of Chrysotechnus.[122] Harvey's tendency to weigh the relative merits of poets and scientists against each other demonstrates the extent to which he regards the technical aptitude of the skilled rhetorician as analogous to the manual and intellectual dexterity of the mechanician. In a catalogue of "illustrious talents" in the margins of his Quintilian, Harvey displays an unwillingness to maintain any disciplinary distinctions between poetry on the one hand and natural and political philosophy on the other. After praising Chaucer, Thomas More, and John Jewel as "vivacious English talents," and John Heywood, Sidney, and Spenser as "three natural geniuses," Harvey groups together various "other illustrious English talents dear to me but more obscure," including "[Thomas] Smith, [Roger] Ascham, [Thomas] Wilson, [Leonard] Digges, [Thomas] Blundeville, [Richard] Hakluyt, my little dears."[123] Mean mechanicians and distinguished poets and humanists side by side, the list unfolds the logic according to which Harvey judges literature, elucidating his persistent conflation of mechanical and rhetorical subtlety.

Many sixteenth-century readers recognize Chaucer as a "universal scholler" whose mastery of astronomy allows him to transcend his status as a poet and earns his *Treatise on the Astrolabe* a frequent place in collections of scientific manuscripts assembled during the period.[124] In the prologue to his 1513 translation of the *Aeneid*, Gavin Douglas praises "venerabill Chauser" as an "orlege" and a "dyall," allusions, perhaps, to the pragmatic, technical emphasis of his treatise on the astrolabe or his attention to astronomical material in *The Franklin's Tale* and *The Nun Priest's Tale*.[125] The Tudor historian John Leland commends Chaucer as an "able mathematician," and in his *Compleat Gentleman*, Henry Peacham singles out the author of *The Canterbury Tales* as an "excellent mathematician, as plainly appeareth by his discourse of astrolabe to his little son Lewis."[126] For some of Chaucer's readers, Harvey included, his mathematical talent is part and parcel of his quick wit: in his dedication to William Thynne's 1532 *editio princeps* of Chaucer's works, Sir Brian Tuke admires Chaucer's "sharpnesse or quycknesse in conclusyon," an acuity that finds expression in his rhetorical and scientific skill alike.[127]

Harvey likewise recognizes Chaucer's "witt" and his "cunning art," but his appreciation of Chaucerian subtlety expresses itself in a preoccupation with the mechanical objects and scientific practices depicted in Chaucer's texts. In his Periegetes, Harvey summarizes several of the *Canterbury Tales*, paying almost exclusive attention to Chaucer's mechanical, astrological, and occult knowledge. *The Franklin's Tale* becomes, in Harvey's synopsis, an "Artificial description of a cunning man, or Magician, or Astrologer," while he describes the principal attractions of *The Squire's Tale* as its "Fowre presents of miraculous vertu: An horse, a sword; a glasse; & a ring" and abridges *The Canon Yeoman's Tale* simply as "the discoverie of the counterfait Alchymist."[128]

When Harvey annotates his copy of the Speght Chaucer in around 1598, he continues to dwell almost exclusively upon the mechanical, alchemical, and magical aspects of Chaucerian poetry. He describes *The Canon Yeoman's Tale* as a "chymical discourse, & discoverie of a cunning impostor," a morality tale which cautions against the use of "cunning withowt effect." *The Franklin's Tale* is about "a cunning man, & arch-Magician," while *The Squire's Tale* is essentially a technical treatise teaching "Cunning Compositions bie Natural Magique."[129] He carefully underlines each mention of a mechanical device in *The Squire's Tale*, including the "*engine or windlas*" and the "*queint mirrors*," and cross-references Chaucer's descriptions of what Harvey calls "slie reflections and of prospectives" with "Bacons perspective," the Oxford friar's work on optics. Harvey also notes allusions to clocks: in *The Man of Lawes Prologue*, he notes how "the time of the day [is] astronomically described" by Chaucer's host, who observes that it is "ten of the clock," and in *The Tale of the Nonnes Priest*, he underlines the "*clocke*" and the abbey "*orloge*" to which Chauntecleer's time-telling capabilities are compared, commenting in the margins, "the cockes astronomie." Chaucer's translation of Jean de Meun's *Roman de la Rose* provokes two sole words from Harvey – "fine optiques" – no doubt a reference to the optical devices and clocks frequently and meticulously described by the French poet.[130]

Conspicuously absent from Harvey's marginal glosses is any of Chaucer's own concern, evident intermittently throughout *The Canterbury Tales*, that mechanical magic might be (in the words of *The Franklin's Tale*) "agayns the process of Nature."[131] Harvey's summaries of the tales constitute an unequivocal celebration of the subtle strategizing and mechanical cunning deployed by Chaucer's more morally questionable characters such as *The Squire's Tale*'s strange knight. There is a demonic glee in Harvey's tone as he rhapsodizes in the margins of Speght's edition about the amoral scientific cunning celebrated by the *Manciple's Tale*: "No Tales like the Tales of cunning Experiments, or straung exploits, or queint surprises, or stratagems."[132] Notable for their unflagging fascination with mechanical devices and magic tricks, Harvey's thumbnail interpretations of *The Canterbury Tales* are symptomatic of his dedication to a disenchanted, Machiavellian set of political attitudes in that they reflect his perceived capacity to distinguish legitimate science from imposture. Reading Chaucer allows Harvey to exercise the Eudromian, skeptical acuity about which he boasts in a 1598 letter to Robert Cecil, writing that Thomas Smith once taught him "not to contemn . . . the true Chymique without imposture" and other "effectual practicable knowledge."[133] A similar pride in distinguishing counterfeit from true science permeates his readings of *The Canterbury Tales*, in which Harvey boasts of his ability to see through the ruses and "stratagems" of characters such as Chaucer's Canon Yeoman, whose astrological "cunning" is fradulent according to Harvey because it is "without effect."[134]

The Canterbury Tales offers Harvey some powerful lessons in deploying the "wisdom of the serpent" and detecting the "forgeries, experiments, & collusions of Impostors" whose exposure he praises in his *Commonplace Book*.[135] Harvey's admiration for Chaucer's cunning is inseparable from the context in which the Speght edition is produced. It is the polytechnical "M. secretarie Cecill" who sponsors the edition and becomes the "new patron of Chawcer," a role cemented by Cecil's association with political expediency and technical knowledge, qualities which, from Harvey's perspective, help to revive Chaucerian cunning in Elizabethan England.[136]

In addition to providing a canonical, English foundation for the Italianate political and technical subtlety that Harvey descries and celebrates throughout his marginalia, the works of Chaucer provide Harvey with a model for his Ramist pedagogical program.[137] Addressed to his son Lewis, Chaucer's *Treatise on the Astrolabe* is purportedly written as a response to his son's "bisi preyere in special to lerne the tretis of the astrelabie." Chaucer continues by outlining a plan for teaching his son the use of the astrolabe, a plan which must have been dear to Harvey for its methodical progression and its emphasis upon repeated practice or "rehearsal" of the instrument. First, Chaucer will show his son how to "reherse the figures & the membres of thin[e] Astrolabie, by-cause that thow shalt han the grettre knowyng of thin owne instrument," and he will then proceed to the "verrey practik" of the device "as ferforth & as narwe as may be shewyd in so smal an instrument portatif-a-boute."

After introducing the plan of the work, Chaucer apologizes for his "rewde endytyng" and his "superfluite of wordes," explaining that he has used a simple, repetitious style because "curio[u]s enditing & hard sentence Is ful hevy atones for swich a child to lerne" as well as because children are more apt to remember what they read several times over.[138] The principles behind the repetitious, patronizing tone of Chaucer's treatise inform and elucidate Harvey's concerns about pedagogical efficacy as well as the temperament of his marginal notes themselves. Throughout his notes, Harvey continually counsels himself to practice, repeat, and rehearse his knowledge in all areas of human endeavor, "everie day better, & better . . . continuall improovement of everi part." Frequently reminding himself that diligent exercise is the key to knowledge, Harvey urges himself to "repeat, repeat, repeat" in the margins of his volume of Domenichi's *Facetie*: "Daily read, read; but daily repeat, repeat, repeat [Quotidie lege, lege; sed quotidie repete, repete, repete]." Even as it depends upon effortless *sprezzatura*, learning also depends upon what Harvey, in the above passage, calls "soverain repetition," and he prides himself on his "dailie & almost hourlie conference" with his books.[139] Not surprisingly, Harvey's preoccupation with repetition as a pedagogical principle is articulated forcefully in his volume of Ramus' *Ciceronianus*, in which he boasts that "I redd over this Ciceronianus twice in twoo dayes."[140] When Harvey begins to undertake the study of the law in around 1580, his zeal for repetition and practice reaches a fever pitch, as befits the demands of the discipline. To ensure that his studies are poised like weapons at the ready in the brutish world of the law, Harvey aspires to be a living book-wheel: "No sufficient or hable furniture, gotten by unperfect posting, or superficial overrunning: or halfelearning: but by perpetual meditations, repetitions, recognitions, recapitulations, reiterations . . . for praegnant & curious reddines, at every lest occasion."[141]

Chaucer's *Treatise on the Astrolabe* appeals to Harvey because the "repetitions" and "recapitulations" necessary for effective learning are already built into the text (and the instrument) itself. Subtitled "Bred and Mylk for Children," it promises to instruct its little readers with the same gentle facility proffered two centuries later by treatises such as Blagrave's *Mathematicall Jewell*. Yet Chaucer addresses his readers with a patriarchal, stern tone. The narrator persistently chides his filial audience: "forget not thys, litel Lewis," "now I have told thee twyes." Seth Lerer has argued that the infantilizing tone used throughout the *Treatise on the Astrolabe* is typical of the "advisory" stance that informs many of Chaucer's works, a patronizing authority which "subjects" its readers and "subjugates them into childhood or incompetence."[142] Harvey recognizes the pedagogical value in Chaucer's condescension, even incorporating a similarly patronizing tone into the frequent marginal remarks directed at his own scholarly shortcomings. In these comments, Harvey internalizes Chaucer's paternalistic pedagogy, exhorting himself to repeat and recapitulate and scolding himself when he fails to do so. Harvey sees the *Treatise on the Astrolabe* as an exemplary model of his own pedagogical convictions, even praising Chaucer as a good educator for having "initiated his little sonne Lewis with such cunning & subtill conclusions, as sensibly, & plainly expressed, as he could devise."[143]

Apparently indifferent to the gentler pedagogical practices advocated by sixteenth-century humanists including Erasmus and Ascham, Harvey exalts rigor in education: "good bringing up," he writes in the margins of the *Synopsis Politica*, "we call breaking, as well in children, scholars, and servants, as young coultes, &c. which can not be withowt sum mixture of severity."[144] His admiration for Chaucer's pedagogical techniques surely informs Harvey's comments in his *Commonplace Book* upon the education of "Ower little Hubert," a nephew whom Harvey taught "to discourse reddily . . . in Arithmetique, Geometry, ye Sphaere" by means of "often repetition. & practis, upon every light occasion."[145]

Harvey's faith in the pedagogical efficacy of repetition and practice is challenged only by his fascination with courtly *facilità*. While he asserts that "that is never too often repeated, wch is never learned, or practised enowgh," Harvey is also attracted to the contrary principle that certain arts may be learned with extraordinary speed and facility: "I dowt not, but a sensible man may learne ye use of his weapon in a day, or two; of his horse in a day, or two . . . Any serviceable poynt, ether civil, courtly, or militar, is very soone lernid, by Art & practis."[146] Torn between the allure of rigor and the attractions of effortless virtuosity, Harvey undercuts his own emphasis upon practice by proposing that "any Art, or science, liberal, or mechanical may summarily be lernid for ordinary talke, in *three dayes*; for use, practis, & profession, in *six*: any language, to understande, in *six*: to speake and write, in *twelve*."[147] In the margins of his *Oikonomia*, he elaborates on this cognitive theory: "the only brave way to lerne althings" is "with no study, & much pleasure." One must learn to "learn, as it were, by the way," concealing one's diligence with a show of *disinvoltura*.[148]

Like Blagrave's *Mathematicall Jewell*, the works of Geoffrey Chaucer promise to reconcile Harvey's competing invocations of Eutrapelian, courtly facility and the assiduous labor of the "polypragmatical" mechanician. At the end of Chaucer's biography in the Speght edition, Harvey elevates the medieval writer and customs official to noble status and praises his works as "excellent in everie veine & humour: & none so like him for gallant varietie . . . as Sir Philip Sidney."[149] *The Knight's Tale* and *The Man of Lawes Tale* teach "heroical pageants" and "courtlie practises" according to Harvey's marginal summaries of these tales. In Harvey's hands, Chaucer's playful jesting and his "sociable intercourse of Tales, stories, discourses, & merriments" are firmly embedded in a courtly milieu that aligns them with Elizabethan courtier-poets such as Sidney.

Harvey takes the art of courtly jesting seriously, painstakingly annotating Castiglione's treatment of decorous joke-telling in Book II of *The Book of the Courtier* in the hope of cultivating the Eutrapelian wit of his favorite courtly makers. Yet he is never quite capable of striking the balance between gravity and levity central to the courtly culture of serious play. It is a truism that Renaissance culture delights in the conflation and the juxtaposition of the trivial and the serious. From Erasmus' *Praise of Folly* to the *ludi* of seventeenth-century natural philosophy, as Rosalie Colie has so brilliantly illustrated, the "ambiguous, the paradoxical, the joco-serious played an essential part in [Renaissance writers'] considerations of God, of nature, and of themselves."[150] Yet achieving that synthesis proves difficult for Harvey, who struggles throughout his life to effect the "secret metamorphosis" of turning "serious matters" into "jests" and vice versa, even inventing a character, Eutrapelus, who has mastered the art of drawing "the salt of the earth and the light of the world into jests [iuvat in iocis haurire salem terrae, et lucem mundi]."[151]

This spirit of intellectual jocularity never ceases to elude Harvey. Calling eloquence an "engine" and ironic wit a "machine," he violently misconstrues the instrumentalities of the ideal courtier, whose weapons of wit, sharp poniards as they are, must never pierce the skin. Nashe recognizes Harvey's misunderstanding of wit in *Strange Newes*, describing his rival's "invention" as "over-weaponed." The instrumental metaphors common to Harvey's discussions of rhetorical combat radiate through Nashe's satire of Harvey, for while he "hath some good words," Nashe mocks, "he cannot writhe them and tosse them to and fro nimbly, or so bring them about, that hee maye make one streight thrust at his enemies face."[152] While Nashe's depiction of Harvey in *Strange Newes* suggests that he lacks a certain subtlety in the deployment of his courtly devices, in *Have With You to Saffron Walden*, Nashe suggests that Harvey's intellect is *too* subtle, excessively focused on minutiae like those "certaine rare Mathematicall experimentes; as for example, that of tying a flea in a chaine." Rather than depict Harvey as a man who sifts through vain subtleties to accumulate pragmatic, urbane knowledge, as Harvey depicts himself in his margins, Nashe describes Harvey's intellectual capacity in terms of that most infamous of *nugae* discussed by Cardano's *De Subtilitate*, scoffing that all of Harvey's knowledge can be "comprehended . . . like *Homers Iliads* in the compasse of a nut-shell."[153] Comparing Harvey's intellectual methods to the gratuitous intricacy of minute technical objects, Nashe recognizes the reductive and limiting nature of the mechanical and intellectual subtlety so prized by Harvey.

CHAPTER 5

Homer in a nutshell: George Chapman and the mechanics of perspicuity

When John Keats first looks into Chapman's Homer, he beholds a "wide expanse" which he likens to the discovery of a panoramic vista:

> Then felt I like some watcher of the skies
> When a new planet swims into his ken;
> Or like stout Cortez when with eagle eyes
> He star'd at the Pacific –.[1]

Keats' comparison between the experience of reading "deep-brow'd" Homer and the sharp-sighted vision of an explorer is apt given the earliest readers of Chapman's Homer. Chapman identifies two contemporary scientists, Thomas Hariot and Robert Hues, as his principal critics for his translation of the *Iliad*. In his preface to the 1611 edition, Chapman relates that he showed his work "to my worthy and most learned friend, M. Harriots . . . whose judgement and knowledge in all kinds I know to be incomparable and bottomlesse," and he mentions "Robert Hews," a friend of Hariot best known for his 1594 treatise on globes, as another figure of "my confest conference touching Homer."[2]

This chapter argues that mechanical practices and objects mediate Renaissance culture's relationship to Homeric epic by cultivating a set of critical strategies aimed at refining the interpretation of Homer's texts. It evolved from a series of questions prompted by the spectral editorial presence of Hariot and Hues in Chapman's text. How do two men chiefly occupied with manufacturing telescopes and globes, rather than literary interpretations, come to serve as such "incomparable" readers of Homer? How do their mechanical inventions confer upon them particular capacities as critics or shed light upon Chapman's attitude towards his literary endeavors? Drawing upon the prefaces and glosses to his Homeric translations, the first half of this chapter argues that the techniques Chapman uses to read and translate Homer, as well as the skills he demands of his readers, are informed by Hariot's and Hues' instruments and techniques.

Chapman's understanding of the practice of translation, his grasp of the structure of Homeric epic, and his conception of an ideal, "deep searching" reader are each shaped by Hariot's and Hues' work on optics, atomism, and stereographic projection.

Like the previous chapter, which examined Gabriel Harvey's interest in mechanics in light of his reading practices, this chapter traces one facet of the mutually supportive evolution of mechanical practices and reading strategies during the Renaissance. For Chapman, who invokes the "perfect eye" of Hariot's telescope as a model for his ideal, perspicacious reader, optical instruments alter, and sometimes improve upon, the relationship between readers and texts, while Hues' work on globes promises to resolve some of the challenges met by Chapman as a translator. Yet unlike Harvey, who regards mechanics as the cornerstone of a Ramist intellectual program in which the reader strives to condense and clarify his learning in order to put it into practice, Chapman idealizes the difficulty of written texts, disdaining the didactic transparency which Harvey seeks. With a Neoplatonic, even orphic, penchant for what Gerald Snare has termed "mystification," as well as a neo-Stoic fondness for obliquity, Chapman imagines his ideal readers as "serching" spirits capable of penetrating the subtle mysteries of his arcane texts. If learning is not directed towards a contemplative *gnosis*, according to Chapman, it turns the scholar into a "walking dictionarie" and an "articulate Clocke," apt metaphors for the perfunctory, instrumentalized learning of the Harveian polymechanist.[3]

"Reading," as Chartier has observed, "is not uniquely an abstract operation of the intellect," but rather is "always a practice embodied in acts, spaces, and habits," mediated by the body, by social conditions, and by machinery.[4] Homeric texts and machinery participate together in the creation of a new kind of reader at the end of the sixteenth century, a reader distinguished by emergent intellectual virtues such as perspicuity and subtlety. Optical devices such as spectacles, microscopes, and telescopes are perhaps the most obvious examples of instruments that modify the relations between readers and their texts, but globes and miniaturized machines, insofar as they function *as* texts, also discipline the reader's eye to make subtle and detailed observations.

From the development of disciplines such as entomology, anatomy, and archaeology to a polyvalent fondness for subtleties both fabricated and natural, Renaissance culture delights in inscrutability. This fascination with the difficult-to-read is sanctioned by a wide variety of philosophical and aesthetic traditions, from a Platonic exaltation of the ineffable and a hermetic delight in arcana to the scrutiny that attends the pursuit of scientific objectivity and the artistic virtuosity exercised by the detail-oriented arts of limning and goldsmithing. Renaissance culture's fascination with the inscrutable is borne out by its frequent invocations of the paradox of *multum in parvo*, or much in little, which posits that the smallest spaces are more replete, and thus symbolically larger, than more expansive ones. The logic that prefers a well-wrought urn to a half-acre tomb privileges a scrutiny necessary to penetrate the deep nooks of minute, densely packed spaces which demand closer inspection than the "perviall," or intelligible, texts disdained by Chapman.[5]

By altering what can and cannot be discerned, optical devices and other mechanical instruments challenge established norms of scrutability, thus affecting the interpretive strategies that Renaissance readers bring to all texts. While an instrument such as a microscope may afford its user a clearer view of the impenetrable recesses of nature, it also alters our standards of scrutability by magnifying remote or indistinct objects. As mechanical instruments improve our ability to read the book of nature, they also modify norms of legibility, thus stimulating other changes in reading practices. For many Renaissance readers, Homer's texts aggravate concerns about legibility, requiring a degree of scrutiny unparalleled except by the most intricate technical objects. The second half of this chapter explores the critical strategies necessitated by Chapman's Homer alongside those cultivated by an odd family of "subtle" texts and objects, including epigrams, mock encomia, pocket watches, insects, and technical *minuterie*, all of which test their readers' abilities to "search" or read closely. Some of these objects serve as mock textual spaces that reproduce Homeric techniques or duplicate the effect of reading Homer: copies of the *Iliad* written inside a nutshell, miniature clocks, or epigrams upon mechanical devices rival the density and the intricacy of Homeric poetry in a different medium.

Chapman met both Hariot and Hues through the circle of scholars who assembled around Henry Percy in the early 1590s, a group which also includes Ralegh, Marlowe, and (at its fringes) Francis Bacon.[6] Collectively inclined towards esoteric intellectual pursuits, this diverse group is best characterized by the same "love of obscurity and erudition" that Grafton detects in Kepler's Prague.[7] While catchy epithets such as the "School of Night" and the "Three Magi" have been discarded for their undue emphasis upon hermeticism, the intellectual habits of Percy's circle are governed by a predilection towards difficulty and abstruseness.[8] Like Kepler, Hariot loves verbal esoterica, making Latin anagrams of his own name and relying upon murky symbols and allegories in his mathematical investigations.[9] To

some extent, the diverse moral and natural philosophies embraced by the
so-called School of Night – including pneumatic, atomistic, and occult
habits of thought – are united by their collective affirmation of obscurity
and subtlety as aesthetic and intellectual virtues. Conceived as an intellectual system organized around the partially discernible *minima* of atom,
monad, and point, the atomism espoused by Thomas Hariot and Walter
Warner exists largely as a vehicle for the more pivotal act of descrying
and extolling subtlety. For Chapman, as well as for Percy, Neoplatonic
and neo-Stoic philosophy are reconcilable, despite the profound moral and
metaphysical differences between them, insofar as they intersect at the axis
of the reverence of the inscrutable.

Percy is singled out by contemporaries for his perspicacious mind that
relishes abstruse knowledge. In his 1609 *Humour's Heav'n on Earth*, a work
of Stoic consolation dedicated to Percy's son, John Davies praises Percy
senior as "A Perfect Pierc-ey that in darknesse cleeres," a "piercing Eie"
capable of penetrating the most esoteric intellectual and moral conundra.[10]
George Peele's 1593 "Honour of the Garter" also depicts Percy as a beacon
of hermetic knowledge, a mage who "clothest Mathesis in rich ornaments"
and follows the "ancient revered steps / Of Trismegistus and Pythagoras, /
Through uncouth ways and unaccessible."[11] Alternately sage or mage, Percy
possesses a capacity to mystify and demystify that assumes both Stoic and
hermetic dimensions.

It is this preoccupation with perspicuity which motivates the Earl's own
attraction to the works of Silver Age writers such as Tacitus and Seneca,
whose appeal resides largely in their "aculeate" style, an anti-Ciceronianism
that shuns "all that is obvious, direct, and natural" in favor of a "brevity
pushed to the verge of obscurity."[12] The poets and historians of the Silver
Age offer exercises in perspicuity, turning their Renaissance readers into
sharp-sighted Lynceuses. For Percy and Chapman, the intellectual appeal
of classical texts "uttered stoicallie in darke words" (as the Elizabethan
translator of Epictetus puts it) is part of a much more widespread set of
obscurantist practices including allegory, the art of perspective, emblematics, and cryptography, a favorite discipline of the young Percy.[13]

The group's collective interest in atomism provides further insight into
its multi-faceted commitment to perspicuity. Disseminated principally
through Hariot, Warner, and Torporley, this particular brand of atomism differs from the later seventeenth-century atomism of Gassendi or
Charleton, which excludes occult explanations and accounts for all physical phenomena mechanically. Instead, it relies upon Giordano Bruno's
concepts of *minima* and *maxima* in the service of studying and extolling

the particulate inscrutability of the cosmos.[14] Like the mitigated atomism of Francis Bacon's early writings, in which a natural philosophy based upon matter and void is profitable, according to Rees, insofar as it sanctions Bacon's "key concept of 'subtlety,'" Hariot and his colleagues are drawn to atomism as a model for intellectual strategies of discernment even if they do not adopt that atomism wholesale as a discrete theory of matter.[15] Working from a conviction in the "inextricable connection between the ordering of mental processes and the order which regulates the natural world," Bruno's English followers strive to *think* atomistically – to "contract yourself into an atom," as Hariot himself puts it in a letter to Kepler, in order to "enter easily" through the "doors of nature's mansion, where her secrets are hidden."[16]

In the *Novum Organum*, Bacon associates such penetrating habits of mind with the atomism of Democritus, who "delved further into Nature than others" and whose natural philosophy privileges the close observation of the "wonderful and exquisite subtlety of Nature."[17] Yet while Percy, Hariot, and their circle acknowledge no concomitant dangers in ferreting out the inscrutable depths of nature, Bacon admits the potential for error in atomistic thinking, for the Epicurean physics of Leucippus and Democritus is so thoroughly "taken up with the minute parts of things that it almost overlooks the structure."[18] What for Bacon constitutes excessive subtlety is, for Chapman, an exemplary critical strategy and the organizing principle of an atomistic, occult poetic sensibility. Hilary Gatti argues that Percy and his entourage are "deeply concerned with the problem of expression," and Chapman is no exception, as is evident from his love of allegory and his copious, mannered use of metaphor.[19] Chapman's attention to problems of representation also extends to his interest in cartography and stereography (globe-making), the art of perspective, optics, and other practices involving the transposition or mediation of images or objects. Although habitually troubled by the distortions wrought upon a text by readers or translators, Chapman strives not for clarity in his writings but rather for obscurity, favoring unusual diction, intricate syntax, esoteric symbolism, and other qualities that heighten the difficulty of poetic language. The reader able to penetrate his cloudy interpretations and turns of phrase is exemplified by the "perfect eye" cast by Hariot, an eye enhanced by a telescopic lens and trained to scrutinize atoms. The science of optics, in particular, provides Chapman with a rich symbolic vocabulary for the exigencies of interpretation and the errors of human judgment. One of the problems contemplated by Hariot in his unpublished work on angles of refraction, the *baculus in aqua*, appears as the emblem on the title-page of Chapman's 1595 *Ovids Banquet of Sence*: the image, a straight stick partially immersed in water which appears to bend as it enters the water, demonstrates the unreliability of sense impressions.[20] Likewise, Hariot's and Hues' telescopes and globes pose, and at times promise to solve, some of the formal and philosophical questions faced by Chapman as a poet and translator.

Better known today for his *briefe and true report of the new found land of Virginia* and for his implication as an atheistical "doubting Thomas" in Richard Baines' testimony against Christopher Marlowe, Hariot was also the most prominent English producer of optical glasses during the first two decades of the seventeenth century. In addition to his work in the fields of gunnery, navigation, and theoretical mathematics, Hariot made important advances in optics and lens-grinding. He and his assistant, Christopher Tooke, are often credited with the invention of the earliest working English telescope, and Hariot's correspondence with William Lower, from 1607 onwards, contains some of the first descriptions of celestial observations made with the new devices.[21]

For Chapman, Hariot's perspective trunks provide a model for the perspicacious reader invoked throughout his poems and Homeric translations. In a dedicatory epistle to his 1598 edition of *Achilles Shield*, Chapman appeals to Hariot's mechanically enhanced eye as the ideal reader for his earliest translation of Homer, a fragment from Book XVIII of the *Iliad*. Invoking the "perfect eye" of Hariot's telescope, Chapman implores his Lyncean friend to "pierce / Into that Chaos whence this stiffled verse / By violence breakes."[22] Penetrating into the "palpable night" of Chapman's obscure and difficult poetry, Hariot's perfect eye operates with the same invasiveness as the keen minds of "Ingenious Darbie and deepe-searching Northumberland," men whose "radiant, and light-bearing intellect" earns them a place among the discerning readers singled out by Chapman's dedicatory epistle to *Ovids Banquet of Sence*.[23]

Chapman persistently describes the efforts of his acute readers in instrumental terms. Acquitting himself from the accusations of obscurity made by certain "empty, and dark spirits, [who] wil complaine of palpable night," he protests in the preface to *Ovids Banquet of Sence* that "in my opinion, that which being with a little endevour serched, ads a kind of Majestie to Poetrie . . . rich Minerals are digd out of the bowels of the earth, not found in the superficies and dust of it."[24] Likening the dark conceits of his "strange poems" to the subterranean spaces of caves and mines, he calls upon the same defense employed by contemporary treatises on metallurgy such as Georgius Agricola's 1556 *De Re Metallica*, which defends mining by asserting that "greater wealth . . . lies hidden beneath the ground . . . than is visible and apparent above ground." It is in these very terms that Ben Jonson, in an epigram upon Chapman's 1618 translation of Hesiod's *Georgicks*, chooses to commend his fellow poet's "deep-searching" methods:

> Whose work could this be, Chapman, to refine
> Old Hesiod's ore, and give it us; but thine,
> Who hadst before wrought in rich Homer's mine?[25]

Chapman's translation of Hesiod is dedicated to none other than Francis Bacon, a writer whose entire project to advance human knowledge rests upon the conviction that "the truthe of Nature lyeth hydde in certaine deepe mynes and caves" in order to be "found out" by men. Yet while Bacon is ultimately skeptical of an excessively meticulous, Democritean attention to natural recesses and subtleties, Chapman experiences a "rapture of delight in the deepe search of knowledge," as he puts it in the preface to his *Shadow of Night*.[26]

Hariot's "bottomlesse" knowledge is the perfect instrument for probing the "deep mines" of Chapman's texts, and "deep-brow'd" Homer its most appropriate object. Throughout his prefatory material, Chapman works to create an illusion of textual depth, using perspectival metaphors to represent the allied poetic virtues of intellectual profundity and rhetorical inscrutability. Rather than create a text which will "prostitutely shew them her secrets, when she will scarcely be lookt upon," Chapman obliges his readers to mine his texts, thus conferring upon his writings an imperceptibility and an opacity that mimic nature as viewed by the atomist or the metallurgist.[27]

Chapman readily admits that his texts are "accounted darke and too much laboured" by many of his readers, yet these very qualities guarantee their difficulty and exclusivity. In his embarrassingly snotty preface to *Ovids Banquet of Sence*, Chapman dismisses the "profane multitude" of readers and "onlie consecrate[s] my strange Poems to these serching spirits," a sentiment he recapitulates in his preface to *Achilles Shield*, which likewise offers itself only to the most penetrating audience. Addressing himself to "you [who] are not every bodie," he scorns those readers who are not "comprehensible of an elaborate Poeme."[28] Chapman constructs e*labo*rate poetry in the most literal sense of the term – intricate, detailed, but also requiring the labor of its readers.

Chapman's idea that Hariot's telescope might prove his perfect reader is one of many contemporary descriptions of perspective glasses that implicates such devices in explicitly literary fantasies, fantasies about readers able to make out distant or obscure texts. In his *Magia Naturalis*, Porta describes a perspective glass which enables its user to read an edition of the Gospel of Saint John "writ so smal, in so litle place, that it was no bigger than a small pimple," while Thomas Digges relates how his father Leonard used "proportionall Glasses" in order to "discover things farre off, [and] read letters" up to seven miles away.[29]

The earliest reports of magnifying lenses focus insistently upon texts or letters, rather than planetary bodies, as their objects of scrutiny. Moreover, the texts singled out by these early telescopes are often either secret documents or "great works" such as Homer and the Bible. The context of one of the first appearances of the word *perspicil*, one of a number of terms used to refer to perspective glasses during the period, reveals how such devices reproduce the deep-searching reader imagined by Chapman. In Tomkis' *Albumazar*, one character offers another a demonstration of the instrument: "Sir, 'tis a perspicil . . . With this I'll read a leaf of that small *Iliad* . . . twelve long miles off."[30] Alluding to the miniature editions of Homer's *Iliad* analyzed in the second half of this chapter, Tomkis mocks the celebrated illegibility of Homeric texts, texts whose interpretive difficulties are compounded by the relative obscurity of ancient Greek and by the challenge of developing a legible Greek typeface.[31] One common solution during the sixteenth century is to print Greek texts entirely in capital letters, thus magnifying them like *Albumazar*'s perspicil. Envisioning Homer's texts as virtually unreadable without the mediation of instruments, *Albumazar*'s shrunken, then amplified, edition of the *Iliad* also illustrates how optical devices refract the humanistic impulse to clarify and enlarge upon, but also perhaps to dwarf, classical texts.

By supplanting the ubiquitous leitmotif that shortsighted moderns must stand upon the shoulders of giants in order to see further, optical devices diminish the perceived discrepancy in perspective between Renaissance humanists and their classical predecessors. It is thus with a "digression on eyeglasses" that Constantijn Huygens frames a debate over the relative intellectual achievements of ancients and moderns in his *Autobiography*, in which he cites spectacles and other optical instruments as proof of modern superiority.[32] Sharing Chapman's disdain for "perviall" texts, Huygens praises the new optical devices for discovering a "new world" of objects that "elude all human eyesight." For Huygens, the appeal of the microscope is that it creates dark conceits, texts whose interpretations have yet to be revealed: "satiated with the wonders of nature that up till now have been obvious to everyone . . . we are led into this second treasure-house of nature" by the view afforded through the microscope.[33] Yet while it affords us an unfamiliar view of nature, the microscope is limited in that, as Bacon observes in the *Novum Organum*, it is "only useful for looking at very small things." By focusing our vision solely upon "fine details," the microscope blinds us to a wider perspective from which to observe natural processes – precisely why Democritus, Bacon's exemplar of atomistic ways of seeing, would have "jumped for joy" at the invention of the microscope.[34] As visual and pedagogical models for a microscopic hermeneutic that privileges intense scrutiny, glasses exemplify the perspicacious reader but also caricature him, emblematizing his biased interpretations or his obsessive attention to "exact knowledge about minute details of ancient texts," as Grafton describes the reading strategies of the fifteenth-century scholar Buonaccorso Massari.[35] This is certainly the implication of Jan van der Straet's engraving *Conspicilla* (see the cover of this book) in which virtually everyone in the scene sports eyeglasses, their own eyes eerily obscured from view. While the text accompanying the engraving boasts that spectacles have illuminated the dark mists before our eyes ("quae luminum obscuriores detegunt caligines"), the figures themselves suggest otherwise: a man in the right foreground holds a book within inches of his face, while a figure in the background walks with a dog and cane, reflecting the incurable blindness of those around him. Optical instruments can mitigate the limitations of human sight, but they can also magnify the minute irregularities of objects around us and increase our awareness of the imperfection of our own instruments of sight.

Optical devices both correct and perpetuate the defects of human vision: the microscope allows its users to "see and discover the smallest objects and the subtilest," as one seventeenth-century writer describes it, but it also reproduces, and even aggravates, the strain of a myopic gaze. In a 1622 treatise on eyesight, Richard Banister describes nearsightedness in terms of the excessive studiousness of a zealous reader: those who suffer from myopia "are constrained when they reade, to look very nigh, imagining oftentimes that they behold little bodies, like to flies, or motes which flie in the aire, as wee see it happeneth to those which have looked very long on their bookes."[36] Akin to the excessive diligence of the "deepe searching" reader, shortsightedness is not the opposite of sight but rather its constant companion. According to Chapman, Hariot's "comprehensive eye" shows "cleare / What true man is, and how like gnats appeare," and it illuminates "this lumpe of blindnes . . . this despisde, inverted world." Optical devices oblige their Renaissance users to confront human frailty, exposing an "inverted world" in the most literal sense when their lenses reflect figures with "their heades downwardes, and theyre feet upwardes, theire righte hande turned to theyre lefte hande" as William Bourne explains.[37]

According to Percy, the discipline of optics ideally aims to "solve all diversities of appearances to the eye" by normalizing visual distortions. Yet in practice, Renaissance optical devices augment the errors and irregularities of human vision, turning the outside world into a veritable fun house by making an object seem "less in bignes, then yt ys" according to Bourne, and another "small thynge to seeme bigge."[38] Even those devices designed to improve eyesight possess liabilities that offset their potential value: Bacon observes that magnifying spectacles make visible the "latent and invisible fine details of bodies, and their hidden schematisms and motions," so that objects appear larger but also more flawed and individuated. Under a microscope, Bacon argues, "a straight line drawn by a pen or pencil is perceived . . . to be quite irregular and crooked."[39] In this respect, the microscope's magnifying capacity is an asset, at least insofar as it draws our attention to those "crooked" or aberrant aspects of nature which are the cornerstones of Baconian scientific inquiry. Moving from particular observations to general principles, Bacon's method focuses upon nature's latent details, thus inverting the priority between large and small by granting the least discernible phenomena the greatest evidentiary authority: "meane and small things discover great, better than great can discover the small: and therefore *Aristotle* noteth well, *that the nature of every thing is best seene in his smallest portions*."[40] This conviction leads Bacon to embrace a group of particulate rhetorical and intellectual techniques such as the "knowledge broken" of the aphorism, a form designed to guide us through the similarly compact and fractured world of nature's subtleties, its "minute worms," saffron threads, drops of ink, and "gilded wire." Yet by focusing our eye upon minutiae, optical devices and the particulate techniques and rhetorical strategies that mimic them can also breed that "meticulous subtlety" so abhorrent to Bacon.[41]

The first two installments of Chapman's Homer, *Seaven Bookes of the Iliades* and *Achilles Shield*, are both printed in 1598.[42] While also an attempt to reproduce what Chapman assumes to be the originary, pre-Lycurgan state of Homeric epic "disseuered into many workes," his dissection of Homeric epic into its constituent parts is a response to the daunting size and density of Homer's text. Virgil's *Aeneid*, which only contains "twelve imperfect bookes," is dwarfed by Homer's "eight and fortie perfect" according to Chapman's reckoning, a length that demonstrates the fantasy of Albumazar's perspicil, with its capacity to magnify an illegible, tiny *Iliad*, to reflect the anxieties of Homer's Renaissance readers. In one of the prefaces to his 1611 edition of the *Iliad*, Chapman recounts an ancient legend about "a Library in the Pallace of the king at Constantinople that contained a thousand a hundred and twentie bookes, amongst which there was the gut of a dragon of an hundred and twentie foote long in which, in letters of gold, the *Iliads* and *Odysses* of Homer were inscribed."[43] Both magnified and condensed by its odd container, this rendition of Homeric epic concretizes Chapman's own dilemmas as a translator as well as the limitations of his readers, unable to comprehend Homer except in reductive and diminished form.

Chapman also begins by translating *Achilles Shield* because this famous fragment from Book XVIII of the *Iliad* exemplifies a group of rhetorical strategies that enable Chapman and his readers to follow Bruno's advice and "contract [themselves] into an atom." It is Chapman's distaste for obvious or "perviall" texts that informs his decision to begin with one of the densest, most tightly packed morsels of epic poetry, a passage that, according to George Sandys, is virtually impervious to critical elucidation.[44] In his commentary upon Book XIII of Ovid's *Metamorphoses*, which depicts the contest between Ajax and Ulysses for Achilles' shield, Sandys repeats the objections of critics who find the shield "too heavy" but also "mysticall" and "not . . . to bee penetrated." What to Sandys is impenetrable is, for Chapman, an exemplary model of the rhetorical principle of *multum in parvo* which demonstrates that paradox because it is a brief fragment that comprises more than the *Iliad* as a whole. As W. J. T. Mitchell has noted, *Achilles Shield* is "larger than the epic in which it is contained" such that "the entire action of the *Iliad* becomes a fragment in the totalizing vision provided by Achilles' Shield."[45] Chapman himself implies as much in his preface to *Seaven Bookes of the Iliad*, arguing that the brief extracts of Homer he offers are, like the results of an alchemical distillation, denser and more concentrated than a longer text: there is "so much quintessence to be drawne from so little a project," he writes, that his 1598 translations "will aske as much judgement to peruse worthily as whole volumes of more *perviall* inventions."[46]

By testifying to the existence of the *multum in parvo* as a physical principle of matter, the Brunonian atomism espoused by Hariot and Warner confirms Chapman's valorization of small but "imperviall" textual fragments such as *Achilles Shield*. Bruno's theory of matter posits the existence of three *minima*, monad, atom, and point: these *minima*, or minimum units of mathematical and physical being, are conceived of as the first principles of existence, and they coincide with "the ultimate maximum, the all-embracing one."[47] As suggested by the frequent allusions to a copy of the *Iliad* inscribed in a nutshell or on a grain of rice, Homeric epic satisfies

Bruno's notion that the antipodal realms of the infinitesimal and the infinite coincide. Chapman recognizes that Homer reigns as king of infinite space even when he is bounded in a nutshell: *Achilles Shield* shows Homeric epic to possess a *minima* and a *maxima* that converge, thus turning topsy-turvy the relationship between the monumental and the minute.

Renaissance fantasies of reading Homeric epic through the magnifying lens of the telescope, written on the hide of a giant dragon, or transcribed *in parvo* on a grain of rice reveal the extent to which the challenges inherent in reading and translating Homer are imagined in spatial or perspectival terms. In his prefaces and glosses, Chapman associates Homer with heavy or voluminous objects – the "hard heights" of a mountain, a monumental statue, a "bottomlesse fountaine," a burdensome load impossible to lift "by my weake arme." Chapman's effort to "compass" Homer in English, all the more formidable given the failed efforts of Thomas Wilson, Thomas Drant, and Arthur Hall earlier in the century, is repeatedly formulated in terms of physical or magnitudinal problems, problems to be rectified by scientific instruments or techniques. Calling upon Hariot as "you whose depth of soule measures the height, / And all dimensions of all workes of weight," Chapman suggests that the "rich mine of knowledge" preferred by Homer is better explored by the piercing eye of his telescope than by the scrutiny of the humanistic scholar. Famously meticulous about the accuracy of his instruments, Hariot brings to Chapman's Homer the "eagle eyes" of the legendary Lynceus, his optical devices providing the proper perspective from which to read – not "for a few lynes with leaves turned over capriciously in dismembred fractions, but throughout – the whole drift, weight, and height of [Homer's] workes."[48]

Chapman views *Achilles Shield* as the embodiment of a specifically Homeric kind of rhetorical virtuosity: the ability to represent a large amount of matter in a small space. Paraphrasing Jean de Sponde's commentary to his 1583 edition of Homer, Chapman praises the compact space of *Achilles Shield* for its capacity to contain "the universall world . . . so spatious and almost unmeasurable, [in] one circlet of a shield." Chapman's English contemporaries likewise focus upon the shield's analogical, macrocosmic quality: Thomas Heywood calls the "orbicular shield" "massie," a "globe-like compasse" that depicts "a thousand sundry objects made by art," while Sandys describes the "orbicular forme of the shield" as containing "the whole world."[49] Evoking the shape and density of a globe, *Achilles Shield* blurs the distinction between textual and technical object. Its rhetorical virtuosity mirrors the perspectival and spatial skills exercised by Hariot and Hues in their designs for the construction of globes – artifacts that reproduce the universe in minute and proportional detail. "None like Homer hath the world enspher'd," writes Chapman in his dedicatory sonnet to Robert Cecil, praising in one breath the shield, the copiousness of Homeric epic, and the poet's mastery of a divine "Proportion, that doth orderly dispose . . . / Till all be circular, and round as heaven."[50]

Singling out *Achilles Shield* for the "high serches" of Hariot's "serious eyes," Chapman makes an implicit analogy between the scrutiny required to read Homer's ekphrasis and the magnifying powers of the telescope.[51] Chapman regards the shield as a synecdoche for Homeric epic – a "little circlet" which contains, in contracted form, all the attributes of the larger text. Regarding *Achilles Shield* as a "dismemberd fraction" which represents the "whole drift" of Homer, Chapman's critical strategy resembles what has come to be called close reading, a technique of interpreting an entire text by enlarging upon brief yet intricate passages. Ekphrasis and close reading both imagine texts as well-wrought urns, elaborate artifacts designed to be subjected to the magnifying lens of the perspicacious reader. Demanding a shift in focus from the whole to the part, ekphrastic texts privilege the "observation of particulars," encouraging atomistic habits of thought and often inviting intense scrutiny from their fictional Renaissance readers.[52] Spenser's Britomart and Shakespeare's Lucrece are both transfixed in front of *tableaux vivants*, ekphrases comparable to *Achilles Shield* for their capacity to "beguil[e] attention, char[m] the sight." The ekphrastic object absorbs its beholder with detail: Britomart spends almost an entire canto of Book III of *The Faerie Queene* "beholding earnestly" the walls of the House of Busyrane to satisfy her "greedy eyes," while Lucrece "gaz'd, and gazing still" at a depiction of the Trojan War.[53]

Ekphrastic description is bound up with the construction of a perspicacious reader or beholder intent upon discerning details. Hidden behind his spear, the image of Achilles studied by Lucrece is mostly "left unseen, save to the eye of mind: / A hand, a foot, a face, a leg, a head / Stood for the whole to be imagined."[54] The "conceit deceitful" of Shakespeare's Achilles involves foreshortening, the painterly illusion of manipulating perspectival space such that a part represents the whole. In his 1612 *Graphice*, Henry Peacham defines foreshortening as "when by art the whole is concluded into one part . . . the rest imagined hid." By contracting large objects into a small space, foreshortening "represents many things in a little roome," creating an illusion of depth and plenitude.[55]

Chapman rhetorically reproduces the foreshortened images of the painter by fostering an illusion of shadowy depth. In his preface to *Ovids Banquet of Sence*, Chapman explains how the "absolute poet" must create the appearance of profundity: he must "lymn, give luster, shaddow, and heightening," thus duplicating the painterly *chiaroscuro* which modulates between shadow and light.[56] Particularly amongst late sixteenth-century neo-Stoics, who regard textual obscurity as a means of focusing and exercising the intellect, foreshortening is the visual equivalent of the opacity and obliquity cultivated by writers such as Tacitus and Seneca. Lipsius describes how he modeled his own style upon the foreshortened images of the painter Timanthes, while Joseph Hall compares the brevity of Tacitus to miniature portraits and to "worlds of Countryes described in the compasse of small mappes," a technique of projection, or cartographic foreshortening, studied by Hues and Hariot.[57]

Influenced by the neo-Stoicism popularized in England during the 1590s, Chapman appreciates depth as an aesthetic virtue and conceptualizes his own rhetorical obliquity in perspectival terms.[58] His ideal reader is the humanistic equivalent of the late sixteenth-century readers of mathematical and scientific texts who rectify the "perviall" quality of their texts according to the rules of perspective. In his translation of Euclid's *Elements*, Henry Billingsley affixes paper tabs to the diagrams in Book XI, the introductory chapter on geometrical solids or "bodely figures," so that his readers can "erect perpendicularly" the forms described in each proposition and "more clearly conceive the . . . construction and demonstration" of each proof.[59]

Chapman praises Percy as one such "deepe searching" reader, an attribute intimately related to the Earl's scientific activities.[60] In particular, Percy's construction of an "elaboratorie," as the space was commonly called during the period, acts as a site for exercising "deepe searching" intellectual strategies, a space whose very etymology reveals its affinities with Chapman's elaborate, labor-intensive, poetry. In the early seventeenth-century vocabulary, to elaborate is to perform something painstakingly or minutely, "to worke exactly, doe a thing fully, and finely."[61] Works of poetry can be elaborate, such as Chapman's "elaborate poeme" of Homer or his version of Hesiod, "translated elaborately out of the Greek." Technical objects are also often described as elaborate: Burton mentions "those elaborate maps of Ortelius, Mercator, Hondius, &c" in his *Anatomy of Melancholy*, and Tycho Brahe boasts of the "elaborately constructed [elaborare constitui]" astronomical instruments made in his laboratory at Uraniborg.[62]

In each instance, the emphasis is upon a careful assembly of words or objects, a process of intricate composition that links the rhetorical virtuosity of the poet or translator to the techniques put to use in the Renaissance elaboratorie – a space which is Homeric in origin. Subterranean spaces like the underground workrooms of Brahe's Uraniborg or the "large and deep caves" in Bacon's Salomon's House evoke the "hollow cave" where Hephaestus spends nine years making "a number of well-arted things, round bracelets, buttons brave, / Whistles, and Carquenets." The Renaissance laboratory legitimates techniques whose semantic and technical roots lie in the *daidala* of Hephaestus' furnace – the coiled chains and rings, Thetis' "exceedingly elaborate" footstool, and the "dancing place / All full of turnings" depicted on Achilles' shield, an object whose own textual and technical complexity testifies to the Homeric origins of the association between rhetorical and technical virtuosity.[63]

The technical skills of the Renaissance *elaboratorie* privilege an attention to detail that resembles the "perfect eye" demanded by Chapman. Like Bacon, who writes in "distinct and disjointed aphorisms" in order to arouse his readers' perspicuity and "invite men to enquire farther," Chapman's "disordered Iliads" offer a similar kind of "knowledge broken" by initiating a process of analytical scrutiny to be continued by the reader.[64] Chapman arouses the perspicuity of his readers with *Enargia*, a rhetorical device he defines in his preface to *Ovids Banquet of Sence* as a "cleereness of representation" that bestows upon a text the illusion of "motion, spirit, and life."[65] Chapman compares this dynamic vividness to *chiaroscuro*, the painter's technique of using both light and shadow in order to grant a canvas depth. Like the "skillfull Painter," Chapman explains, the "absolute poet . . . must lymn, give luster, shaddow, and heightening; which though ignorants will esteeme spic'd, and too curious, yet such as have the judiciall perspective, will see it hath motion, spirit, and life."[66]

The key qualities of "motion" and "life" fostered by *Enargia* are explained by Chapman and his contemporaries in terms of the "artificial motions" of machinery. By creating an illusion of motion, *Enargia* approximates the marvelous lifelikeness of machinery, a verisimilitude epitomized, for Renaissance readers, by Homer's description of Achilles' shield. In his preface to *Achilles Shield*, Chapman entertains the idea that the shield *is* a machine on account of its remarkable lifelikeness: the description is "so lively proposde as not without reason many in times past have believed that all these thinges have in them a kind of voluntarie motion, even as those Tripods of Vulcan and that Daedalian Venus αυτοχινητεοσ [autokinetic, or self-moving] . . . for so are all things here described by our divinest Poet, as if they consisted not of hard and solid mettals but of a truely living and moving soule."[67] The nature of Homer's poetic genius is in essence autokinetic: like the self-moving devices designed by Hephaestus, the tripods and "handmaids of gold" that move with "strengthes and motions voluntary," the poet animates his subject with a "free furie."[68] Chapman's analogy between artistic

inspiration and the animation of machinery is by no means unique during
the period: in his *Trattato dell'Arte*, translated into English in the same year
as Chapman's *Achilles Shield*, Lomazzo similarly defines "motion" or *virtù*
as a key criterion of artistic virtuosity: it is the vivacity of a work of art,
its "whole spirite and life." According to Lomazzo, Leonardo Da Vinci is
the artist best able to represent "*motions . . .* as doe most neerely resemble
the life," a quality embodied by his paintings but also by his "artificiall
motions," or machines, devices similar to "those of Daedalus, which
(as *Homer* writeth) cometh to the battel of themselves. Or *Vulcanes Tripodes*
mentioned by Aristotle."[69]

Not merely a "curious" trick of the eye, *Enargia* enforces a "judiciall
perspective" in order to mitigate the subjective nature of the act of reading. Preoccupied with his own status as an object of misconstrual or censure, Chapman conceives of a "perfect eye," a single, impartial perspective
from which to read his texts so as to normalize the eccentricities of his
readers' critical faculties. His preoccupation with "perspective metaphors
and analogies" is attended by a typically Stoic wariness about the dangers
of wavering opinion or unsound judgment. In his *Tragedy of Chabot*, for
instance, Allegre compares his master Chabot to "a picture wrought to optic
reason" in that both are viewed from multiple and competing perspectives:

> And, till you stand, and in a right line view it,
> You cannot well judge what the main form is;
> So men, that view him [Chabot] but in vulgar passes,
> Casting but lateral, or partial glances
> At what he is, suppose him weak, unjust,
> Bloody, and monstrous . . .

Distorted except when viewed from "the right laid line / Of truth," the
anamorphic Chabot symbolizes the "enchanted glass" of a kaleidoscopic
court where value and status are in perpetual flux.[70]

Chapman imagines his own texts as enchanted glasses, anamorphic perspectives that appear distorted without the correct judgment of the deep-
searching reader. Like the glasses described by Bourne, which only show
the "trewe forme and shape of your face, or any thinge, that standeth
directly right against it," Chapman regards his texts as deformed by the
"lateral, or partial glances" of faulty readers.[71] This awry glance is personified by "squint-ey'd Envie," Renaissance culture's allegorized version
of the short-sighted Zoilus, whose vitriolic critique of Homer makes his
name synonymous with biased, malicious criticism. Chapman seizes upon
the ancient grammarian's optical defect as a metaphor for more common

habits of misreading: his strabismus, or squint-eye, a pathology defined in contemporary treatises on ophthalmology as "when the naturall figure of the eye is perverted," or as a "wresting, or writhing, which draweth the sight unequally," symbolizes the reader's failure to penetrate directly into a text.[72] Hariot's singular perfect eye is, of course, the antidote to Zoilus' squint, its focused, piercing stare a corrective to a wall-eyed or myopic gaze that neglects to see objects except through lateral or partial glances.

In the prefaces and dedicatory epistles to his Homeric translations, Chapman imposes an "optic reason" upon his readers. Dismissing his critics by relativizing the oblique perspective from which they judge his work, he strips his detractors of absolute authority: "there is nothing either good or bad, hard or softe, darke or perspicuous, but in respect, and in respect of men's light, sleight or envious perusalles."[73] Singling out those rare readers who interpret his texts from the "right laid line" of vision, rather than by what *Chabot*'s Allegre calls "vulgar passes," Chapman imagines his audience's capacity for judgment as dictated by the laws of visual perspective.

Yet Chapman's optical metaphors obviate the clarity they imply as symbols of perspicuity and judiciousness. Insofar as they relativize the distance or size of their objects, Renaissance optical devices question the very existence of a perfect eye, human or mechanical, thus supplying Renaissance writers, particularly those with skeptical inclinations, with compelling metaphors for the fallacies of the human understanding. Cornelius Agrippa looks to the "affections" and "deceits" of perspective glasses to attest to the vanity of human knowledge, while Donne's "broken glasses show / A hundred lesser faces" to symbolize the distorting effects of human passion. More than once, Bacon describes intellectual error in terms of the distorting convexities and concavities of a mirror. "Just as an uneven mirror," he writes, "distorts the rays of things, so the mind also, when it is acted upon by things through the sense, treacherously implants and mixes its own nature into the nature of things, in the process of forming its own erroneous notions."[74] Optical devices not only replicate the idols of the mind, but they also exacerbate the deceptive capacity of our senses. Constantijn Huygens finds that telescopes and microscopes impair our intrinsic sense of proportional size and distance: commenting upon the view afforded through Cornelius Drebbel's microscope, Huygens remarks "that the estimation which we commonly make of the size of things is variable, untrustworthy, and fatuous insofar as we believe that we can . . . discern any great difference in size merely by the evidence of our senses." Able to magnify the most distant or minute objects, optical glasses yield an uncompromisingly relativistic view of nature in which no one object is the measure of all others. "It is impossible," Huygens concludes, "to call anything 'little' or 'large' except by comparison."[75]

Like Drebbel's microscope, Hues' globes and Hariot's perspective trunks alter the relative distances and magnitudes of objects, thus eroding the possibility of an impartial perspective from which to read the book of nature. Involving complex formulae of proportional contraction termed "projections," globes demand a virtuoso foreshortening of textual space comparable to Achilles' shield, whose "orbiguitie," according to Chapman, evokes the "roundnesse of the world." In his 1594 *Tractatus de Globis et Eorum Usu*, a treatise written to accompany a set of terrestrial and celestial globes made by Emery Molyneux, Hues defines a globe or sphere as "an analogicall representation" invented by artificers in order to express "the beautifull and various fabricke of the whole universe" in the miniature form of a "little circlet."[76]

If Hariot's perspective glasses symbolize Chapman's exemplary deep-searching reader, Hues' globes offer Chapman an altogether different lesson in how to read and translate Homeric epic. Globes are texts, engraved and printed by the same artisans responsible for producing books and other printed matter. Furthermore, globes are "analogicall" and ekphrastic texts – a notion which certainly did not escape Donne, for whom globes (like tears, beds, fleas, and well-wrought urns) are symbols for contracting the "whole world's soul" into his poems to make "one little room an everywhere." For Elizabethan and Jacobean fans of the aculeate style, maps and globes are models for what Henry Cuffe refers to as *magnum in parvo*, the rhetorical technique that achieves "much matter in few words, every short golden sentence and particle thereof containing incredible store of most pure substance." In a neo-Stoic *consolatio* printed in 1607, Cuffe compares his terse style, in which the "circuit of a small period, comprehend[s] substance sufficient to fill whole volumes," to the cartographic skills of "cunning *Cosmographers*, [who] draw the whole compasse of the wide *World*, into the narrow precincts of a small *Mappe*."[77] Globes are texts in a more mundane sense as well: products of a burgeoning print culture, Renaissance globes often contain indices, tables, and even prefaces to the reader, such as the passage beginning "ai lectoris [to the reader]" visible on one of Molyneux's terrestrial globes, printed by Jodocus Hondius in 1592, and owned by Henry Percy. The idea of a preface affixed to a globe is delightfully odd, however, since globes are texts without a beginning or ending: like epic, one is obliged to plunge in *in medias res*.

The art of globe-making presents certain technical difficulties which shed light upon Chapman's concerns about producing an English translation of

Homer. Both stereography and translation entail an unavoidable distortion and reduction: globes must radically reduce the size of what they represent without sacrificing detail, and they must replicate the proper proportions of the original, a task that speaks to Chapman's own considerations as a translator as he weighs them in his prefatory material. Hariot and Hues are both troubled by the representational challenges of globe-making – the difficulty of maintaining an adequate sense of detail in a small space, as well as the difficulty involved in representing a round object on flat pieces of paper which are then pasted onto a round surface. There is substantial room for error in this two-step process of translation, a concern reflected in Hues' observation that Tycho Brahe has made a "coelestiall globe . . . so coldly and elaborately framed and every way exactly answering it selfe."[78]

Globes require translating a three-dimensional space onto a two-dimensional surface and then back onto a three-dimensional surface, the "round ball" which, as Donne observes, "quickly make[s] that, which was nothing, all." Round objects will never quite translate onto a flat surface, however, and Renaissance geographers and mathematicians grapple with various ways to eliminate the distortion. Like Hues, Hariot participates in this project: after having studied the "lately reformed Mappes, Globes, Sphaeres, and other Instruments" at Oxford with Richard Hakluyt in the late 1570s, Hariot worked for Ralegh, during which time he became interested "in the problems of stereographic projection, of translating the globe's surface on to a two-dimensional surface, and the reverse."[79] Despite Hariot's preoccupation with the accuracy of his instruments, the task proved impossible, for while the distortions of any given projection can be mitigated, they cannot be eliminated entirely. In his *Mathematicall Jewell*, Blagrave explains why it is mathematically impossible to reduce a globe into a "plaine forme," since "a flat superficies cannot be equally answerable to a globes superficies in all pointes." Because "there is no affinitie or proportion of a streight line to a crooked, nor of a globe to a plaine," the cartographer's only alternative is to rely upon "the art opticke, commonly called prospective," thus rectifying the incompatibility between straight and crooked lines by means of an optical trick.[80]

Once regulated by the laws of artificial perspective, the distortions of the map and the globe are rationalized by means of a projection, a perspectival grid that "translates" one plane to another, thus partially reconciling the disparity between divergent "superficies." The principal dilemma of stereographic projection is that it demands a compromise between various distorting pressures, none of which can be minimized except at the expense of increasing others. While perfect correspondence is impossible, projection at least regulates the translative errors it cannot otherwise eradicate.

Chapman encounters similar problems of accommodation as he strives to make his translation "consent, / In sense and elocution" with Homer's Greek text. Chapman regards the task of translating Homer as an inevitably reductive process, at its worst resulting in the "impalsied diminution of Homer" by his French translators. One of his deepest concerns is to ensure that his translation preserves the same proportions as the original text, and not to take "more license from the words, then may expresse / Their full compression, and make clear the Author." A good translation is as much a matter of quantity as it is of quality, a difficult matter given the divergent size, or volume, of Greek and English. While Chapman indicts some of Homer's translators as having "fail'd to search his deepe, and treasurous hart," he is every bit as troubled by the physical size of Homeric translations, which err in rendering the text more compact or more attenuated than the Greek original.[81] Struggling to find the appropriate space in which to contain Homeric epic, Chapman vacillates between different verse lengths, using the roomier fourteener for his 1598 *Seaven Bookes of the Iliad*, switching to heroic couplets for the *Achilles Shield* fragment, returning to the fourteener in 1616 for his complete translation of the *Iliad*, and switching back to heroic couplets once more for his complete *Odyssey*.

An even more pressing dilemma for Chapman as translator is that Greek and English are impossible to project onto one another perfectly. The two languages will never correspond fully because, like round globes and flat maps, they are not "answerable" to each other at every grammatical superficies. Chapman scoffs at the fruitless "paines and cunnings" of translators who try "word for word to render / Their patient Authors; when they may as well, / Make fish with fowle, Camels with Whales engender."[82] For Chapman, literal translation yields incongruous joinings, and he uses the Horatian vocabulary of monstrosity to convey the grotesque, hybrid progeny produced by the "distinguisht natures" of the two languages.[83] Like any inflected language, Greek conveys more matter with fewer words than are required to convey the same matter in English. Translating Greek into English thus requires transferring a fixed amount of poetic substance from a larger container into a smaller one without altering the size or density of the original text.

Chapman objects to the forced fit of "word-for-word traductions" and, resistant to the temptation to cram Homer into English, he defends his tendency to "use needful Periphrases."[84] In a prefatory epistle first printed in his 1609 *Iliads*, Chapman launches an extended critique against the "forced Glose" of literal translation, especially those French and Italian translators whose "many syllables in harsh Collision / Fall as they brake their necks." Tripped up by too many words and syllables, writers like "grave Salel," who translated the first ten books of the *Iliad* into French in 1555, stumble through Homer's densely packed text like fencers fighting in a studiolo:

> . . . me thinkes, their long words
> Shew in short verse as in a narrow place
> Two opposites should meet with two-hand swords
> Unweildily, without use or grace.[85]

By contrast, Chapman preserves the "free grace" of the original with digressions and periphrases, occupying Homer's text in a manner which Jonson likens to a colonial venture:

> such passage hast thou found, such réturns made,
> As, now, of all men, it is called thy trade.

It is an apt metaphor for Chapman's struggle to carve out some *Lebensraum* with what he calls his "beyond-sea manner of writing," creating a text so expansive that Keats imagines himself needing the "eagle eyes" of Cortez to scan its oceanic depths.[86]

The challenge of producing a translation of Homer that preserves the plenitude of the Greek text is answered by the keen interest Renaissance culture manifests in creating and imagining minute versions of the *Iliad* and the *Odyssey*. The second half of this chapter unravels the threads of an interrelated group of objects and texts that verbally, visually, or mechanically reproduce Homer's texts in contracted or miniaturized forms. Miniature objects such as the Iliad-in-a-nutshell, the parodic miniaturizations of the *Iliad* by the pseudo-Homeric *Batrachomyomachia* and its Renaissance imitations, and the "privy" version of Homer in Harington's *Metamorphosis of A JAX* all serve as vehicles for privileging the kind of scrutiny exemplified by Hariot's perfect eye. The artifice particular to inscrutable objects, from miniaturized mechanical devices and minute insects to Homeric minuterie, works to cultivate "subtlety," a complex quality central to the intellectual and aesthetic sensibilities of Chapman and his age.

The enthusiasm for diminutive reproductions of Homer is nowhere more evident than in the numerous Renaissance allusions, often based upon Pliny's description, to a minute volume of the *Iliad* "written in a piece of parchment, which was able to be couched within a nut-shel."

Pliny's account of the Iliad-in-a-nutshell appears in a chapter of his *Natural History* that furnishes various "examples of good Eie-sight," such as a man who could "see and discerne out-right 135 miles," and works by artists skilled in minuterie – a model ship "no bigger than a little bee might hide it with her wings," or Callicrates' tiny, ivory ants.[87]

References to the Iliad-in-a-nutshell surface in a bafflingly wide variety of Renaissance texts, from encyclopaedic works of natural philosophy by Cardano and Burton to courtesy literature and epigrams. Frequently denigrated as trivial or excessively artful, minutiae such as the Iliad-in-a-nutshell reflect the preciosity or idleness of their owners. Thomas Powell, whose 1661 *Humane Industry: A History of Most Manual Arts* provides accounts of various technical minutiae, acknowledges that while "these knacks are but little useful, and take up more time then needed to be lost, yet they discover a marvelous pregnancy of wit in the Artificers."[88] Occupying the vacant hours of idle emperors or aristocrats, minute devices are both symptom and cure for an epidemic ennui that finds solace in the self-absorbing contemplation of excessively intricate objects. Burton prefaces his catalogue of mechanical devices that "rectify" melancholy with that "elaborate and curious buckler made by Vulcan," identifying the compact space of Achilles' shield as the ancient prototype for the trifling gadgets that crowd the Renaissance *Kunstkammer*. Providing comfort for the death of Patroclus, the shield makes Achilles "infinitely delighted" in the same way that "artificiall workes, perspective glasses," and the making of "mappes, modelles, dials, &c" are "intricate and pleasing" to the Jacobean melancholic.[89] The cramped, detail-packed spaces of elaborate devices (mechanical or rhetorical) fill a metaphysical emptiness, their inutility emblematic of the idle frivolity of their users.

Miniature objects exemplify a technical virtuosity that, insofar as it symbolizes the *plenitudo potestatis* of sovereign power, is easily harnessed to absolutist ideologies. As Powell observes with respect to the pendant watches "made in the Collet or Jewel of a ring" owned by Charles V and James I, "there is more Art and Dexterity in placing so many Wheels and Axles in so small a compass."[90] Even the most toy-like devices, such as the ring dials designed by John Cheke and William Buckley for the young Edward VI and his sister Elizabeth, service explicitly absolutist fantasies as symbols of the future monarchs' consolidated, sovereign power. Several of the more than one hundred clocks and watches in the inventory of the Emperor Charles V's possessions after his abdication are miniatures set into rings and cameos. King James I, Emperor Rudolf II, and other heads of state also collect miniature devices; according to contemporary accounts, Charles I even took a small silver watch dial, made by Richard Delamain, to his own execution, handing it over moments before his death to be given to his son as if the instrument held the distilled essence of sovereign power in its small compass.[91]

While one might view the Iliad-in-a-nutshell as an effort to depreciate Homer's text by diminishing its magnitude, the technique of miniaturization has the opposite effect, condensing the text into a smaller physical space in order to allow it to occupy a larger symbolic space. In another story from Pliny, paraphrased by Chapman in the preface to his 1611 *Iliads*, Alexander the Great places the infinite riches of "Homer's bookes" into a casket so that "the most precious worke of all men's minds / In the most precious place might be preserv'd."[92] Like Alexander's casket, the nutshell acts as a reliquary, protecting the *Iliad* from the violence of reductive interpretation.

The Iliad-in-a-nutshell is also a virtually illegible text, and its small size exaggerates the difficulty involved in reading Homer. Apart from books intended for children, it is only the most imposing or ubiquitous texts, such as Homer and the Bible, which are commonly rendered in minute forms during the Renaissance. Texts such as Robert Greene's 1″ by 1.25″ *Tale of Troy* (1604), or editions of the Lord's Prayer written on pennies or in shells, confirm Susan Stewart's argument that while minute writing diminishes its object in size, "the labor involved multiplies, and so does the significance of the total object."[93] An object requiring great discernment to make and read, the Iliad-in-a-nutshell reproduces the difficulties of reading Homeric texts, for its unreadability underscores the scrutiny required to penetrate the layers of allegorical meaning that Chapman refers to as Homer's "depth."[94]

Sixteenth-century encyclopaedic scientific texts such as Cardano's *De Subtilitate* (1553), Guido Pancirolli's *De Rerum Memorabilium* (1599), and Porta's *Magia Naturalis* (1589), all of which contain chapters or extended passages on technical minutiae, follow Pliny's lead in treating miniature objects as evidence of excellent eyesight in the maker or the beholder. What unites these otherwise disparate objects into a discrete category is that, like Chapman's "serching" texts, they exercise intellectual faculties of discernment. Pancirolli describes Callicrates' ants as "hardly legible" creatures that "by reason of their exquisite and extreme Exility, do almost fly the sight."[95] This exility, or fineness, nurtures the perspicuity prized by the Stoics, so much so that Plutarch mentions Callicrates' ants alongside the sharp-sighted Lynceus in his satiric account of the super-subtle logic of Stoic philosophers, who "wind out of these difficulties and untie these knots . . . verie subtilly and valiantly."[96]

In the culture of the Renaissance court, miniature machines nurture the key courtly virtue of subtlety, or *acutezza recondita*. In *The Compleat Gentleman*, inscrutable devices including a nutshell *Iliad*, a "cherry stone cut in the form of a basket" containing fifteen pairs of dice, Callicrates' ants, "and other suchlike small creatures of ivory" function in a manner similar to the "conceits of wit and pleasant invention, as ingenious Epigrams, Emblemes, [and] Anagrams" endorsed by Peacham as the proper sphere of the Jacobean gentleman.[97] Minute and compact literary devices are the rhetorical counterparts of the diminutive and elaborate technical curiosa described by Peacham: both exercise the wit and dexterity of their makers or beholders.

With a tacit understanding of the correspondences between rhetorical and mechanical subtlety, Renaissance writers use the compact genres of epigrams, emblems, and ekphrases to depict mechanical devices. Epigrammatic accounts of machines are so common, particularly after around 1610, that they begin to assume their own subgenre with particular conventions, specifically the topos of the *multum in parvo*. Many of these "machine epigrams" are indebted to one ancient prototype, Claudian's epigram upon the sphere of Archimedes, which was translated into English three times during the seventeenth century. Archimedes' sphere, or "heaven of small glass [in parvo cum cerneret aethera vitro]," as Henry Vaughan translates the opening line, evokes the structure of the epigram, its translucent and "frail orb" mirroring the literary genre that Puttenham calls "shorte and sweete . . . [and] shews a sharp conceit in few verses."[98] Epigrams about mechanical devices describe their objects as a happy coexistence of brevity and amplitude: Thomas Campion's "De Horologio Portabili [Of a Portable Clock]" describes a miniature clock as it interprets or unfolds time: "time's interpreter, wrought into a little round [temporis interpres, parvum congestus in orbem]," accompanies the poet everywhere, counting the hours with its "moving wheels [mobilius rotulis]." The clock is clearly a metaphor for Campion's epigrammatic style – "congestus," or small but replete. In the preface to his *A Booke of Ayres*, Campion writes that epigrams, like airs, are "in their chief perfection when they are short and well seasoned," but then qualifies that "where there is full volume, there can be no imputation of shortness."[99] What epigrams lack in length, they make up for in depth, their "little rounds" as densely packed as the minute gears of a clock or the crowded surface of Achilles' shield.

Several art historians have argued that ekphrasis involves an "intermedial" rivalry, a *paragone* between the mediums of painting and poetry.[100] Machinery enters into this paragonal contest during the Renaissance, serving as another, rival medium that competes with visual and textual forms of expression. Ekphrastic machines such as pocket watches offer new methods for containing infinite riches in little room, rivaling texts and paintings to achieve an effect of *multum in parvo*. Self-moving devices such as Archimedes' "brasen heaven," Archytas' "wooden dove," and Regiomontanus' iron eagle and fly provide classical and Renaissance poets with an occasion to celebrate an intricacy that operates both textually and mechanically. Archimedes' sphere prompts a "witty epigram" by Claudian, while Archytas' dove, a flying automaton made of wood, is described by Aulus Gellius, and Regiomontanus' automaton is invoked in Du Bartas' *Divine Weekes and Workes*.[101] The machines anatomized by these poems are vehicles for showcasing verbal wit, opportunities for rhetorical, and not mechanical, invention.

The Renaissance attraction to intricate machinery resides largely in the narrative pleasure derived from displaying and describing it. Peacham's descriptions of mechanical devices demonstrate a *plaisir de conter* similar to that which Steven Mullaney identifies in Thomas Platter's 1599 account of Walter Cope's cabinet of curiosities. Platter's travel journal, like contemporary narratives by Hentzner, Waldstein, and Coryate, seizes upon mechanical objects as a means to flaunt the writer's capacity for an extended *descriptio*.[102] Objects such as clocks, *jets d'eaux*, or spinning wheels, all of which feature prominently in the above narratives, challenge the descriptive faculties of these writers, demanding not only a new and exotic idiom but also a Lyncean attention to detail. As both a miniature object and a full text, the Iliad-in-a-nutshell merely condenses into a single, immediate gesture the process by which a technical artifact demands minute, verbal description. The tiny *Iliad* and its kin rival the techniques of Homeric ekphrasis, arousing the kind of wonder expressed by Renaissance readers of Homer, who marvel at the capacity of *Achilles Shield* to contain, in contracted form, the universe of Homeric epic.

It is in precisely these terms that Du Bartas praises Regiomontanus' autokinetic iron fly:

> O devine wit, that in the narrow wombe
> Of a small Flie, could finde sufficient roome
> For all those springs, wheeles, counterpoize, & chaines,
> Which stood in steed of life, and spurre, and raines.[103]

The automaton is marvelous not because it can fly, but rather because of the rhetorical skill of Regiomontanus' "devine wit," which can condense so much matter into a "narrow wombe." Whether or not they are physically small, Renaissance machines embody *copia*, their plenitude often overwhelming to the beholder. The narrator of Francesco Colonna's *Hypnerotomachia Poliphili* persistently suffers from the inability to describe the machines and devices strewn about his dream, even as he delights in the exotic vocabulary of their gadgetry: "with what Cranes, winding beames, Trocles, round pulleys, Capres bearing out devices, and Poliplasies, and drawing frames, and roped tryces, therein being unskilful, I slip over it with silence."[104] When an Italian ambassador visiting the Spanish court in 1571 attempts to describe a clock made by Juanelo Turriano for Charles V, he is overcome by a similar abundance of detail, writing in his journal that "to sum up [the clock] contains so many things that there is not sufficient time to see it . . . or memory to remember it or words to describe it."[105]

Turriano's clock arouses reactions similar to those elicited by the astronomical clock in Strasbourg Cathedral, constructed in the latter half of the sixteenth century and depicted in several contemporary engravings. William Hole, who also engraved the title-pages of Chapman's 1611 and 1616 editions of Homer, produced an illustration of the clock that appears in the 1611 edition of Coryate's *Crudities*. In its copious detail, the image demonstrates how Renaissance machines function like miniatures in provoking verbal and visual narratives which, as Stewart puts it, are "automatically verbose."[106] The textual nature of the clock's intricacy does not elude Burton, who praises "the steeple and clocke at Strasburrough" in the same breath as those "elaborate maps" of Ortelius and Hondius, and the "exquisite descriptions" and "pleasant Itineraries" of Hakluyt, Sandys, and Camden, since each kind of item promises an "infinite delight" with the pleasing variety of objects that it offers.[107]

Like the machines encountered by Colonna's Poliphilo, the Strasbourg clock echoes and mimics the rhetorical challenges of Coryate's travel narrative, a genre which demands a meticulous attention to detail and the assimilation of an Odyssean diversity of experience. Praised as "Britains Perspicil" and as "Britains Ulysses" in the commendatory verses to the *Crudities*, Coryate possesses the scrutiny and prolixity required to record his prolific observations – the very skills needed to narrate an "epic" machine such as the Strasbourg clock. Elaborate machines reproduce the *copia* generated by the travel narrative and even come to resemble the traveler himself, who is transformed into a machine as he churns out a seemingly endless supply of text. Several commendatory epistles to the *Crudities* compare Coryate's verbosity and precision to the steady motion of machinery, depicting the author as a "skrewed engine mathematicall," a "turn-spit jacke," and a "perpetuall motion" whose "industrious Toes" and "ready Fingers" seek out and record a wealth of detail.[108]

Another account of the Strasbourg clock, written in a 1581 letter by Stephen Powle, contends with a different set of narrative difficulties. Powle is overwhelmed by the "rare heith" of the 600-foot tower and its "many and sundry parts," which induce in him a "tremblinge terror." Powle's account offers a nascent glimpse of the Burkeian sublime, producing the emotional state that results from what the eighteenth-century writer calls "greatness of dimension" as well as from "the last extreme of littleness." "When we attend to the infinite divisibility of matter," Burke writes, "we become amazed and confounded at the wonders of minuteness, nor can we distinguish in its effect this extreme of littleness from the vast itself."[109] This is precisely what happens to Powle when he attempts to describe the "divers incredible motions" of the clock: his eyes are "unable to arrest the object . . . which, beinge veary swifte, escapeth," an experience he compares to "lookinge on a whirlinge wheele, wee discerne not the spookes therof, nor on birdes flyinge we see no fethers." Certain that his description falls short of the machine itself, "wherein lie hidden more misteries than I have manifested unto you in theise few lines," Powle must foreshorten the towering clock in order to portray it, asking his reader to augment his incomplete description "with your judgement, which like the skillful geometrician, canne by one smale part proportionably gather the whoale boddie."[110] One can only imagine that the miniature model of the Strasbourg clock, made in 1589 by Isaac Habrecht, would prove that much more trying for Powle's descriptive faculties, since it reproduces all the features and motions of the original clock in a space only around five feet high.

That the intricacy of Renaissance machinery often hinders its technological effectiveness is of little concern given that the chief purpose of such machinery is to exercise intellectual and rhetorical faculties rather than perform physical operations. One striking example is the "Nef," or mechanical ship, made by Hans Schlottheim for the Emperor Rudolf II in about 1580. Ostensibly a clock, the Nef's sole dial, approximately 2.5″ in diameter, is lost among a profusion of distracting detail, so much so that one can barely tell the time amid the throngs of self-moving figures. The Nef is no more a timepiece than is Campion's epigram really about a clock: rather, they are both specimens of the cult of *difficultà* that is a hallmark of the aesthetics of the late sixteenth and early seventeenth centuries.

R. J. W. Evans has argued that one of the chief concerns of the Mannerism of Rudolfine Prague is the "model and its relationship to the real," a preoccupation also evident in the scientific and artistic pursuits undertaken in the court of Henry, Prince of Wales, who was himself an avid collector of model ships, timepieces, and planetary models.[111] Planetary models in particular are prized for their analogical significance within a Neoplatonic framework that views spheres and celestial models as a means of accommodating divine order to the human intellect by translating "heavenly material" into a visible form. Marsilio Ficino regards planetary spheres as proof that "man could also make the heavens, could he only obtain the instruments and the heavenly material, since even now he makes them, though of a different material, but still with a very similar order." Corporeal by nature but divine by analogy, mechanical models invest their collectors and users with "almost the same genius as the Author of the heavens" according to Ficino, and they legitimate notions of kingship predicated upon similarly analogical logic.[112] The prince who plays with model ships or miniature clocks lays bare divine mysteries as well as his own *corpus mysticum*, the transcendent aspect of his twinned nature. Furthermore, in the hands of rulers, mechanical models exemplify the "minute techniques" upon which political power relies during the seventeenth century, exercising its authority by means of what Foucault calls "small acts of cunning" endowed with a "great power of diffusion." As the Nef's heralds and electors, drummers and trumpeters, move in procession before the diminutive, enthroned Emperor who nods to them in acknowledgment, they portend the advent of that "meticulous king of small machines," as Foucault terms Frederick II of Prussia, a ruler whose power depends upon regulating his subjects with a tyrannical scrutiny. "No immensity," observes Foucault, "is greater than a detail."[113]

A good number of the minute devices described by sixteenth- and seventeenth-century writers – Callicrates' pismires, Walchius' iron spider, Regiomontanus' fly, and various accounts of chains and locks made for fleas – assume the form of insects. Insects, whose very name (*insectum*, or cutting up) links them with anatomical techniques of scrutiny and dissection, mediate Renaissance culture's cultivation of a deep-searching reader. Several scholars have noted the Elizabethan fondness for insects in textual and decorative motifs: Queen Elizabeth owned a dress embroidered with spiders, flies, and other insects, a design which mirrors the curious network spun by Acrasia's "subtile web" in Spenser's Bower of Bliss.[114] As minute replicas of human society or as metaphors for the meticulous artifice of elaborate texts, insects are the ekphrases of the natural world, containing a remarkable amount of detail in a contracted space. In his *Natural History*, Pliny marvels at the "industrie and subtilitie of Nature" in making insects: "How hath she bestowed all the five senses in a Gnat? . . . can there be devised a thing more finely & cunningly wrought than the wings set to her body?"[115]

Made newly visible by the microscope in the early decades of the seventeenth century, insects are also the natural counterparts of machines, the elaborate objects through which man recreates and rivals nature's subtlety. Rhapsodizing about the "greatnes half-seen" of nature, who "shuts up her Minuter bodies all / In curious frames, imperceptibly small," the seventeenth-century poet Richard Leigh, in imitation of Du Bartas, compares the intricate "Workmanship" of an insect to the complex network of cogs and wheels in a miniature clock:

> What skill is in the frame of insects shown?
> How fine the threads, in their small textures spun?
> How close those instruments and engines knit,
> Which motion, and their slender Sense transmit?
> Like living watches, each of these conceals
> A thousand springs of life, and moving wheels.[116]

Organic prototypes for the meticulous techniques of Renaissance clock-makers, insects nestle alongside automata, optical devices, and portable scientific instruments in the collections of natural philosophers such as Ulisse Aldrovandi, who according to Findlen sought to elevate the discipline of entomology to a science worthy of a "learned and discerning eye." Their breath and blood invisible to the naked eye, insects resemble automatic machinery in that both occupy a liminal space between the natural and the artificial, the living and the merely lifelike. In the *Kunstkammer* at Schloss Ambras, a collection begun in the 1570s by Archduke Ferdinand of Tirol, insects are displayed inside boxes called *Schüttelkasten*: when the containers are agitated, the animals inside twitch, displaying the same eerily lifelike movements as the "landscapes of automatons" displayed in the same collection.[117]

Exposed to wonders entomological and mechanical, Renaissance visitors to Schloss Ambras or to Aldrovandi's studio receive a two-pronged lesson in perspicuity nurtured by nature and art alike. Like Bacon's "disjoynted" aphorisms, the "disjoyned" wasps' bodies illustrated in entomological texts such as Thomas Moffett's *Theater of Insects* stimulate the critical strategies inculcated by Chapman.[118] Perhaps this is why several sketches of insects in Moffett's *Insectorum sive minimorum animalium theatrum* (1634) are represented as marginalia, occupying the textual space where readers make their minute observations. Moffett's assertion that "there is nothing wherein Nature and her whole power is more seene . . . than in the least creatures of all" is kindled by the same aesthetic and intellectual convictions that arouse his culture's interest in machinery, in difficult or detailed texts, and in Daedalian structures such as labyrinths and winding stairs. The "artificiall composition" of insects' bodies, which Moffett depicts as "sphaericall and heavenly . . . a counterfeit similitude of heaven," is a natural archetype for the "ring composition" or circular narrative of Homeric epic, a shape duplicated in miniature by the "orbicular" form of Achilles' shield with its dancing maze "all full of turnings."[119]

The Renaissance term which links natural subtlety and rhetorical artistry to the structural complexity of mechanical devices is "Daedalian," a near-synonym for intricate, expertly crafted, or cunning.[120] The consummate Daedalian structure is, of course, the labyrinth, a form that offers Renaissance culture a compelling symbol for intellectual difficulty, aesthetic complexity, or trickery. Glossing the figure of Daedalus in his translation of Ovid, Sandys explains that the term "dedalian" refers to any of the "delicate structures" constructed by the "rare artificer," particularly the automated statues that "would goe by themselves." In his allegorical interpretation of the Cretan engineer in the *De Sapientia Veterum*, Bacon similarly interprets Daedalus' labyrinth as a metaphor for the moral ambiguity and intellectual complexity of mechanics by virtue of the structure's "subtilty and divers intricate passages . . . which by the eye of iudgement can hardly be guided and discerned."[121] With their potential to cause confusion and entanglement, Daedalus' subtle devices train Renaissance readers to negotiate the "intricate passages" of texts to seek out threads and clues.

Moffett was a poet as well as an entomologist, and in his *The silkwormes, and their flies* (1599), a verse epistle celebrating the artistry of the silkworm, he invokes Nature as a "Daedalian mouldresse," praising small creatures as well as intricate machines as evidence that "greatest worths in smallest things appeare."[122] Moffett's text is one of a number of Renaissance mock encomia that enlists machinery in extolling the superior artifice of insignificant creatures or objects. The intricacy of machinery and the Daedalian cunning necessary to make and use it permit and encourage the subversion of epic proportions by inverting the priority between large and small, thus breathing new life into the Homeric *agon* between force and cunning. Along with Harington's *Metamorphosis of A JAX* (1596), Peter Woodhouse's *The Flea* (1605), and translations of the pseudo-Homeric *Batrachomyomachia* by William Fowldes (1603) and Chapman (1624), Moffett uses the "infinite subtility" of mechanical devices as a vehicle to travesty and subvert epic principles. Moffett begins his poem with an explicit parody of the opening lines of both the *Iliad* and the *Aeneid*: "I neither sing Achilles' baneful ire, / Nor Man, nor Armes, nor Belly-brothers warres . . . / I sing of little Wormes and tender Flies."[123] Like the "precious place" of a nutshell or of Alexander's chest, Moffett's poem diminishes the *Iliad* while simultaneously demonstrating that "little caskets hold our richest goods." To do so, Moffett invokes Regiomontanus' iron fly, the ekphrastic machine that rivals the rhetorical technique of *multum in parvo*:

> Ingenious Germane, how didst thou convey
> Thy springs, thy scrues, thy rowells, and thy flie?
> Thy cogs, thy wardes, thy laths, how didst thou lay?

Enthusiastically developing Du Bartas' notion that "in smallest things . . . greatest wonders be," Moffett offers a catalogue of intricate devices such as Theodorus' tiny sculpted self-portrait with his "paire of compasses and squire." The description is a self-conscious celebration of the technical virtuosity demanded by minutiae whose details are so "lively made, that one might see them all: / Yet was the whole worke than a flie more small."[124]

The most intriguing item in Moffett's catalogue of mechanical minutiae is an automated flea circus, "made so by art, that art imparted life" by one Gawen Smith in 1586. Like the "exility" of Callicrates' ants or the twitching creatures inside the *Schüttelkasten*, Smith's performing fleas act "like things that were alive": they "skippe" and appear to "let out bloud" from a "secret sheathe."[125] Fashioning tiny chains and locks, the locksmith harnesses the fleas to a miniature coach which they pull like tiny horses. By increasing the power of minute creatures by technical means, Moffett's flea circus operates in conformity with the pseudo-Aristotelian *Mechanical Problems*, which defines a machine as a means to enable things possessing little weight to move heavy weights.[126]

Moffett's *Silkwormes, and their flies* is one of several Renaissance mock encomia which incorporates mechanical power into its parodic rereading of Homeric epic, treating machinery as an aspect of *metis* in that it enhances the power of the weak against a stronger or swifter adversary. Like the paradoxical encomium, which operates by inverting natural hierarchies and collapsing distinctions in size, machinery rearranges the scale of creation by virtue of its capacity to alter the outcome of conflicts between possessors of natural and artificial strength. Chapman calls the pseudo-Homeric *Batrachomyomachia* a "ridiculous poem of Vermin" depicting Greeks and Trojans as frogs and mice but giving them "nobility of birth, valorous elocution not inferior to his [Homer's] heroes."[127] Inasmuch as they assist in the victory of cunning over force, machines and devices play a pivotal role in

Renaissance parodies of epic. In the pseudo-Homeric *Batrachomyomachia*, the mice arm themselves with a variety of found objects including pine needles ("like strong pikes") and walnut shells, used "for helmet" rather than to conceal minute editions of the *Iliad*.[128] As a tiny yet ostentatiously elaborate object, the Iliad-in-a-nutshell is the consummate token of parody, its capacity for magnitudinal inversion and transposition evoking the dislocations of normative size effected by the parodic mode. Samuel Parker thus subtitles his 1700 translation of the *Batrachomyomachia* "Homer in a nutshell," while Thomas Browne includes among the "antiquities and rarities" of the mock cabinet of curiosities in his *Musaeum Clausum* an edition of the "*Batrachomyomachia*, or the Homerian battel between Frogs and Mice, neatly described upon the Chizel bone of a large Pike's Jaw."[129] By enhancing the size and grandiloquence of "ridiculous Vermin," the generic effects of the paradoxical encomium are actualized by the power of a machine such as the microscope to magnify its objects, thus revealing the vast complexity of the smallest creatures. Looking into his microscope, Huygens proclaims that he will "draw my lessons . . . from little flowers, midges, ants and mites," echoing Moffett's promise to "sing of little wormes and tender flies" rather than about gods and heroes. By undermining natural hierarchies, Moffett's text challenges our fixed sense of size in the same manner as Drebbel's microscope when it demonstrates to Huygens that the tiniest creatures "may be so greatly magnified by lenses . . . [and] magnified more by other lenses, and then still by others, and so on endlessly."[130]

Sir John Harington's *A New Discourse of a Stale Subject, or the Metamorphosis of A JAX* (1596) seizes upon the alliance between mechanical power and the parodic, subversive power of the paradoxical encomium. Frequently dismissed as a Rabelaisian trifle propelled by an extended pun on the name of the Homeric hero and "a-jakes," the Elizabethan term for a toilet, Harington's proposal for the invention of a flush lavatory travesties the rhetorical and pictorial conventions of the Elizabethan technical treatise. Its pseudonymous narrator Misacmos (hater of filth) refers to the work as a "fantasticall treatise" in which it is "declared, explaned, and eliquidated, by pen, plot, and precept, how unsaverie places may be made sweet, noysome places made wholesome, filthie places made cleanly." While largely satirical, Harington's work never loses sight of the basic utility of the invention, frequently stressing its "publicke benefit."[131] Like Henry Percy, who worked on a plumbing system for Syon House during the late 1590s, Harington intends his "homely" invention for serious use, having built similar devices at Richmond Palace and in his own home at Kelston several years before writing *A JAX*. The second part of the treatise, *An Anatomie of the Metamorpho-sed A JAX*, was probably written not by Harington but by his personal servant Thomas Combe. Written in the style of a technical treatise, the *Anatomie* provides a do-it-yourself guide for building a rudimentary toilet, complete with engravings: one depicts "Don A JAX house, of the new fashion, all in sunder, that a workeman may see what he hath to do," and on the following page, the device is shown once again, "all put together, that the workeman may see if it be well" (figure 5.1).

The design for "Don A JAX house" works by forcing dirty water "by a small pype" out of the cistern, after which it is "convayed under the seate in the hinder part thereof (but quite out of sight)," while at the same time forcing fresh water into the cistern by a "Cocke or a washer to yeeld water with some pretie strength, when you would let it in."[132] In short, Harington's privy functions according to the hydraulic principles laid down by Archimedes and Hero of Alexandria, and developed by Renaissance engineers, in order to raise water by mechanical means – to drain fens, to divert water from canals, rivers, or wells, or to build garden machinery and automata powered by the forced displacement of water. In Ramelli's *Le Diverse et Artificiose Machine*, more than half of the text's 195 engravings depict machines for raising water, as Ramelli describes again and again, from "low" places to "high" ones.

Raising its lowly subject aloft, Harington's mock encomium functions in a similar manner as his toilet. While the privy works by means of a "force" or plunger that drives water upwards and against its natural course, the encomium uses a comparable force, breaching decorum by elevating a low subject with a high style and "tell[ing] a homelie tale of this in prose as cleanlie." Harington acknowledges the connection between his device and the mock encomium, which seizes upon a base or homely topic and "make[s] it all manerlie." In a prefatory letter, he writes that "I do compare my buildings and my writings together," since both "extoll . . . the basest roome of my house . . . afore the best." The jakes is a species of *metis*, an adversarial power that inverts natural hierarchies between strong and weak and between high and low. Aptly, the "little cost and great facilitie" of Harington's device is modeled upon the inventions of the "rare enginer" Archimedes, famous for his ability to lift heavy weights easily with the help of machinery.[133]

Nowhere do conflicts between natural and artificial strength arise as persistently as they do in Homeric epic, and Harington's privy reenacts one of the most famous Homeric contests between force and cunning, the competition between Ajax and Ulysses for the possession of Achilles' shield. In Book XXIII of the *Iliad*, cited here from Chapman's translation,

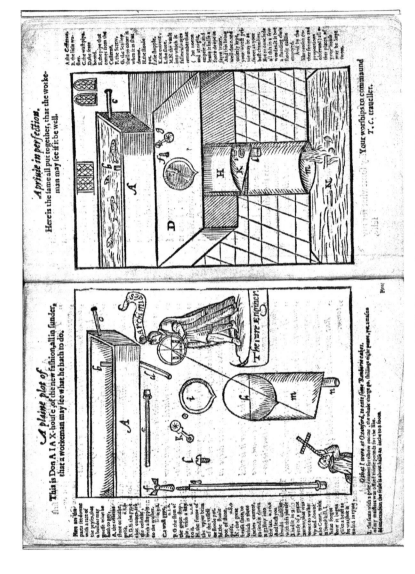

5.1 John Harington, *An Anatomie of the Metamorphos-ed Ajax*, two views of Don Ajax's house

Ajax, "huge in strength," loses a footrace to "craftie" Ulysses, "as huge in sleight," when Minerva trips Ajax so that he tumbles "Amidst the ordure of the beasts," leaving him "all besmear'd," a humiliation that leads him to commit suicide, at which point he is "turnd into a Hyacint." Reinterpreting the "ruthfully smer'd" Ajax as excrement "eliquidate[d]" by its adversary, Harington's toilet restages the footrace in *Iliad* XXIII by recasting Ulysses' cunning as the "device" of the privy, his "sleight" or craftiness symbolized by the toilet's "vaults and secret passages made under ground, to convey away both the ordure & other noisome things." Ajax, in turn, is transmuted into excrement, his metamorphosis into an aromatic flower allegorized in Harington's text by the toilet's capacity (after its own "metamorphosis" or improved addition of flush and seal) to make unsavory odors "sweet" and "wholesome." The jakes thus becomes a new Ulyssean hero, able to flush down his excremental adversary.[134]

Narratives of *metis* in which wit or subtlety triumph over force shape Renaissance culture's understanding of the auxiliary power of machinery, which compensates weaker forces with *engin* and *virtù*. Hephaestus, the lame but technically adept god responsible for crafting Achilles' shield and various automata, grants a mythographic foundation to the alliance between classical narratives of *metis* and Renaissance attitudes towards mechanical power. In Chapman's version of Book VIII of Homer's *Odyssey*, Vulcan's "craft," a translation of Sponde's *techne*, assists and supplements his native defects so that "Lame Vulcan" entraps Mars and Venus, and "the slow outgoes the swift."[135] The mechanically enhanced dexterity of the "both-foot halting" god serves a prosthetic function: his "handmaids of gold" help him walk, thus obscuring his "native lamenes," while the "dancing place" depicted upon Achilles' shield constitutes "a triumph over disfigurement for the smith who cannot dance."[136] For Hephaestus, machinery is quite literally a "prosthetic god," and his technical subtlety the compensatory power of the subjected.

Like his sister Minerva, Hephaestus is a master of spider-like techniques – nets, traps, and spiral bonds that mimic his own circular gait. Powell compares the workmanship of the miniature locksmith Mark Scaliot, who fabricates tiny chains to be "fastened and put about a fleas neck," to the "admirable chains and nets which Vulcan made to apprehend *Mars* in conjunction with his *Venus*, which were so fine and subtille . . . that the wanton Lovers could not see them till they felt them."[137] Lying in wait for Venus and Mars, or ensnaring Hera in her throne, Hephaestus resembles Pliny's spider, who makes webs that are "held and tied fast by knots that cannot be undone."[138] Homer and Ovid both liken the trap laid for Mars and Venus to a spider-web, a "net of wire" which Chapman describes as "pure, as of a spider's loom / The woof before 'tis woven. No man nor God / Could set his eye on it, a sleight so odd / His art shew'd in it."[139] Pretending to return to his furnace while he lies in wait for the adulterous couple, Hephaestus duplicates the cunning of the spider, a creature who, according to Pliny, tends to "retire into a corner so far from the midst, making semblance as though she meant nothing lesse than that she doth, and as if she went about some other businesse."[140] Pliny terms this quality "subtilitie."

Insects, epigrams and emblems, miniature machines, deep-searching readers, and Hephaestus' artifice are united by their mutual cultivation of subtlety. Hephaestus' net is "subtle" in the most literal sense of the word: while the term is used to describe various substances, from delicate particles like sand to the intricacy or complexity of machines, texts, and arguments, subtlety is principally the quality of fineness as applied to threads or wires. Insects, whose small size shows forth nature's subtlety to its best advantage, spin webs which Pliny and Moffett describe, respectively, as "thin and subtil" and "thinne, fine, glystering, and subtile." In the hands of a virtuoso metalworker, subtlety results from a process of drawing out iron or gold so as to be virtually invisible – "like gold to aery thinness beat," as Donne writes in that most attenuated and subtle metaphor of "A Valediction: Forbidding Mourning." Subtle objects are so delicate or rarified that they elude the hand, the eye, or the understanding: Golding describes Hephaestus' "net of Wire so fine and slight" as "much more fine than any handwarpe oofe [*sic*]," while Natale Conti emphasizes its invisibility, "an iron wire so subtle and delicate that it could not be seen [filé de fer si subtil & si delié, qu'on ne le pouvoit veoir]." In French, *subtil* is actually two distinct words: according to Randle Cotgrave's 1611 French–English dictionary, the masculine noun *subtil* is a "kind of small gold or silver thread," while as an adjective *subtil* signifies "subtil, craftie, wilie, wittie, cunning." Since the two senses overlap in English, Cotgrave defines *subtilier* as "to subtilize, extenuate, make thinne, fine" but also "to plot, invent, contrive, devise, imagine, mase."[141]

Applied to objects, subtlety denotes exility, refinement, or anything which, due to its small size or complexity, escapes the sense or the intellect. As an intellectual power, subtlety is the ability to discern whatever is indistinct or obscure. Renaissance educational treatises use the term "subtlety" to describe the particular kind of intellectual acuity capable of perceiving difference or detail, as opposed to the intellect which excels in spotting resemblance. In his *De Tradendis Disciplinis*, Vives distinguishes between "sharp" and "slow" wits in that the former have "very great power in discerning separate and scattered things." Rather than accept "as joined those things which they see together," the sharp wit perceives objects and ideas as divisible, and, according to Vives, is able to "analyse things into their separate parts by a close examination, which is called subtlety."[142]

Subtlety is also used to refer to the intricate skills of the metalworker and the goldsmith. Cellini's *Trattato dell'Oreficeria* uses the term *virtù* to refer to general technical excellence, but *sottigliezza* is the principal laudatory term applied to meticulous procedures such as limning or filigree work (*limatura*) and *lavorare di minuteria* – elaborate, miniature sculptures such as Cellini's own salt-cellar, that virtuoso example of Renaissance goldsmithing.[143] When Chapman defines *Enargia* as the ability to "lymn, give luster, shaddow, and heightening," he engages the idiom of the miniaturist and the goldsmith to articulate his theories of textual subtlety. Chapman adopts the idiom used by Elizabethan limners such as Nicholas Hilliard, describing the "admirable luster" of sharp readers in terms of the opaque and lustrous surface of miniature portraits. In *The Arte of Limning*, Hilliard stresses the importance of drawing "very lightly . . . with a very small pensile, that it scarce at first maye be discerned," and of using "the same discretion to shadow," applying "the pointe of the Pencell with littel light touches." Unlike the painter, the limner uses real gold and silver leaf in order to "give the true lustre" of his object, a technique "which so enricheth and innobleth the worke that it seemeth to be the thinge it selfe."[144]

Chapman aims to reproduce this technique of creating "lustre" in his translations of Homeric epic, verse that "so farre outshin[es]" other poetry that it appears to consist "not of hard and solid metalls but of a truely living and moving soule." Whether they refer to metals or to the figurative threads and lines of texts, techniques such as filing and limning produce a gloss that evokes the golden luster of Achilles' shield, its depiction of men "clad in shining steele" and wearing coats whose "colours did reflect / Glosses like oyle," or Hephaestus' other resplendent artifacts, Achilles' "shining Greaves" and his Curace "that did for light out shine / The blaze of fire."[145] Objects and surfaces which dazzle or refract light are referred to by Homer as *poikile*, a term which means glittering, dappled, intricate, subtle, or evasive. In spite of the extraordinary range of meanings for the term, *poikilos* constitutes a distinct aesthetic and intellectual category in both classical and Renaissance culture. Lomazzo's *Trattato dell'Arte* includes a chapter on "Refracted or Broken Light," addressing the effect of light "as it falleth upon glasses, Christals, water, armour, and such like shining thinges," objects that possess either a "subtile watrinesse" or a "resplendencie and glittering." Yet *poikile* can also denote a crafty person whose subtle evasions produce an "interplay of reflections," a protean identity that wavers like the reverberation of a flame. Fire, light, and glass all exemplify the "shimmering sheen and shifting movement" that is characteristic of *poikile*, thus linking Hephaestus' materials with the attributes of his female companions: Charis, or radiance, and Thetis with her "christall feet."[146]

Chapman's poetic theory is founded upon this key Homeric quality of *poikilos*, his subtle, elusive texts reproducing the variegated radiance and gloss of Achilles' shield. The meaning of the English word "gloss" results from the conflation of two initially distinct words, the Greek γλοσσια (language) and the Old High German for glass: different as they are, both mediums have the capacity to clarify or distort the objects mediated through them. Like an image filtered through a perspective glass, verbal "glossing" enlarges and elucidates its object, but it also distorts meaning with specious arguments or smooth talk. Both attracted to and distrustful of verbal subtlety, Elizabethan and Jacobean writers evoke the techniques of limners, metalworkers, and glaziers to describe the potentially demonic virtuosity of the human tongue. Comparing our instrument of speech to the tool of a metalworker, Ben Jonson praises Shakspeare's "well-turnèd, and true-filèd lines" even as that image of eloquence comes perilously close to that of Spenser's "subtill Archimago," who "could file his tongue as smooth as glas."[147]

In sixteenth- and early seventeenth-century culture, arguments and works of art are termed subtle when deemed too intricate or abstruse, signaling anxieties about artifice, the ruses of specious logic, or the moral vacuity of aestheticism. Bacon describes these "unprofitable subtilitie[s]" as "Copwebs [*sic*] of learning, admirable for the finesse of thread and worke, but of no substance or profite," thus allying Hephaestian *techne* with a category of nugatory objects and practices, including mechanical devices, minuterie, and deliberately obscure texts, known collectively as "vain subtleties." At least two sixteenth-century texts, Montaigne's essay entitled "Of Vaine Subtilties" and a chapter of Cardano's *De Subtilitate* devoted to "uncertain and useless subtleties [subtilités incertaines et inutiles]," both denounce (albeit with a thinly veiled delight) activities and objects "invented out of an ostentation of spirit and understanding, and not for any use [inventées à l'ostentation de l'esprit et entendement, non pour aucune utilité]." From acrostics and water-clocks to the Iliad-in-a-nutshell, these two anatomies of subtlety compile imaginary *Kunstkammern* of objects prized for their "rarenesse" or "difficultie" rather than for "goodnesse or profit."[148]

At the beginning of *De Subtilitate*, Cardano defines subtlety as "that which seems very open and easy, but which is very obscure [(ce que) peut sembler apert & facile, qui est tresobscur]." Predicated upon a discontinuity between outward simplicity and inner complexity, subtlety sets into motion a conflict between appearance and reality, and between the exoteric and the esoteric, that pervades Renaissance culture. Many of Cardano's examples of subtlety generate friction between their outward semblance and inner essence, often by means of an ostentatious display of their inner workings. Among these are self-winding clocks, whose workings are "well-hidden [excellens cachées]," a machine made of glass, to show "the beauty of the work [la beauté de l'oeuvre]" and the anatomical drawings of Vesalius and Da Vinci, which "manifest the excellent imitation of the entire human body [manifeste . . . l'excellent imitation de tout le cors humain]."[149]

As defined by Cardano, the notion of subtlety dramatizes what Katherine Maus has called a "dialectic of vision and concealment," an interplay between interiority and exteriority staged by Renaissance writers through dramatic character, in religious discourse and political philosophy, and through scientific objects and practices.[150] From the fourteenth century onwards, the concept of subtlety reveals and works to refine a triangulation of political, intellectual, and mechanical artifice: Chaucer and Jean de Meun use phrases such as "subtle device" and "subtle engine" to describe mysterious or obscure mechanisms as well as crafty plots, clever intellects, and wily characters such as the "subtile tregetours" of Chaucer's *Franklin's Tale*, one of several Chaucerian texts which demonstrates the intersection of anxieties aroused by mechanical subtlety and those aroused by the ruses of a specifically Homeric *metis*. In *The Squire's Tale*, Chaucer reincarnates that most cunning of Greek engines, the Trojan horse, a device which Caxton later describes as made "so subtylly that wyth oute forth no man coude perceive ne see entree ne yssue."[151] An archetype of pathological interiority, the Trojan horse yokes demonic mechanical virtuosity to Greek cunning. When Chaucer's strange knight arrives at the Mongol court with his Homeric engine, "maad more subtilly" than his audience can comprehend, the onlookers assume the device to be powered by "queynte mirours" and "slye reflexiouns," but they also imagine it to possess a demonic interiority in that, like the "Grekes hors Synon," it contains "men of armes . . . thereinne."[152]

Its mechanical exterior concealing a living interior, the Trojan horse is the quintessence of subtlety. Its composite nature is the inspiration for Renaissance engineers, whose anxious delight at the prospect of eroding the boundary between the human and the mechanical is reflected in designs for tanks, underwater devices, and similar modes of covert transport. An ominous resurrection of the Trojan horse appears in several sixteenth-century editions of Valturio's *De Re Militari*: an anthropomorphic tank, complete with whiskers and tail, reveals an eerie eye peering out from within (figure 5.2).

5.2 Roberto Valturio, *De Re Militari*, whiskered tank

Arabica machina ad expugnationem vrbium, magna & ingens
viris, pontibus, fcalis, variifque inftrumentis bellicis referta.

5.3 Roberto Valturio, *De Re Militari*, fire-breathing dragon

As the final chapter of this book explores at greater length, Renaissance machinery resurrects the classical past, habitually returning to the mythical contrivances of Daedalus, Archytas, Hephaestus, or Archimedes and assuming their antique garb. On stage, in pleasure gardens, and in the arena of war, creatures of myth and legend inhabit machines. A grotto designed by Salomon de Caus contains an automated tableau that restages the myth of Polyphemus and Galatea. A 1536 French edition of Vegetius depicts an underwater diver and his breathing device alongside Neptune, while sixteenth-century editions of Valturio's *De Re Militari* imagine a virtual dragon that breathes real fire, a mechanically sophisticated adversary for the modern St. George (figure 5.3). These machines at once corroborate and supplant the mythological figures they resuscitate, bringing to life the most outlandish fictions of the past. Speaking at the foundation of Gresham College in 1588, Thomas Hood persuades his audience of the utility and dignity of mechanics by arguing that the discipline possesses the power to reanimate classical legend: "these be no fables that I tell," Hood remarks of Homeric automata such as Hephaestus' tripods and Daedalus' statues, for "our present age affirmeth them true."[153] Machinery promises to turn myth into truth as the followers of Daedalus and Hephaestus invent flying machines, robots, and other marvels that once existed only in the poetic imagination.

The fusion of the animate and the inanimate effected by its machinery has the capacity to erode Renaissance culture's most essential and hard-won assumptions about human nature. At times, Renaissance hybridizations of humans and machines expose and censure the inhuman impulses which lurk within Renaissance humanism's own idealized image of humanity, from the technological sophistication of its warfare and the coercive pressures of its intellectual and corporeal disciplines to its political and philosophical instrumentalities. These are the concerns of the next chapter, which argues that Talus, Artegall's iron servant in Book v of Spenser's *Faerie Queene*, exposes the potentially dehumanizing effects of the militarism, the juridical rigor, and the Stoic ideal of invulnerability upon which Spenser's Essexian humanism is partially predicated.

CHAPTER 6

Inhumanism: Spenser's iron man

O wherfore is my steely heart so hard?
Why am I made of mettall unrelenting?

Robert Devereux, 2nd Earl of Essex[1]

Spenser's stated aim in writing *The Faerie Queene* is to "fashion a gentleman," but in Book v he does just the opposite, inventing a character
who, both in body and in spirit, is made of unrelenting metal. Through
Talus, the "yron man" assigned to execute Astraea's "stedfast doome" in her
absence, Spenser questions whether the precondition of humanity is essential or detrimental to the consummation of heroic virtue. In the first four
books of Spenser's epic, we encounter heroes who, howsoever much they
represent moral abstractions, are humanized by their vulnerability. They
succumb to despair and doubt, to the enticements of lust, and to mercy
and pity. Immune to the encumbrances of mortal flesh and the debilities
of a human soul, Spenser's Talus complicates *The Faerie Queene*'s project
to fashion a "gentleman or noble person in vertuous and gentle discipline,"
for his inhuman constitution and his barbarity reveal the potentially dehumanizing effects of that project.[2] As a machine, Book v's iron man is a
grotesque distortion of Spenser's humanistic and chivalric values, undermining *The Faerie Queene*'s valorization of courtliness and heroic action by
pushing those ideals to a literal extreme. While Talus certainly exemplifies
the effortlessness and the fortitude of the perfect courtly instrument, his
disobedience and his lack of capacity for human feeling call into question
the possibility and the desirability of fashioning human beings according
to his iron mold (v.i.12).

Spenser by no means abandons his courtly ideals in *The Faerie Queene*.
Quite the contrary: Book v's disturbing narrative of a political instrumentalism gone awry is followed by the enthusiastic recuperation of courtesy
in Book vi, which smoothes out the previous book's tense treatment of
political instrumentality. Yet the moral dilemmas which arise as Spenser

lays down his troubling ideals of justice in Book V oblige the poet to reevaluate what constitutes "true curtesie," and to differentiate carefully between the civility embodied in Calidore and the virtues attendant upon Book V's champion of Justice (VI.Proem.5). The first canto of Book VI takes great pains to point out that while human affection and *misericordia* may well prove detrimental to Astraea's agents of Justice in Book V, these impulses are absolutely central in upholding Book VI's Arcadian fantasy of courtliness. As Calidore is quick to remind us, Talus' inhumanity is hostile to courtly ideals even if his violence is not, for there is "no greater shame to man then inhumanitie" (VI.i.26). In his confrontation with Briana and Crudor, Calidore threatens to punish those who "breake bands of civilitie" or otherwise bring dishonor to "noble arms and gentle curtesie," thereby justifying brutality as the essential safeguard of civility (V.vi.9). Book VI labors to exonerate courtesy by transcending the instrumentalism of its violence in the name of preserving humanity from its own barbaric acts. Yet as Book V has already demonstrated by means of the strained relationship between Artegall and his iron groom, the instrumental means upholding *The Faerie Queene*'s ethical and political ideals are difficult, if not impossible, to transcend. Thus even as Book V is girded and contained by Book IV's impassioned defense of love and Book VI's appeals to human kindness, the inhumane instruments of Justice demonstrate virtues such as mercy and compassion to be impractical and illusive in the "present time" of Book V.

As a mechanism designed to exact Justice without suffering from the infirmities of human feeling, Talus vexes Spenser's critique of the "Stoicke censours" indicted in the proem to Book IV for their refusal to acknowledge that human affection is an essential component of heroic action. The machinery of Book V, Talus included, both epitomizes and challenges the dangerously seductive ideologies of Stoicism and the militaristic ethos that accompanies that philosophy in late Elizabethan England. Spenser literalizes but also complicates the Stoic fantasy of the iron man in Talus' impenetrable frame: "albe he wanted sence / And sorrowes feeling," Spenser writes of Talus, yet he "did inly chill and quake" (V.vi.9), his tremors corroborating Gordon Braden's argument that Stoic *apatheia* is "continuously and deeply involved with the most paralytic kind of anger."[3] His invulnerable metal body an allegorical embodiment of Stoicism taken to a disturbing and at times absurd extreme, Talus exposes the ethical hazards of the ideologies and tactics that inure the soldier to his own violent acts.

Talus' lust for violence provides a stark contrast to Artegall, whose efficacy as an instrument of Justice is tempered by his capitulation to tenderness and mercy as well as by his confidence in a chivalric code that is peculiarly out of place in his corner of Faerie Land, permeated as it is with brutality and fraud. Yet Artegall's iron groom undercuts the chivalric ideals embodied by his master in various ways. Shunning hand-to-hand combat, Talus engages in the increasingly common siege-style warfare of Spenser's day and performs the military duties not of a living soldier but rather of a war machine, an instrument that threatens to supersede the chivalric knight and thus reveal courtliness to be incompatible with the methods and values of modern militarism.

In an essay on the etiquette of wearing armor, Montaigne laments that the ancient Parthians, "men of yron," exceeded us in "military discipline."[4] The iron man – stronger, more disciplined, and more invulnerable to suffering than his fleshy counterpart – is a commonplace late sixteenth-century fantasy fueled by the militarism of the age and the attendant revival of Stoic philosophy. Out of the carnage of the French Wars of Religion and the Dutch War of Independence emerge new virtues to be cultivated by war, particularly an emotional and physical insusceptibility to war itself. For many neo-Stoic writers of the period, warfare is uniquely suited to exercising the indifference or *apatheia* central to that philosophy. Robert Johnson compares the battlefield to "a Schoole where the body ought to be inured" and taught to "endure all corporall adversities," while Lipsius argues in *De Constantia*, a text composed to "teach survival amid the suffering and chaos" of war, that violent times demand "complete detachment" from all affections, even pity and patriotism.[5]

On both sides of the Channel, the 1570s and 1580s witness the rise of what William Sherman has called "military humanism." In addition to emphasizing practice and discipline, military leaders including Essex, Leicester, and (in Holland) Prince Maurice of Nassau encourage the enthusiastic revival of classical works of military tactics, paving the way for the emergence of the genre that Gerhard Oestreich refers to as "politico-technical literature."[6] Military treatises by men such as Thomas Digges, who was Leicester's musket-master in the Low Countries, voice Fluellian defenses of the "disciplines of the pristine wars of the Romans." Despite the "late invention of Artillerie," Digges writes, "the Antique Romane and Grecian Discipline Martiall doth farre exceed in Excellency our Moderne," a sentiment he may have inherited from Lipsius, whose *De Militia Romana* argues that while guns have superseded ancient "engines of battery," an ancient army could still rout a modern one with ease.[7]

The conviction that modern soldiers lack the discipline of their classical ancestors shapes contemporary debates regarding the relative efficacy of the gun and the crossbow, a controversy that reaches a fever pitch during the early 1590s as Spenser writes the latter three books of *The Faerie Queene*. England's battle of the ancient and modern instruments begins in 1574 with Barnabe Rich's *Right excelent and pleasaunt dialogue, betwene Mercury and an English souldier*, in which the god of cunning inventions argues that the superiority of the musket has "altogether altered" the "order of the wars." Although, as Rich acknowledges, sixteenth-century guns are only moderately effective, they are nonetheless useful because "the strength of man is generally decayed," and he must therefore rely increasingly upon machinery in order to supplement his dwindling powers.[8] Advocacy of the musket grows in the last decade of the century as professional soldiers such as Roger Williams, a distinguished servant of Leicester and of Essex in the Netherlands and France respectively, witness first-hand the efficacy of modern weapons. In his 1590 *Briefe Discourse of Warre*, Williams claims that 500 musketeers could easily vanquish three times that number of archers, and those who disagree either "allege antiquity without other reasons" or lack actual experience in battle.[9] Yet as John Smythe argues in his 1590 *Certain Discourses Military*, guns are more effective than bow and arrow only in theory, and not in practice, for the new instruments, unpredictable in their aim, are only as reliable as their users, who "do commonly discharge their pieces without taking any certain sight at point and blank."[10]

In the years after 1590, defenses of the bow and arrow flood Elizabethan presses: Humphrey Barwick's *Brief Discourse concerning the Force and Effect of all Manual Weapons of Fire* (1591); Matthew Sutcliffe's 1593 *Practice, Proceedings, and Laws of Arms*; Smythe's 1595 *Instructions*; R.S.'s 1596 *Brief Treatise*. For these writers, the decay of archery is both cause and symptom of the erosion of social hierarchies and of traditional manly virtues such as valor. So long as the crossbow survives, so too does the lone knight: as the distillment of a nostalgic longing for the waning military proprieties of the past, the crossbow emblematizes an epoch (real or imagined) when war was a stage for the exhibition of courtly ideals. As Castiglione advises, "where the Courtyer is at a skirmishe" he should "undertake his notable and bould feates . . . with as litle company as he can, and in the sighte of noble men." With the advent of the gun and the attendant introduction of siege warfare, the courtier-soldier forfeits his chance to "shewe feates of Chivalrie."[11]

In medieval warfare and in the world of Renaissance romance, single combat is the norm.[12] By the end of the sixteenth century, however, it becomes increasingly difficult to view war as a vehicle for reinforcing courtly ideals, a point driven home nowhere more emphatically than by Philip

Sidney's death on the battlefield at Zutphen. Chivalric tournaments no longer offer sufficient training for the battlefield, particularly since there are "everie day newe inventions . . . and all sort of engins newly invented and corrected dailie," as Roger Williams observes. The majority of these inventions place an increased emphasis upon defensive strategies, turning war into a series of blockades in which victory is granted to the more devious tactician.[13] By 1595, the Privy Council is encouraging the commissioners of musters in Buckinghamshire to replace their bows with calivers and muskets "because they are of more use than the bows." Chivalric military exploits still live on, and even thrive, in "celebration and recreation," as Whigham observes, but in actual warfare, the "armed chivalric knight" and his "individual feats of socially distinctive heroism" become increasingly obsolete.[14]

Book v of Spenser's *Faerie Queene* is uneasy about these new methods of warfare and the virtues and social values associated with them. Spenser's discomfort with the physical and emotional inurement to pain advocated by late sixteenth-century neo-Stoics and Essexian militarists alike is evident in his representation of instruments of war, devices that expose his uneasiness about the immunity to "sense" and "feeling" epitomized by Talus. Yet Spenser is no less uneasy about the burden of human affection that characterizes Artegall's imperfect execution of Justice.

David Norbrook has called *The Faerie Queene* the "fullest poetic embodiment of the political ideals of Sidney and his circle," and Book v in particular constitutes Spenser's "sustained defense of the Leicester–Essex foreign policy."[15] Yet Spenser's responses to the political methods and dispositions of his successive patrons are neither blindly loyal nor homogenous. At the core of Book v's complex and divergent attitudes towards the policies and philosophical attitudes embraced by Leicester, Essex, and Grey lies Talus, the perverse, inhuman mascot of Elizabethan military humanism and its devastating array of newfangled machines and strategies.

In the early 1590s, Spenser is deeply entrenched in the intellectual values and aristocratic codes of honor cultivated by the Earl of Essex and his secretariat. In a dedicatory sonnet to the 1590 edition of *The Faerie Queene*, Spenser promises Essex that he will be featured in the allegory at some later date, and several episodes from Books v and vi are read as allusions to the Earl's chivalry, his involvement in French politics, and what Mervyn James calls his "devoted adherence to military profession."[16] Even so, Spenser struggles to embrace the Essexian model of political and military leadership, admitting as early as 1590 that he cannot represent the "good governour and a vertuous man" in the same person and instead must "dissever" the one from the other.[17] While Spenser's original aim appears to have been to follow Virgil and Ariosto in reconciling the virtuous hero and the good governor in the figure of Arthur, the poem never achieves this reconciliation between ethics and politics.

The cleavage between virtue and good government is most pronounced in Book v of *The Faerie Queene*, in which Talus represents the means and methods used to exact Justice, while Artegall represents the noble and rightful ends of that virtue. Envisioning Talus as Artegall's "right hand" or instrument ("powre is the right hand of Justice truely hight"), Spenser represents Justice as a *gemina persona*, made up of two distinct yet conjoined bodies (v.iv.1). Subject to passion and injury, Artegall represents the "body natural" of the law, while Talus represents the legal "body politic," susceptible neither to passion nor to corporeal harm.[18] Like the mystical body of Tudor kingship, the body politic of Justice as it is instantiated in Talus is immune from decay and reproach, wiping away the faults of Justice's "body natural" as they are embodied in the conciliatory, merciful Artegall. As an embodiment of the *lex talionis*, Talus is an instrument for exacting the full rigor of the law. He represents the physical force necessary to ensure the just implementation of the law, demonstrating how, in the words of Federico Commandino, mechanics is the "right hand [bracchio destro]" of good government.[19] Yet Spenser periodically questions the Knight of Justice's reliance upon Talus' mechanical power, a power both instrumental to and at odds with the imagined ends of Justice as they are personified by Artegall.

By representing Talus as a literal instrument, Spenser's text adheres to a legal instrumentalism characteristic of much late sixteenth-century political thought, which imagines the law as a tool to be manipulated in the manner of a mechanical device. Asserting that "Kings are not above the Law," the *Vindiciae contra Tyrannos* argues that monarchs profit from the regulatory instrumentalism of the laws circumscribing their actions just as scientists profit from the use of mechanical instruments: "those kings are ridiculous and worthy of contempt, who repute it a dishonour to conform themselves to law, as those surveyors who think themselves disgraced, by using of a rule, a compass, a chain, or other instruments . . . or a pilot who had rather fail, according to his fantasie and imagination, than steer his course by his needle and sea-card." The comparison between a ruler's use of the law and the operation of a mechanical device turns out to be particularly apt given Spenser's representation of Justice, since according to the author of the *Vindiciae*, the proper enforcement of the law demands a cold-blooded rationality, "free from all perturbations, not subject to be moved with choler, ambition, hate."[20] Devoid of sense and feeling, Talus alternately encourages and vexes this powerful juridical fantasy of the perfect legal instrument, untouched by passion or mercy.

By "dissevering" his allegory of Justice between Artegall and Talus, Spenser explores the assets and liabilities of merciful and rigorous Justice, the latter characterized by the unemotional hardness of Talus' iron frame and the brutality of his methods. Book v is commonly read as a continued allusion to the Irish regime under Arthur, Lord Grey, who served as Lord Deputy of Ireland for Queen Elizabeth between 1580 and 1584, and for whom Spenser reluctantly acted as secretary. Accused of excessive violence against the Irish and removed from his post, Lord Grey was perceived as a "bloody man," yet according to Spenser's *View of the Present State of Ireland*, he was "most gentle, affable, loving, and temperate."[21] The discrepancy between the actual and the perceived Lord Grey, or between the noble aims of his enterprise and the brutality of its implementation, is teased out by the intimate but intermittently discordant partnership between the merciful Artegall and his iron-fisted groom, a reading which turns Book v into a critique of the means, but not the ends, of Elizabeth's colonial ideology.[22] Representing, respectively, the spirit and the letter of the law, Artegall and Talus enforce the morally tenuous distinction between intent and act as Spenser labors to dissociate the ethically high-minded motivations of the Irish campaign from the barbarity of Lord Grey's actual regime.

Book v of *The Faerie Queene* is often regarded as a companion text to *A View of the Present State of Ireland* in that both texts are critical of "Elizabeth's 'soft' attitude toward [the] control and subjection" of the Irish.[23] Both texts are indeed distrustful of "softness," of the emotional involvement that hinders the stern, objective dispensation of Justice. In *A View*, one of the interlocutors asserts that "it is dangerous to leave the sense of a law unto the reason or will of the judges who are men and may be miscarried by affections and many other means, but the laws ought to be like to stony tables, plain, steadfast, and unmoveable."[24] While Artegall is all too easily mollified by his adversaries, Talus clearly solves the juridical challenges posed by the miscarriage of the affections in that he is not a man but an automaton, "immoveable, resistlesse, without end" (v.i.12). In his dogged fixity and his fury, Talus resembles the fierce and "stubborne" Irish as depicted by Spenser, even as he also resembles the "immoveable" rigor of English law itself, which the Irish do "especially rage at and rend in pieces as most repugnant to their liberty and natural freedom."[25] Wrathful and impetuous but also stubborn and unfeeling, the character of Talus reveals Spenser to be as uneasy about hardness as he is about softness and leniency. As in *A View*, where Spenser mediates between severity and gentleness in his project to "soften and temper the most stern and savage nature" of the Irish, Book v weighs the ethical and political liabilities of both rigor and mercy, guided throughout by the hypothesis that the eradication of the affections might be every bit as dangerous as their miscarriage.[26]

Spenser explores this problem through Talus' "iron hand," his master metaphor for the instrumentality of the law as well as for its potentially dehumanizing effect upon its executor. The periodic friction between Talus and Artegall reflects an underlying conflict within the *gemina persona* of Spenser's concept of Justice, one produced by the two competing demands of the virtue. Jean Bodin observes in his *Six bookes of a common-weale* that "nothing is more contrarie unto true justice, than pitie; neither any thing more repugnant unto the office and dutie of an upright judge, than mercie . . . So that a prince sitting in judgement must take upon him *two contrarie persons*, that is to say of a mercifull father, and of an upright magistrat; of a most gentle prince, and of an inflexible judge."[27] While Artegall is the "mercifull father," easily mollified by the enemy and betrothed to Britomart (whose affiliation with Equity distances Artegall further from the letter of the law), Talus, by contrast, is the "upright magistrat" whose want of feeling makes him a perfectly detached arbiter of the law.

Contemporary iconography supports Bodin's argument that Justice is best dispensed by "two contrarie persons" rather than by a unified, coherent human form. In contradistinction to other manifestations of Justice, represented by living figures, Ripa's *Iconologia* depicts "Giustitia Rigorosa" as a female skeleton holding a flail or whip; like death, the rigor of the law cannot be swayed by the stirrings of the flesh.[28] The classical figure after whom Spenser's Talus is fashioned is an archetype for the commonplace Renaissance notion that arbiters of Justice should assume inhuman characteristics. *Don Quixote*'s Sancho Panza remarks that judges and governors ought to be made of brass, an observation probably indebted to Erasmus' *Adages*, where the epithet "Chalcenterus," or brass-intestines, is used to ridicule the resolve of men who undertake tasks as if they possessed "innards of brass, as was feigned of Talus, the custodian of the island of Crete [insigniter patiens laborum atque indefatigabilis, velut habens aerea intestina, qualem fabulae narrant fuisse Talo custodem insulae cretae]."[29] *Measure for Measure*'s unyielding and merciless Angelo, who acts as deputy for the overly lenient Duke, is said to piss congealed ice; his "very blood is snow-broth" according to the hot-blooded Lucio.[30] Yet *Measure for Measure* is ultimately distrustful of the inflexible dispensation of the law proposed by its title, and Angelo is even somewhat redeemed by his stirrings of lust, testimony to his common humanity, if not his superior moral and juridical probity. Even as Spenser gives life to the idea in Talus, Book v of *The Faerie Queene* is also troubled by the notion that Justice is best dispatched by a body immune from human passion.

The classical legends of Talus upon which Spenser bases his iron man idealize the insensate objectivity of the law. According to Plato and Hesiod, Talus was a brass or iron man who guarded the laws of Crete. Hesiod writes that he was descended from a "brasen race, sprung from ash-trees" who loved "deeds of violence" and were "hard of heart, like adamant, fearful men." Incredibly strong, "their armour was of bronze, and their houses of bronze, and of bronze were their implements."[31] Spenser's Talus inherits this adamant hardness: first described by Spenser as "made of yron mould, / Immoveable, resistlesse, without end," he manifests extraordinary resolve throughout Book v, taking on each new "tumultuous rout" and "raskall crew" he meets with an indefatigable vigor. Like the "perfect metall" of Artegall's sword Chrysaor, which is "so firme and hard," Talus is invulnerable to the demands of a human body (v.i.10). While guarding Britomart after she learns of Artegall's captivity to Radigund, Talus does not "suffer sleepe to seaze / His eye-lids sad, but watcht continually . . . / Like to a Spaniell wayting carefully" (v.vi.26). At least in this respect, Talus is a model soldier according to the standards of Spenser's day, adhering to the prescriptions set out by texts such as the 1599 *Lawes and Orders of Warre*, a treatise addressed to the Earl of Essex "for the good conduct of the service in Ireland" which stipulates that "no man beeing set Sentinel shall sleepe, or . . . shal depart and forsake that place without warrant, upon paine of death."[32] With his superhuman fortitude, Talus is also an exemplary Stoic: like the ideal soldier described in Thomas Digges' *Stratioticos*, he is able to "abide both heate and cold, hunger and thirst, travell and watching," and to "put on a Resolution to abide all kind of hardnesse."[33]

The imperviousness of Spenser's iron man is the literalization of a metaphor common to ancient and Renaissance Stoicism alike. Diogenes Laertius describes Zeno, the founder of the old Stoa, as a man with an "iron frame" who possessed the "utmost endurance" to pain, and sixteenth-century neo-Stoics imagine the key virtue of *apatheia* in similar terms.[34] In *The Morale Philosophie of the Stoicks*, Guillaume Du Vair writes that the wise man should "not be mooved a whit" by things indifferent to him, but rather assure himself that "this thing toucheth me not at all, it concernes not me." If we govern ourselves, Du Vair continues, "we cannot be wounded at all," a quality epitomized by Artegall's adamantine assistant.[35] On stage and off, would-be Stoics aspire to the durability of Talus' iron body, often invoking metal, marble, and similarly sturdy materials to showcase their resolution in adversity. Having mastered the Stoic values of her Roman captors, Shakespeare's Cleopatra proclaims herself "marble-constant" in her "resolution," while, disgusted with his "penetrable flesh," Chapman's Bussy yearns to become "like a Roman statue . . . / Till death hath made me marble."[36] Yet as Diogenes Laertius points out, and as many Renaissance writers recognize, *apatheia* is not always a virtue, and it can turn into callousness or excessive severity. Talus mediates between these two aspects of *apatheia*, at times possessing the detached constancy of the Stoic sage, but at times exhibiting a perniciously inhuman impassivity.

More so than marble, iron exemplifies the hard yet resilient disposition of the ideal Stoic, since as natural philosophers commonly note, iron is "very soft, malleable, and ductile" and yet cannot be liquified like softer metals, so that even stronger stones and minerals "submit to the power of iron."[37] In Dekker's *London's Tempe*, a Lord Mayor's Pageant sponsored by the Society of Ironmongers, a singing troupe of smiths celebrates the malleability of "brave iron" by endowing the metal with a Stoic resistance to adversity: "the more it suffers, the more it smoothes offence; / In drudgery it shines with patience."[38] Iron externalizes the simultaneous demand for fixity and flexibility in the passionless sage. From Plato's *Ion* onwards, iron is also associated, by dint of its magnetic power, with the maintenance of political and cosmic order: according to Dekker's ironmongers, "By iron's strong charmes / Ryotes lye bound."[39] Yet iron proves a peculiar emblem of civic order, since its unique makeup makes it both malleable and intractable. Pliny explains that while iron seems "dull" and stiffe," it is nonetheless both responsive and willful: "What can we devise more stubborne and rebellious in its own kind, than the hard yron, yet it yeelds, and will abide to be ordered: for loe, it is willing to be drawne by the load stone."[40]

Appropriate to his iron constitution, Talus enforces order and rule in a world turned upside down. Described as Artegall's "gard and government," Talus is in fact Astraea's mediatory instrument: upon departing the earth at the onset of the Iron Age, the demigoddess of Justice "willed him with Artegall to wend, / And doe what ever thing he did intend" (v.i.12). Yet like his classical ancestors, Talus takes his own initiative with greater frequency as Book v unfolds, and in the final two cantos, he is only tenuously under his leader's control. Talus' metamorphosis from a conjoined to a separate instrument begins when he is divided from the enslaved Artegall; left to his own devices, Talus massacres Radigund's entire troop as Britomart looks on, her heart quaking at the appalling sight (v.vii.36). When Talus attacks

Grantorto's "raskall many" in Canto 2, Artegall tells him to desist from his "cruell deed" (v.xi.65). Yet this first command does not suffice, for at the beginning of the next canto, Talus massacres Grantorto's troops with such gusto that "Artegall him seeing so to rage, / Willd him to stay, and signe of truce did make" (v.xii.8). At the end of the final canto, the Knight of Justice must once again restrain Talus when, upon meeting the Blatant Beast, he "would her have chastiz'd with his yron flaile, / If her Sir Artegall had not preserved, / And him forbidden, who his heast observed" (v.xii.43). In showing Artegall to disapprove of Talus' cruel methods, Spenser represents those methods as outside Artegall's authority, thus exculpating Lord Grey from the charges of excessive brutality that prompt his removal from his position.

Dissociated from the cruelty and impetuosity of his groom, Artegall in fact errs towards the other extreme, disdaining to fight certain of his enemies and entering into armed conflict only after a thorough consideration of the situation. While Artegall relies upon his powers of eloquence to persuade the giant of Canto 2 to desist from his dangerous relativism, Talus quickly wearies of the giant's verbal subtleties, and rashly tosses him off a cliff (v.ii.49). Though Artegall's reluctance to fight at first appears praiseworthy in contradistinction to Talus' Terminator-like approach, it proves more troubling when the "lawlesse multitude" rises up in support of the giant, and he is paralyzed by indecision: "when Artegall did vew, / He much was troubled, ne wist what to doo." (v.ii.52). Artegall's inaction is motivated not by pity but by a strict adherence to chivalric decorum, "for loth he was his noble hands t'embrew / In the base blood of such a rascall crew." His solution is to send Talus in his place "truce for to desire," but the iron man instead disperses the "raskall rout" with his flail, thus extricating Artegall from a delicate situation (v.ii.52–54). Even when he acts according to Artegall's wishes, Talus invariably takes the initiative in battle, confirming Spenser's description of Talus as "the true guide of [Artegall's] way and vertuous government" (v.viii.3). In this revealing epithet, Spenser may be suggesting that, like Shakespeare's Antony, "our leader's led / and we are women's men," for not only does Artegall submit to a woman but, more ominously, he surrenders to his own instrumental means.[41]

Talus externalizes a commonplace Stoic fantasy, yet he ultimately interrogates and even mocks Stoic ideals rather than endorsing them. With his impenetrable body and his frenzied outbursts, Talus bears a close resemblance to the Senecan madman, whose invulnerability is "one manifestation of a drive that, swerving in the other direction, leads to . . . uncontrollable rage."[42] In his depiction of Artegall's servant and the attendant challenges he poses to political instrumentality, Spenser is perhaps thinking of the Earl of Essex, a man whom Francis Bacon underhandedly praises as "the fittest instrument to do good to the State" even though that instrument ought to have been more "obsequious." Despite his popular reputation for courtesy, Essex is also described by contemporaries as a man "full of vehement and unrestrained passion," and as early as 1596, Bacon proclaims that he is a "man of nature not to be ruled."[43] Essex's willfulness is complemented by impressive physical prowess, so much so that one of the Earl's co-competitors in a leaping contest remarks that he had "a body . . . made of yron, supporting travaile and passioned in all extremities, that following him [in leaping] did tyre our bodies, that are made of flesh and bone."[44] His mettle notwithstanding, Essex is often depicted as incapable of repressing passion and rage, and like Spenser's metal man, his demeanor confirms Braden's argument that the aspiring Stoic tends to "swerve" away from resolve and towards immoderate affection.[45]

An automaton without "sence" or "feeling," Talus exhibits a fury that Spenser depicts as the unavoidable counterpart of his immovable nature. Swinging his iron flail as his resolute façade gives way, Talus enacts the concerns which many Elizabethan and Jacobean writers bring to the "stonie philosophie" and its inadequacy or failure to inculcate metal men.[46] In Chapman's *Revenge of Bussy d'Ambois*, Clermont portrays the Earl of Oxford as a "Rare, and most absolute" man, yet also out of control, "passionate, insulting, raging, / Labour[ing] with iron flailes, to thresh down feathers / Flitting in ayre."[47] Armed with iron flails, Stoicism's metal men are supposed to be stubborn, but also yielding. Joseph Hall imagines the "Patient Man" as able to meet the "fiercest paines with strength of resolution"; he should be made of metal, but "of a metall not so hard as flexible."[48] Yet Talus, like Chapman's Earl of Oxford, lacks the essential ductility to temper his hardness. Comparing the "unruly affections" to the "stubborne metall" which "scorne[s] the ferule," Hall's essay on the "Patient Man" demonstrates the instability of the concept of the "iron man" in which metal represents both unbridled passion and the philosophical therapies used to discipline that passion.

Talus exposes the more sinister implications of Stoicism's fantasies of impenetrability, fantasies which have the potential to erode Renaissance humanism's most fundamental assumptions about what it means to be human. A suspicion of Stoic apathy, influenced by several ancient philosophers, accompanies the revival of Stoicism during the Renaissance.[49] Seneca recognized that *apatheia* can be taken to a dangerous extreme: in a section of *De Constantia* entitled "That a wise man cannot feel any injury or insult [nec injuriam nec contumeliam accipere sapientem]," he compares the invulnerability of the wise man to very hard stones "impervious to steel," yet later in the essay he repudiates his own metaphor, qualifying that the Stoic should not be "harde and stupide, like a flint or as a barre of iron" but rather "have a sence" of what he suffers.[50] According to Seneca, Stoical constancy develops in response to sentient feelings, rather than in an affective vacuum: rather than circumvent sentience, the sage confronts and conquers it, thus making Stoicism an adversarial philosophy that is only fully articulated when it is threatened. This is perhaps why, in the writings of Cicero, Plutarch, and Diogenes Laertius, as well as in the plays of Shakespeare, Jonson, and Chapman, the Stoic hero is depicted in the process of breaking down, the dissolution of his philosophical attitudes a result of the fact that the violent emotion inimical to Stoic apathy is also its inescapable partner.[51]

Because the attainment of Stoic ideals is dependent upon the affections those ideals seek to repress, many Renaissance writers protest that the Stoic sage is an impossible fiction, a philosophical chimera who, in the words of Erasmus, "never was and never will be in existence anywhere."[52] Many Renaissance writers skeptical of what Calvin terms the "iron philosophy" look to the anti-Stoic essays of Plutarch, which censure the Stoics for the impracticality and inconsistency of their ethical and physical doctrines. For Plutarch, the central contradiction of Stoicism is that it extinguishes and abolishes the soul of man in a misguided attempt to govern it. Attacking the implausibility of Stoic *apatheia*, he reproves Pindar for devising a man of "impassibilitie" with a "bodie so hard, as it could not be pierced."[53] Spenser commits precisely this absurdity with Talus, but he does so in order that Talus' "resistlesse" frame might expose the inadequacies of the neo-Stoic militarism outlined by writers including Lipsius and Du Vair and epitomized, at least for a time, by Essex. Talus is the monstrous issue of a philosophy "intent on confecting some perverse substitute for what we were meant to be," a philosophy which, for sixteenth-century opponents of Stoicism, creates subjects who are "seriously out of touch with what is most valuably and essentially human."[54]

Fearful that Stoicism turns men into "blocks and stocks and senseless stones," sixteenth-century writers ponder the question of how completely one must eliminate sense and feeling to fulfill Seneca's paradoxical dictum that "to subdue passion is to be truely a man."[55] Initially attracted to Stoicism for its capitulation to Fate, Calvin ultimately rejects the notion that "patiently to bear the cross is to be utterly stupefied and to be deprived of all feeling of pain," thus distinguishing true Christian suffering from the philosophy which "turns patience into insensibility" and the "valiant and constant man into a stock." Fellow Calvinists echo him, asserting that God does not wish us to be "altogether benumbed."[56] Its advocates and critics alike recognize that the very nature of Stoicism depends upon pinning down the nebulous yet crucial distinction between managing one's affections and eradicating them. Edward Reynolds, one of Essex's secretaries, explains that the key to governing the passions "is not to be without them, but above them," yet he acknowledges that the subtlety of that distinction results in misguided attempts to extinguish the passions, leaving "scarce any thing in [a man] which he may command and governe."[57] When prompted to imagine the consequences of such a misconstrual, English Renaissance writers invariably envision the results of Stoicism's miscarriage as inanimate or quasi-animate creatures. The man who suppresses his passions entirely, according to the early seventeenth-century writer Owen Felltham, is not a human being but a "motive statue" or a "speaking stone," while Richard Greenham and William Cornwallis caution their audiences, respectively, against the "numnes" and the "blockish conceit, that would have men to be without all affection."[58]

For many Renaissance opponents of the philosophy, Stoicism creates "a marble statue of a man, devoid of sense and any sort of human feeling," and it is this desire to transcend, cast off, or repress the fundamental conditions of humanity that makes the philosophy so unpalatable both to humanists such as Erasmus and Calvinists such as Thomas Gataker, who protests that Stoicism "strippeth men of humanitie."[59] The degeneration into what Gataker calls a "brutish inhumanitie" is palpably evident in both the moral and the physical landscape of Book v of *The Faerie Queene*, where humanity's degradation is imagined as a process of petrification. Book v begins with an account of how the world has "runne quite out of square" since the Golden Age, and has now become a "stonie" age:

> And men themselves, the which at first were framed
> Of earthly mould, and form'd of flesh and bone,
> Are now transformed into hardest stone.
>
> (v.Proem.2)

Made of iron rather than "earthly mould," Talus is a persistent reminder of the cosmic and moral decay that permeates Book v as a whole – a mascot for the Iron Age. The most horrifying consequence of Astraea's flight is that it strips humans of their essential humanity: in her absence, the human race is "backward bred," devolving into stone and thus reversing the process of creation initiated by "Pyrrha and Deucalione" (v.Proem.2). While Talus contributes to the restoration of political and cosmic order in Book v, a world in which "Right now is wrong, and wrong that was is right," his disobedience and his belligerence exacerbate rather than alleviate the natural and social disorder endemic to Spenser's Iron Age, where stars "doe at randon rove / Out of their proper places" and animals "from their course astray" (v.Proem.4; 6).

Talus' predilection towards violence and cunning reminds us that the inhabitants of Book v have irrevocably forsaken that "Golden Age" when "no man was affrayd / Of force, ne fraud in wight was to be found: / No warre was knowne" (v.Proem.9). As a guardian of the law, Talus' very presence is symptomatic of humanity's "degendered" state (v.Proem.2), for as Richard Hooker points out, "laws of arms" are "built upon depraved nature," and consequently neither laws nor weapons were necessary during the Golden Age.[60] Talus occupies a peculiar position with respect to the depravity of the Iron Age, since he both emblematizes and combats its brutality, its cunning, and its technologically sophisticated methods of warfare.

In its setting, its thematic concerns, and its imagery, Book v erodes the moral and physiological boundaries between humans and non-humans (machines, animals, stones) in order to consider which qualities, if any, demarcate humanity from, or elevate it above, its bestial and mechanical counterparts. While his Protestant emphasis upon the inevitability of sin and the total sufficiency of grace never permits Spenser to exalt humanity to the extent of a Pico or a Manetti, *The Faerie Queene* licenses and even encourages a view of humanity capable of fashioning itself according to a divine model. Moreover, Spenser emphasizes the centrality of trial in making virtuous and noble heroes out of his human protagonists: Redcrosse Knight and Guyon attain their respective status as exemplars of Faith and Temperance only after those virtues have been hard won in the caves of Despair and Mammon. Yet the virtue of Justice as it is embodied jointly in Artegall and Talus is not interrogated to the same degree: in Talus, at least, it simply exists, *sui generis*, and is never imperiled by the infirmities of flesh or spirit that debilitate Spenser's human heroes. Unmoved and "unexercised" by the world around him, Talus never comes to possess that uncloistered virtue for which Milton's *Areopagitica* praises Book II's intermittently intemperate Sir Guyon.[61] The epic intended to fashion virtuous gentlemen, and thus to enable corrupt humanity to transcend its failings and its natural affections with divine intervention, discipline, and education, has circumvented this process with Talus, encased him in metal, and then recoiled at the result.

After striving throughout Book IV to prove to his "Stoick censours" that heroism is reconcilable with love and "naturall affection," Spenser forsakes this project in Book V by suggesting that Justice must be implemented by a body devoid of human feeling, a conviction which comes perilously close to that voiced by the "frosen hearts" indicted in the proem to Book IV (IV.Proem.I–2). Set in a "degendered" present, Book V complicates Spenser's project of recuperating and ennobling human affection. While Guyon's wrath in the Bower of Bliss, like that of Chapman's Achilles, is transformed from a perturbation into a heroic passion of the mind, Talus' wrath never dignifies him, but rather acts as a synecdoche for the "stonie," brutish world which he inhabits.

The tensions and apertures evident in the instrumental relationships of Book V demonstrate that the militaristic ethos of hardness and fortitude epitomized by Talus is difficult or even impossible to reconcile with the obedience to authority essential to the successful mediation of Justice through Astraea's human and inhuman instruments. Artegall and Talus are certainly not unique amongst Spenser's characters in their mediatory role as the instruments of an absent yet authoritative will, for all the titular virtues of *The Faerie Queene* are, in one way or another, passive instruments of both sovereign and divine will. Yet the characters who serve as the mediating instruments of Redcrosse Knight or Sir Guyon – Una, the dwarf, Arthur, and the Palmer – never resist their appointed roles as blatantly as Talus thwarts Artegall's command. As Spenser represents it in Book V, Justice is a doubly mediated virtue, a baton passed from Astraea to Artegall and from Artegall to Talus that recedes further from the will of the dread sovereign goddess at each remove.

In its relationship between its two protagonists, as well as through villains such as Malengin, Grantorto, and the giant of Canto 2 complete with his weighing device, Book V of *The Faerie Queene* demonstrates the hazards of political, legal, and mechanical instrumentalism. Together with and independent of their associations with the dehumanizing effects of Stoic militarism, the engines and devices of Book V reflect Spenser's pervasive anxieties about the legitimate use of artifice and cunning in the arena of war. Unlike *A View*, where the Irish resist colonization with stubborn intractability, *The Faerie Queene* consistently imagines metamorphosis as the most effective and menacing means of resistance. Duessa, Archimago, Acrasia, and Proteus, among others, perform their evil acts by transforming themselves or the world around them through art, magic, disguise, or the creation of illusions or false dreams. Able to fight fraud with fraud by imitating the metamorphic capacity of his adversaries, Talus complicates the poem's attitudes towards artifice and machination, for while he represents the divinely sanctioned "right hand of Justice," he also adopts the tricks and ruses of Astraea's enemies, following Malengin "apace" in spite of his ever-changing form and cunningly evading Britomart's questions until she flatly accuses him of deception (v.ix.16; v. vi.16). In his pursuit of Malengin, whose very name confirms the demonic, guileful aspects of machinery that haunt Book v as a whole, Talus counters his every metamorphosis:

> Into a Foxe himself he first did tourne;
> But [Talus] him hunted like a Foxe full fast.
> Then to a bush himselfe he did transforme,
> But he the bush did beat, till that at last
> Into a bird it chaung'd, and from him past . . .
>   (v.ix.17, 1–5)

Often interpreted as an allegory for the guerilla warfare practiced by the Kerns, the Irish rebels who move swiftly amongst the caves and bogs of their native land in order to evade their English enemies, Malengin's capacity for metamorphosis, as well as Talus' adaptability to this method, underscores the violence and deception necessitated by the Iron Age.[62]

By setting Book v in a "stonie," contemporaneous age, Spenser contextualizes the perverse Stoic ideal of adamantine resolve within a culture permeated by dissimulation and artifice both political and mechanical. Spenser and his contemporaries imagine the last age of mankind as governed by cunning as well as by violence and injustice. Thomas Heywood imagines the Golden Age as devoid of artifice: "men were governd more by *Will*, then *Art*," Heywood writes, and there was no fraud, no guile, and no capacity for the reproduction of images, coins, or texts: "Before smooth *Cunning* was to ripenesse growne, / Or divellish *Wax* and *Parchment* yet were knowne."[63] Talus is complicit in this devolution of nature into *techne*, honesty into fraud, and singularity into the proliferation of simulacra and counterfeit reproductions. The demand for increasingly elaborate and deadly instruments of war is both cause and symptom of the Iron Age, and while Talus ensures against the encroachment upon property rights in a grasping age, his status as a war machine also implicates him in the induration he combats. In his capacity to mimic the devious methods of his adversaries, Talus is the consummate enemy of guile but also its *Doppelgänger*, thus complicating Spenser's repudiation of artifice in *The Faerie Queene*.

Throughout the *The Faerie Queene*, and particularly in Book v, epic identity is governed by objects and instruments. The poem's persistent focus upon the lineage, circulation, and deployment of swords, shields, and other weapons of war suggests that epic characters are measured by the sum of their instruments, instruments which are exchanged, inherited, counterfeited, and stolen.[64] In their normative use, weapons confer nobility and ancestry upon Spenser's heroes, thus contributing to *The Faerie Queene*'s project of distinguishing the "difference / Betweene the vulgar and the noble seed" (ii.iv.1). Yet as in the case of Braggadochio, whose stolen weapon is "reft" by Talus in Book v, instruments of war can also undermine the enforcement of social distinctions when they abet the "valorous pretence" of villains attempting to impersonate authentic nobility and virtue.

Like so many of *The Faerie Queene*'s human subjects who manifest themselves in both true and false forms (Una and Duessa, Florimell and the false or snowy Florimell, and so on), many of Spenser's instruments and devices also have both genuine and fake counterparts. In Book ii, Mammon's shield is a forgery of those wielded by Guyon and Artegall, its "yron coate, all overgrowne with rust" and "filthy dust" concealing a new and "glistring glosse" so as to make the weapon appear "to have beene of old" (ii.vii.4). Its fresh polish hidden behind an antique patina, the upstart shield forges its own ancestry. Enchased with "antickes and wild Imagery," the grotesque technical virtuosity of Mammon's shield is a demonic imitation of Artegall's Homeric shield, but also of Spenser's own ersatz "anticke" style.

Feeding his hundred furnaces with his iron tongs and bellows, Mammon is a sham counterpart of Vulcan, the god who epitomizes technical ingenuity for Spenser and his contemporaries. Unlike the shield forged for Achilles by the smith-god, Mammon's shield is the apogee of art's perversion of nature, threatening to corrupt the normative instrumentality exemplified by the heroes of Spenser's poem. Churning out counterfeit antiquities, Mammon's furnace provides the first clue that Guyon has stumbled upon a degenerate court ruled by extravagant artifice. Through Mammon, Sir Guyon meets the "sturdy villein" Disdayne, a man fabricated "all of golden mould" who exemplifies the dehumanizing effects of courtly artifice: he is, in short, the literal embodiment of a courtly *sprezzatura* that has degenerated back into its etymological root, *sprezzare* (to scorn or disdain). Although he possesses "life" and "sence," Disdayne is clearly akin to Talus in that no "mortall steele" can "emperce his miscreated mould" (ii.vii.40–42). His invulnerability exposes both the impossibility and the cruelty of the courtly ideal of negligent diligence according to which courtiers must perform every act "without pain, and (as it were) not mynding it."[65] If Talus' iron body reproves the extreme hardness necessitated by war and the stern rationality demanded by Justice, then Disdayne's golden frame censures the essential inhumanity of the courtly decorum that turns men into instruments. As George Peele points out, Spenser was himself a victim of "Courts Disdaine, the enemie to Arte," a theme he returns to at the end of Book v with the Blatant Beast, a personification of the contemptuous back-biting that colored Spenser's experience of life at court.[66]

In Book v, Spenser's attitudes towards courtly instrumentality are mediated by instruments and devices which, since they are so easily stolen, relinquished, or otherwise misused, have the capacity to destabilize courtly values as well as uphold them. Braggadochio is exposed and disgraced for having stolen a shield later "blotted out" by Talus, while Burbon shamelessly abandons his shield in the heat of battle and Artegall is "disarmed" in both senses of the term by the female Radigund. Each of these episodes demonstrates how Book v reveals heroism and chivalric virtue to be perilously contingent upon the rightful possession and proper use of instruments. Yet Spenser also stages periodic moments of confusion between his heroes and their instruments that culminate in Book v's uneasy pairing of Artegall and Talus as the agent and instrument of Justice.

As early as Book III, when Artegall is first spied by Britomart in her "wondrous myrrhour," she cannot see the Knight of Justice through his metal armor, catching only the faintest glimpse of his "manly face" through his "ventayle lifted up on hye" (III.ii.24). Britomart cannot even determine whether the creature in her mirror is a "living wight," since, wholly encased in metal, Artegall resembles his iron groom (III.ii.38). Spenser's description of Artegall's full body armor is odd, if not downright ridiculous, on a number of counts. First, there was a substantial reduction in the protective armor worn during the second half of the sixteenth century, making the Knight of Justice's equipment utterly obsolete for the modern warfare waged throughout Book v. By the 1590s, authors of military treatises such as Roger Williams regularly recommend making armor "so light as you can devise."[67] Since musket shot could pierce through even the thickest armor, the increased movement and speed permitted by lighter armor protect the Elizabethan soldier better than a bulky metal suit, a dangerous encumbrance either on foot or on horseback. Even so, other writers cling to the armorial conventions of old: John Smythe derides those "new fantasied men of war [who] despise and scorn our ancient arming of ourselves." Smythe blames Philip Sidney's death on the "unsoldierlike and fond arming" that comes into fashion during the Dutch Wars of Independence, maintaining that Sidney would have survived had he worn the heavy cuisses, or thigh-guards, that were abandoned during the previous half century.[68]

By arraying Artegall in an obsolete style of armor prized largely for its nostalgic rather than its protective value, Spenser endangers his hero at the expense of preserving the military conventions and attendant social values of a waning chivalric age, particularly the distinguishing acts of individual heroism in which Artegall engages even to his own detriment. To complicate matters, Artegall inherits his armor from Achilles, the wrathful and intemperate hero of the *Iliad* who is a singularly inappropriate model for Spenser's merciful Knight of Justice. Of "antique mould," Artegall's armor is inscribed "with cyphers old, / *Achilles armes, which Arthegall did win*" (III.ii.25). The association between Achilles and Artegall makes sense insofar as the Earl of Essex, one of Spenser's principal models for the hero of Book V, was regarded as a latter-day Achilles and his shield a symbol of the Earl's military prowess and his adamantine resolve. In Artegall's hands, Achilles' shield both represents and ensures the proper government of the passions as it also does for Guillaume Du Vair, who compares Stoic *apatheia* to "that great, stately, and impenetrable buckler which *Vulcan* forged for *Achilles* . . . as Achilles went to schoole unto Chiron to learne the use of that buckler: so we must go to schoole to Philosophy, to know the right use of Wisdome" and to "purge our minds of all such passions as do arise in them."[69] Chapman's 1598 translations of the *Iliad* recuperate the character of Achilles by tempering his extreme wrath with a correspondingly powerful restraint, thus converting his ire into a "heroic passion of the mind" that can be harnessed for virtuous use.[70] Spenser seems to hope that Artegall, and by extension Essex, have inherited Achilles' martial prowess without his excessively passionate nature, and throughout Book V, he labors to demonstrate that Artegall's capacity for affection is a mark of virtue and benevolent civility rather than the sign of an unbridled will.

While Artegall's composure, his equanimity, and his restraint distinguish him from the wrathful Achilles, the rashness and ire associated with Homer's hero is transferred to Talus over the course of Book V. Though Artegall declines to defend himself against the Blatant Beast, Talus is poised to attack, thus prompting a strange exchange of roles in which the "resistless" Talus cannot resist the "bitter wordes" of envious back-biters while his master "past on, and seem'd of them to take no keepe" (V.xii.42). Ironically, the iron man turns out to be more susceptible to Detraction, and more easily provoked, than his sensitive, human counterpart. His rash impetuosity is the undesirable byproduct of Talus' resolve, for as Castiglione points out, while the soldier must "be utterlye resolved" and "arme [himself] as thoughe [he] shoulde go against the shotte of a Cannon," he must not "runne rashely to these combattes" lest he appear reckless to the point of folly.[71]

The periodic role reversals between Artegall and Talus explain what has justifiably been called one of the most "preposterous" battle scenes of *The Faerie Queene*. When Artegall disguises himself to enter the Souldan's court, Arthur takes on the Souldan in single combat while Artegall takes on a "warlike rout" of "nigh a hundred knights," chasing them about with "cowheard shame" until conquering every last one of them (v.viii.50). Artegall singlehandedly overcomes an entire militia, undertaking the kind of epic yet menial violence that Book v usually credits to Talus. Talus stands idly by as Artegall *becomes* Talus, and as Michael West has observed, "just as the Don and Sancho gradually exchange roles in *Don Quixote*," Book v momentarily inverts the roles between master and servant and between human and instrument, a reversal which has "ominous implications for Spenser's theory of Justice."[72]

The fact that Artegall and Talus intermittently incorporate aspects of each other's temperaments underscores the antithetical qualities demanded by the militaristic ethos of late Elizabethan culture: the exemplary courtier-soldier must be temperate yet impassioned, merciful yet cruel, human yet impervious. In the process of disclosing the incongruity of a militaristic, neo-Stoic ethic when circumscribed by the larger mandates of Christian humanism, Spenser exposes the difficulties involved in the project of fashioning a virtuous man who is also a model soldier. These contradictions are reticulated in the temperamental discrepancies and correspondences between Artegall and Talus, as well as in Artegall's own vacillation between justice and mercy and between cruelty and compassion.

The result of the friction between Book v's discrepant models of manly *virtù* is a style of warfare whose tactics are inconsistent and sometimes downright odd. In the battle against Grantorto, Artegall swings pendulum-like from leniency to cruelty in what amounts to a total volte-face in policy. At first, Artegall tries to restrain Talus' rage, calling a truce and explaining that "not for such slaughters sake / He thether came" (v.xii.8). Artegall then issues a chivalric challenge to Grantorto – a courtly gesture of kindness, one presumes, until Grantorto is decapitated. Even as the liberated army runs "with greedie joyfulnesse" to Irena's feet, Artegall punishes them, condemning "all such persons, as did late maintayne / That Tyrants part" (v.xii. 24–25). The inconsistency between Artegall's initial benevolence and his ultimate severity exposes the discord among the conflicting moral, sociopolitical, and religious principles underpinning his two divergent courses of military action.

Spenser's representation of war machinery in Book v is every bit as incoherent as the battle tactics of its adversaries. Few of Spenser's mechanical caprices resemble actual devices, and those that do often serve a radically different function in the context of the poem. Given its ability to thresh out "falshood," and to "truth unfould," Talus' "strange weapon" is, as Spenser admits, "never wont in warre" (v.i.12; v.iv.44), though it does resemble an automatic threshing machine, a device described in Barnabe Googe's translation of Conrad Heresbach's work on husbandry as a "lowe kind of Carre with a couple of wheeles, and the Front armed with sharp Syckles, which forced by the beast through the Corne, did cut downe al before it."[73] With his metal body and his iron flail, Talus also resembles a wheel-lock pistol, a small, self-igniting gun whose spring mechanism operates by means of a "miniature vise or clamp at the end of a moveable arm holding a piece of hard stone, usually iron pyrites." According to J. R. Hale, late sixteenth-century guns possessed a "mysterious personality of their own," firing capriciously and with erratic aim.[74] Talus' predilection towards rage and disobedience is implicitly connected to his status as a machine, one of several wayward instruments populating Book v which demonstrate the exigencies of political instrumentalism by means of the erratic behavior of Renaissance war machinery.

Like the "new fantasied" soldiers bemoaned by John Smythe, Spenser's war machines are largely the product of fantasy and ideology, not military necessity: whimsical and often defective, they nevertheless possess a powerful capacity to complicate the relationship between sentient humanity and non-sentient machinery, categories whose instability vexes Spenser's theories of justice. By probing both the resemblance and the difference between human and machine, Spenser explores the possible threats posed by machinery's capacity to perfect, alter, or arrogate human characteristics and values.

One of the more fantastical war machines of Book v is the Souldan's "charret," a chariot or battle-wagon armed with "yron wheeles and hookes" (v.viii.28). Michael West argues that, with its "grapples," the chariot recalls the "high-pooped Spanish galleons" that towered over English ships during the Armada. These craft were intended for sea-battle, however, and not ground warfare, perhaps explaining why the device malfunctions, its iron hands attacking its operator:

> At last they have all overthrowne to ground
> Quite topside turvey, and the pagan hound
> Amongst the yron hookes and graples keene,
> Torne all to rags, and rent with many a wound . . .
>
> (v.viii.42)

Backfiring against its commander, the Souldan's "topside turvey" engine offers an ironic reworking of Philip II's *impresa*, which depicts the Spanish King as Apollo driving the chariot of the sun.[75] In Spenser's hands, the chariot of the sun-god is hijacked by Phaeton, turning into an unruly device that mutinies against its master.

Artegall, of course, undergoes a similar struggle with his instrument. While laboring to restrain Talus, he reminds us of the Sorcerer's Apprentice in his hapless attempt to control the ever-multiplying brooms of *Fantasia*, a modern allegory of technics-out-of-control that imagines a reversal of power between master and servant similar to those effected in Book v. Both scenarios are perhaps inspired by classical descriptions of the automated statues of Daedalus, which in Plato's *Meno* are said to "do all sorts of good so long as they stay in their place" but when "untethered . . . give you the slip like a runaway slave."[76] Like Daedalus' potentially unruly machines, Talus and the Souldan's cart reveal both the assets and the liabilities of instrumental means – the tools, strategies, and intermediaries through which commanders and rulers exercise their military and political power. In other books of *The Faerie Queene*, the titular heroes possess an unmediated and rather seamless relationship to their instruments: Redcrosse Knight never has to chastise his dwarf, nor does Guyon have to correct the actions of his Palmer – if anything, it is the other way round. In Book v, Spenser reverses the system of heroic mediation that informs the poem as a whole, thus challenging the commonplace mandate of late sixteenth-century political philosophers that rulers can and should avail themselves of instruments.

Spenser's representations of war machines in Book v, Talus included, reveal a persistent interest in devices that mechanically simulate the operation of hands, arms, and similarly tactile instruments. The grapples, hooks, and other simulated appendages that protrude from so many of Artegall's adversaries, human and inhuman, reflect a pervasive concern about the potentially anthropomorphic quality of machinery as well as a preoccupation with the exigencies of instrumental relationships. The grapples on the Souldan's battle cart possess a symbolic, and not a military, function: with its autonomous, humanoid extremities, the machine forges the kind of disturbingly tight coupling between human and machine that haunts Book v as a whole, informing its attitudes towards the experiences of "sence" and "feeling" which (in theory, at least) distinguish humans from their machines.

The lifelikeness of Book v's machinery underscores the degenerative transformation of men from "earthly mould" into "hardest stone," exposing some of the more disturbing implications of that metamorphosis. As men devolve into stone and machines take on the characteristics of animate creatures, the erosion of distinctions between human and machine reflects an underlying concern that humans have *become* machines – that the experience of war, or the demands of Stoicism, or the legal and political instrumentalism of the age have conspired to rupture the barrier between the vital and the mechanical. That Spenser's machines assume eerily animate shapes reflects his recognition that, in the words of Jacques Ellul, "technique is entirely anthropomorphic because human beings have become thoroughly technomorphic."[77] Book v of *The Faerie Queene* communicates both the delight and the horror of this two-pronged metamorphosis: as machinery perfects humanity, it threatens to dismantle the very category of the human.

Often the product of hybridization between human (or animal) and machine, designs for Renaissance war machinery effect a similar dissolution of boundaries with similarly playful yet disturbing effects. Sixteenth-century editions of works of military tactics by writers including Roberto Valturio and the late antique author Renatus Flavius Vegetius contain numerous depictions of machines in quasi-animate forms. In a 1535 French edition of Vegetius, one illustration depicts a tank or chariot crowned by a bald, human head, protruding spikes radiating outward like the thorns of a porcupine (figure 6.1). Sixteenth-century editions of Valturio's *De Re Militari* contain illustrations of *testudine*, or giant shields, in the shape of turtles, a nod to the etymology of the term as well as to the device's structural and functional resemblance to the tortoise's natural defense mechanism. In an illustration from the 1535 French edition of Valturio's text, an uncannily human eye peeps out from inside a tank: encased in metal like Artegall inside his helmet, the device effects a grotesque union between human and machine (see figure 5.2). Like the *capricci* of Pieter Brueghel, Giuseppe Arcimboldo, or François Desprez, in which wheels replace feet, windmills protrude from heads, and scientific instruments supplant the features of human faces, depictions of military machines create grotesque jumbles of the animate and inanimate realms. In his manuscripts, the late medieval German engineer Conrad Kyeser depicts grappling devices that resemble cats and other clawed animals, and the machines introduce themselves to the reader with proper names: "I am Philoneus," one pyrotechnic engine proclaims, "made of copper, silver, bronze, clay, gold, or other sturdy stuff. When I am empty I do not burn, but set my body, filled with turpentine or strong wine, on the hearth, and then, when warmed, I emit fiery sparks."[78] As the name Philoneus (Φιλο–νευς, or love of novelty) suggests, Kyeser's invention is self-consciously new even as it is also grounded in the casual familiarity of human discourse. Disguised as animate creatures, these and

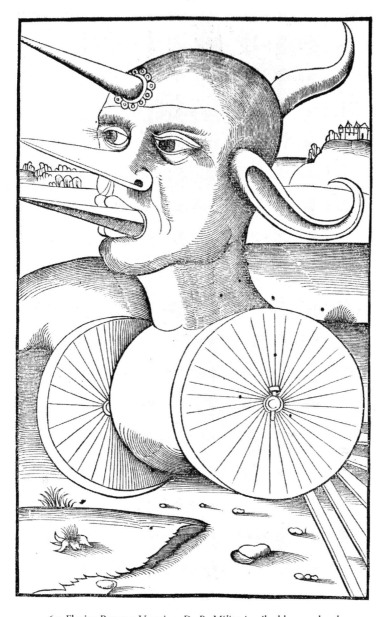

6.1 Flavius Renatus Vegetius, *De Re Militari*, spiked human head

other war machines both reflect and camouflage the transformations in military tactics and engineering taking place during the Renaissance, in which face-to-face conflict between individual human soldiers is replaced by the kind of impersonal, mechanical violence perpetrated by Talus. In an attempt, perhaps, to conceal or diffuse the increasing anonymity of mechanized warfare, sixteenth-century engineers humanize and aestheticize their designs, enchasing cherubs on pistols and creating similarly incongruous couplings so as to "make the gun beautiful," as the Italian artillerist Vanoccio Biringuccio puts it.[79]

As Book v struggles to reconcile chivalric conventions and values with the mechanically enhanced militarism of a "stonie" age, Artegall emerges as the principal champion of a chivalric ethic either disregarded or threatened both by his enemies (Radigund, Malengin, the Souldan) and by his own iron groom, whose inhuman indifference proves hostile to Spenser's courtly project of fashioning gentlemen. As he contemplates whether an excess or a dearth of human feeling poses a greater threat to a just society, Spenser ponders the assets and liabilities – moral, political, and spiritual – of both human weakness and mechanical invulnerability. While the ease with which Artegall is mollified supports a theory of heroic virtue consistent with the proem to Book iv, Talus' inviolability complicates that theory, for he lacks the susceptibility to feeling that is the unavoidable and often troublesome companion of the Knight of Justice.

Spenser explores these questions through a symbolic idiom of hardness and softness that saturates Book v and in particular informs its most protracted episode of singlehanded combat, the fight between Artegall and Radigund in Canto 5. While Talus' method of combat is predicated upon the de-individuation and multiplication of the enemy into "raskall crews" and "tumultuous routs," Artegall remains in the uneasy position of being able to see, touch, and count his adversaries. When the combat begins, Spenser imagines Artegall "Like as a Smith that to his cunning feat / The stubborne mettall seeketh to subdew" (v.v.7). Likening the Knight of Justice to a blacksmith who toils against Radigund "as if she had an yron andvile beene" (v.v.8), Spenser initially represents this battle with the same relentless, objectifying aggression applied by Redcrosse Knight, whose fierce blows to the dragon are compared to "sparckles from the Anduile" made by "heavie hammers" (i.xi.42). Yet unlike Redcrosse, who never sees the dragon as anything more animate than an "infernall fournace," Artegall comes to recognize that Radigund is not a machine made of "steely armes" that emits "flakes of fire," but rather a fleshy, living woman (i.xi.44). When his sword shears away her helmet, he discovers "a miracle of natures goodly grace, / In her faire visage" (v.v.8; v.v.12). Throwing down his sword, Artegall stands flustered "with emptie hands all weaponlesse," recoiling from a conflict suddenly infused with emotional and tactile feeling:

> At sight thereof his cruell minded hart
> Empierced was with pittifull regard,
> That his sharpe sword he threw from him apart,
> Cursing his hand that had that visage mard . . .
>
> (v.v.14, v.v.13)

No longer in possession of the instruments of physical distantiation that make violence possible for him, Artegall is mollified by Radigund, subdued by her "ruth of beautie" even as Radigund remains ruthless and stubborn, attacking him with "huge redoubled strokes" (v.v.13–14). The smith-and-metal analogy inverted, Artegall is softened and made a "womans slave," an office he performs with "true subjection" (v.v.23; 26).

Yet the remainder of the episode complicates the initial opposition between Artegall's susceptibility to feeling and Radigund's heartlessness. Like Talus' odd inner "quake," Radigund's apparent immunity to affection masks a fervor within: full of "outrage" and "ire" in war, she struggles to repress her growing tenderness for Artegall:

> . . . still the more she strove it to subdew,
> The more she still augmented her owne smart,
> And wyder made the wound of th'hidden dart.
>
> (v.v.28)

Spenser's lesson is clear: affection will out, and Radigund's "stubborne handling of her love-sicke hart" is both a fruitless effort and a violent misconstrual of the injunction to govern one's affections. As Radigund and her maid are touched by Artegall, Canto 5 ends as every human character is mollified by their passions as if they had taken a communal dip in the pond that strips Redcrosse Knight of his manly courage and turns him "feeble fraile" (I.vii.6). Only Talus escapes Radegone untouched: when the Amazon's army "thought on Talus hands to lay," he disperses them with his flail, preserving the physical and psychic distance essential to the execution of his violent acts (v.v.19). Canto 5 thus reassesses Spenser's thesis in the proem to Book IV that military valor and love are mutually supportive virtues:

> . . . all the workes of those wise sages,
> And brave exploits which great Heroes wonne,
> In love were either ended or begunne.
>
> (IV.Proem.3)

Artegall's capture and Talus' subsequent triumph interrogate the extent to which "naturall affection" is profitable or even necessary for the "brave exploits" of war (IV.Proem.2).

In its insistence upon the centrality of feeling to human experience, the battle between Artegall and Radigund participates in Book V's larger undertaking to delineate and enforce the physical and epistemological perimeters of the human subject. As a quasi-animate machine, Talus plays a crucial role in this scheme by upsetting the maintenance of distinctions between the human and the inhuman. The classical ancestors of Spenser's Talus are associated with the protection of boundaries: in Plato's *Minos* and Apollodorus' *Library*, Talus is the bronze man of Crete who guards its laws and its borders; in the *Argonautica*, he throws stones at voyagers as they approach the island, just as Spenser's Talus throws rocks at Malengin (V.ix.17).[80] In a more unusual version of the legend, which appears both in Ovid's *Metamorphoses* and in Apollodorus' *Library*, Talus is the nephew and apprentice of Daedalus, and he does not guard physical boundaries but rather patrols the threshold between nature and artifice. Incurring his uncle's envy for the invention of a saw, copied in iron from the pattern of the backbone of a fish, he is thrown off a cliff by Daedalus, and in Ovid's account is transformed into a *perdix*, or partridge.[81] Talus' uncanny ability to create a carpenter's instrument modeled after an organic prototype, as well as his own capacity for metamorphosis, dissolves the distinction between living creatures and insensate objects, upsetting the priority of nature over *techne* that *The Faerie Queene* so frequently asserts. The fate of Ovid's Talus becomes a warning to those who seek to effect metamorphic transformations between organic and mechanical realms, an art that his uncle practices with similarly inauspicious results.

Given Talus' ability to slip between the margins of the human and the non-human, one might add to the complicated ancestry of Spenser's iron man a possible Latin pun: *talus* is the Latin for knucklebone, the anatomical feature on the hind feet of certain animals which one Renaissance anatomist likens to "the wheele of a pulley."[82] While *tali* distinguish one group of animals from another, they also distinguish all animals from man, as Erasmus points out in his colloquy on the subject: "man alone is without *tali* for a double reason: first, because he is a biped, secondly, because he has feet split by five toes."[83] Spenser's Talus performs a similar function in that he contributes to the demarcation of boundaries between human and non-human creatures and objects.

Klaus Theweleit has characterized the Fascist soldier as a man who kills "in order to maintain a fragile sense of [his] own bodily boundaries."[84] As invulnerable as he appears, Spenser's Talus may perform his violent acts in response to a similar threat of internal incoherence or fragility. In several accounts of the Cretan Talus, he possesses a fatal flaw in his otherwise impenetrable metal frame. The *Argonautica* describes how "in all the rest of his limbs was he fashioned of bronze and invulnerable; but beneath the sinew by his ankle was a blood-red vein; and this, with its issues of life and death, was covered by a thin skin." In Apollodorus' version, Hephaestus constructs Talus with "a single vein extending from his neck to his ankles, and a bronze nail was rammed home at the end of the vein." Like Achilles, this Talus meets his fate by a fragile patch in his heel, either grazing his ankle on a jagged rock (in the *Argonautica*) or (in Apollodorus' *Library*) falling for a trick of Medea, who "drew out the nail, so that all the ichor gushed out and he died."[85]

Spenser translates this fatal defect of the iron man in Book v by making hands, feet, and artificial appendages sites of tension and violence, the vulnerable spots of a text that nervously explores the thin membrane between the animate and the inanimate realms. Armed with his "iron paw," Talus is a key participant in the displacement of hands by their inhuman or ersatz counterparts, a task he accomplishes, more often than not, by dismemberment – decapitating Pollente and Grantorto, cutting off Munera's hands and feet, and so on.[86] Talus' own appendages are of course synthetic, his "iron paw" and flail substitutes for the hands that so many of his adversaries also enhance by mechanical means. Almost no one in Book v has a genuine set of hands, and the artificial limbs scattered about Book v habitually serve as instruments and as casualties of violence. Munera's hands and feet are gold and silver, but these are "chopt off, and nayld on high" by Talus, an apt punishment for the thefts she has committed – literally, it appears – "by hooke and crooke" (v.ii.26–27). The Souldan uses his "yron hookes and graples keene" in battle, but they turn against him, rending his "faire limbs" such that "no whole peece of him was to be seene" (v.viii.42–43). Malengin, the master of "slights and jugling feates," holds a "huge long staffe . . . arm'd with many an yron hooke," supplemental appendages that symbolize his "legierdemayne" or devious ingenuity (v.ix.11,13). Geryoneo shares Malengin's deftness as he wields a "huge great yron axe" among his six hands:

> He could his weapon shift from side to syde,
> From hand to hand, and with such nimblesse sly . . .
> . . . Behinde, beside, before, as he it list apply.
>
> (v.xi.5–6)

With their depraved, mechanically enhanced dexterity, Geryoneo and Malengin demonstrate a mastery of their weapons that the heroes of Book v lack. Arthur, Artegall, and Burbon all drop their weapons on at least one occasion, and their clumsiness suggests that like the ancient Sir Sergis, they have "long since aside had set / The use of armes, and battell quite forgone" (v.xi.37).

Renaissance writers follow Aristotle in regarding the human hand as the "instrument of instruments," the natural prototype for all other tools: the hand is "an instrument that represents many instruments," for it is "as good as a talon, or a claw, or a horn, or again, a spear or a sword, or any other weapon or tool: it can be all of these, because it can seize and hold them all."[87] In Peter Apian's 1533 *Instrument Buch*, a chapter on the "naturlich Instrument die Finger der Hande" follows several chapters concerning the construction of quadrants and sectors, thus establishing a continuity between the human hand and its inorganic counterparts. The French mechanician Joseph Boillot elaborates upon this analogical instrumentality in his 1598 *Modelles Artifices de Feu*, writing that the original "instruments" are the senses, such as sight and touch; then come the hands, and finally machinery.[88] A crucial yet flexible midpoint in the spectrum between nature and artifice, the Renaissance hand – and even more its prosthetic imitations – places the "machine into a close and uneasy relation with the organic."[89]

The proliferation of hands and their artificial replacements reflects Book v's pervasive concerns about the legitimacy and efficacy of political instrumentality – about the mediation of diplomatic, juridical, or military actions through instruments both living and lifeless, including hands, weapons, servants, and machines. The tools of the body politic, hands and feet are common metaphors for political instrumentality during the Renaissance. James I advises his son in the *Basilikon Doron* to follow the "microcosme of your owne body" in his political conduct: "having two hands and two feete, with many fingers and toes for quicke execution, in employing all instruments meet for effectuating your deliberations."[90] By contrast, Artegall's failure to manipulate his tools, from his dropped sword to the disobedient Talus, calls into question the Knight of Justice's reliance upon his other auxiliary instruments. If political authority is most effective, according to one sixteenth-century writer, when we cannot "distinguish the end of the instrument" from its agent, then Book v reveals the hazards of delegating authority as it passes from Astraea to Artegall to Talus, becoming more diluted at each remove.[91]

Designs for Renaissance war machinery reveal a self-conscious recognition of both the continuity and the friction between natural and artificial instruments. In Valturio's design for grappling hooks, a disembodied hand grasps the crenellations at the roof of the castle, an eerie reminder of the human appendage after which grappling tools are modeled (figure 6.2). Yet nowhere does war machinery generate more confusion about the displacement of the human hand by its mechanical supplements than in Taccola's *De Ingeneis* ("Of Engines"), a fifteenth-century Sienese treatise on mechanical devices that depicts animals and machines side by side in order to establish structural or functional correspondences between organic and inorganic instruments.[92] Many of the animals depicted in *De Ingeneis* are exotic creatures such as unicorns and rhinoceri; others have their weaponry built into their bodies. By representing tusked and horned animals alongside depictions of machinery, Taccola's treatise traces the continuity between the animate and the inanimate while also intimating the potential displacement of the former by the latter. Opposite a page depicting a phantasmagoria of grapples, cranes, and similar grasping instruments, a grazing giraffe uses his long neck to reach the leaves of a tall tree without any hands, a natural analogue to the hooks and clamps beside him. In another illustration, a porcupine confronts a siege engine, its protruding quills readied for action and clearly akin, in both aim and design, to the defensive spikes on Renaissance chariots and tanks.

It is for similar tactical reasons that Spenser's Malengin morphs himself into a hedgehog, a particularly cunning defensive maneuver since, when Artegall grabs on to the prickly creature, it "prickt him so, that he away it threw" (v.ix.18). Slipping through Artegall's fingers, Malengin deflects the touch of his enemies, an evasion of physical contact which, like that of Talus, sheds light upon the military tactics of Book v. War in Book v is in essence tactile, consisting in the ability to grab, hook, or touch one's adversary while simultaneously protecting oneself from being disarmed – from injury or loss of weapons, but also from the physical sensation that arouses the affections. Talus and Malengin arm themselves against any infringement upon their sacrosanct physical and emotional space, reproducing the Stoic indifference that Du Vair sums up in the attitude, "this thing toucheth me not at all." The untouchability they seek not only cultivates Stoic *apatheia* but also assures the inviolability of sovereign power, as Louis XII of France must have recognized when he chose for his emblem a hedgehog accompanied by the motto *Cominus et eminus*: hand-to-hand and out of reach.[93] His *impresa* imagines royal power as Briarean, actualizing the commonplace morsel of political advice that princes ought to have "many eyes and long arms" in order to "exercise" power from "afarre off."[94] By extending the reach of the human hand, mechanical instruments bolster the fantasy of

6.2 Roberto Valturio, *De Re Militari*, grappling hooks

an all-touching yet untouchable and inviolate sovereignty. Calling Louis' porcupine emblem a "flying arsenal," Emmanuele Tesauro compares it to "the javelin, the arquebus, and above all Archimedes' engine, which (as we said) wounded near and afar." Assailing their targets without necessitating the proximity of agent and recipient, these mechanical devices effect so exemplary a political instrumentality that, according to Tesauro, "one might have painted that very engine [constructed by Archimedes], with the same words *Eminus et cominus*."[95]

The artful distantiation of Talus and Malengin dramatizes the increasingly estranging and dehumanizing effects of war during the Renaissance. While the hand-to-hand combat practiced by Artegall runs the risk of fostering intimacy between combatants and eroding the emotional and physical distance necessary to fight, Talus embodies the military technologies and tactics that preserve and enhance the distance between adversaries. Spenser recognizes both the appeals and the dangers of Talus' capacity to strip war of its tactile nature, for the insensate hardness that makes Talus a model soldier also inures him to pain and to pity, qualities central to the essentialist humanism of *The Faerie Queene*. Although Spenser never arrives at an explicit critique of Essexian militarism in Book v, Talus' insensibility demonstrates that while war may inspire heroic passion, it also dehumanizes its participants. In this respect, Spenser would agree with Pierre Charron that while valor is the "greatest, the most generous and heroicall virtue of all others," the inurement to violence necessitated by war has a profoundly estranging effect: "the arte and experience of undoing one another, of killing, ruinating, destroying our owne proper kinde," Charron writes, "seemes to be unnaturall and to proceed from an alienation of our sence and understanding."[96] Allegorizing that alienation of sense through Talus' iron paw, Spenser defines human nature as the capacity to feel pain, to experience the "sense of feeling" which, as Montaigne argues at the end of his *Apology*, "doth so often confound and re-enverse all these goodly Stoicall resolutions," corroding the fantasy of the iron man.[97]

Conclusion

Spenserian allegory is characterized by what Michael Murrin has called an "absurdity principle," an element of ridiculousness that reaches its climax in Book v.[1] Despite its cynical view of war and its depiction of moral and cosmic decay, the legend of Justice is undeniably comical, even absurd, on account of its protagonists' ability to escape injury with such remarkable ease. With his cartoon-like invulnerability, Talus is the heir of Ariosto's Orrilo, able to pop his decapitated limbs right back onto his body, or of Rabelais' Master Gasser, who in the *Quart Livre* invents a method "to avoid being wounded or touched by cannon fire [de non estre blessé ne touché par coups de canon]."[2] What makes these characters funny is their exaggerated displays of invulnerability, their participation in a Stoic fantasy that is illusive and often parodic. In "Of Constancie," Montaigne mocks those soldiers who behave like iron men, describing how men "of resolute minde" have been seen to shield themselves from gunfire with their bare hands, a scene which "give[s] their fellowes cause of laughter."[3] In Montaigne's example, as in the case of Talus, the zealous disciple of Stoic resolve becomes a caricature, his hyperbolic fortitude a grotesque distortion of the dignified and godlike elements of humanity.

Despite its comic vein, Book v of *The Faerie Queene* is morally unsettling for its persistent fusion of war and spectacle. In true chivalric – and post-modern – fashion, Spenser conflates violence and recreation in a manner typical of Renaissance technical treatises, which outline the construction and use of war machinery alongside devices intended for private or courtly recreations, drawing attention to the fact that the most violent applications of machinery are similar in design, if not in function, to the most harmless ones. Fireworks, in particular, link the battlefield to the *apparati* of recreative, courtly display. In Book x of his *Pyrotechnia* (1540), Biringuccio explains that "artificial fires" are "fine and useful things in wars" but they likewise appeal to "those who take delight in celebrating holidays with festivities and with fires." Fireworks have a "happy and pleasing effect" according to Biringuccio even though they are "deadly and very injurious to all living things" and may bring "harm and terror" to humankind.[4] The conflation of martial and recreational pyrotechnics is even more pronounced in early seventeenth-century English treatises on the subject such as John White's *Rich cabinet, with variety of inventions*, in which instructions for the manufacture of explosive devices to blow up bridges and fortifications are provided in the same chapter as directions for making a "dragon, or the like [creature] spitting of fire" and for making "Saint George fighting with a dragon in fire," a pasteboard diorama whose figures move by means of hidden magnets.[5]

In his 1635 *Pyrotechnia*, which also contains directions for reproducing the characters of Spenserian romance in fire, John Babington explains the uneasy juxtaposition of war and spectacle typical of this genre of technical literature. While "artillery and fire-workes" are "useful against an enemy in the field," Babington writes, "these halcyon dayes" oblige him to invent machines that "howsoever they may seeme to serve onely for delight and exercise . . . the due consideration of the ordering of them may excite and stirre up in an ingenious minde, sundry inventions more servicable in times of warre."[6] Babington's appreciation that his mechanical inventions exist primarily to stimulate the intellect and the imagination reveals a fundamental difference between Renaissance culture's attitudes towards technology and our own. In Babington's world, machines are tools of thought that produce effects not through their utilization but rather through a "due consideration" of them.

As intellectual recreations or as conceptual tools for philosophers, scholars, and artists, Renaissance machines are only secondarily regarded as objects with specific functions and aims. Machines are means, not ends: they represent ways of doings things rather than things to be done. The most ineffectual or impractical machines are often more compelling to Renaissance culture than machines that "work" in the modern sense of the term. Frequently regarded as unpredictable or mendacious, Renaissance machines do some of their finest work when they fail to work, for in so doing they help their makers and observers understand the nature of courtly artifice or political authority, the uncertainty of the senses, or the frailty and disorder, cosmic and microcosmic, that Donne compares to the erratic movements of a clock: "we scarce live long enough to try, / Whether a true made clock run right, or lie."[7] The staged mechanical catastrophes in James Shirley's *Triumph of Peace* and in Gian Lorenzo Bernini's *The Inundation of the Tiber*, as well as the actual catastrophe during the 1613 performance of Thomas Campion's *Masque of Squires* in which a cloud machine became intrusively visible and audible to the audience, are a source of anxious delight for a culture that relishes the kind of playful negotiation between artifice and *naturalezza* set into motion by the breakdown of machinery.[8] By simulating the collapsing sets, falling curtains, and fires that are an all-too-common feature of the Renaissance theatre, the counterfeit malfunctioning of stage machinery confirms the complex relationship between art and nature noted by Zanni, a wry observer of the mechanical foul-ups in Bernini's *Impresario*: "When a thing looks truly natural, there's got to be some machination behind it [al ghè machina qui sotto]."[9]

In their actual or imagined tendency to break down, Renaissance machines caution against intellectual subtlety, bureaucratic complexity, and human arrogance and pride. Edward Coke compares the English legal system to a clock, since in both contrivances, the malfunctioning of even the smallest wheels can cause the entire mechanism to grind to a halt.[10] In a 1605 text, Thomas Tymme uses a similar analogy to attest to the "shortnesse, frailtie, and miseries of Mans Life" and the "foolishnesse" of our minds, since the "human clocke of life" is just like those clocks "made by arte and skill, with so many wheeles, that if one be staide, all the rest are letted."[11] Far from serving as an analogical model for a divinely appointed universe – or, for that matter, a self-regulating, godless one – the broken clock posits an ideal order only to reduce it to disarray, revealing a world "all in pieces, all coherence gone."[12]

To the dismay of more pragmatic mechanicians such as Salomon de Caus, the fabulous machines depicted in the *Theatrum Mechanorum* of Besson and Ramelli linger in the realm of "vaines imaginations," impossible dreams "invented on paper and ineffectual in practice [inventées sur le papier . . . (et ne) peuvent avoir aucun effet]."[13] Designed for the printed page, Renaissance machines are born out of the demands and concerns of a humanistic culture, contrived to pose and answer intellectual, aesthetic, and moral questions even at the expense of their own effectiveness. Complaining about excessive refinements in Elizabethan infantry tactics, John Smythe scoffs at formations designed according to aesthetic, and not strategic, considerations, those "battles in triangle, and battles in form of stars, with many other such battles of divers shapes and fashions extraordinary, that are rather set forth to fill up books and to please the curious than for any great use."[14] Renaissance military engineers accommodate their inventions to the tastes and expectations of readers, shaping those inventions according to philological and literary concerns: "new names," remonstrates the Italian humanist Flavio Biondo, are invented along with the "invention of new instruments." Primed by the outlandish mechanical marvels of romance,

Renaissance readers relish the exotic novelty of technical vocabulary: "unless they read of battering rams, missiles of burning pitch, slings, and scorpions," Biondo complains, "[they] think the siege no siege at all or, at best, a very inept one [eorum insolentia ideo multos fastidit, quod nisi arietem, fallicaram, scorpionem, fundasque ilico legentes offenderint, nullam aut ineptissimam fuisse oppugnationem existamant]."[15] Renaissance machines are produced by and for the golden world of the imagination, so much so that to machinate (*machiner*), as one early seventeenth-century French dictionary defines it, is synonymous with to contrive, to invent, to dream ("machiner ou songer quelque finesse").[16]

Before seventeenth-century science heeds Bacon's call to regulate the human mind and its scientific experiments "as if by machinery," Renaissance culture understands machination not simply as a tool to impose constraints upon the human intellect, but also as a medium for the unfettered expression of wit and fancy. The descendant of Autolycus and his grandson Odysseus – Odysseus *polymechanos*, as Homer often calls him – the Renaissance *homo mechanicus* tucks his devices away in his deep pockets of inventiveness and resourcefulness. For characters such as Marlowe's Barabas, Spenser's Malengin, and Rabelais' Panurge, the inheritor of Odyssean polymechany who "is always machinating something [tousjours machinoit quelque chose]," machines belong to the province of wily intelligence, tools of that clever, devious wit whose energy powers the most vigorous fictions of the Renaissance.[17]

Since the middle of the seventeenth century, the idea of a mechanistic universe has presupposed what Peter Dear has called a "foundation of metaphysical certainty" for the nature and behavior of matter.[18] Yet unlike later seventeenth-century materialists such as Hobbes, whose devotion to a plenist, mechanistic theory of matter demands restricting the scope of scientific study to the investigation of the mechanical causes of natural processes, sixteenth-century writers do not, for the most part, view a mechanized cosmos as a necessarily predictable, orderly, or material one. Indeed, the most pervasively mechanized worlds of the Renaissance imagination are, quite often, also its most disorderly, fanciful, and grotesque, from the anti-masques of Ben Jonson and the artificial bowers of *The Faerie Queene* to Colonna's *Hypnerotomachia Poliphili* and Rabelais' *Tiers Livre*.

What may be the first reappearance of the ancient Greek term *automata*, in Rabelais' *Gargantua*, confirms this essentially imaginative and recreative power of Renaissance machinery. As a respite from the rigorous educational program designed by his tutor Ponocrates, which places a "severe strain on his spirits," Gargantua constructs automata as part of a lesson in pastoral recreation: after "bantering, making merry, drinking healths, playing, singing, dancing," and reading "Virgil's Georgics, or Hesiod, or Politian's Rusticus," Gargantua and his tutor construct "several little automata, that is to say self-moving engines [plusieurs petitz engins automates, c'est à dire soy mouvens eulz-mesmes]."[19] As suggested by Ponocrates, whose name (from the Greek *ponos*, or toil, and *krateo*, or conquest) denotes the triumph of pleasure and facility over effort, Gargantua's self-moving engines transform the relationship between work and play and between discipline and ease. In so doing, Gargantua's mechanical exercises challenge the quintessentially humanist devotion to exercise and restraint – intellectual, moral, and corporeal – that is both epitomized and parodied by Ponocrates' pedagogical program.

Humanism, Machinery, and Renaissance Literature both confirms and complicates Norbert Elias' assertion in *The Civilizing Process* that technology and education are "facets of the same overall development," confederates in the implementation of "affect-control" and of the various social and moral constraints that affect the civilization of conduct during the Renaissance.[20] Yet the Renaissance *homo mechanicus* is not wholly allied with the forces of civility: witness Jonson's depiction of Comus in *Pleasure Reconciled to Virtue*, the anti-masque counterpart to Daedalus whose mechanical inventions include a grain hopper, an "excellent engine, ye spit," and the "great ordnance" attributed to him as the "father of farts."[21] Comus' extraordinary capacity for machination serves the demands of his voracious appetite; like his ancestor, Master Gasser in Rabelais' *Quart Livre*, he "invents all arts, all machines, all crafts, all engines and subtle devices . . . and all for the belly [invente toutes ars, toutes machines, tout mestiers, tous engins et subtilitez . . . et tout pour la trippe!]."[22] Unlike the mechanized bodies imagined by Descartes' *De l'Homme* or by William Harvey's *De Motu Cordis*, the embodied mechanisms of Comus and Master Gasser denote monstrous hybridity, deviance, and passionate excess.

While there indeed exist "machine-men" before the rise of the corpuscular philosophy, they do not necessarily behave in ways sympathetic to a post-Cartesian understanding of what it means for a human being or an animal to be "like a machine" or, for that matter, what it means for a machine to be lifelike. One of the profoundest yet most imperceptible legacies of the intellectual and scientific revolutions of the seventeenth century is the way in which new systems of classification and discourses of knowledge alter the perceived relationship between humans and machines. In order to accommodate developments in both physics and metaphysics, the repertoire of imagined distinctions and similarities governing that relationship is replenished with a new store of metaphors, transformed by a new sense of what it means to do something "as if by machinery." As the inheritors of this legacy, we may not be predisposed either to discern or to understand the intellectual, ethical, and aesthetic presuppositions that do (or do not) govern Renaissance attitudes towards machinery in the century and a half before the scientific revolution. My simplest, but perhaps also my most ambitious, goal in writing this book was to provide an instrument to help both author and reader transcend those predispositions as well as we are able.

It has become critically fashionable over the past decade to speak of "the Renaissance computer," the "early modern search engine," and similar "knowledge technologies" as forerunners of the machines that govern the distribution, ordering, and retrieval of knowledge in our postmodern and post-print world. In certain respects, the analogy between the emergence of print culture in the sixteenth century and the recent Internet revolution is a useful one: both alter intellectual practices and modes of social and political interaction, nurturing new "technologies of the self" for conceiving and performing human identity. Yet to describe Renaissance technologies in terms of contemporary concepts such as hypertext or cyberspace is to obscure the radical polyvalence of machines in the pre-machine age. As tools of humanist self-examination, Renaissance machines are endowed with a forceful heteroglossia: working in league with competing ethical, political, and aesthetic values, they have the power both to arrange and to disarrange the neat rows of dualisms – reason and passion, art and nature, humanity and inhumanity – that confer order upon the mental world of the Renaissance.[23]

Notes

INTRODUCTION: SUBTLE DEVICES: RENAISSANCE HUMANISM
AND ITS MACHINERY

1. Balthasar de Gracián y Morales, *Oraculo Manual y Arte de Prudencia*, ed. L. B. Walton (New York: Dent, 1962), Aphorism 15; Simon Sturtevant, *Metallica, or, The Treatise of metallica, briefly comprehending the doctrine of diverse new metallical inventions* (London: George Eld, 1612), chapter 5, 55.

2. Sturtevant, *Metallica*, preface, A2v; Av; Sturtevant, *Dibre Adam, or Adams Hebrew Dictionarie: a rare and new invention, for the speedie atteyning, and perfect reteyning, of the Hebrew, Chaldee, and Syriack tongues* (London: Felix Kingston, 1602).

3. Sturtevant, *Dibre Adam*, Preface, B2r–v.

4. Peter Ramus, *Scholae in Liberales Artes* (Basel: Eusebium Episcopium, 1578), Preface to the reader, A2r; on his use of the term *technologia*, see Walter Ong, *Ramus, Method, and the Decay of Dialogue* (Cambridge, MA: Harvard University Press, 1958), 197–98; Timothy Reiss, *Knowledge, Discovery, and Imagination in Early Modern Europe: The Rise of Aesthetic Rationalism* (Cambridge: Cambridge University Press, 1997), 77–89.

5. BL C.60.f.9: Gabriel Harvey's copy of *M. Tullii Ciceronis Epistolae ad Atticum* (Venice: Paulus Manutius, 1563), 208, 211.

6. Caspari Streso, *Technologia Theologica Exemplo Illustrata* (Lyons: David Lopes, 1634); for this latter use of *technologia*, see Christoph Scheibler, *Philosophia Compendiosa* (Oxford: William Turner, 1639), chapter 1, A2v: "Technologia est Artium & Scientarum methodica Descriptio ad mentem informandam."

7. Thomas Blundeville, *The true order and methode of wryting and reading hystories* (London: William Seres, 1574), Dedication to the Earl of Leicester, B1r; *M. Blundeville his Exercises* (2nd edn., London: John Windet, 1597), Preface.

8. Conrad Dasypodius, *Institutionem Mathematicarum* (Strasbourg: Iosias Rihelius, 1593), "Elementa Mechanicae," 42; compare *Spiritali di Herone Alessandrino*, tr. Alessandro Giorgi (Urbino: Ragusii, 1592), translator's preface, 3; Bernardino Baldi, *Mechanica Aristotelis Problemata Exercitationes* (Mainz, 1621), Preface.

9. Francis Bacon, *The Great Instauration*, Preface, in *Novum Organum*, ed. and tr. Peter Urbach and John Gibson (Chicago and LaSalle: Open Court Press, 1994), 12, 23.

10. On method, see Neal Gilbert, *Renaissance Concepts of Method* (New York: Columbia University Press, 1960); Ong, *Ramus*, 163–72; Reiss, *Knowledge, Discovery, and Imagination*, 73–134.

11. R. Malcolm Smuts, *Court Culture and the Origins of a Royalist Tradition in Early Stuart England* (Philadelphia: University of Pennsylvania Press, 1987), 147–49; Steven Shapin, *A Social History of Truth. Civility and Science in Seventeenth-Century England* (Chicago: University of Chicago Press, 1994); Hélène Vérin, *La Gloire des ingénieurs: l'intélligence technique du XVIe au XVIIIe siècle* (Paris: Albin Michel, 1993), 102–11. On virtuosity and technique, also see Walter E. Houghton, Jr., "The English Virtuoso in the Seventeenth Century," *Journal of the History of Ideas* 3 (1942), 51–73 and 190–219; John Shearman, *Mannerism* (London: Penguin, 1967); Paolo Rossi, *Philosophy, Technology and the Arts in the Early Modern Era*, tr. Salvator Attanasio (New York: Harper & Row, 1970); R. J. W. Evans, *Rudolf II and his World: a Study in Intellectual History, 1576–1612* (2nd edn., Oxford: Clarendon Press, 1973); Roy Strong, *Henry, Prince of Wales and England's Lost Renaissance* (London: Thames & Hudson, 1986).

12. Patricia Fumerton, *Cultural Aesthetics: Renaissance Literature and the Practice of Social Ornament* (Chicago: University of Chicago Press, 1991), 1–3; compare Thomas Hankins and Robert J. Silverman, *Instruments and the Imagination* (Princeton: Princeton University Press, 1995), 13.

13. Horst Bredekamp, *The Lure of Antiquity and the Cult of the Machine: The Kunstkammer and the Evolution of Nature, Art, and Technology*, tr. Allison Brown (Princeton: Markus Weiner Publications, 1995), 7 and throughout.

14. Francesco Sansovino, *The Quintessence of Wit, being A corrant comfort of conceites maximes, and poleticke devises*, tr. R[obert] H[itchcock] (London: Edward Allde, 1590), Aphorism 565, 66r.

15. Cyprian Lucar, *A Treatise Named Lucar Solace* (London: Richard Field, 1590), Book IV, chapter 12; Hugh Plat, *The jewell house of art and nature conteining divers rare and profitable inventions* (London: Peter Short, 1594), Preface to the Reader, Br.

16. Marcel Detienne and Jean-Pierre Vernant, *Cunning Intelligence in Greek Culture and Society*, tr. Janet Lloyd (Chicago: University of Chicago Press, 1991), 3.

17. *Ibid.*, 34–37. Compare Michel de Certeau, *The Practice of Everyday Life*, tr. Steven Rendall (Berkeley: University of California Press, 1984), Preface, xix; 37; and Vérin, *La Gloire des ingénieurs*, 19–26.

18. John Dee, *Euclids Elements of Geometrie, with the Mathematicall Preface of John Dee*, tr. Henry Billingsley (London: John Daye, 1570), D1r.

19. Aristotle, *Mechanical Problems*, in *Minor Works*, tr. W. S. Hett (Cambridge, MA: Harvard University Press, 1963), 331.

20. Giovanni Tortelli, *De Orthographia dictionem e graecis tractarum* (Rome, 1471), "horologium." On Tortelli's clock, see Alexander Keller, "A Renaissance

Humanist Looks at 'New' Inventions: the Article 'Horologium' in Giovanni Tortelli's *De Orthographia*," *Technology and Culture* 11 (1970), 345–65: 345–47.

21. Tortelli, *De Orthographia*: "Ut sciamus verum esse quod Aristoteles & alli quidam scripscrunt pauperum proprium esse cum mali sunt dolo uti: divitum vi: ideoque alterum vulpeculae: alterum leoni componatur." On the *metis* of the fox, see Detienne and Vernant, *Cunning Intelligence*, 34.

22. Dasypodius, *Inst. Math.*, 42; Vitruvius, *On Architecture*, 2 vols, tr. Frank Granger (Cambridge: Heinemann, 1999), vol. II, Book X, 1, 275. Compare Guido Ubaldo del Monte, *Le Mecchaniche*, tr. Filippo Pigafetta (Venice, 1581), Preface, which defines mechanics as "cosa fatta con artificio de movere, come per miracolo, & fuori dell'humana possanza grandissimi pesi con piccola forza [a thing made artificially to move, as if by a miracle, and beyond human power, very great weights with little force]."

23. Bacon, *The New Atlantis*, in *The Oxford Authors: Francis Bacon*, ed. Brian Vickers (Oxford: Oxford University Press, 1996), 485.

24. Randle Cotgrave, *A Dictionarie of the French and English Tongues* (London, 1611, rpt. and ed. William S. Woods [Columbia: University of South Carolina Press, 1950]), sig. Ddd 4r, "engin"; John Florio, *Anna's World of Words* (London: E. Blount, 1611) and his *Vocabulario Italiano & Inglese* (London: T. Warren, 1659), *ingegno*; Guillaume Budé, *Commentarii Linguae graecae* (Paris: Iodoco Badio Ascensio, 1529), 677; *Lexicon Graecolatinum Ioannis Crispini* (London: Henry Bynneman, 1581), Zzz3r; on the same page, Crespin defines *technologia* as "arte loquor, artificiosè disputo, argutor." On the origins of the term technology, see Jacques Guillerme, "Les Liens du sens dans l'histoire del la technologie," in *De la technique à la technologie* (Paris: Centre Nationale de la Recherche Scientifique, 1984), 24–27; Vérin, *La Gloire des ingénieurs*, 19–27; 144–58.

25. Girolamo Cardano, *De Subtilitate libri xxi* (Nürnberg, 1550), tr. Richard le Blanc as *Les Livres . . . de la subtilité* (Paris: Charles l'Angelier, 1556), Book 14, 290 and throughout. On Cardano and J. C. Scaliger, see Ian MacLean, "Montaigne, Cardano: The Reading of Subtlety / The Subtlety of Reading," *French Studies* 37 (1983), 143–56; Anthony Grafton, *Cardano's Cosmos: the Worlds and Works of a Renaissance Astrologer* (Cambridge, MA: Harvard University Press, 1999), 161–63.

26. Cardano, *De la subtilité*, Preface, 1.

27. Francis Bacon, *Phenomena Universi sive Historia Naturalis ad Condendam Philosophiam* (1611), in *Philosophical Studies, 1611–1618*, ed. and tr. Graham Rees, vol. VI of *The Oxford Francis Bacon* (Oxford: Clarendon Press, 2000), 2–5. On Bacon's interest in subtlety, see Graham Rees, "Atomism and 'Subtlety' in Francis Bacon's Philosophy," *Annals of Science* 37 (1980), 549–71: 566–70.

28. Bacon, *Phenomena Universi* and *Descriptio Globi Intellectualis*, in *Philosophical Studies*, 6–7; 166–67.

29. Bacon, *The Advancement of Learning*, ed. Michael Kiernan, vol. IV of *The Oxford Francis Bacon* (Oxford: Clarendon Press, 2000), 24.

30. Bacon, *Filium Labyrinthi sive Formula Inquisitionis*, in *Philosophical Studies*, 416; *Novum Organum*, ed. and tr. Urbach and Gibson, Book II, Aphorism 39, 225.

31. Bacon, *De Sapientia Veterum*, tr. Sir Arthur Gorges as *The Wisdome of the Ancients* (London, 1619; rpt. New York: Garland, 1976), Fable 19, 94.

32. Francis Bacon, *The New Atlantis*, in *Francis Bacon*, ed. Vickers, 484–87; "Of Simulation and Dissimulation," in *The Essayes or Counsels, Civill and Morall*, ed. Michael Kiernan, vol. xv of *The Oxford Francis Bacon* (Oxford: Clarendon Press, 2000), 21. On machinery in *The New Atlantis*, see Amy Boesky, "Bacon's *New Atlantis* and the Laboratory of Prose," in *The Project of Prose in Early Modern Europe and the New World*, ed. Elizabeth Fowler and Roland Greene (Cambridge: Cambridge University Press, 1997), 138–53.

33. Bacon, "Of Simulation and Dissimulation," in *Essayes*, 20. On Bacon's Tacitism, see Edward Benjamin, "Bacon and Tacitus," *Classical Philology* 60 (1965), 102–10; Morris Croll, *"Attic" and Baroque Prose Style*, ed. J. Max Patrick and Robert O. Evans (Princeton: Princeton University Press, 1969); F. J. Levy, "Hayward, Daniel, and the Beginnings of Politic History in England," *Huntington Library Quarterly* 50 (1987), 1–34; J. H. M. Salmon, "Stoicism and Roman Example: Seneca and Tacitus in Jacobean England," *Journal of the History of Ideas* 50 (1992), 199–225; Mary Tenney, "Tacitus in the Politics of Early Stuart England," *Classical Journal* 37 (1941), 151–63.

34. Bacon, "Of Masques and Triumphs," in *Essayes*, 117.

35. Glenn Burgess, *Absolute Monarchy and the Stuart Constitution* (New Haven: Yale University Press, 1996), 53; also see Smuts, "Court-Centered Politics and the Uses of Roman Historians, *c.* 1590–1630," in *Culture and Politics in Early Stuart England*, ed. Kevin Sharpe and Peter Lake (Stanford, CA: Stanford University Press, 1993), 22–27.

36. On the Stoicism of the Earl of Essex and his circle, see Salmon, "Stoicism and Roman Example," 205–17; Smuts, "Court-Centered Politics," 22–27; Burgess, *Absolute Monarchy*, 53–61. On Percy's Stoicism, see Stephen Clucas, " 'Noble Virtue in Extremes': Henry Percy, Ninth Earl of Northumberland, Patronage, and the Politics of Stoic Consolation," *Renaissance Studies* 9 (1995), 267–91, esp. 268–85. On Leicester's and Essex's interest in machinery, see Mordechai Feingold, *The Mathematicians' Apprenticeship: Science, University, and Society in England, 1560–1640* (Cambridge: Cambridge University Press, 1984), chapter 6; E. G. R. Taylor, *Mathematical Practitioners in Tudor and Stuart England* (Cambridge: Cambridge University Press, 1954), chapter 2.

37. On the popularity of Tacitus in England during the 1590s, see David Womersley, "Sir John Hayward's Tacitism," *Renaissance Studies* 6 (1992), 46–59 and his "Sir Henry Savile's Translation of Tacitus and the Political Interpretation of Elizabethan Texts," *Review of English Studies* 42 (1991), 313–42; Burgess, *Absolute Monarchy*, 54–61; Levy, "Hayward, Daniel, and the Beginnings of Politic History," 10–26; Alan Bradford, "Stuart Absolutism and the 'Utility' of Tacitus," *Huntington Library Quarterly* 46 (1983), 127–55; Salmon, "Stoicism and Roman Example," 205–17.

38. On the Earl of Essex and his circle, see Paul E. J. Hammer, *The Polarisation of Elizabethan Politics. The Political Career of Robert Devereux, Second Earl of Essex, 1585–1597* (Cambridge: Cambridge University Press, 1999), 294–303 and his "The Uses of Scholarship: The Secretariat of Robert Devereux, Second Earl of Essex, *c.* 1585–1601," *English Historical Review* 109 (1994), 26–51. On Essex as patron, see Mervyn James, "At a Crossroads of the Political Culture: the Essex Revolt, 1601," chapter 9 of his *Society, Politics, and Culture: Studies in Early Modern England* (Cambridge: Cambridge University Press, 1986), 418–63. On the Earl of Leicester and his circle, see Hammer, "The Uses of Scholarship," 42; Salmon, "Precept, Example, and Truth: Degory Wheare and the *ars historica*," chapter 2 of *The Historical Imagination in Early Modern Britain*, ed. Donald Kelley and David Harris Sacks (Cambridge: Cambridge University Press, 1997), 13–18.

39. Henry Percy, Ninth Earl of Northumberland, *Advice to his Son*, ed. G. B. Harrison (London: Ernest Benn, 1930), 67, 71.

40. For Percy's account, see P.R.O., S.P. Domestic James I, vol. ii, no. 9 (*c.* 1606), rpt. in G. R. Batho, "Thomas Harriot and the Northumberland Household," *1991 Thomas Harriot Lecture, Oriel College* (Oxford, 1992); see also Clucas, " 'Noble Virtue in Extremes,' " 269.

41. Richard Tuck, *Philosophy and Government 1572–1651* (Cambridge: Cambridge University Press, 1992), 108; Bacon, *The Advancement of Learning*, Book 2, 58–59.

42. Aristotle, *Politics*, in *Aristotle XXI*, tr. H. Rackham (Cambridge, MA: Harvard University Press, 1977), Book 1, 1253b. My translation, based on Rackham: Aristotle uses the term κυβερνοσ (pilot, governor) for my sailor, and οργανον (organon) for my "instrument."

43. *Ibid.*, Book 1, 1253b.

44. Plutarch, *The philosophie, commonlie called, the morals . . . translated out of Greeke into English . . . by Philemon Holland* (London: Arnold Hatfield, 1603), "Precepts of Policie," 350; compare Justus Lipsius, *Six Bookes of Politickes or Civil Doctrine*, tr. William Jones (London: Richard Field, 1594), Book v, chapter 17, 175.

45. Plutarch, *Morals*, tr. Holland, "Precepts of Policie," 359.

46. On political patronage of, and interest in, mechanics, see Gerhard Oestreich, *Neostoicism and the Early Modern State*, tr. David McLintock (Cambridge: Cambridge University Press, 1982), 71–85; Jason Saunders, *Justus Lipsius. The Philosophy of Renaissance Stoicism* (New York: Liberal Arts, 1955), 28 and throughout; Robert Bireley, *The Counter-Reformation Prince. Anti-Machiavellianism or Catholic Statecraft in Early Modern Europe* (Chapel Hill: University of North Carolina Press, 1990), 79–85; E. J. Dijksterhuis, *Simon Stevin: Science in the Netherlands around 1600* (The Hague: Martinus Nijhoff, 1970), 10; Evans, *Rudolf II*, 163–228; José A. García-Diego, *Juanelo Turriano. Charles V's Clockmaker: the Man and the Legend*, tr. David Ley (Madrid: Castalia, 1986); M. Mignet, *Charles quint: son abdication, son séjour et sa mort au monastère de Yuste* (Paris: Perrin, 1891), 207–15; Roy Strong, *Splendour at Court*.

Renaissance Spectacle and the Theater of Power (Boston: Houghton Mifflin, 1983) and his *Art and Power. Renaissance Festivals, 1450–1650* (Woodbridge, Suffolk: Boydell, 1984).

47. Oestreich, *Neostoicism*, 1–2.

48. *Justi Lipsi Poliorceticon. Sive de Machinis. Tormentis. Telis. Libre Quinque* (Antwerp: Plantijn, 1596), dedication; on Lipsius and Rubens, see Mark Morford, *Stoics and Neostoics: Rubens and the Circle of Lipsius* (Princeton: Princeton University Press, 1991), 142 and throughout.

49. *C. Cornelius Tacitus ex. 1. Lipsii* (Lyons: Elzevier, 1634), preface, 2: Lipsius also describes Tacitus as better able than any other historian to "penetrate deeply into the mysteries of state and the falls of empires [Nemo arcana Principium, & ruentis imperii fata altius penetravit]."

50. Saunders, *Justus Lipsius*, xiii; 125.

51. Steven Shapin, *The Scientific Revolution* (Chicago: University of Chicago Press, 1996), 13; compare E. J. Dijksterhuis, *The Mechanization of the World Picture*, tr. G. Dijkshoorn (Oxford: Oxford University Press, 1961), 401. On Stoicism and Renaissance science, see Peter Barker, "Stoic Contributions to Early Modern Science," in *Atoms, Pneuma, and Tranquility: Epicurean and Stoic Themes in Early Modern European Thought*, ed. Margaret Osler (Cambridge: Cambridge University Press, 1991), 135–54: 136.

52. On the "protoscientific" quality of Taciteanism and its investigation of "causal mechanisms," see Salmon, "Precept, Example, and Truth," 13–14; Oestreich, *Neostoicism*, 5. Compare Peter Burke, "Tacitism," chapter 7 of *Tacitus*, ed. T. A. Dorey (New York: Basic Books, 1969), 151–68.

53. Francesco Guicciardini, *Ricordi*, ed. Emilio Pasquini (Rome: Garzanti, 1999), Aphorism 18, 28: "Insegna molto bene Cornelio Tacito a chi vive sotto a' tiranni el modo di vivere e governarsi prudentemente, così come insegna a' tiranni e modi di fondare la tirannide," tr. as *Maxims and Reflections*, tr. Mario Domandi (New York: Harper & Row, 1965), Aphorism 18, 45.

54. Traiano Boc[c]alini, *I Ragguagli di Parnasso: or Advertisements from Parnassus, in Two Centuries, with the Politick Touch-Stone*, tr. Henry Earl of Monmouth (London: Humphrey Moseley, 1656), Part II, 71st Advertisement, 347–48.

55. On Grotius' "mathematics of politics," see Ernst Cassirer, *The Myth of the State* (New Haven: Yale University Press, 1946), 156; compare Tuck, *Philosophy and Government*, 279–98; Roger D. Masters, *Machiavelli, Leonardo, and the Science of Power* (South Bend, IN: University of Notre Dame Press, 1996), 195–98; Levy, "The Background of Hobbes' *Behemoth*," chapter 10 of *The Historical Imagination*, 243–65.

56. Boccalini, *Advertisements*, Part II, 348.

57. Plutarch, *Morals*, "Of Morall Vertue," 68.

58. John Dee, *General and Rare Memorials Pertayning to the Perfect Arte of Navigation* (London: John Day, 1577), title-page; B4r; on the relationship between natural and political philosophy in the work of Dee, see William Sherman, *John Dee: the Politics of Reading and Writing in the English Renaissance* (Amherst: University of Massachusetts Press, 1995), 150–54.

59. Niccolò Machiavelli, *Discourses Upon Livy*, tr. Edward Dacres (London, 1641), Epistle Dedicatory, A4r.
60. Thomas Digges, *An Arithmeticall Warlike Treatise named Stratioticos* (2nd edn., London: Richard Field, 1590), Dedication to the Earl of Leicester, A2r.
61. Digges, *Stratioticos*, Preface to the Reader, B2r–v.
62. Lipsius, *Politickes*, tr. Jones, Book I, chapter 7, 11; Book III, chapter 1, 41; compare Jean Bodin, *Methodus ad Facilem Historiarum Cognitionem* (Paris, 1566), in *Corpus général des philosophes français*, vol. v, no. 3, tr. Pierre Mesnard (Paris: Presses Universitaires de France, 1951), 283A, lines 50–59.
63. On Machiavellian *virtù* as flexibility, see Victoria Kahn, "*Virtù* and the Example of Agathocles in Machiavelli's *Prince*," chapter 8 of *Machiavelli and the Discourse of Literature*, ed. Albert Ascoli and Victoria Kahn (Ithaca, NY: Cornell University Press, 1993), 195–217: 206–11.
64. Fulke Greville, *A Treatie of Humane Learning*, in *Poems and Dramas of Fulke Greville*, ed. Geoffrey Bullough (London and Edinburgh: Oliver & Boyd, 1939), 178–79, lines 605; 611–16.
65. Boccalini, *The New-Found Politicke Disclosing the Secret Nature and Dispositions as well of Private Persons as of Statesmen and Courtiers*, tr. John Florio and William Vaughan (London, 1626), Part II, Advertisment 23, 39–46.
66. Baldassar Castiglione, *The Book of the Courtier*, tr. Thomas Hoby and ed. Virginia Cox (London: Dent, 1994), Book IV, 318. On flexibility as a courtly virtue, see Daniel Javitch, *Poetry and Courtliness in Renaissance England* (Princeton: Princeton University Press, 1978), 32 and his "*Il Cortegiano* and the Constraints of Despotism," in *Castiglione. The Ideal and the Real in Renaissance Culture*, ed. Robert Hanning and David Rosand (New Haven: Yale University Press, 1983), 20.
67. Descriptions of Drebbel's perpetual motion machine from accounts by D. Antonini (in a 1612 letter to Galileo) and Heinrich Hiesserle von Chodaw, both cited in Jennifer Drake-Brockman, "The *Perpetuum Mobile* of Cornelius Drebbel," in *Learning, Language, and Invention: Essays Presented to Francis Maddison*, ed. W. D. Hackmann and A. J. Turner (Paris: Variorum, 1994), 124–47: 137, 128–29.
68. Bacon, *Novum Organum*, Preface, 38. On the Vatican obelisk, see Alexander Keller, "Mathematical Technologies and the Growth of the Idea of Technical Progress in the Sixteenth Century," in *Science, Medicine, and Society in the Renaissance*, ed. Allan Debus (New York: Science History Publications, 1972), 21; William B. Parsons, *Engineers and Engineering in the Renaissance* (Cambridge, MA: M.I.T. Press, 1939), 169–71.
69. Bacon, *Novum Organum*, Preface, 38.
70. Bacon, "Of Fortune," in *Essayes*, 123.
71. Thomas Nashe, *The Unfortunate Traveller*, in *The Works of Thomas Nashe*, 5 vols., ed. Ronald McKerrow (Oxford: Basil Blackwell, 1958), vol. II, 283. On the corporeal etiquette of Renaissance court culture see Georges Vigarello, "The Upward Training of the Body from the Age of Chivalry to Courtly Civility," in *Fragments for a History of the Human Body*, 3 vols., ed. Michael

Feher (Cambridge: Zone Books, 1989), vol. II, 151; Mark Franko, *Dance as Text: Ideologies of the Baroque Body* (Cambridge: Cambridge University Press, 1993), chapter 1; Jay Tribby, "Body/Building: Living the Museum Life in Early Modern Europe," *Rhetorica* 10 (1992), 139–63.

72. Christopher Hill, *Intellectual Origins of the English Revolution* (Oxford: Clarendon Press, 1965), 64.

73. Anthony Levi, *French Moralists: the Theory of the Passions, 1585–1649* (Oxford: Clarendon Press, 1964), 11. On Renaissance neo-Stoicism, see Geoffrey Miles, *Shakespeare and the Constant Romans* (Oxford: Clarendon Press, 1996), 6–75; Gilles Monsarrat, *Light from the Porch: Stoicism and English Renaissance Literature* (Paris: Didier, 1984); Reid Barbour, *English Epicures and Stoics: Ancient Legacies in Early Stuart Culture* (Amherst: University of Massachusetts Press, 1998), Introduction and chapter 3; Gordon Braden, *Renaissance Tragedy and the Senecan Tradition: Anger's Privilege* (New Haven: Yale University Press, 1985), 17–30; 71, and throughout.

74. Robert Johnson, *Essaies; or, Rather imperfect offers* (London, 1607), ed. Robert Hood Bowers (Gainsville, FL: Scholars' Facsimiles and Reprints, 1955), Essay 12, F3r–4r.

75. *Ibid.*, Essay 2, A2v.

76. Thomas Wright, *The Passions of the Minde in General*, ed. Thomas Sloan (Urbana: University of Illinois Press, 1971), Book 1, chapter 1, 5.

77. Plato, *Phaedrus*, 253E, in *Plato 1*, tr. Harold North Fowler (Cambridge, MA: Harvard University Press, 1990), 495.

78. Wright, *The Passions of the Minde*, Book II, chapter 1, 49.

79. Jan van der Straet (Stradanus), *Nova Reperta* (2nd edn., Antwerp, 1600), 15; Ben Jonson, *News from the New World Discovered in the Moon* (London, 1620), in *Works*, vol. VII, ed. C. H. Hereford, Percy Simpson, and Evelyn Simpson (Oxford: Clarendon Press, 1941), 516.

I AUTOMATOPOESIS: MACHINERY AND COURTLINESS IN RENAISSANCE URBINO

1. Desiderius Erasmus, *A Declamation on the Subject of Early Liberal Education for Children* [*De pueris statim ac liberaliter instituendis declamatio*], tr. Beert C. Verstraete, in *Collected Works of Erasmus*, vol. XXVI, ed. J. K. Sowards (Toronto: University of Toronto Press, 1985), 317.

2. Cesare Ripa, *Nova Iconologia* (Padua, 1618), ed. Piero Buscaroli (Milan: Tascabili, 1992), Part 1, 30–31.

3. Ripa, *Nova Iconologia*, 30–31, paraphrasing Aristotle, *Mechanical Problems*, 331.

4. *Ibid.*; Castiglione, *The Book of the Courtier*, Book 1, 53. On the influence of the *Mechanical Problems* in Renaissance Italy, see Stillman Drake and I. E. Drabkin, *Mechanics in Sixteenth Century Italy: Selections from Tartaglia, Benedetti, Guido Ubaldo del Monte, and Galileo* (Madison: University of Wisconsin Press, 1969), Introduction; R. D. Laird, "The Scope of Renaissance Mechanics," *Osiris*, 2nd series, 2 (1986), 43–68; P. L. Rose, *The Italian Renaissance of Mathematics*.

Studies on Humanists and Mathematicians from Petrarch to Galileo (Geneva: Droz, 1975), esp. 45–47; 87–89; 105–06.

5. Castiglione, *The Book of the Courtier*, Book I, 53.

6. On technical virtuosity in Renaissance court culture, see Feingold, *The Mathematicians' Apprenticeship*; Mario Biagioli, *Galileo, Courtier. The Practice of Science in the Culture of Absolutism* (Chicago: University of Chicago Press, 1993); Strong, *Henry, Prince of Wales*, 86–137; 184–219; Smuts, *Court Culture*, 139–59. On the related concepts of civility and discipline in the Renaissance court, see Norbert Elias, *The Civilizing Process*, tr. Edmund Jephcott (New York: Urizen Books, 1978); Michel Foucault, *Discipline and Punish: the Birth of the Prison*, tr. Alan Sheridan (New York: Vintage Books, 1979); Frank Whigham, *Ambition and Privilege: the Social Tropes of Elizabethan Courtesy Theory* (Berkeley: University of California Press, 1984), 33 and throughout; Tribby, "Body/Building," 140–43; Vigarello, "The Upward Training of the Body," 171.

7. *Aristotelis Mechanica*, tr. Henri de Monantheuil (Paris: Jeremiah Perier, 1599), Preface to Henri IV.

8. Johannes Kepler to Michael Mästlin, 1/11 June 1598, in Kepler, *Gesammelte Werke*, 20 vols., ed. Walther Van Dyck and Max Caspar (Munich: C. H. Beck, 1937–59), vol. XIII, 222. On the *Kunstkammer* of Rudolf II, see Bredekamp, *The Lure of Antiquity*, 31–34; Thomas Da Costa Kaufmann, "Remarks on the Collections of Rudolf II: the Kunstkammer as a form of *Representatio*," *Art Journal* 38 (1978), 22–28.

9. Castiglione, *The Book of the Courtier*, Book I, 54.

10. On Kepler's mechanical models, see Bredekamp, *The Lure of Antiquity*, 37.

11. Wayne Rebhorn, *Courtly Performances: Masking and Festivity in Castiglione's "Book of the Courtier"* (Detroit, MI: Wayne State University Press, 1978), 35; Desiderius Erasmus, *De Pueris Instituendis*, tr. Richard Sherry as *That Chyldren oughte to be taught and brought up gently in vertue and learnynge* (London: John Day, 1550), 152.

12. Castiglione, *The Book of the Courtier*, Book IV, 335.

13. On παρασκευν (instrumentalities) see Plato, *Republic*, 495A, 2 vols., tr. Paul Shorey (Cambridge, MA: Harvard University Press, 1946), vol. II, 47.

14. On the "escapist" nature of Castiglione's text, see Christine Raffini, *Marsilio Ficino, Pietro Bembo, Baldassare Castiglione. Philosophical, Aesthetic, and Political Approaches in Renaissance Platonism* (New York: Peter Lang, 1998), 95; Attilio Momigliano, *Storia della letteratura italiana dalle origini ai nostri giorni* (8th edn., Milan, 1968), 187, calls the text "idyllic"; Joseph Mazzeo, *Renaissance and Revolution: the Remaking of European Thought* (New York: Pantheon, 1965), 134, calls it a "kind of Utopia" or "Arcadia." On the text's "cynical" pragmatism, see Joseph Falvo, *The Economy of Human Relations. Castiglione's "Libro del Cortegiano"* (New York: Peter Lang, 1992), xiii.

15. See Lauro Martines, *Power and Imagination: City-States in Renaissance Italy* (New York, 1979), 330; Eduardo Saccone, *Le buone e le cattive maniere: letteratura e galateo nel Cinquecento* (Bologna, 1992), 82.

16. Castiglione, *The Book of the Courtier*, Book IV, 362.

17. Thomas Hoby, "The Epistle of the Translator," dedicated to Lord Henry Hastings; Thomas Sackville, "In Commendation of the Worke," both in Castiglione, *The Book of the Courtier*, 9; 2.

18. Hoby, "The Epistle of the Translator" and "A Breef Rehersall," both in Castiglione, *The Book of the Courtier*, 4–5; 366–71.

19. On *The Book of the Courtier* as a "technical treatise," see Tribby, "Body/Building," 144; on the "plodding" quality of Aristotle, see James Hankins, *Plato in the Italian Renaissance*, 2 vols. (Leiden: E. J. Brill, 1990), vol. 1, 325.

20. "Nam de ceteris quidem rebus, etsi more paedagogorum certas regulas non tradiderit, quo pacto scilicet vel orandum sit vel disputandum vel huiusmodi aliquid agendum, in dialogis tamen, quos summo artificio singularique doctrina conscripsit, plurima atque utilissima omnium fere bonarum artium ac disciplinarum praecepta inseruit." Cardinal Bessarion, *In Calumniatorem Platonis* (Venice: Aldus Manutius, 1502), Book 1, chapter 2, cited in Hankins, *Plato*, vol. 1, 256.

21. Hankins, *Plato*, vol. 1, 350–51.

22. Castiglione, *The Book of the Courtier*, "The Epistle of the Author," 17. On the relationship between the ideal and the real in Castiglione, see Eduardo Saccone, "Grazia, Sprezzatura, Affettazione in *The Courtier*," in *The Ideal and the Real in Renaissance Culture*, ed. Robert Hanning and David Rosand (New Haven: Yale University Press, 1983), 46–54.

23. Castiglione, *The Book of the Courtier*, "The Epistle of the Author," 17. On Plato's pedagogical inefficacy, see Hankins, *Plato*, vol. 1, 255–57.

24. Castiglione, *The Book of the Courtier*, "The Epistle of the Author," 17.

25. *Ibid.*, Book 1, 37.

26. *Ibid.*, 51–2.

27. *Ibid.*, 53.

28. On the debate between arms and letters, see *ibid.*, Book 1, 82–3; Book IV, 316.

29. *Ibid.*, Book IV, 334; 316; both spoken by Lord Octavian.

30. On the worldliness of Bembo's Platonism, see Raffini, *Marsilio Ficino*, 137.

31. On Italian Renaissance Neoplatonism, see Hankins, *Plato*, vol. 1, 267–359; Michael Allen, *The Platonism of Marsilio Ficino* (Berkeley: University of California Press, 1989); Paul Oskar Kristeller, *Eight Philosophers of the Italian Renaissance* (Stanford, CA: Stanford University Press, 1954), chapter 3, and his *The Philosophy of Marsilio Ficino* (Gloucester, MA: Peter Smith, 1964), esp. chapter 6. On the Platonism of Cardinal Bessarion, see Hankins, *Plato*, vol. 1, 167–74, 236–63; Carlotta Labowsky, *Cardinal Bessarion and the Biblioteca Marciana: Six Early Inventories* (Rome: Edizioni di Storia e Letteratura, 1979), introduction.

32. On the building of the Ducal Palace, see D. S. Chambers, *Patronage and Artists in the Italian Renaissance* (London, 1971), 164–66; Antonio Manno, "Architettura e Arte Meccaniche nel Fregio del Palazzo Ducale di Urbino," in *Federico da Montefeltro: Lo Stato, Le Arti, La Cultura*, ed. Giorgio Cerboni Baiardi (Rome: Bulzoni, 1986), 94–96.

33. On Duke Federico's interest in mathematical science, see James Dennistoun, *Memoirs of the Dukes of Urbino Illustrating the Arms, Arts, and Literature of Italy from 1440 to 1630*, 3 vols. (London: Longman, Brown, Green, and Longman, 1851), vol. I, 216.

34. On the foundation of these institutions, see Chambers, *Patronage and Artists*, 164–66; Cecil Clough, "The Library of the Dukes of Urbino," *Librarium* 9 (1966), 101–05, rpt. as chapter 6 of Clough, *The Duchy of Urbino in the Renaissance* (London: Variorum Reprints, 1981). On Luca Pacioli, see Alfred W. Crosby, *The Measure of Reality: Quantification and Western Science, 1250–1600* (Cambridge: Cambridge University Press, 1997), 214–18.

35. On the library of the Dukes of Urbino, its patrons, and its scholars, see Clough, "The Library of the Dukes of Urbino," 101–05. On Bessarion, see Marino Zorzi, *La Libreria di San Marco. Libri, lettori, società nella Venezia dei Dogi* (Milano: Arnoldo Mondadori, 1987), 53 and throughout. On the importance of the Urbino library for foreign scholars, see also Clough, "The Relations between the English and Urbino Courts, 1474–1508," *Studies in the Renaissance* 14 (1967), 202–27.

36. Giorgio Valla, *De Expetendis et Fugiendis Rebus* (Venice: Aldus, 1501), esp. Book XIII.10; on Valla, see P. L. Rose, "Bartolomeo Zamberti's Funeral Oration for the Humanist Encyclopaedist Giorgio Valla," chapter 16 of *Cultural Aspects of the Italian Renaissance. Essays in Honour of Paul Oskar Kristeller*, ed. Cecil Clough (Manchester: Manchester University Press, 1976), esp. 299–303. On *De Rebus Expetendis* see also Rose, *The Italian Renaissance of Mathematics*, 46–49.

37. On Bembo's studies with Poliziano and Tomeo, see Raffini, *Marsilio Ficino*, 61–62.

38. "Angeli Politiano praelectio: cui titulis Panepistemon," in *Omnia Opera Angeli Politiani, et alia lectu digna* (Venice: Aldus Manutius, 1498), Z2v; the *Panepistemon* was first printed one year earlier in Giorgio Valla, *Euclides Cleonidae Harmonicum Introductorium* (Venice: Simon Papiensis, 1497).

39. On Plato's attitude towards the mechanical arts, see *The Republic*, 495D, vol. II, 49.

40. The copy of Ptolemy's *Geography* is Bibl. Marc. Ms. Gr. Z.388, fo. 6v; rpt. in Anthony Turner, *Early Scientific Instruments, 1400–1800* (London: Sothebys Publications, 1987), 41.

41. Hankins, *Plato*, vol. I, 296.

42. On the astrolabe made by Regiomontanus for Bessarion in 1462, see Derek de Solla Price, "The First Scientific Instrument of the Renaissance," *Physis* I (1959), 26–30: 27–29.

43. *Aristotelis Mechanica*, tr. Niccolò Leonico Tomeo (Venice, 1525), cited in Laird, "The Scope of Renaissance Mechanics," 66. On Leonico Tomeo's edition of Aristotle's *Mechanical Problems* and the reception of the work, see Laird, "The Scope of Renaissance Mechanics," 47–50; Drake and Drabkin, *Mechanics*, 5; Rose, *The Italian Renaissance of Mathematics*, 49.

44. Castiglione, *The Book of the Courtier*, Book II, 120; Aristotle, *Mechanical Problems*, 331.

45. Guido Ubaldo, *Le Mechaniche*, tr. Filippo Pigafetta (Venice, 1581), Dedicatory Letter of Filippo Pigafetta, cited in Drake and Drabkin, *Mechanics*, 249.

46. On *operazioni*, see *The Book of the Courtier*, Book II, 133.

47. *Ibid.*, 179.

48. *Aristotelis Mechanica*, tr. Tomeo, cited in Laird, "The Scope of Renaissance Mechanics," 49.

49. Aristotle, *Mechanical Problems*, 331.

50. Proclus, *A Commentary on the First Book of Euclid's Elements*, tr. Glenn R. Morrow (Princeton: Princeton University Press, 1970), Prologue to Part I, chapter 8, 17. On Proclus' scientific attitudes, see Morrow's introduction, xx–xxxiv; Rose, "The Accademia Venetiana: Science and Culture in Renaissance Venice," *Studi Veneziani* II (1969), 191–242: 197 and his "A Venetian Patron and Mathematician of the xvith Century: Francesco Barozzi (1537–1604)," *Studi Veneziani*, new series I (1977), 119–49: 125; Lucas Siovanes, *Proclus: Neoplatonic Philosophy and Science* (Edinburgh, 1966), 118–19; 225; Laurence Jay Rosan, *The Philosophy of Proclus. The Final Phase of Ancient Thought* (New York: Cosmos Books, 1949), 44–45.

51. Proclus, *Commentary*, Part I, chapter 13, 33–34; 50.

52. Niccolò Tartaglia, *Quesiti e Inventioni Diverse* (Venice, 1546), cited in Drake and Drabkin, *Mechanics*, 106–07.

53. Guido Ubaldo, *Mechanicorum Liber* (Pesaro, 1577), Author's Preface to Francesco Maria II, Duke of Urbino, in Drake and Drabkin, *Mechanics*, 245.

54. Guido Ubaldo, *Le Mecchaniche*, dedicatory letter of Pigafetta, in Drake and Drabkin, *Mechanics*, 248.

55. Bernardino Baldi, *Cronica de matematici overo epitome dell'istoria delle vite loro* (Urbino: A. A. Monticelli, 1707), 2 (Pitagora); 14 (Platone); 7 (Archita); 26–27 (Archimede).

56. Baldi, *In Mechanica Aristotelis problemata exercitationes* (Mainz: Johannes Albinus, 1621), Preface; *De Herone Alessandrino De Gli Automati, overo Machine Semoventi, libri due*, tr. Bernardino Baldi (Venice: Girolamo Porro, 1589), 4v; 6v.

57. *De Herone Alessandrino De Gli Automati*, 10–10v; 8–8v.

58. *Ibid.*, 12–12v.

59. Francesco Maurolico, *Cosmographia*, dedicatory epistle to Bembo, translated in Laird, "The Patronage of Mechanics and the Theory of Impact in Sixteenth-Century Italy," in *Patronage and Institutions: Science, Technology, and Medicine at the European Court 1500–1750*, ed. Bruce Moran (Rochester: Boydell and Brewer, 1991), 57–8.

60. On the treatment of mechanics and machinery in Maurolico's treatise, see his *Cosmographia Francisci Maurolyci* (Venice: Lucae Antonii Iuntae, 1543), Dedication to "Reverendissimo Domino D. Pietro Bembo," sig. ā 7r.

61. Castiglione, *The Book of the Courtier*, Book I, 52.

62. *Ibid.*, 51. On the concealment of effort, see Whigham, *Ambition and Privilege*, 33.
63. Guido Ubaldo, *Mechanicorum Liber*, dedicatory epistle to Francesco Maria II, Duke of Urbino, in Drake and Drabkin, *Mechanics*, 241.
64. *Ibid.*, 241; 243.
65. Cicero, *Orator* XXIII.78, in *Cicero v: Brutus and Orator*, tr. H. M. Hubbell (Cambridge, MA: Harvard University Press, 1997), 363.
66. *Ibid.*; compare Quintilian, *Institutio Oratoria*, 4 vols., tr. H. E. Butler (Cambridge, MA: Harvard University Press, 1996), vol. I, I. II.2–3; 185.
67. Cicero, *Orator* XXIII.76, in *Cicero v*, 363; Castiglione, *The Book of the Courtier*, Book I, 75.
68. Castiglione, *The Book of the Courtier*, Book I, 54.
69. Quintilian, *Institutio Oratoria*, 1.10.49; 183.
70. Cicero, *De Natura Deorum*, II.34–35, in *Cicero XIX: De Natura Deorum* and *Academica*, tr. H. Rackham (Cambridge, MA: Harvard University Press, 1994), 207–08.
71. Cicero, *Tusculan Disputations* 1.25, in *Cicero XVIII*, tr. J. E. King (Cambridge, MA: Harvard University Press, 1996), 75.
72. On Renaissance scientific illustration, see Samuel Edgerton, "The Renaissance Development of the Scientific Illustration," in *Science and the Arts in the Renaissance*, ed. John Shirley and F. David Hoeniger (Washington: Folger Shakespeare Library, 1985), 177–84 and his *The Heritage of Giotto's Geometry: Art and Science on the Eve of the Scientific Revolution* (Ithaca: Cornell University Press, 1991), 22–44. On Roberto Valturio and Francesco di Giorgio Martini, see Bertrand Gille, *Engineers of the Renaissance* (Cambridge, MA: M.I.T. Press, 1966), 80–119. On the notebooks of Francesco di Giorgio Martini, see *Renaissance Engineers: From Brunelleschi to Leonardo Da Vinci* (Florence: Palazzo Strozzi, June 22, 1996–January 6, 1997), ed. Paolo Galluzzi (Florence, Istituto e Museo di Storia della Scienza, 1996), 166–67.
73. Baldi's list of his written works can be found in the "Syllabus Librorum" appended to his 1621 *In Mechanica Aristotelis . . . exercitationes*. On Baldi's 1589 translation of Hero's *Automata*, see Rose, *The Italian Renaissance of Mathematics*, 247.
74. Baldi, "Descrizione del Palazzo Ducale d'Urbino," rpt. in Castiglione, *Il Cortegiano* (Florence: Barbèra, 1889), 299; 319. For Baldi's 1601 biography of Duke Federico, see Baldi, *Vita e Fatti di Federigo di Montefeltro, duca di Urbino*, ed. Francesco Zuccardi, 3 vols. (Bologna: Turchi Veroli, 1826), vol. II.
75. Baldi, "Descrizione del Palazzo Ducale d'Urbino," chapter 16 ("Artifizi del palazzo"), 319.
76. Castiglione, *The Book of the Courtier*, Book II, 179.
77. Baldi, *Cronica*, 97 (Giovanni di Monteregio); 107 (Luca Pacioli); 134–35 (Pietro Ramo).
78. Roger Ascham, *The Schoolmaster*, ed. Lawrence V. Ryan (Charlottesville, VA: Folger Shakespeare Library, 1967), 21; compare Juan Luis Vives, *Vives: On Education. A Translation of the De Tradendis Disciplinis*, ed. and tr. Foster

Watson (Cambridge: Cambridge University Press, 1913), 73–75. On negative attitudes towards quick or mathematical wits, see Mordechai Feingold, "The Mathematical Sciences and New Philosophies," in *Seventeenth-Century Oxford*, ed. Nicholas Tyacke (Oxford: Clarendon Press, 1997), 364–67.

79. Juan Huarte, *Examen de Ingenios para las sciencias* (Baeza, 1575), 395–96.
80. Antonio Persio, *Trattato dell'Ingegno dell'Huomo* (Venice: Aldus Manutius, 1576), 15; 8.
81. Pierre Charron, *Of Wisdome*, tr. Samson Lennard (London: Edward Blount, 1608), Book I, chapter 15, 55; Book III, chapter 1, 358.
82. *Ibid.*, Book I, chapter 15, 55–58.
83. Michael de Montaigne, "Of Vaine Subtilties, or Subtill Devices," in *The Essayes*, tr. John Florio (London, 1606; rpt. New York: Modern Library, 1933), Book I, chapter 54, 268–69.
84. Charron, *Of Wisdome*, Book I, chapter 15, 61–62. For the French version of this passage, see Charron, *De La Sagesse*, ed. Barbara de Negroni (Paris: Fayard, 1986), Book I, chapter 14, 139–40.
85. Timothy Bright, *Treatise of Melancholie* (London: John Windet, 1586), 62.
86. Baldi, *Le Vite de Matematici*, ed. Elio Nenci (Milan: Franco Angeli, 1998), 495; 517–18. (This is a different version of the *Cronica*, a revised version of the medieval and Renaissance sections of Baldi's earlier text.)
87. Laird, "Archimedes Among the Humanists," *Isis* 82 (1991), 629–38: 630.
88. Baldi, *Cronica*, 27 (Archimede); Monte, *Mechanicorum Liber*, cited in Drake and Drabkin, *Mechanics*, 243.
89. Vitruvius, *De Architectura*, Book X, 1, 3: "Ergo est organa et machinarum ratio ad usum sunt necessaria, since quibus nulla res potest esse non inpedita."
90. Plutarch, "Life of Marcellus," in his *Lives of the Noble Grecians and Romans*, 3 vols., tr. Sir Thomas North (London, 1579; rpt. 1895), vol. II, 350. Compare the similar accounts in Athenaeus, *The Deipnosophists*, v.206–07, 7 vols., tr. Charles Burton Gulick (Cambridge, MA: Harvard University Press, 1987), vol. II, 433–35; and *Polybius*, 6 vols., tr. W. R. Paton (Cambridge, MA: Harvard University Press, 1922), vol. III, Book 8, 453–61.
91. Plutarch, *Lives*, vol. II, 350–51.
92. *Ibid.*, 353.
93. *Ibid.*, 354; 356.
94. On Besson, see Jean Taisnier, *A very necessarie and profitable Booke concerning Navigation*, tr. Richard Eden (London: Richard Jugge, 1575), Epistle Dedicatory to William Winter, *3r; on Drebbel, see Thomas Tymme, *A Dialogue Philosophicall* (London: Clement Knight, 1612), 63; on Briggs, see John Aubrey, "Life of Henry Briggs," in *Lives*, ed. Oliver Lawson Dick (Ann Arbor: University of Michigan Press, 1960), 39.
95. Giorgio Vasari, "Life of Leonardo Da Vinci," in *Lives of the Most Eminent Painters, Sculptors & Architects*, 10 vols., tr. Gaston C. De Vere (London: Philip Lee Warner, 1912–14), vol. IV, 89–91; Plutarch, "Life of Marcellus," in *Lives*, vol. II, 349.

96. Daniel Javitch, "*Il Cortegiano* and the Constraints of Despotism," in *The Ideal and the Real*, 24–25.

97. Plutarch, "Life of Marcellus," in *Lives*, vol. II, 353–54.

98. Castiglione, *The Book of the Courtier*, Book I, 54.

99. Plutarch, "Life of Marcellus," in *Lives*, vol. II, 351–52.

100. Anthony Blunt, *Artistic Theory in Italy*, cited in Saccone, "Grazia, Sprezzatura, Affettazione," in *The Ideal and the Real*, 46.

101. Castiglione, *The Book of the Courtier*, Book IV, 334; Hoby glosses the passage "Virtus in actione."

102. For Machiavelli's use of the term *virtù*, see his *The Prince*, tr. Mark Musa (New York: St. Martins, 1964), Introduction, x–xv. On the connections between *virtù* and *techne*, see Kahn, "*Virtù* and the Example of Agathocles," 211, and her *Machiavellian Rhetoric from the Counter-Reformation to Milton* (Princeton: Princeton University Press, 1994), 93. On the meaning of the term *virtù*, see also Neal Wood, "Some Common Aspects of the Thought of Seneca and Machiavelli," *Renaissance Quarterly* 21 (1968), 11–23; John Plamenatz, "In Search of Machiavellian *Virtù*," chapter 7 of *The Political Calculus: Essays in Machiavelli's Philosophy*, ed. Anthony Parel (Toronto: University of Toronto Press, 1972), 157–78.

103. Castiglione, *The Book of the Courtier*, Book IV, 313.

104. On the scientific meanings of the term *virtù* in the Renaissance, see A. C. Crombie, *Augustine to Galileo: the History of Science, AD 400–1650* (London: Falcon Press, 1952), 82.

2 ARTIFICIAL MOTIONS: MACHINERY, COURTLINESS, AND
DISCIPLINE IN RENAISSANCE ENGLAND

1. John Dee, *The elements of geometrie of the most auncient philosopher Euclide of Megara. Faithfully translated into the Englishe toung, by H. Billingsley, citizen of London . . . With a very fruitfull praeface made by M. I. Dee, specifying the chiefe mathematicall scie[n]ces, what they are, and wherunto commodious* (London: John Daye, 1570), D1.

2. Nashe, *The Unfortunate Traveller*, in *Works*, ed. McKerrow, vol. II, 282–83; Robert Dallington, *A Survey of the Great Dukes State of Tuscany in the Year of Our Lord 1596* (London: Edward Blount, 1605), 12–13; 60–61.

3. Wright, *The Passions of the Minde*, The Preface unto the Reader, lxi; G.B.A.F., *A Discovery of the great subtilitie and wonderful wisdome of the Italians* (London: John Wolfe, 1591), B1v.

4. On Linacre and Pole, see Zorzi, *La Libreria di San Marco*, 103–07; George B. Parks, *The English Traveller to Italy*, 2 vols. (Stanford, CA: Stanford University Press, 1954), vol. I, 451–91; Owen Hannaway, "Georgius Agricola as Humanist," *Journal of the History of Ideas* 53 (1992), 553–60. On English students in Padua, see Jonathan Woolfson, *Padua and the Tudors: English Students in Italy, 1485–1603* (Toronto: University of Toronto Press, 1998).

5. On Castiglione's embassy to England, see Clough, *The Duchy of Urbino*, 774–79.

6. On Dee's work with Commandino, see Dee, *A Letter, Nine Yeeres since, written and first published Containing a most Briefe Discourse Apologetical* (London, 1603), A4v–Br; Peter French, *John Dee: the World of an Elizabethan Magus* (London: Routledge, 1972), 37; Rose, *The Italian Renaissance of Mathematics*, 199–200; Enrico Rambaldi, "John Dee and Federico Commandino: An English and Italian Interpretation of Euclid During the Renaissance," in *Italy and the English Renaissance*, ed. Sergio Rossi and Dianella Savoia (Milan: Unicopli, 1989), 125–26.

7. Dee, *Preface*, C3v.

8. *Ibid.*, D1r.

9. Machiavelli, *The Prince*, chapter 25, 208–09; on the connection between political and mechanical *virtù*, see Masters, *The Science of Power*, 25–27, 188–89; Lynn White, Jr., "The Iconography of Temperantia and the Virtuousness of Technology," rpt. in *Action and Conviction in Early Modern Europe: Essays in Memory of E. H. Harbison*, ed. T. K. Rabb and J. E. Siegel (Princeton: Princeton University Press, 1969), 197–219; Otto Mayr, *Authority, Liberty, and Automatic Machinery in Early Modern Europe* (Baltimore: Johns Hopkins University Press, 1986), 37 and throughout.

10. Sherman, *John Dee*, 24–45; Dee, *Preface*, A4v.

11. Dee, *Preface*, C4v. In BL C.122.bb.35, Dee's edition of *Elementorum Libri xv* (Paris, 1557), he underlines Euclid's account of this exchange between Archimedes and Hiero.

12. Dee, *Preface*, A1r–v.

13. *Ibid.*, *1v.

14. Dee, *Monas Hieroglyphica*, in "A Translation of John Dee's 'Monas Hieroglyphica,'" ed. C. H. Josten, *Ambix* 12: 2–3 (June–October 1964), 131; 133.

15. Dee, *Preface*, *1v; C3v.

16. Plato, *The Republic*, vol. II, Book VII, 526B; Dee, *Preface*, *v.

17. Guido Ubaldo, *Mechanicorum Liber*, Dedication to Francesco Maria II, cited in Drake and Drabkin, *Mechanics*, 241.

18. BL MS Sloane 15, "Doctor Dee his Instructions and Annotations upon Euclids Elements," 2v; 18r; 8r. (Dated December 10, 1569 on 21v.)

19. Peter Ramus, *Scholarum Mathematicum* (Frankfurt: Andreas Wechel, 1599), Book 1, 28.

20. Dee, *Preface*, A3r; Strong, *Henry, Prince of Wales*, 213.

21. On Essex's interest in mechanical devices, see Feingold, *The Mathematicians' Apprenticeship*, 201–09; on his pocket-dial, see F. R. [R]aines, "The Pocket Dial of the Earl of Essex," *Notes and Queries* fourth series 9 (1872), 9–10.

22. On clocks belonging to Leicester and Elizabeth I, see Feingold, *The Mathematicians' Apprenticeship*, 201–09; 197; on instruments made for Elizabeth I by Humphray Cole and William Buckley, see R. T. Gunther, "The Great Astrolabe and Other Scientific Instruments of Humphray Cole," *Archaeologia* 76 (1926–27), 302 and his "The Astrolabe of Queen Elizabeth," *Archaeologia* 86

(1936), 65–72; Taylor, *Mathematical Practitioners*, 169. On Elizabeth's collection of clocks, see J. Nichols, *The Progresses and Public Processions of Queen Elizabeth*, 3 vols. (London, 1823), vol. I, 294; vol. II, 249; 300; E. J. Wood, *Curiosities of Clocks and Watches from the Earliest Times* (London, 1886), 252–55.

23. On the clock at Hampton Court, see Frederick, Duke of Wirtemberg, "A True and Faithful Narrative (1602)," rpt. in William Benchley Rye, *England as Seen by Foreigners* (London: John Russell Smith, 1865), 19. On the machinery at Whitehall, see Paul Hentzner, *Travels in England During the Reign of Queen Elizabeth* (1598; rpt. London, 1797), 23–24 and *The Diary of Baron Waldstein, a Traveller in Elizabethan England* (1600), tr. G.W. Gross (London: Thames & Hudson, 1981), 59.

24. See the discussion of technical education in W. S., *Discourse of the Common Weal of this Realm of England*, ed. Elizabeth Lamond (Cambridge: Cambridge University Press, 1929), 13; 25–7.

25. Ramus, *Scholarum Mathematicum*, 14.

26. BL MS Landsdowne 101, fos. 17–21 (from Richard Eden to Lord Burghley), 18b; BL MS Lands. 101, fos. 69–76 (from Emery Molyneux to Lord Burghley), 72a (dated March 4, 1596 on 70b).

27. BL MS Lands. 101, fos. 56–59, Thomas Hood, "To the Right Honorable Sir William Cecill Knight / Lorde Burleighe Lorde Treasurer of Englande."

28. On Burghley's scientific patronage, see B. W. Beckingsale, *Burghley, Tudor Statesman, 1520–1598* (New York: St. Martin's Press, 1967), 261; Feingold, *The Mathematicians' Apprenticeship*, 205–10.

29. Sherman, *John Dee*, 190–91.

30. On Theobalds, see *The Diary of Baron Waldstein*, 83; Strong, *The Renaissance Garden in England* (London: Thames & Hudson, 1979), 53; Feingold, *The Mathematicians' Apprenticeship*, 204.

31. William Bourne, *Inventions or devises very necessary for all generalles and captaines, or leaders of men* (London: Thomas Woodcocke, 1578), Device 113, 98–99.

32. BL MS Lands. 101, Richard Eden to Lord Burghley, fo. 20a; Roger Bacon, *Frier Bacon His Discovery of the Miracles of Art, Nature, and Magick. Faithfully translated out of Dr. Dees own Copy, by T. M. and never before in English* (London: Simon Miller, 1659), chapter 1, 2; chapter 8, 36; chapter 4, 17; 19.

33. Edmund Worsop, *A Discoverie of Sundrie Errors and Faults Daily Committed by Landemeaters* (London: Henrie Middleton, 1582), title-page; Bourne, *Inventions or devises*, 99.

34. On the scientific use of the vernacular, see William Eamon, *Science and the Secrets of Nature: Books of Secrets in Medieval and Early Modern Culture* (Princeton: Princeton University Press, 1994) and his "From the Secrets of Nature to Public Knowledge: the Origins of the Concept of Openness in Science," *Minerva* 23 (1985), 321–47; Elizabeth Eisenstein, *The Printing Press as an Agent of Change: Communications and Cultural Transformations in Early Modern Europe* (Cambridge: Cambridge University Press, 1979), 444–50.

35. Worsop, *A Discoverie of Sundrie Errors and Faults*, A2v; E3r; G2r.

36. Georg Philipp Harsdörffer, *Delitiae mathematicae et physicae* (Nuremberg, 1651), 348–49, tr. Mayr, *Authority, Liberty, and Automatic Machinery*, 44.
37. Arnold Clapmar, *De Arcanis Rerumpublicarum Libri Sex* (Bremen: J. Wessel, 1605), 9. On late sixteenth-century treatments of *arcana imperii* and sacral theories of kingship, see Peter Donaldson, *Machiavelli and Mystery of State* (Cambridge: Cambridge University Press, 1988), esp. 111–85; Ernst Kantorowicz, *The King's Two Bodies: a Study in Medieval Political Theology* (Princeton: Princeton University Press, 1957) and his "Mysteries of State: an Absolutist Concept and its Late Medieval origins," *Harvard Theological Review* 47 (1955), 65–91; Tuck, *Philosophy and Government*, chapter 3; Kenneth Schellhase, *Tacitus in Renaissance Political Thought* (Chicago: University of Chicago Press, 1976), esp. chapter 6; and Jonathan Goldberg, *James I and the Politics of Literature: Jonson, Shakespeare, Donne, and their Contemporaries* (Stanford, CA: Stanford University Press, 1988), chapter 2.
38. Tommaso Campanella, *Del Senso delle Cose e Della Magia*, ed. Antonio Bruers (Bari, 1925), 242.
39. *Ibid.*, 241–42. On similar skeptical attitudes towards natural magic during the Renaissance, see William Eamon, "Technology as Magic in the Late Middle Ages and the Renaissance," *Janus* 70 (1983), 171–212.
40. Gabriel Naudé, *Apologie pour tous les grands personnages qui ont esté faussement soupçonnez de magie* (Paris, 1625), chapter 3, 77–79.
41. On Drebbel's inventions, see Tierie, *Cornelius Drebbel, 1572–1633*, 8–13; Drake-Brockman, "The *Perpetuum Mobile* of Cornelius Drebbel," esp. 128–33; Strong, *Henry, Prince of Wales*, 141–58. On the uses of machinery and natural magic in the Jacobean court, see Frances Yates, *The Rosicrucian Enlightenment* (London: Routledge & Kegan Paul, 1972), chapters 1 and 2; Vaughan Hart, *Art and Magic in the Court of the Stuarts* (New York: Routledge, 1994), chapters 1 and 2; William Huffman, *Robert Fludd and the End of the Renaissance* (New York: Routledge, 1988), Introduction and chapter 1.
42. Cornelius Drebbel, Dedicatory Letter to King James I, in *Wonder-vondt van eeuwighe bewigingh* (Alkmaar, 1607), sigs. A4r–B2r, and cited in Drake-Brockman, "The *Perpetuum Mobile* of Cornelius Drebbel," 129–30.
43. Thomas Tymme, *A Dialogue Philosophicall. Wherein Natures Secret Closet is Opened . . . Together with the wittie invention of an Artificiall perpetuall motion, presented to the Kings most excellent Maiestie* (London, 1612), 60–62; James VI and I, *His Majesties Declaration, Touching his Proceedings in the Late Assemblie and Convention of Parliament* (London, 1622), in *Political Writings*, ed. Johann Somerville (Cambridge: Cambridge University Press, 1994), 250.
44. Heinrich Hiesserle von Chodaw, "Raiss Buch und Leben," Prague Nat. Mus. MS vi A 12, fos. 48v–50v, cited in Drake-Brockman, "The *Perpetuum Mobile*," 128–29.
45. *Ibid.*, 129.
46. James VI and I, *Basilikon Doron*, in *King James VI and I: Political Writings*, ed. Johann P. Somerville (Cambridge: Cambridge University Press, 1994), 59.

47. Simon Schaffer, "The Show That Never Ends: Perpetual Motion in the Early Eighteenth Century," *The British Journal of the History of Science* 28 (1995), 157–89: 161.

48. John Johnston, *An History of the Constancy of Nature*, tr. John Rowland (London: John Streater, 1657), 110–11. On seventeenth-century attitudes towards perpetual motion, see Arthur W. J. G. Ord-Hume, *Perpetual Motion: the History of an Obsession* (New York: St. Martin's Press, 1977), 177 and throughout; Henry Dircks, *Perpetuum Mobile; or, A History of the Search for Self-Motive Power, from the XIIIth to the XIXth Century* (Amsterdam: B. M. Israel, 1968); Mary Louise Gill and James G. Lennox, *Self-Motion from Aristotle to Newton* (Princeton: Princeton University Press, 1994).

49. Edward Somerset, Sixth Earl and Second Marquis of Worcester, *A Century of the names and scantlings of such Inventions as at present I can call to mind to have tried and perfected, which . . . I have . . . endeavoured now in the year 1655, to set these down in such a way as may sufficiently instruct me to put any of them in practice* (London: J. Grismond, 1663), Invention 98, 66–67. On Somerset's work with perpetual motion, see Ord-Hume, *Perpetual Motion*, 31–34; 65–67.

50. Cornelius Drebbel to King James I, undated letter (*c.* 1610) rpt. in Abbotsford Club *Miscellany* vol. 1 (1837), 111–13, and cited in Drake-Brockman, "The *Perpetuum Mobile* of Cornelius Drebbel," 130–31.

51. Strong, *Splendour at Court*, 190.

52. Taisnier, *A Verie Necessarie and Profitable Book Concerning Navigation*, tr. Eden, Dedicatory Epistle to William Winter, *3r. Compare Simon Stevin, *De Weeghdaet* [The Practice of Weighing], in *The Principal Works of Simon Stevin*, 5 vols., ed. E. J. Dijksterhuis (Amsterdam: C. V. Swets & Zeitlinger, 1955–66), vol. 1, 371–73.

53. John Blagrave, *The Mathematicall Jewell, shewing the making, and most excellent use of a singuler instrument so called: in that it performeth with wonderfull dexteritie, whatsoever is to be done, either by quadrant, ship, circle, cylinder, ring, dyall, horoscope, astrolabe, sphere, globe, or any such like heretofore devised* (London: Walter Venge, 1585), title-page; Thomas Fale, *Horologiographia. The Art of Dialling* (London: Felix Kyngston, 1627), Preface.

54. Blagrave, *The Mathematicall Jewell*, title-page; Dedication to Sir William Cecil; Castiglione, *The Book of the Courtier*, Book 1, 49; 56.

55. Shapin, *A Social History of Truth*, 120.

56. Henri de Suberville, *L'Henry-metre, Instrument Royal, et Universel* (Paris: Adrien Perier, 1598); Octavio Strada de Rosberg, *La Première Partie des Desseins Artificiaux de Toutes Sortes de Moulins . . . et aultres inventions, pour faire monter l'eau au hault, sans beaucoup de peine & despens* (Frankfurt: Paul Jacques, 1617).

57. Robert Tanner, *A Mirror for Mathematiques, a golden gem for geometricians . . . and an auncient antiquary for astronomers and astrologians* (London: J. C. for Richard Watkins, 1587), title-page; Aaron Rathborne, *The surveyor in foure bookes* (London: William Stansby, 1616), title-page; Castiglione, *The Book of the Courtier*, Book 1, 53.

58. Patricia Parker, "Rude Mechanicals," in *Subject and Object in Renaissance Culture*, ed. Margreta De Grazia, Maureen Quilligan, and Peter Stallybrass (Cambridge: Cambridge University Press, 1996), 45–6.

59. James VI and I, *Basilikon Doron*, 58; 56. Compare Henry Peacham, *The Compleat Gentleman* (London, 1634), ed. Virgil Barney Heltzel (Washington, DC: Folger Shakespeare Library, 1962), chapter 1, 23. On the aristocratic disdain for mechanics, see Hill, *Intellectual Origins of the English Revolution*, 64.

60. Niccolò Tartaglia, *Quesiti e Inventione Diverse*, tr. Cyprian Lucar as *Three Books of Colloquies concerning the Arte of Shooting* (London: John Harrison, 1588), Dedication to Henry VIII.

61. Bourne, *The Treasure for Travelers* (London, 1578, rpt. Amsterdam and New York: Theatrum Orbis Terrarum, 1979), Preface; Leonard Digges, *A Geometrical Practise, named Pantometria . . . with sundry strange conclusions both by instrument and without, and also by Perspective glasses* (London: Henrie Bynneman, 1571), Preface to the reader, A2v; Whigham, *Ambition and Privilege*, 106.

62. Javitch, *Poetry and Courtliness in Renaissance England*, 80; compare Whigham, *Ambition and Privilege*, 122.

63. Bourne, *Inventions or devises*, Preface, ¶3v; Digges, *Pantometria*, D2r; frontispiece.

64. Bourne, *Inventions or devises*, Preface, ¶3r; Thomas Hill, *A Briefe and Pleasant Treatise, entituled, Naturall and Artificiall Conclusions* (London: John Kyngston, 1581), Preface.

65. On Renaissance science and the *gioco serio*, see Paula Findlen, "Jokes of Nature and Jokes of Knowledge: The Playfulness of Scientific Discourse in Early Modern Europe," *Renaissance Quarterly* 43 (1990), 292–331; Thomas DaCosta Kaufmann, *The Mastery of Nature. Aspects of Art, Science, and Humanism in the Renaissance* (Princeton: Princeton University Press, 1993), chapter 4, esp. 101–02; Bredekamp, *The Lure of Antiquity*, 67–72. On the Renaissance concept of recreation, see Rosalie Colie, *Paradoxia Epidemica: the Renaissance Tradition of Paradox* (Princeton: Princeton University Press, 1966), 309–18.

66. Worsop, *A Discoverie of Sundrie Errors*, C1v.

67. Denis Henrion, *Collection, ou Recueil de Divers Traictez Mathematiques* (Paris: Fleurry Bourriquant, 1621), Dédication à Monsieur Frère du Roy.

68. Nicolas Hunt, *Newe Recreations of the Mindes Release and Solacing* (London: Luke Faune, 1631), title-page.

69. Henry Van Etten, *Mathematicall Recreations or a collection of sundrie excellent Problemes . . . Both usefull and recreative* (London: T. Cotes for Richard Hawkins, 1633), Dedicatory Poem; this text is a translation of Jean Leurechon, *Recréations Mathematiques, composées de plusieurs problèmes plaisans & facetieux* (Rouen: Charles Osmont, 1629).

70. Aubrey, "Life of Henry Savile," in *Lives*, 267–68.

71. William Oughtred, *The Circles of Proportion and the Horizontal Instrument*, tr. William Forster (London: Augustine Matthews, 1633), Forster's dedication to Kenelm Digby.

72. Oughtred, *The Circles of Proportion*, "To the English Gentrie, and all others studious of the Mathematicks . . . the Just Apologie of Wil. Oughtred, against the slanderous insimulations of Richard Delamain, in a pamphlet called *Grammelogia*," A3r.

73. *Ibid.*, D2v; B2r–v.

74. Michel de Montaigne, *Travel Journal*, tr. Donald Frame (San Francisco: Northpoint Press, 1983), 36–37. French text cited from Montaigne, *Journal de Voyage*, ed. Louis Lautrey (Paris: Librairie Hachette, 1909), 125.

75. Montaigne, *Travel Journal*, 37; Montaigne, *Journal de Voyage*, 125.

76. On de Caus' Richmond Palace machinery, designed in 1611, see Strong, *Henry, Prince of Wales*, 107–08 and his *Renaissance Garden in England*, 97–103. On Ware House's machines, designed in 1613, see *A History of the King's Works 1485–1600*, 3 vols., ed. H. M. Colvin, (London: HMSO, 1982), vol. II, 231–32. On Drebbel's perpetual motion, see Henry Peacham, "To the famous Traveller ever to be esteemed the joy of his Somersetshire, Thomas Coryate of Odcombe," in Thomas Coryate, *Coryats Crudities. Hastily gobled up in five Moneths travells in France, Savoy, Italy . . . some parts of high Germany, and the Netherlands; Newly digested in the hungry aire of Odcombe* (London, 1611, rpt. London: Scolar Press, 1978), k4v.

77. Angelo Poliziano, "A Letter to Bartolomeo Scala in Defence of the Stoic Philosopher Epictetus" (1479), in *Cambridge Translations of Renaissance Philosophical Texts*, 2 vols., ed. Jill Kraye (Cambridge: Cambridge University Press, 1997), vol. I, 194. On corporeal discipline during the Renaissance, see Norbert Elias, *The Court Society*, tr. Edmund Jephcott (New York: Pantheon, 1983), 397–98.

78. Christóbal de Villalón, *Ingeniosa Comparación entre lo antiguo y lo presente* (Madrid, 1539), ed. Manuel Serrano y Sanz (Madrid: Sociedad de Bibliófilos Españoles, 1898), 173–74.

79. Giovan Paolo Lomazzo, *A tracte containing the artes of curious painting carvinge [and] Buildinge*, tr. Richard Haydocke (Oxford: Joseph Barnes, 1598), Book 2, chapter 1, 1–2.

80. Leonardo Da Vinci, *Notebooks*, 2 vols., ed. and tr. Jean-Paul Richter (New York: Dover, 1970), vol. II, Book 19, Aphorism 1154; on the Mannerist aesthetics of motion, see Evans, *Rudolf II*, 244–74; Shearman, *Mannerism*, 81–118.

81. John Wilkins, *Mathematicall Magick* (London: Samuel Gellibrand, 1648), Book I, chapter 5, 28–9.

82. John Davies, *Orchestra, or a Poeme of Dauncing*, in *The Poems of Sir John Davies*, ed. Robert Krueger (Oxford: Clarendon Press, 1975), 120–21.

83. Wilkins, *Mathematicall Magick*, Book II, chapter 1, 145–46.

84. Villalón, *Ingeniosa Comparación*, 173–74; Ambrosio de Morales, *Las Antigüedades de las ciudades de España* (Alcalá, 1575), 93v, also cited in Garcia-Diego, *Juanelo Turriano*, 101.

85. On the temperance of clocks and other machines, see White, "The Iconography of *Temperantia*," 204–17; Mayr, *Automatic Machinery*, 44–50.

86. Aristotle, *Nicomachean Ethics*, in *Aristotle* xix, tr. Arthur Rackham (Cambridge, MA: Harvard University Press, 1982), i.x.ii; Plutarch, "Precepts of Policie," *Morals*, tr. Holland, 359.

87. Castiglione, *The Book of the Courtier*, Book iv, 313.

88. Antonio de Guevara, *The Diall of Princes*, tr. Thomas North (London: John Waylande, 1557), Prologue; Richard Delamain, *Gramelogia, Or, the Mathematicall Ring* (London: John Haviland, 1630), Dedicatory Epistle to King Charles I.

89. Sturtevant, *Metallica*, 49.

90. Ripa, *Nova Iconologia*, ed. Piero Buscaroli (Milan: Tascabili, 1992), "Esercitio," 502–03.

91. Peacham, *The Compleat Gentleman*, full title; chapter 7, 69.

92. On the intellectual culture of Prince Henry's court, see Salmon, "Stoicism and Roman Example," 207–08; Burgess, *Absolute Monarchy*, 54. On the study of mechanics in Henry's court, see Smuts, *Court Culture*, 145–52; Strong, *Henry, Prince of Wales*, 86–137.

93. On Wright, see Strong, *Henry, Prince of Wales*, 212; 215–18; Lesley Cormack, "Twisting the Lion's Tail: Practice and Theory at the Court of Henry Prince of Wales," in *Patronage and Institutions*, 71–8.

94. Peacham, *Graphice or the Most Auncient and Excellent Art of Drawing and Limning* (2nd edn., London: W.S. for John Browne, 1612); *The Compleat Gentleman*, chapter 7, 76–77.

95. Peacham, *The Compleat Gentleman*, chapter 9, 84; chapter 17, 144.

96. *Ibid.*, chapter 9, 85.

97. *Ibid.*, chapter 9, 88; 17, 144.

98. Thomas Blundeville, *M. Blundeville his Exercises* (2nd edn., London, 1597), To the Reader. On the treatises reprinted in the *Exercises*, see Taylor, *Mathematical Practitioners*, 173; 331. Peacham mentions the work in *The Compleat Gentleman*, 69 and 89.

99. Aubrey, "Francis Bacon," in *Lives*, ii.

100. Salmon, "Precept, Example, and Truth," 18; Blundeville, *True order and methode*, Dedication to the Earl of Leicester, Bi.

101. Henry Savile, "Annotations Upon the First Book of Tacitus," in *The Ende of Nero and the Beginning of Galba. Fower Books of the Histories of Tacitus. The Life of Agricola* (Oxford: Richard Wright, 1591), Book i, note 18, 5. Compare Robert Johnson, *Essayes*, D2v, who praises Tacitus for discovering "not only the sequels of things but also the causes & reasons."

102. Savile, *The Ende of Nero and the Beginning of Galba*, 7.

103. On Savile's European journey, see Bodl. MS Gr. Misc. e.8 [Henry Savile, Notebook compiled during Continental Tour, *c.* 1581]; R. B. Todd, "Henry and Thomas Savile in Italy," *Bibliothèque d'Humanisme et Renaissance* 58 (1996), 439–44; J. R. L. Highfield, "An Autograph Commonplace Book of Sir Henry Savile," *Bodleian Library Record* 7 (1963), 73–83; Womersley, "Sir Henry Savile's Translation of Tacitus," 313. On Savile's scientific scholarship, see Feingold, *The Mathematicians' Apprenticeship*, 126–37; Ian Philip, *The*

Bodleian Library in the Seventeenth and Eighteenth Centuries (Oxford: Claren-
don Press, 1988), 2–23. On the scientific texts collected and owned by Savile,
see Bodl. MS. Savile 107 (Catalogue of Books and Manuscripts in Henry
Savile's Library), fos. 1–22; Bodl. MS Add. C.296 (Catalogus Librorum
Manuscriptorum of Henry Savile), fos. 172r–173v. On his 1620 bequest to
the Bodleian, see Philip, *The Bodleian Library*, 2–8; R. W. Hunt, ed., *A
Summary Catalogue of Western Manuscripts in the Bodleian Library at Oxford*
(Oxford: Clarendon Press, 1953), vol. 1, 104–05.

104. Philip Sidney, *The Complete Works*, 4 vols., ed. Albert Feuillerat (Cambridge:
Cambridge University Press, 1923), vol. 3, letter XLII, 130–33.

105. Bodl. MS Top Oxon. e 525 [*An Oration Made Before her Sacred Majesty at
Oxford, ye 23 of September 1592 by Henry Savile & now translated into English
by F.D., 1603*], fo. 11; fos. 1–2. The Latin version of Savile's oration can be
found in Bodl. MS e Musaeo 190 (*Habita Oxonii. anno 1592 Septemb. 23.
coram Regina Elizabeth.*)

106. Bodl. MS Top Oxon e 525 (Savile's *Oration*), fos. 12–13; fo. 10.

107. Bodl. MS Savile 28 (Henry Savile's Latin version of Ptolemy's *Almagest*), 1r–v;
10v.

108. Bodl. MS Savile 45 (Dell'Utilità che si traggono della Mechanica & de suoi
Instromenti); Bodl. MS Savile 17 (*Aristotelis Mechanica*, tr. Henri de Monantheuil), Dedicatory Epistle to King Henri IV, a3r.

109. Bodl. MS Savile 29 (Henry Savile, *Prooemium Mathematicum*), fo. 29r.

110. *Ibid.*, fo. 16r; fo. 31r.

111. Savile, *Praelectiones Tresdecim in Principium Elementorum Euclidis* (Oxford:
John Litchfield & Jacob Short, 1621), 20–22; 30; 29.

112. Percy, *Advice to his Son*, ed. Harrison, Part 1, 71. On Percy's Stoicism, see
G. R. Batho, Stephen Clucas, and Anna Beer, *Prison Writings of Sir Walter
Raleigh and the Ninth Earl of Northumberland. Durham Thomas Harriot Seminar: Occasional Paper 19* (1991), 18–19; Clucas, "'Noble Virtue in Extremes,'"
280–82. On Percy's knowledge of mechanics and his acquaintances in the
field, see Feingold, *The Mathematicians' Apprenticeship*, 130–33; 204–07; John
W. Shirley, "Walter Ralegh and Thomas Harriot," chapter 2 of *Thomas Harriot, Renaissance Scientist*, ed. Shirley (Oxford: Clarendon Press, 1974), 15–31;
James McConica, "Elizabethan Oxford: The Collegiate Society," Chapter 10
of *The History of the University of Oxford*, vol. III: *The Collegiate University*,
716–19; Philip, *The Bodleian Library*, 11–17.

113. Percy, *Advice to his Son*, Part 1, 67; 72; Cicero, *De Finibus Bonorum et Mal-
orum*, tr. H. Rackham (Cambridge, MA: Harvard University Press, 1983),
IV.V.II.

114. John Hall, *Paradoxes* (London, 1650), ed. Don Cameron Allen (Gainesville,
FL: Scholars' Facsimiles and Reprints, 1956), Paradox 2, 53–54.

115. Percy, *Advice to his Son*, Part 1, 69.

116. Stephen Clucas, "Thomas Harriot and the Field of Knowledge in the English
Renaissance," *1994 Thomas Harriot Lecture Oriel College, Oxford* (Oxford:
Oxford University Press, 1995), 21.

117. On Percy's edition of Guido Ubaldo and his experiments at Syon House, see Clucas, "Thomas Harriot and the Field of Knowledge," 20. For Hariot's correspondence with Percy, see BL MS Add. 6789 (Thomas Hariot, *Mathematical Papers*, vol. VIII), fo. 524v ("De Pondere aquae quo premuntur y, quibus altius incumbit. Quaestio ab illustrissimo Domino Henrico Comite Northumbriae proposita, et ventilata"); for Torporley's letter, see BL MS Add. 4458, "Torporley's Answer to Percy's Scientific Questions," fo. 4r. On the contents of Percy's library, see G. R. Batho, "The Library of the 'Wizard' Earl: Henry Percy, Ninth Earl of Northumberland (1564–1632)," *The Library*, fifth series, 15 (1960), 246–61: Appendix 1, 259–60.

118. See John Peacock, "The 'Wizard Earl' Portrayed by Hilliard and Van Dyck," *Art History* 8:2 (June 1985), 139–57: 140.

119. Poliziano, "Letter to Bartolomeo Scala," in *Cambridge Translations*, ed. Kraye, vol. I, 195.

120. Peacock, "The 'Wizard Earl,' " 143.

121. BL MS Sloane 1333 (Poliorcetica/Sive/De Machinis & Scientia Militari), fo. 98v: "Si libera brachia sunt proportionalia ponderibq. in eiq. appensis virq., libra collocata . . . poratta pondera aquaeponderabunt."

122. Robert Recorde, *The Pathway to Knowledge* (London: R. Wolfe, 1551), Preface; Z2r.

123. On Percy's undated "dissertation on love, and on its incompatibility with the pursuits of learning," see *Calendar of State Papers, Domestic Series, of the Reign of James I* (1603–10), ed. Mary Anne Everett Green (London: Longman, Brown, 1857), vol. XI, 9, 183, and rpt. in Frances Yates, *A Study of "Love's Labor's Lost"* (Cambridge: Cambridge University Press, 1936), 208.

124. *Ibid.*, 209.

125. Plutarch, "No Pleasant Life According to Epicurus," *Morals*, 590.

126. Plutarch, "That Aged Men Ought to Govern the Common-Wealth," *Morals*, 387; *Lives*, vol. II, 262; compare Plutarch's account of Euclid in "How to Bridle Anger," *Morals*, 130.

127. William Cornwallis, *Essays*, ed. Don Cameron Allen (Baltimore: Johns Hopkins University Press, 1946), Essay 37, 142.

128. John Ford, *The Golden Meane*, in *The Nondramatic Works of John Ford*, ed. L. E. Stock, Gilles Monsarrat, Judith Kennedy, and Dennis Danielson (Binghamton, NY: Renaissance English Text Society, 1991), 269.

129. Geoffrey Whitney, "Tunc tua res agitur, paries cum proximus ardet," to M. Thomas Wheteley, lines 1–4, in *A Choice of Emblemes* (Leyden: Christopher Plantyn, 1586), ed. John Manning (Aldershot: Scolar Press, 1989), Part 2, 208.

130. Nashe, "Pasquil's Returne to England" (London, 1589), in *Works*, vol. I, 84; Jonson, *Cynthia's Revels*, II.3.99–100, in *Works*, vol. IV, 73; on the mendacity of clocks during the Renaissance, see Mayr, *Authority, Liberty, and Automatic Machinery*, 50–52.

131. George Chapman, *Bussy d'Ambois*, ed. Nicholas Brooke (London: Methuen, 1964), III.1.53–58.

132. Guillaume Du Vair, *The Morale Philosophie of the Stoicks*, tr. Thomas James (London, 1598), ed. Rudolf Kirk (New Brunswick, NJ: Rutgers University Press, 1951), 62; Johnson, *Essays*, Essay 12, F3v–F4r.

3 INANIMATE AMBASSADORS: THE MECHANICS AND POLITICS OF MEDIATION

1. Jean-Jacques Boissard, *Icones Quinquaginta Virorum illustrium . . . cum eorum vitis descriptis*, 2 vols. (Frankfurt: Theodore de Bry, 1597), vol. 1, frontispiece.
2. Plutarch, "Precepts of Policie," *Morals*, 350; 359.
3. Azo of Portius (d. *c.* 1230), *Summa* (Venice, 1594), Book IV, chapter 50, cited in Keith Hamilton and Richard Langhorne, *The Practice of Diplomacy. Its Evolution, Theory and Administration* (New York and London: Routledge, 1995), 22.
4. William Shakespeare, *Hamlet*, III.ii.369–71. All citations of Shakespeare are from *The Complete Works of Shakespeare*, ed. David Bevington (4th edn., New York: Longman, 1997).
5. L[eonardo] Ducci, *Ars Aulica or the Courtiers Arte* (London: Edward Blount, 1607), chapter 1, 3.
6. Antonio Ponce de Santa Cruz, cited in Daniel Sennert, Nicholas Culpeper, and Albiah Cole, *Thirteen Books of Natural Philosophy* (London: Peter Cole, 1660), Book IV, chapter 5, 474–75.
7. On changes in Tudor intelligence, see John Michael Archer, *Sovereignty and Intelligence: Spying and Court Culture in the English Renaissance* (Stanford, CA: Stanford University Press, 1993), 46–47; 124; Beckingsale, *Burghley: Tudor Statesman*, 220–26; James Westfall Thompson and Saul K. Padover, *Secret Diplomacy: Espionage and Cryptography, 1500–1815* (2nd edn., New York: Frederick Ungar, 1963).
8. Bernard du Rosier, *Ambaxiator Brevilogus* (1436), cited in Donald Queller, *The Office of Ambassador in the Middle Ages* (Princeton: Princeton University Press, 1967), 60; also see Garrett Mattingly, *Renaissance Diplomacy* (Boston: Houghton Mifflin, 1955), 29–31.
9. Bacon, "Of Cunning" and "Of Negociating," *Essayes*, 73; 145.
10. Charron, *Of Wisdome*, Book III, chapter 1, 361; French text cited from Charron, *De la Sagesse*, Book III, chapter 2, 558.
11. Lipsius, *Six Bookes of Politickes*, Book IV, chapter 14, 119; compare Montaigne, "A Tricke of Certaine Ambassadors," *Essayes*, Book I, chapter 16, 42.
12. Walter Ralegh, *The Arts of Empire and Mysteries of State Discabineted in Political and Polemical Aphorisms* (London, 1692), chapter XXV, 117.
13. Castiglione, *Book of the Courtier*, Book II, 121–22.
14. Joseph Hall, *Characters of Vertues and Vices* (London, 1606), ed. Kirk, Epistle 1608: "A Description of a Good and Faithful Courtier," 203.
15. Chaucer, *Troilus and Criseyde*, in *The Riverside Chaucer*, ed. Larry Benson (Boston: Houghton Mifflin, 1987), Book IV, 132–33; George Puttenham, *The Arte of English Poesie*, ed. Gladys Doidge Willcock and Alice Walker (Cambridge: Cambridge University Press, 1936), Book III, chapter 18, 186; 193–95.

16. Bacon, "Of Cunning," *Essayes*, 70–72.
17. On Mercury in the Renaissance, see Sherman, *John Dee*, 12–14; Joseph Porter, *Shakespeare's Mercutio: his History and Drama* (Chapel Hill: University of North Carolina Press, 1988); Noel Purdon, *The Words of Mercury: Shakespeare and English Mythography of the Renaissance* (Manchester: Institut für Englische Sprach und Literatur, 1974); Douglas Brooks-Davies, *The Mercurian Monarch: Magical Politics from Spenser to Pope* (Manchester: Manchester University Press, 1983), Introduction and chapter 1.
18. On Hermes' deceitfulness, see Detienne and Vernant, *Cunning Intelligence*, 308–09.
19. On James I's statue, see Victor Thoren, *The Lord of Uraniborg: a Biography of Tycho Brahe* (Cambridge: Cambridge University Press, 1990), 336; on Cellini's Mercury see Bredekamp, *The Lure of Antiquity*, 2. On automata in the shape of Mercury, see Lomazzo, *A tracte containing the artes*, Book II, chapter 1, 2.
20. Cuthbert Tunstal to King Henry VIII (BL MS Vit. B. xx 163) and Cuthbert Tunstal to Cardinal Wolsey (R. O. Ellis, 3 Ser. I, 231), both dated October 12, 1520 and rpt. in J. S. Brewer, ed., *Letters and Papers, Foreign and Domestic, of the Reign of Henry VIII: Preserved in the Public Record Office, the British Museum, and Elsewhere in England*, 21 vols. (London: Longman, Green, Longman, & Roberts, 1862–1932), vol. III, part I, 1018–19.
21. Alberico Gentili, *De Legationibus, libri tres* (London, 1585), 2 vols., tr. Gordon Laing (Oxford: Oxford University Press, 1924), vol. II, 145–46; Ermolao Barbaro, *De Officio Legati*, rpt. in V. E. Grabar, *De Legatis et Legationibus tractatus varii* (Dorpat, 1905), 100r. On the education of Renaissance ambassadors, see Mattingly, *Renaissance Diplomacy*, chapter 23.
22. Angel Day, *The English Secretorie* (2nd edn., London, 1599), rpt. in *English Linguistics 1500–1800*, vol. XXIX (New York: Scolar Press, 1967), 127.
23. On jugglers and barbers as ambassadors, see Queller, *The Office of Ambassador*, 155.
24. Tunstal to Wolsey, in *Letters and Papers*, vol. III, part I, 1019.
25. On Kratzer, see Taylor, *Mathematical Practitioners*, 12–13; Feingold, *The Mathematicians' Apprenticeship*, 196–204; Pearl Hogrefe, *The Sir Thomas More Circle* (Urbana: University of Illinois Press, 1959), 37 and throughout.
26. MS Bodl. 504 (Nicholas Kratzer, *Canones Horopti, c.* 1523–35), fo. IV. On Kratzer as instrument-maker, see Sydney Anglo, *Spectacle, Pageantry, and Early Tudor Policy* (Oxford: Clarendon Press, 1969), 218; R. T. Gunther, *Early Science in Oxford*, 15 vols. (Oxford: Oxford University Press, 1920–1967), vol. II, 101–06.
27. John Rastell, *A New Interlude and a merry of the nature of the Four Elements* (London, 1519), in *A Select Collection of Old English Plays*, ed. W. Carew Hazlitt (London: Reeves & Turner, 1874), vol. I, 27. On natural philosophy in the Tudor morality play, see A. W. Reed, *Early Tudor Drama. Medwall, the Rastells, Heywood, and the More Circle* (London: Methuen, 1926), 13–20; *Three Rastell Plays. Four Elements, Calisto and Melebea, and Gentleness and Nobility*, ed. Richard Axton (Cambridge: D. S. Brewer, 1979), introduction.
28. On Rastell's scientific sources, see M. E. Borish, "Source and Intention of *The Four Elements*," *Studies in Philology* 35 (1938), 149–57; Elizabeth Nugent,

"Sources of John Rastell's *The Nature of the Four Elements*," *PMLA* 57 (1942), 74–88; George B. Parks, "Rastell and Waldseemüller's Map," *PMLA* 58 (1943), 572–74; Taylor, *Mathematical Practitioners*, 312.

29. Rastell, *Four Elements*, 19; 40.
30. *Ibid.*, 45–46; 21.
31. Anglo, *Early Tudor Policy*, 217–19.
32. Peter Gillis to Desiderius Erasmus, Antwerp, January 18, 1517, rpt. as letter 515 in *Correspondence of Erasmus, Letters 446–593 (1516–1517)*, vol. IV of *Collected Works of Erasmus*, tr. R. A. B. Mynors and D. F. S. Thomson (Toronto: University of Toronto Press, 1977), 185. On Kratzer's and Holbein's errands, see Mary Hervey, *Holbein's "Ambassadors": the Picture and the Men* (London: George Bell, 1900), 76; Lisa Jardine, *Worldly Goods: A New History of the Renaissance* (New York: Doubleday, 1996), 357–60.
33. Nicholas Kratzer to Thomas Cromwell, rpt. in *Letters and Papers*, ed. Brewer, vol. XIII, pt. I, 179.
34. Norman Bryson, *Looking at the Overlooked*, 61, cited in *Subject and Object*, 3.
35. Greenblatt, *Renaissance Self-Fashioning*, 9; 17–21.
36. Hervey, *Holbein's "Ambassadors,"* 223–26; also see Jardine, *Worldly Goods*, 299–307; 357–58; Kenneth Charlton, "Holbein's *Ambassadors* and Sixteenth-Century Education," *The Journal of the History of Ideas* 21 (1960), 99–109. On the relationship between Kratzer and Holbein, see Anglo, *Early Tudor Policy*, 217–19; Otto Pächt, "Holbein and Kratzer as Collaborators," *Burlington Magazine* 74 (1944), 134–39.
37. Jardine, *Worldly Goods*, 306; on commerce and trade as themes of Holbein's painting, see *ibid.*, 431–32; 436.
38. On the etymological connections between emblem(atura), mosaic, and museum, see Paula Findlen, *Possessing Nature: Museums, Collecting, and Scientific Culture in Early Modern Italy* (Berkeley: University of California Press, 1994), 50; on the related concept of social "emblematics" or bricolage, see Shapin, " 'A Scholar and a Gentleman,' " 279–327; Biagioli, *Galileo, Courtier*, 11.
39. Findlen, *Possessing Nature*, 296; for similar arguments, see Tribby, "Body/Building," 152; Susan Stewart, *On Longing: Narratives of the Miniature, the Gigantic, the Souvenir, the Collection* (Durham, NC: Duke University Press, 1993), 152–54.
40. Tribby, "Body/Building," 152; Hervey, *Holbein's "Ambassadors,"* 56, note 1; 75.
41. Paris Bibl. Nat. Coll. Dupuy, vol. 726 (Jean de Dinteville to his brother François, dated May 23, 1533), fo. 46v, rpt. in Hervey, *Holbein's "Ambassadors,"* 80.
42. Suberville, *L'Henry-metre: Instrument Royale*, Dedication to Henri IV; Jacques Besson, *Théâtre des Instrumens Mathematiques et Mechaniques* (2nd edn., Paris, 1579), Dedication by François Beroald, A3r.
43. Alciati, *Emblemata*, cited in Hervey, *Holbein's "Ambassadors,"* 229–31: "Unaque si fuerit non bene tenta fides, / Ruptave (quod facile est) perit omnis gratia

concha / Illique praecellens cantus ineptus erit"; on the theme of discord in Holbein's painting, see also Jardine, *Worldly Goods*, 425.

44. On the terrestrial globe, see Hervey, *Holbein's "Ambassadors,"* 212–14.

45. On Selve's secret visit to England, see *ibid.*, 76.

46. Jardine, *Worldly Goods*, 299; Johannes Trithemius, *Polygraphie et Universelle Escriture Cabalistique*, tr. Gabriel de Collange (Paris: Jacques Kerver, 1561), 239v. On lemons and armagnac as cryptographic devices, see 235v.

47. On Holbein, Kratzer, and German steelyard workers, see Jardine, *Worldly Goods*, 357–60; T. H. Lloyd, *England and the German Hanse, 1157–1611. A Study of their Trade and Commercial Diplomacy* (Cambridge: Cambridge University Press, 1991). On the use of German as code, see Hervey, *Holbein's "Ambassadors,"* 75–6; Mattingly, *Renaissance Diplomacy*, 248–49.

48. On More's relationship to Holbein's *Ambassadors*, see Greenblatt, *Renaissance Self-Fashioning*, chapter 1, esp. 17–27; Nicholas Harpsfield, *Lyfe and Death of Sir Thomas Moore*, ed. Elsie Vaughan Hitchcock. Early English Text Society, vol. CLXXXVI (London: E.E.T.S., 1932), 21; Thomas More, *Utopia*, tr. Robert Adams (2nd edn., New York: W. W. Norton & Co., 1992), 7–8.

49. Cuthbert Tunstal, *De Arte Supputandi libri quattuor* (London: Richard Pynson, 1522), dedicatory letter to Thomas More. On Tunstal as mathematician, see Charles Sturge, *Cuthbert Tunstal: Churchman, Scholar, Statesman, Administrator* (London: Longmans, 1938), 71–73. On double-entry bookkeeping, see Mary Poovey, *A History of the Modern Fact: Problems of Knowledge in the Sciences of Wealth and Society* (Chicago: University of Chicago Press, 1998), chapter 2; Crosby, *The Measure of Reality*, chapter 10.

50. On Erasmus' and More's influence upon their portraits by Holbein, see Lisa Jardine, *Erasmus, Man of Letters: the Construction of Charisma in Print* (Princeton: Princeton University Press, 1993), chapter 1.

51. Thomas Powell, *Humane Industry; or, a History of Most Manual Arts* (London: Henrie Herringman, 1661), chapter 7, 76–77. On anamorphosis, see also Jurgis Baltrusaitis, *Anamorphoses ou magie artificielle des effets merveilleux* (Paris: Olivier Perrin, 1969); Colie, *Paradoxia Epidemica*, 312–15.

52. Puttenham, *The Arte of English Poesie*, Book 1, chapter 27, 54; Richard Fly, *Shakespeare's Mediated World* (Amherst: University of Massachusetts Press, 1976), 8.

53. Montaigne, "A Tricke of Certaine Ambassadors," in *Essayes*, Book 1, chapter 16, 40–42; Puttenham, *Arte of English Poesie*, Book III, chapter 23, 266; 271.

54. Sansovino, *The Quintessence of Wit*, Aphorism 65, 8r.

55. On the legitimacy of "honest and laudable deceipt," see Lipsius, *Six Books of Politickes*, Book IV, chapter 13, 114.

56. Thomas Tomkis, *Albumazar* (London: Nicholas Okes, 1615), 1.3, A4v–Br; 1.4, Bv.

57. Ben Jonson, *Volpone, or the Fox*, in *Works*, vol. V, II.i.78–89.

58. *Ibid.*, IV.i.115–24; V.iv.44–51.

59. Jonson, Epigram XCII ("The New Cry"), in *The Complete Poems*, ed. George Parfitt (London: Penguin, 1988), 65, lines 25–28.

60. Porta, *De Furtivis Literarum Notis Vulgo: De Ziferis Libri IIII* (Naples, 1563), 1.8.26.

61. *Ibid.*, III.7.70–73; Giovanbattista Palatino, *On Cryptography; the Treatise Dalle Cifre from Palatino's Writing Book of 1540*, tr. A. S. Osley (Wormley, England: Glade Press, 1970), 14–20.

62. Trithemius, *Clavicule*, in *Polygraphie*, 212b.

63. Trithemius, *Polygraphie*, 3r (Pythagoras); 164v (Zoroaster; Hermes); 184r–v (alchemists).

64. Trithemius, *Clavicule*, in *Polygraphie*, 226b.

65. Trithemius, *Polygraphie*, Prologue, 5v; *Epistre sur la Steganographie*, in *Polygraphie*, 243a. The "figures Planispheriques" are represented on fos. 252a–57a.

66. BL MS Add. 4403, fos. 154–64 (Henry Reginald, "Two Mathematicall . . . An Invention for briefe speedie and Secrete Intelligence), fos. 154–55.

67. BL MS Add. 4403, fos. 154–55. On Trithemius' "algarithmes," see *Clavicule*, in *Polygraphie*, 296a.

68. BL MS Add. 4384, fos. 67a–92a (Henry Reginald, "Architectiones Seu Inventiones Sex," dated 1603), fo. 72a.

69. BL MS Add. 4384, fo. 78b. On Archimedes' cryptographic devices, see *Polygraphie*, IV; 229b; Trithemius' source is Aulus Gellius, *Noctes Atticae*, XVII, 9.

70. Roger Bacon, *Discovery of the Miracles of Art, Nature, and Magick*, chapter 4, 20.

71. Leonard Digges, *Pantometria*, Preface by Thomas Digges, A3v; compare Thomas Digges' account in *Longimetria*, where he explains how one may use glasses to "discerne any trifle, or read any letter lying there open, especially if the sonne beames may come upon it," cited from Brian Ford, *Images of Science: A History of Scientific Illustration* (New York: Oxford University Press, 1993), 152–53.

72. Biagioli, *Galileo, Courtier*, 122–25.

73. Stephen Orgel, *The Illusion of Power: Political Theater in the English Renaissance* (2nd edn., Berkeley and Los Angeles: University of California Press, 1991), 10–11; Suberville, *L'Henry-metre*, Dedication to Henri IV.

74. BL MS Lands. 77, Art. 59 (Edmund Jentill to Lord Burghley, dated October 1, 1594), rpt. in Halliwell, *A Collection of Letters Illustrative of Early Science in England* (2nd edn., London: Historical Society of Science, 1965), 35.

75. Bacon, *Discovery of the Miracles of Art, Nature, and Magick*, chapter 5, 19.

76. Van Etten, *Mathematicall Recreations*, Problem 78, 160; Problem 66, 101.

77. On Drebbel's perspective glasses, see Cornelis van der Woude, *Kronyck van Alckmaar* (Gravenhage, 1746), 102, cited in Tierie, *Cornelius Drebbel*, 49; compare Porta, *Magia Naturalis*, Book 17; Van Etten, *Mathematicall Recreations*, Problem 66, 100; and the examples in Lynn Thorndike, *A History of Magic and Experimental Science*, 8 vols. (New York: Macmillan, 1923–58), vol. VI, 496.

78. Van Etten, *Mathematicall Recreations*, Problem 77, 144–46; Martin Heidegger, *The Question Concerning Technology and Other Essays*, tr. William Lovitt (New York: Garland, 1977), 11.

79. Montaigne, *An Apologie of Raymond Sebond*, in *Essayes*, Book II, chapter 12, 532.

80. *Ibid.*, 534.

81. Robert Burton, *The Anatomy of Melancholy*, 6 vols., ed. Thomas C. Faulkner, Nicholas K. Kiessling, and Rhonda L. Blair (Oxford: Clarendon Press, 1992), vol. I, 424 (1.3.3.1); Wright, *The Passions of the Mind*, Book II, chapter 1, 49.

82. Frances Godwin, *Nuncius Inanimatus, or The Mysterious Messenger*, printed with his *The man in the moone, or, A discourse of a voyage thither* (London: Joshua Kinton, 1657), 1.

83. *Ibid.*, 3.

84. *Ibid.*, 12.

85. *Ibid.*, 2–3.

86. Charron, *Of Wisdome*, Book I, chapter 10, 41; chapter 3, 15; French text cited from Charron, *De la Sagesse*, Book I, chapter 9, 112; Book I, chapter 3, 63.

87. Godwin, *Nuncius Inanimatus*, title-page; *Ambassades du Roy de Siam envoyé à l'excellence du Prince Maurice, arrivé à la Haye le 10.Septemb. 1608*, in *The Unsung Hero and the Origin of the Telescope*, ed. Stillman Drake (Los Angeles: Zeitlin & Ver Brugge, 1976), 3; 5–7.

88. See Sextus Julius Frontinus, *The Strategemmes, Sleyghtes, and Politics of Warre* (London, 1539), Book II, chapter 13; *The Foure Bookes of Flavius Vegetius Renatus*, tr. J[ohn] Sadler (London: Thomas Marshe, 1572), Book II, chapter 19.

89. John Wilkins, *Mercury: or the Secret and Swift Messenger, Shewing How a Man may with Privacy and Speed communicate his Thoughts to a friend at any distance* (London: John Norton, 1641), Preface to the Reader; title-page. On the use of arrows, birds, and bullets as "swifter" than "corporeall messengers," see *ibid.*, chapter 16, 123–24; on enchanted glasses, see chapter 19, 152.

90. *Ibid.*, chapter 17, 133–37.

91. Richard West, "To his Honoured Friend J. W. on . . . the Secret and Swift Messenger," in *ibid.*, A4v.

92. *Ibid.*, Preface to the Reader; chapter 18, 141.

93. Burton, *The Anatomy of Melancholy*, vol. I, 426 (1.3.3.1): "artificiall devices to over-hear their confessions, like that whispering place of Glocester with us, or like the Dukes place at Mantua in Italy, where the sound is reverberated by a concave wall."

94. West, "To his Honoured Friend J. W.," in Wilkins, *Mercury*, A4v.

95. Timothy Bright, *Characterie, an arte of shorte, swifte, and secrete writing by character* (London, 1588), A3r–v; Trithemius, *Polygraphie*, 5v.

96. Miguel de Cervantes, *Don Quixote*, tr. J. M. Cohen (London: Penguin, 1950), part 2, 869.

97. *Ibid.*, 878.

98. Salomon de Caus, *Les Raisons des Forces Mouvantes, avec diverses Machines tant utiles que plaisants* (Frankfurt: J. Norton, 1615), Book III.

99. Shakespeare, *Twelfth Night; Or, What You Will*, 1.IV.32–33; Raymond Williams, *Keywords. A Vocabulary for Culture and Society* (New York: Oxford University Press, 1976), "Organic," 227.

100. *The Diary of Master Thomas Dallam* (*c.* 1599–1600), rpt. and ed. J. Theodore Bent, *Early Voyages and Travels in the Levant* (London: Hakluyt Society, 1893), Introduction, xii–xiii; xvi.

101. *Ibid.*, 62; 64.

102. *Ibid.*, 66.

103. *Ibid.*, 15; Ong, *Rhetoric, Romance, and Technology*, 35 and 1–8.

104. *The Diary of Thomas Dallam*, 67.

105. *Ibid.*, 68.

106. *Ibid.*, 68–69; Elias, *The Court Society*, 101.

107. *The Diary of Thomas Dallam*, 73; 69–70.

108. *Ibid.*, 71; Puttenham, *Arte of English Poesie*, Book III, chapter 24, 294: "such as retire from the Princes presence [in the Ottoman court], do not by & by turne tayle to them as we do, but go backward or sideling for a reasonable space, til they be at the wal[l] or cha[m]ber doore."

109. *The Diary of Thomas Dallam*, 70; Aristotle, *Politics*, Book 4, 1253b.

110. *The Diary of Thomas Dallam*, 70; Cornwallis, Essay 33, "Of Silence and Secrecie," in *Essayes*, 117.

111. *The Diary of Thomas Dallam*, 70. On Wilkins' work with deaf-mutes, see *Mercury*, Introduction; Barbara Shapiro, *John Wilkins 1614–1672: An Intellectual Biography* (Berkeley: University of California Press, 1969), 121.

112. Puttenham, *Arte of English Poesie*, Book III, chapter 18, 193.

113. Tuvill, *The Dove and the Serpent*, chapter 13, 71.

114. *Ibid.*, chapter 4, 23.

115. Bacon, "Of Cunning," *Essayes*, 69; 71.

116. *Ibid.*, *Essayes*, 70; 72; 71.

117. Bacon, "Of Counsell," *Essayes*, 64–65.

118. Bacon, *Novum Organum*, Preface, 38.

119. *Ibid.*

120. Bacon, Preface to *The Great Instauration*, in *ibid.*, 13.

121. *Ibid.*, Book I, Aphorism 18, 47.

122. On the cracks in cabinet councils, see Bacon, "Of Counsell," *Essayes*, 65; on the failure of magnifying instruments, see Bacon, *Novum Organum*, Book I, Aphorism 50, 60.

123. Bacon, *Novum Organum*, Book II, Aphorism 39, 224–26.

124. Christopher Marlowe, *The Jew of Malta*, in *Doctor Faustus and Other Plays*, ed. David Bevington (Oxford: Oxford University Press, 1995), II.iii.187–90.

125. *Ibid.*, v.ii.111–14.

126. Anthony Copley, *A Fig for Fortune* (London: Richard Johns, 1596), 16–17, lines 375; 391–3.

127. Marlowe, *Jew of Malta*, v.ii.116; I.i.115.

128. Shakespeare, *Anthony and Cleopatra*, II.v.100–01.

129. Thomas Heywood, "Epilogue Spoken at Court" (1633), in Marlowe, *Jew of Malta*, 322.

130. Marlowe, *Jew of Malta*, I.i.187.

131. Stephen Greenblatt, "Marlowe, Marx, and Machiavelli," in *Learning to Curse. Essays in Early Modern Culture* (New York and London: Routledge, 1990), 53–5; Katherine Maus, *Inwardness and Theater in the English Renaissance* (Chicago: University of Chicago Press, 1995), 35.
132. The term "means" is spoken by Barabas at i.i.35, v.i.61, and v.i.92.
133. Ben Jonson, Epigram cxv, "On the Town's Honest Man," lines 25–26, in *Complete Poems*, 79; on attitudes towards Renaissance engineers, see Vérin, *La Gloire des ingénieurs*, 112–13.
134. Leonardo Da Vinci, letter to Lodovico Sforza, Duke of Milan, cited in Jardine, *Worldly Goods*, 239–40.
135. See Jonson, Epigram xcvii, "On the New Motion"; "An Expostulation with Inigo Jones"; and "To Inigo, Marquess Would-Be, A Corollary," in *Complete Poems*, 68; 345–48.
136. Marlowe, *Jew of Malta*, v.v.35–36.
137. *Hamlet*, i.ii.47–49.
138. *Ibid.*, iv.ii.69; v.ii.319.
139. *Ibid.*, iii.ii.363–71; iii.ii.367; ii.ii.595.
140. *Ibid.*, ii.i.64–67.
141. *Ibid.*, i.ii.36–38.
142. *Ibid.*, i.v.38; 36; 68.
143. *Ibid.*, iii.i.187–88; iii.iii.29; ii.ii.565–66.
144. *Ibid.*, iv.ii.16–22.
145. *Ibid.*, v.ii.32; 49.
146. *Ibid.*, iii.iv.212–14.
147. *Ibid.*, v.ii.309; ii.ii.124.

4 THE POLYMECHANY OF GABRIEL HARVEY

1. Epigraph from Harvey's copy of Niccolò Machiavelli, *Arte of Warre*, tr. Peter Whithorne (London, 1573), A2r (STC 17165); Gabriel Harvey, *Pierces Supererogation*, in *The Complete Works*, 3 vols., ed. Alexander Grosart (London, 1884; rpt. New York, AMS Press, 1964), vol. ii, 211.
2. Harvey's copy of Joannes Ramus, *Oikonomia seu Dispositio Regularum utriusque Juris in Locos Communes brevi interpretatione subjecta* (Cologne, ad intersignum Monocerotis, 1570), 15, cited in *Gabriel Harvey's Marginalia*, ed. G. C. Moore Smith (Stratford-upon-Avon: Shakespeare Head Press, 1913), 148 (hereafter referred to as *Marginalia.*).
3. Detienne and Vernant, *Cunning Intelligence*, 28.
4. *Ibid.*, 46–48; 115.
5. Harvey, *Commonplace Book*, 17r, cited in *Marginalia*, 91. On Roger Bacon's mechanical inventions, see Wayne Shumaker, "Accounts of Marvelous Machines in the Renaissance," *Thought: a Review of Cultures and Ideas* 51 (1976), 255–70: 255; William Eamon, "Technology as Magic in the Late Middle Ages and the Renaissance," *Janus* 70 (1983), 171–212.

6. On Dandalo's "Doggtrick," see Harvey, *Commonplace Book*, 23r; 17r; 25r, cited in *Marginalia*, 97; 91; 100–01; Machiavelli, *The Prince*, chapter 18, 145: "a uno principe è necessario sapere bene usare la bestia e l'uomo."

7. Folger MS H.a.2(1), Harvey's copy of Ludovico Domenichi, *Facetie, motti, e burle, di diversi signori e persone private* (Venice: Andrea Muschio, 1571), 31v, also cited in Stern, *Gabriel Harvey*, 187.

8. On "right artificiality," see Harvey, *Foure Letters and Certain Sonnets*, in *Works*, vol. I, 218.

9. On Harvey's personae see Stern, *Gabriel Harvey*, 126–28; 175–90; James Nielson, "Reading Between the Lines: Manuscript Personality and Gabriel Harvey's Drafts," *Studies in English Literature* 33 (1993), 43–82: 78 and throughout.

10. Detienne and Vernant, *Cunning Intelligence*, 18; on Odysseus' epithets, see, for instance, *Iliad* XXIII, 314 (*pantoie*), *Odyssey* VI, 234 (*techne pantoie*), *Iliad* XI, 482 and *Odyssey* III, 163 (*poikilometis*).

11. Ευδρομοσ literally means "running well," while Ευτραπελοσ literally means "easily turning" and, by extension, with dexterity. On the term *polytechnos*, see Johannes Scapula, *Lexicon Graecolatinum novum* (London: Bibliopolarum, 1619), sig. Yy2v, which defines it as skill in many arts, or the possession of varied artifices ("multa arte accuratus, multum artificii habens: vel, valde artificiosus").

12. BL 533.k.1, Harvey's copy of Joannis de Sacrobosco, *Textus de Sphaera . . . cum compositione Annuli astronomici Boneti Latensis* (Paris: Simon Colinaeus, 1527), A2r.

13. Harvey's copy of T. Livii Patavini, *Romanae Historiae Principis, Decades Tres* (Basel: Jonnes Hervagios, 1555), 93, cited in Stern, *Gabriel Harvey*, 150; BL Add. MS 42518, Harvey's copy of *The Woorkes of our antient and lerned English Poet, Geffrey Chaucer*, ed. Thomas Speght (London: George Bishop, 1598), 422v.

14. [STC 11128] Harvey's copy of Joannes Foorth, *Synopsis Politica* (London: H. Bynneman, 1582), title-page.

15. *Ibid.*, TT1r; UU1v; TT3r.

16. BL C.60.e.13, Achilles Pirminus Gassar[us], *Historiarum et Chronicorum Totius Mundi Epitome* (Basel?, 1538), signed "Gabriel Harvejus, 1576," title-page; 52; 202; 263; 255–56.

17. Harvey's copy of Gassarus, *Historiarum*, 263; on the "little finger of Pollicy," see Harvey, *Pierces Supererogation*, in *Works*, vol. II, 315.

18. Nashe, *Have With You to Saffron Walden*, in *Works*, vol. III, 79.

19. On Harvey's defeat by Perne, see his account in *Foure Letters*, in *Works*, vol. I, and cited in Stern, *Gabriel Harvey*, 53.

20. Harvey, *Foure Letters*, in *Works*, vol. I, 136–37.

21. On Harvey's attitudes towards courtiership, see Stern, *Gabriel Harvey*, 17–22; John Lievsay, *Stefano Guazzo and the English Renaissance* (Chapel Hill: University of North Carolina Press, 1961), 88–96; Ruutz-Rees, "Some Notes of Gabriel Harvey's in Hoby's Translation of Castiglione's *Courtier*," 608–39.

22. STC 4778, Harvey's copy of Baldassar Castiglione, *The Courtyer of Baldessar Castilio; divided into foure bookes . . . done into Englyshe by Thomas Hoby* (London: Wyllyam Seres, 1561), E2v; compare YY3v, where Harvey captures the meaning of *sprezzatura* in the aphorism, "The rarest men extend their utterest possibilitie, with a fine (as it were) familiar sleight."

23. BL C.60.l.11, Harvey's copy of *M. Fabii Quintiliani Oratoris Eloquentissimi, Institutionem Oratoriarum Libri xii* (Paris: Robert Estienne, 1542), dated 1579, 45; 313. The latter comment appears in Book 6, chapter 4 of Quintilian's text, in a section entitled "De Risu [On Laughter]," next to Quintilian's description of Demosthenes.

24. BL C.175.i.4, Harvey's copy of Thomas Blundevill[e], *The foure chiefest Offices belonging to Horsemanship* (London: Henrie Denham, 1580), A1v; compare his comments in STC 884, his copy of John Astley, *The art of riding, set foorth in a breefe treatise* (London: H. Denham, 1584), verso of title-page, where Harvey commends both Astley and Blundeville as "two right proffitable, & gallant Writers, in the excellent veine of Xenophon."

25. Castiglione, *The Book of the Courtier*, Book 1, 55.

26. Harvey's copy of Castiglione, *The Book of the Courtier*, ZZ1r–v; Harvey's copy of Blundeville, *Offices*, 5r.

27. Folger H.a.2(I), Harvey's copy of Domenichi, *Facetie*, 32v; Harvey's copy of Castiglione, *The Book of the Courtier*, ZZ1v.

28. Harvey's copy of Blundeville, *Offices*, A1v.

29. Sir Philip Sidney, *An Apology for Poetry*, in *Elizabethan Critical Essays*, ed. Smith, vol. 1, 150.

30. Harvey, *Pierces Supererogation*, in *Works*, vol. ii, 99.

31. Sidney, *Apology*, in *Elizabethan Critical Essays*, vol. 1, 195.

32. *Ibid.*, 159; 203; my italics.

33. Harvey's copy of Quintilian, *Institutio Oratoriarum*, 393; 567.

34. Harvey's copy of Blundeville, *Offices*, 11v; 51v.

35. Castiglione, *The Book of the Courtier*, Book 1, 52.

36. Sidney, *Apology*, in *Elizabethan Critical Essays*, vol. 1, 161.

37. Harvey, *Foure Letters*, in *Works*, vol. 1, 227–28.

38. On the significance of "Eutrapelia," see Aristotle, *Nicomachean Ethics*, ii.vii.13; Folger MS H.a.2(3), Gabriel Harvey's copy of Lodovico Guicciardini, *Detti et Fatti Piacevoli, et Gravi; Di Diversi Principi, Filosofi, Et Cortegiani . . . Et Ridotti A Moralita* (Venice: Cristoforo de Zanetti, 1571), 82v.

39. Harvey, *Pierces Supererogation*, in *Works*, vol. ii, 50–51.

40. Harvey, *Commonplace Book*, 24v, cited in *Marginalia*, 100.

41. Harvey, *Pierces Supererogation*, in *Works*, vol. ii, 104–05.

42. *Ibid.*, 106.

43. Harvey, *Commonplace Book*, 27v, cited in *Marginalia*, 105.

44. Harvey's copy of Foorth, *Synopsis Politica*, Epistle Dedicatory; 9; 2, cited in *Marginalia*, 192–93; compare *Pierces Supererogation*, in *Works*, vol. ii, 56, where eloquence is a "dubble flayle" and "arguments are swoordes."

45. Castiglione, *The Book of the Courtier*, Book ii, 166; 110.

46. Excluding medical and astrological texts and works of military tactics. For books owned by Harvey, see Stern, *Gabriel Harvey*, 244–48; 264–71.
47. BL C.60.O.7, Harvey's copy of John Blagrave, *The Mathematical Jewel, Shewing the making, and most excellent use of a singular Instrument so called: in that it performeth with wonderfull dexteritie, whatsoever is to be done, either by Quadrant, Ship, Circle, Cylinder, Ring, Dyall, Horoscope, Astrolabe, Sphere, Globe* (London: Walter Venge, 1585), title-page. Harvey signed the text 'gabrielharvey-1585' but a second set of comments were made in or after 1590, when Blagrave published his *Baculum Familiare*, a work Harvey refers to in his later set of notes.
48. Gabriel Harvey's copy of Thomas Hill, *The Schoole of Skil . . . Orderly set forth according to Art, with apt Figures and proportions in their proper places* (London: T. Judson for W. Jaggard, 1599), 267v, cited in Stern, *Gabriel Harvey*, 221.
49. BL 533.k.1, Harvey's copy of Sacrobosco, *De Sphaera*, A2r.
50. Philip Sidney to Edward Denny, May 22, 1580, rpt. in James M. Osborn, *Young Philip Sidney, 1572–1577* (New Haven: Yale University Press, 1972), Appendix 5, 537, my italics.
51. Philip Sidney to Robert Sidney, dated October 18, 1580, in *The Complete Works of Philip Sidney*, vol. III, 132; on Harvey's possible authorship of the letter to Denny, see Grafton and Jardine, " 'Studied for Action': how Gabriel Harvey Read his Livy," *Past and Present* 129 (1990), 30–78: 39.
52. Harvey's copy of Blagrave, *Mathematical Jewel*, Preface to the Reader.
53. *Ibid.*, 11.
54. Harvey's copy of Guicciardini, *Detti et Fatti*, 40v: "Ociosis [*sic*] tam professoribus quam scholasticis infinitas tot auctorum nugas relinquit."
55. Harvey's copy of Blagrave, *Mathematical Jewel*, title-page. On the instruments made by Kynvin, Cole, Reynolds, and Read, see Taylor, *Mathematical Practitioners*, 171–72 and throughout.
56. On Thomas Gemini, see Taylor, *Mathematical Practitioners*, 20; D. J. Bryden, "Evidence from Advertising for Mathematical Instrument Making in London, 1556–1714," *Annals of Science* 49 (1992), 301–36: 301–04.
57. On Kynvin and Cole, see Taylor, *Mathematical Practitioners*, 40–45; Sherman, *John Dee*, 173–76.
58. Harvey, *Pierces Supererogation*, in *Works*, vol. II, 289.
59. *Ibid.*, 289–90.
60. Ramus, *Scholarum Mathematicum*, Book 2, 61: "Haec vere Martis schola est: haec Vulcani officina est." Compare STC 17165 (part 2), Harvey's copy of Peter Whitehorne, *Certeine Wayes for the ordering of Souldiors in Battelray* (London: John Wight, 1573), D3v; Bacon, *Advancement of Learning*, Book II, 58; *Novum Organum*, Book II, 141.
61. Gabriel Harvey to Robert Cecil, in *Works*, vol. I, Introduction, xxvii.
62. On Harvey's Ramism and his editions of Ramus' *Ciceronianus*, see Stern, *Gabriel Harvey*, 21 and throughout; Gerald Snare, "Satire, Logic, and Rhetoric in Harvey's Earthquake Letter to Spenser," *Tulane Studies in English* 18 (1970), 17–33; Kendrick Prewitt, "Gabriel Harvey and the Practice of Method," *Studies in English Literature* 39 (1999), 19–39. On Ramus' influence in Elizabethan

England, see Wilbur Howell, *Logic and Rhetoric in England: 1500–1700* (New York, 1961), 146–281.

63. Ramus, *Scholarum Mathematicum*, Book 1, 38. On the Ramist concept of method, see Miller, *The New England Mind*, 116–21; Ong, *Ramus*, 115–97; *William Temple's "Analysis" of Sir Philip Sidney's "Apology for Poetry,"* ed. and tr. John Webster (Binghamton, NY: Center for Medieval and Early Renaissance Studies, 1984), Introduction, 16–21.

64. For these definitions of "technologia," see Miller, *The New England Mind*, 121; Ong, *Ramus*, 197.

65. Ong, *Ramus*, 115.

66. BL C.60.f.9, Gabriel Harvey's copy of *M. Tullii Ciceronis Epistolae ad Atticum, Ad M. Brutum, Ad. Quinctum Fratrem* (Venice: Paulus Manutius, 1563), 208. Hopper's dictionary was printed as the *Latino-Graecum dictionarum* (Basel: Hieronymus Curionis, 1563).

67. Harvey's copy of Domenichi, *Facetie*, 10r; 41v.

68. Bacon, *The Advancement of Learning*, Book 11, 58; Harvey's copy of Domenichi, *Facetie*, 10r.

69. On Gardiner and Cromwell, see Harvey's copy of *Oikonomia*, 18, cited in *Marginalia*, 149. On Harvey's Machiavellianism, see Anthony Grafton and Lisa Jardine, *From Humanism to the Humanities: Education and the Liberal Arts in Fifteenth- and Sixteenth-Century Europe* (London: Duckworth, 1986), 189 and throughout; on his possible ownership of John Wolfe's editions of Machiavelli, see Stern, *Gabriel Harvey*, 101–02; 268; Harry Hoppe, "John Wolfe, Printer and Publisher 1579–1601," *The Library*, fourth series 14 (1933), 267–69.

70. Harvey's copy of Guicciardini, *Detti et Fatti*, F5r.

71. Bodl. MS 4°.Rawl.61, Harvey's copy of Luca Gaurico, *Tractatus Astrologicus* (Venice: Curtius Troianus Navo, 1552), YY1r.

72. Harvey's copy of Dionysius Periegetes, *The surveye of the world, or situation of the earth . . . now englished by Thomas Twine* (London: Henrie Bynneman, 1572), 6r, cited in *Marginalia*, 163 (STC 6901).

73. Harvey's copy of Blagrave, *Mathematical Jewel*, "The Author in his Owne Defence," cited in *Marginalia*, 212. The comment appears next to a dedicatory poem by Blagrave in which he mentions his youth and lack of schooling.

74. Harvey's copy of Blagrave, *Mathematical Jewel*, 19; 124.

75. On mathematics at Tudor Cambridge, see W. W. Rouse Ball, *A History of the Study of Mathematics at Cambridge* (Cambridge: Cambridge University Press, 1889), 21–25.

76. Harvey's copy of Joannes Ramus, *Oikonomia*, Cr, cited in Stern, *Gabriel Harvey*, 46. According to Stern, *ibid.*, 47, these annotations were probably made in 1580, though Harvey acquired the text in 1574.

77. Harvey's copy of Ramus, *Oikonomia*, 7, cited in *Marginalia*, 146.

78. *Ibid.*, 5; 10, cited in *ibid.*, 146–47.

79. Harvey's copy of Quintilian, *Institutionem Oratoriarum*, cited in Grafton and Jardine, *From Humanism to the Humanities*, 191.

80. Harvey's copy of Ramus, *Oikonomia*, 10, cited in *Marginalia*, 147.

81. Harvey's copy of Quintilian, *Institutionem Oratoriarum*, T7r.
82. Harvey, *Commonplace Book*, 16r, cited in *Marginalia*, 89.
83. Harvey's copy of Guicciardini, *Detti et Fatti*, 147v; on the useless knowledge contained in books, see Guicciardini, *Maxims and Reflections*, Aphorism 35, 51.
84. Harvey's copy of Blagrave, *Mathematical Jewel*, 1: "Omnes Artes fundatae super sensu, et Ratione, plane constant Ratione, et Sensu. Ratio, anima cuiusque principii. Experientia, anima animae, firmissima demonstratio, et irrefutabile κριτηριον [*kriterion*]. Da mihi ocularem, et radicalem demonstrationem cuiusque principii, experimenti, instrumenti, Geometrici, Astronomici, Cosmographici, Horologiographici; Geographici, Hydrographici; et omnino cuiusvis Mathematici."
85. Grafton and Jardine, " 'Studied for Action,' " 30–31; 44–46. On the book-wheel, see Agostino Ramelli, *Le Diverse et Artifiose Macchine*, tr. and ed. Martha Teach Gnudi and E. S. Ferguson as *The Various and Ingenious Machines of Agostino Ramelli* (Baltimore: Johns Hopkins University Press, 1987), 509; Bert Hall, "A Revolving Bookcase by Agostino Ramelli," *Technology and Culture* 11 (1970), 389–400.
86. On Dee as an "adversarial" reader and annotator, see Sherman, *John Dee*, 73–74.
87. See, for instance, John Feather, "The Book in History and the History of the Book," *Journal of Library History* 21 (1986), 12–26: 15; Roger Chartier, *The Cultural Uses of Print in Early Modern France*, tr. Lydia G. Cochrane (Princeton: Princeton University Press, 1987) and his *Cultural History: Between Practices and Representations*, tr. Lydia G. Cochrane (Cambridge: Polity Press, 1988); Roger Darnton, "First Steps Towards a History of Reading," *Australian Journal of French Studies* 21 (1986), 5–30; Sherman, *John Dee*, esp. 53–78.
88. On Henry VIII's copy of Peter Apian's *Astronomicum Caesarum*, see Taylor, *Mathematical Practitioners*, 17; on the volvelles in Apian's text, see Owen Gingerich, "Astronomical Paper Instruments with Moving Parts," in *Making Instruments Count. Essays on Historical Scientific Instruments Presented to Gerard L'Estrange Turner*, ed. R. G. W. Anderson, J. A. Bennett, and W. F. Ryan (Aldershot: Variorum, 1993), 63–74.
89. Tanner, *A Mirror for Mathematiques*, mentioned alongside Bourne's 1578 *Treasure for travelers* on A8v of Harvey's copy of Jerome Turler's *The Traveiler* (London: Abraham Veale, 1575).
90. Leonard Digges, *A boke named tectonicon briefly shewing the exact measuring, and specific reckening all maner of land, squares, timber, stone . . . with other things pleasant and nesessarie, most conducible for surveyers, landmeaters, joyners, carpenters, and masons* (2nd edn, London: Thomas Gemini, 1562), title-page; Bryden, "Mathematical Instrument Making," 302.
91. Worsop, *A Discovery of Sundrie Errors*, "An Advertisement to the Reader"; also see Lucar, *A Treatise Named Lucar Solace*, "To the Reader"; William Barlow, *The navigators supply, Conteining many things of principall importance belonging to navigation, with the description and use of diverse instruments framed chiefly for that purpose* (London: G. Bishop, R. Newbery, and R. Barker, 1597), title-page.

92. Sears Jayne, *Library Catalogues of the English Renaissance* (2nd edn., Foxbury Meadow, Godalming, Surrey: St. Paul's Bibliographies, 1983), Appendix III (Sample Cambridge Inventories), IV: "List of Books in the 1589 Inventory of Abraham Tilman (CUI 1589–1592)," 187–88.

93. On Percy's library catalogue, see Batho, "The Library of the 'Wizard' Earl," 250; 253–54; on Perne's will, see Gunther, *Early Science in Cambridge*, 142.

94. Giovanbattista Palatino, *The Instruments of Writing* (Rome, 1540), ed. and tr. Henry K. Pierce (Newport: Berry Hill Press, 1953), n.p.; Jonathan Goldberg, *Writing Matter: From the Hands of the English Renaissance* (Stanford, CA: Stanford University Press, 1990), 105 and throughout.

95. Bacon, *Novum Organum*, Book 1, Aphorism 2, 43.

96. On the anti-Ciceronian or "Attic" style, see Croll, *Attic and Baroque Prose Style*, 18–29; 188–198; George Williamson, *The Senecan Amble: Prose from Bacon to Collier* (2nd edn., Chicago: University of Chicago Press, 1966), chapter 4, 89–114; Brian Vickers, *Francis Bacon and Renaissance Prose* (Cambridge: Cambridge University Press, 1968), chapter 3, 60–69.

97. Harvey, *Commonplace Book*, 16r; 21r, cited in *Marginalia*, 89, 95; Harvey's copy of Ramus, *Oikonomia*, 7, cited in *Marginalia*, 146–47.

98. On these texts owned by Harvey, see Stern, *Gabriel Harvey*, Appendix B, 198–241.

99. On miscellanies and their Renaissance readers, see Barbara Benedict, *Making the Modern Reader: Literary Mediation and the Early Modern Miscellany* (Princeton: Princeton University Press, 1996).

100. Robert Recorde, *The Grounde of Artes* (London: Reyner Wolff, 1542), Preface to Richard Whalley, A3r; Plat, *The jewell house of art and nature*, Preface to the Reader.

101. On the assembly of commonplaces and storehouses, see Walter Ong's foreword to Sister Joan Marie Lechner, *Renaissance Concepts of the Commonplaces* (New York: Pageant Press, 1962); Mary Crane, *Framing Authority: Sayings, Self, and Society in Sixteenth-Century England* (Princeton: Princeton University Press, 1993), Introduction.

102. Castiglione, *The Book of the Courtier*, Book 1, 59: "a litle (I will not saie diffycultie) but covered subtilty [*acutezza recondita*] make[s] the reader more hedefull."

103. Harvey's copy of Domenichi, *Facetie*, 42r; compare BL C.60.a.1(1), Gabriel Harvey's copy of Stefano Guazzo, *La Civil Conversatione* (Venice: Gratioso Percachino, 1581), FF3r.

104. Edgerton, *The Heritage of Giotto's Geometry*, 256.

105. Roger Chartier, *The Order of Books: Readers, Authors, and Libraries in Europe Between the Fourteenth and the Eighteenth Centuries*, tr. Lydia Cochrane (Stanford: Stanford University Press, 1994), 9.

106. BL C.60.f.8, Harvey's copy of Thomas Hood, *The Marriners Guide ... wherein the use of the plaine sea card is briefly and plainely delivered* (London: Thomas Est, for Thomas Wight, 1592), bound with William Bourne, *A Regiment for the*

Sea, newly corrected and amended by Thomas Hood (London, 1592); Harvey's copy of Turler, *The Traveiler*, inscribed "Ex dono Edmundi Spenserii . . . 1578" on the title-page.

107. BL 533.k.l, Harvey's copy of Sacrobosco, *De Sphaera*; BL 531.f.8, possibly Harvey's copy of Gemma Frisius, *Gemmae Frisii Medici Ac Mathematici De Astrolabio Catholico Liber quo Latissime patentis Instrumenti multiplex usus explicatur* (Antwerp: Joan. Seelsius, 1556). References to Frisius appear on D5v, D6r, and D7v of his copy of Sacrobosco; on Harvey's probable ownership of the Frisius volume, see Stern, *Gabriel Harvey*, 267.

108. Harvey's copy of Blagrave, *Mathematical Jewel*, title-page.

109. BL MS Add. 42518, Gabriel Harvey's copy of Geoffrey Chaucer, *The Workes of our antient and lerned English Poet* (London: George Bishop, 1598), inscribed "gabrielharvey 1598" on the title-page. See Stern, *Gabriel Harvey*, 126 on Harvey's acquisition of the Chaucer folio.

110. Harvey's copy of Dionysius Periegetes, *The surveye of the world*, notes on verso of the second of seven flyleaves preceding the title-page, also cited in *Marginalia*, 161.

111. *Ibid.*

112. On Chrysotechnus and Axiophilus, see Stern, *Gabriel Harvey*, 126–27; 176–79.

113. Harvey's copy of Chaucer, *Workes*, 422v. On Harvey's difficulties in learning languages, particularly French, see his comments in his copy of Antonio de Corro, *The Spanish Grammer*, tr. John Thorius (London: John Wolfe, 1590), D1r, and cited in Stern, *Gabriel Harvey*, 158.

114. Harvey's copy of Chaucer, *Workes*, 422v; Harvey's copy of Guicciardini, *Detti et Fatti*, 202v.

115. Harvey's copy of Periegetes, *The surveye of the world*, verso of second of seven flyleaves preceding title-page, cited in *Marginalia*, 159–61. On the date of these annotations, see Stern, *Gabriel Harvey*, 126.

116. On attitudes towards scientific didacticism in Elizabethan England, see Robert Schuler, "Theory and Criticism of the Scientific Poem in Elizabethan England," *English Literary Renaissance* 15 (1985), 3–41: esp. 5–10.

117. Harvey's copy of Periegetes, *The surveye of the world*, 3r, cited in *Marginalia*, 161; on 4v of the same volume, Harvey praises the "astrological descriptions" of "admirable Bartas."

118. Webbe, *A Discourse of English Poetrie*, and Sidney, *Apology*, both in *Elizabethan Critical Essays*, vol. 1, 236; 160.

119. Sidney, *Apology*, in *Elizabethan Critical Essays*, vol. 1, 160–61.

120. Harvey's copy of Periegetes, *The surveye of the world*, 5r, cited in *Marginalia*, 162: "Hodiernos poetas tam esse ignaros astronomiae: praeter Buclaeum, Astrophilium, Blagravum: alios perpaucos, Uraniae filios."

121. Richard Mulcaster, *Positions*, ed. R. H. Quick (London and New York: Longmans, Green, 1888), 241; see *Marginalia*, note to page 162, line 31. Harvey knew Mulcaster and mentions him in *Pierces Supererogation*, in *Works*, vol. II, 291.

122. Harvey's copy of Periegetes, *The surveye of the world*, 5r, cited in *Marginalia*, 162–63.

123. BL C.60.l.11, Harvey's copy of Quintilian, *Institutionum Oratoriarum*, T3r: "Tria vividissima Britannorum ingenia, Chaucerus, Morus, Juellus. Quibus addo tres florentes indoles; Heiuodum, Sidneium, Spencerum. Qui quaerit illustriora Anglorum, invenie, obscuriora . . . Smithium, Aschamum, Vilsonumt, Diggesium, Blundevilum, Hacluitum, mea corcula."

124. See, for instance, MS Bodl. 68, fos. 13–25, where an anonymous version of Chaucer's *Treatise on the Astrolabe* is included alongside fourteenth-century scientific manuscripts including a 1328 treatise on an annulus (fos. 1–12) and the *Tractatus ad Faciendam Astrolabium* (fos. 26–34). Bodl. MS E. Museo 116, which contains John Dee's copy of Chaucer's treatise, also binds the work with other scientific manuscripts.

125. Gavin Douglas, *Eneados*, 4 vols., ed. David F. C. Coldwell (Edinburgh: W. Blackwood, 1957–64), vol. 1, Prologue to Book 1, 86, lines 339–342.

126. John Leland, *A Life for Chaucer* (*c.* 1540), cited in Derek Brewer, *Chaucer: the Critical Heritage*, 2 vols. (London: Routledge, 1978), vol. 1, 91; Peacham, *The Compleat Gentleman*, chapter 10, 106.

127. *The Woorkes of Geffrey Chaucer*, ed. William Thynne (London: Thomas Godfray, 1532), Dedication by Brian Tuke. On the textual history of Chaucer in the sixteenth century, see Alice Miskimin, *The Renaissance Chaucer* (New Haven: Yale University Press, 1975), 246–51 and Seth Lerer, *Chaucer and his Readers: Imagining the Author in Late Medieval England* (Princeton: Princeton University Press, 1993), chapter 4.

128. Harvey's copy of Periegetes, *The surveye of the world*, cited in *Marginalia*, 160–61.

129. Harvey's copy of Chaucer, *Workes, Arguments to Every Tale and Book, The Canon Yeoman's Tale*, 16r; *The Franklin's Tale*, 80v; *The Squire's Tale*, 52r.

130. Harvey's copy of Chaucer, *Workes, The Man of Lawes Prologue*, 45r; *The Tale of the Nonnes Priest*, 113r; *The Romaunt of the Rose*, 151v.

131. Geoffrey Chaucer, *The Franklin's Tale*, line 1345, in *The Riverside Chaucer*, 185.

132. Harvey's copy of Chaucer, *Arguments to Every Tale and Book, The Manciple's Tale*, 17r.

133. Gabriel Harvey to Sir Robert Cecil, cited in *Works*, vol. III, xxvii; compare Harvey's comments in BL MS Add. 36674, his copy of "An excellent book of the Art of Magick first begun 22 Mar. 1567," 47v and throughout.

134. Bodl. 4°.Rawl.61, Harvey's copy of Gaurico, *Tractatus Astrologicus*, E4r.

135. Harvey, *Commonplace Book*, 15r, cited in *Marginalia*, 89.

136. On Cecil as Chaucer's "patron," see Harvey's copy of Chaucer, *Workes*, 393v.

137. On Harvey's Ramist pedagogy, see Grafton and Jardine, *From Humanism to the Humanities*, 190–93; Prewitt, "Gabriel Harvey," 19–39.

138. Chaucer, *A Treatise on the Astrolabe, A.D. 1391*, ed. Walter Skeat (London: Early English Text Society, 1872), 1; 3.

139. Harvey's copy of Domenichi, *Facetie*, 8v; 36r.

140. Harvey's copy of Peter Ramus, *P. Rami, Regii Eloquentiae, et Philosophiae Professoris, Ciceronianus* (Paris: Andreas Wechelus, 1557), R7v, cited in Stern, *Gabriel Harvey*, 232.

141. Harvey's copy of Joannes Ramus, *Oikonomia*, A2r, cited in *Marginalia*, 146–47.

142. Lerer, *Chaucer and his Readers*, 18; 5; on Chaucer's didacticism, see also George Ovitt, "History, Technical Style, and Chaucer's *Treatise on the Astrolabe*," in *Creativity and the Imagination: Case Studies from the Classical Age to the Twentieth Century*, ed. Mark Amsler (Newark: University of Delaware Press, 1987), 49.

143. Harvey's copy of Periegetes, *The surveye of the world*, front endpapers, cited in *Marginalia*, 159.

144. Harvey's copy of Foorth, *Synopsis Politica*, cited in *Marginalia*, 194.

145. Harvey, *Commonplace Book*, 16v, cited in *Marginalia*, 90–91.

146. *Ibid.*, 16r; 24r, cited in *ibid.*, 89; 99.

147. *Ibid.*, 16r, cited in *ibid.*, 91.

148. Harvey's copy of Ramus, *Oikonomia*, 32, cited in *Marginalia*, 147.

149. Harvey's copy of Chaucer, *Workes*, *Arguments to Every Tale and Book*, 16r.

150. Colie, *Paradoxia Epidemica*, 307.

151. Harvey's copy of Guicciardini, *Detti et Fatti*, 82v.

152. Nashe, *Strange Newes*, in *Works*, vol. I, 282. For Harvey's use of similar metaphors, see his *Pierces Supererogation*, in *Works*, vol. II, 41, where he refers to Nashe as a "dreadfull enginer of phrases" who shoots "dogboltes, and catbolts," and 56, where Harvey complains of his "cruell Confuters: whose arguments are swoordes; whose sentences, murthering bullets; whose phrases, crosbarres."

153. Nashe, *Have With You to Saffron Walden*, in *Works*, vol. III, 54.

5 HOMER IN A NUTSHELL: GEORGE CHAPMAN AND THE MECHANICS OF PERSPICUITY

1. John Keats, "On First Looking into Chapman's Homer," in *John Keats: The Oxford Authors*, ed. Elizabeth Cook (Oxford: Oxford University Press, 1990), 32, line 5; lines 9–12.

2. George Chapman, *Homer's Iliads* (London, 1611), "The Preface to the Reader," in *Chapman's Homer: The Iliad*, ed. Allardyce Nicoll (2nd edn., Princeton: Princeton University Press, 1998), 15–16, lines 80–82; 89–90.

3. On Chapman's invocation of Hariot's "perfect eye," see his "To My Admired and Soule-Loved Friend Mayster of all essentiall and true knowledge, M. Harriots," in George Chapman, *Achilles Shield* (London: John Windet, 1598), line 41; on his penchant for "mystification," see Gerald Snare, *The Mystification of George Chapman* (Durham, NC: Duke University Press, 1989), esp. 2–5. On Chapman's readers as "serching spirits," see his *Ovids Banquet of Sence*, Dedicatory Epistle to Matthew Roydon, in *The Poems of George Chapman*, ed.

Phyllis Brooks Bartlett (London: Oxford University Press, 1941), 49 (hereafter cited as *Poems*); on Chapman's image of the scholar as a "walking dictionarie" and an "articulate Clocke," see his *Euthymiae Raptus; or The Teares of Peace*, lines 531–33, in *Poems*, 185.

4. Chartier, *The Order of Books*, 3.

5. For Chapman's disdain of "perviall" texts, see his "To the Most Honored . . . Earle of Essex," *Seaven Bookes of the Iliad*, in *Chapman's Homer: The Iliad*, 505.

6. On Chapman's acquaintance with Hariot and Hues, see John W. Shirley, *Thomas Harriot: A Biography* (Oxford: Clarendon Press, 1983), 66–67.

7. On Kepler, see Anthony Grafton, "Humanism and Science in Rudolphine Prague: Kepler in Context," in his *Defenders of the Text: the Traditions of Scholarship in an Age of Science, 1450–1800* (Cambridge, MA: Harvard University Press, 1991), 180.

8. On Percy's scientific pursuits, see John W. Shirley, "The Scientific Experiments of Sir Walter Raleigh, the Wizard Earl, and the Three Magi in the Tower, 1613–1617," *Ambix* 4 (December 1949), 52–66; Hilary Gatti, *The Renaissance Drama of Knowledge* (London and New York: Routledge, 1989), chapters 2 and 3; Frances Yates, *The Occult Philosophy in the Elizabethan Age* (London: Routledge, 1979), 14; 135–44. The epithet the "Three Magi" was first used by Anthony à Wood in his *Athenae Oxoniensis*, 4 vols., ed. Philip Bliss (London: Rivington, 1813–20), vol. I, 390, under his entry for Hariot.

9. On Hariot's anagrams, see BL MS. Add. 6789 (Thomas Hariot's *Mathematical Papers*, vol. VIII) fo. 475v; on his hermeticism, see Shirley, *Thomas Harriot*, 271.

10. John Davies of Hereford, *Humour's Heav'n on Earth* (London, 1609), Dedication to Algernon Percy.

11. George Peele, "The Honour of the Garter," "Ad Maecenatem Prologus," in *The Works of George Peele*, 3 vols., ed. A. H. Bullen (London: John Nimmo, 1888), vol. II, 317.

12. On anti-Ciceronianism during the period, see Williamson, *The Senecan Amble*, 82–83; 187.

13. Epictetus, *The Manuall of Epictetus*, tr. J[ames] S[anford] (London, 1567?), translator's annotations to chapter 25, 13. Porta's 1591 *De Furtivis Literarum Notis vulgo de Ziferis Libri IIII* is dedicated to Percy; on his interest in cryptography, see Batho, "The Library of the 'Wizard' Earl," 249. On Chapman's interest in optics, see Raymond Waddington, *The Mind's Empire: Myth and Form in George Chapman's Narrative Poems* (Baltimore: Johns Hopkins University Press, 1974), 117–37.

14. On the atomism of Percy and his circle, see Robert Kargon, *Atomism in England from Hariot to Newton* (Oxford: Clarendon Press, 1966), 27–47; Gatti, *The Renaissance Drama of Knowledge*, 49–73.

15. On Bacon, see Rees, " 'Atomism' and 'Subtlety' in Francis Bacon's Philosophy."

16. Gatti, *The Renaissance Drama of Knowledge*, 65; 72 (citing Hariot's correspondence with Kepler, also rpt. in Shirley, *Thomas Harriot*, 385–88).

17. Bacon, *Novum Organum*, Book 1, Aphorism 51, 61; Book 2, Aphorism 43, 239.

18. *Ibid.*, Book 1, Aphorism 57, 63.

19. Gatti, *The Renaissance Drama of Knowledge*, 67.

20. On Chapman's use of the *baculus in aqua* as an emblem, see Waddington, *The Mind's Empire*, 144–48.

21. On Richard Baines' accusations against Hariot, see Shirley, "Thomas Harriot and Sir Walter Raleigh," in *Thomas Harriot: Renaissance Scientist*, ed. Shirley, 23–24 and his *Thomas Harriot*, 320; on his scientific investigations, see Shirley, *Thomas Harriot*, 383–404; Taylor, *Mathematical Practitioners*, 182–83. On the connections among Hariot, Hues, Percy, and Chapman, see Batho, "The Library of the 'Wizard' Earl," 246–61; Henry Stevens, *Thomas Hariot the Mathematician, the Philosopher and the Scholar* (London, 1800), 95–113.

22. George Chapman, "To My Admired and Soule-Loved Friend Mayster of all essentiall and true knowledge, M. Harriots," in *Achilles Shield* (London: John Windet, 1598), lines 41–3.

23. Chapman, *The Shadow of Night* (London, 1599), dedicatory epistle to Matthew Roydon, in *Poems*, 19.

24. Chapman, *Ovids Banquet of Sence*, dedicatory epistle to Matthew Roydon, in *Poems*, 49.

25. Georgius Agricola, *De Re Metallica* (Basel, 1556), ed. and tr. Henry and Lou Hoover (New York: Dover, 1950), Preface, xxxi; Ben Jonson, "To my worthy and honoured Friend, George Chapman, on his translation of Hesiod's *Works and Days*," lines 1–3 , in *The Complete Poems*, ed. Parfitt, 262.

26. Bacon, *The Advancement of Learning*, Book II, 80; Chapman, *The Shadow of Night*, dedicatory epistle to Matthew Roydon, in *Poems*, 19.

27. Chapman, *The Shadow of Night*, dedicatory epistle to Matthew Roydon, in *Poems*, 19.

28. Chapman, *Ovids Banquet of Sence*, preface; "To the Understander," *Achilles Shield*, in *Chapman's Homer: The Iliad*, 548. On Chapman's love of obscurity, see Snare, *The Mystification of George Chapman*, 2–5.

29. Porta, *Natural Magick*, Book XVII ("Of Strange Glasses"), 363; L. Digges, *Pantometria*, Preface by Thomas Digges, A3v. Compare Galileo's 1611 account of his demonstration of his telescope, cited in Shapin, *The Scientific Revolution*, 72.

30. Tomkis, *Albumazar*, 1.iii, A4v.

31. On the obscurity of Greek during the Renaissance, see Howard Clarke, *Homer's Readers: A Historical Introduction to the Iliad and the Odyssey* (Newark: University of Delaware Press, 1981), 57; L. D. Reynolds and N. G. Wilson, eds., *Scribes and Scholars. A Guide to the Transmission of Greek and Latin Literature* (Oxford: Clarendon Press, 1991), 146.

32. On Huygens' *Autobiography*, see Svetlana Alpers, *The Art of Describing: Dutch Art in the Seventeenth Century* (Chicago: University of Chicago Press, 1983), 10.

33. Huygens, *Autobiography*, cited in *ibid.*, 9; 7.

34. Bacon, *Novum Organum*, Book II, Aphorism 39, 225.

35. Grafton, *Defenders of the Text*, 25–26.

36. Powell, *Humane Industry*, 137; Richard Banister, *A Treatise of One-Hundred and Thirteene Diseases of the Eyes* (2nd edn., London, 1622), Book II, chapter 8, C5r. On myopia and corrective lenses, see Catherine Wilson, *The Invisible World: Early Modern Philosophy and the Invention of the Microscope* (Princeton: Princeton University Press, 1995), 74; on the history of spectacles, see L. M. Angus Butterworth, "Glass. Lenses and Optical Instruments," in *A History of Technology*, 8 vols., ed. Charles Singer, E. J. Holmyard, A. R. Hall, and Trevor I. Williams (Oxford: Clarendon Press, 1954–84), vol. III, 229–33; Jean-Claude Margolin, "Des Lunettes et des hommes ou la satire des mal-voyants au XVIe siècle," *Annales* 30 (1975), 375–93; John Dreyfus, "The Invention of Spectacles and the Advent of Printing," *The Library*, sixth series, 10 (1988), 93–106.
37. Chapman, "To Harriots," in his *Iliads*, lines 98; 112–13; BL MS Lands. 121 (13), William Bourne, "The Property and Qualytyes of Glaces," fo. 99a.
38. Percy, *Advice to his Son*, ed. Harrison, 69; BL MS Lands. 121 (13), Bourne, "Glaces," fos. 98–99. On the distortions effected by optical glasses, see James Elkins, *The Object Stares Back. On the Nature of Seeing* (New York: Harcourt Brace, 1996), 98.
39. Bacon, *Novum Organum*, Book II, Aphorism 39, 225.
40. Bacon, *The Advancement of Learning*, Book II, 64.
41. Bacon, *Novum Organum*, Book II, Aphorism 43, 239; on the "delight in particularization" in Renaissance culture, see Jonathan Sawday, *The Body Emblazoned: Dissection and the Human Body in Renaissance Culture* (London and New York: Routledge, 1995), Preface, ix; 2–3.
42. Chapman's translation of Books 1–12 of the *Iliad* appeared in 1609, and his complete *Iliad* was entered in the Stationers' Register in 1611 and probably printed in the same year. His translation of Books 1–12 of the *Odyssey* appears in 1614, and a complete *Odyssey* in 1615. His complete translation of both texts, entitled *The Whole Workes of Homer*, was entered in the Stationers' Register in 1616.
43. Chapman, "To the Reader," *Seaven Bookes of the Iliad*; "Of Homer," *Iliads*, both in *Chapman's Homer: The Iliad*, 507; 20.
44. Chapman, *Ovids Banquet of Sence*, Dedicatory Epistle, 11–13: "But that Poesie should be as perviall as Oratorie, and plainnes her speciall ornament, were the plaine way to barbarisme."
45. George Sandys, "Upon the Thirteenth Booke of Ovid's *Metamorphosis*," in his *Ovids Metamorphosis English'd, mythologiz'd, and represented in figures* (Oxford: John Lichfield and William Stansby, 1632), 445; W. J. T. Mitchell, "Ekphrasis and the Other," *South Atlantic Quarterly* 91 (1992), 695–720: 716.
46. Chapman, "To the Most Honored . . . Earle of Essexe," *Seaven Bookes of the Iliad*, in *Chapman's Homer: The Iliad*, 505.
47. Gatti, *The Renaissance Drama of Knowledge*, 59.
48. Chapman, "To Harriots," lines 1–2; 31; "To the Most Honoured . . . Earle Marshall," *Achilles Shield*, in *Chapman's Homer: The Iliad*, 544; on Hariot's concern for the accuracy of his instruments, see Shirley, *Thomas Harriot*, 90–95.

49. Chapman, Dedicatory Epistle to Earl Marshall, *Achilles Shield*, in *Chapman's Homer: The Iliad*, 543; Thomas Heywood, *Troia Britanica: or, Great Britaines Troy* (1609, rpt. Hildesheim and New York: Georg Olms Verlag, 1972), Canto 8, FF2v–FF3r; Sandys, *Ovids Metamorphosis English'd*, 445.

50. Chapman, "To the Most Worthie Earle . . . of Salisbury," *Iliads* (1611), 9; "To the High Borne Prince of Men, Henrie Thrice," *Iliads* (1611), in *Chapman's Homer: The Iliad*, 6–7, lines 105; 123.

51. Chapman, "To Harriots," line 148.

52. Alpers, "*Ekphrasis* and Aesthetic Attitudes in Vasari's *Lives*," *Journal of the Warburg and Courtauld Institutes* 23 (1960), 190–215: 190. On ekphrasis, see also Mitchell, "Ekphrasis and the Other"; James Heffernan, *Museum of Words: The Poetics of Ekphrasis from Homer to Ashbery* (Chicago: University of Chicago Press, 1993), 5.

53. Edmund Spenser, *The Faerie Queene*, ed. Thomas P. Roche, Jr. (London: Penguin, 1987), III.xi.53, lines 1; 4. Shakespeare, *The Rape of Lucrece*, lines 1531; 1576.

54. Shakespeare, *The Rape of Lucrece*, lines 1425–28; line 1423.

55. Peacham, *Graphice*, chapter 10, 37; the term "foreshortening" first appears in the first edition of this work, the 1606 *Art of Drawing*. Compare Giorgio Vasari, *On Technique*, tr. Louisa Maclehose (New York: Dover, 1960), chapter 17; Lomazzo, *A tracte containiug the artes*, Book v, chapter 2, 185–87.

56. Chapman, *Ovids Banquet of Sence*, Preface to Matthew Roydon.

57. Lipsius, *Manuductio* and Joseph Hall, *Epistles in Six Decades*, VI.10, both cited in Williamson, *The Senecan Amble*, 123; 194.

58. On perspective in the context of Renaissance scientific culture, see Erwin Panofsky, "Galileo as a Critic of the Arts: Aesthetic Attitude and Scientific Thought," *Isis* 47 (1956), 3–15 and his *Perspective as Symbolic Form*, tr. Christopher Wood (New York: Zone Books, 1991); also see Edgerton, *The Heritage of Giotto's Geometry*, 35–44; 231–51.

59. On the emendation of the 1533 Euclid, see Edgerton, *Giotto's Geometry*, 165. A 1570 Billingsley translation of Euclid in the Bodleian Library (Savile W5) has extant erected tabs on fos. 332v and 339v.

60. On Percy's laboratory, see Shirley, *Thomas Harriot*, 225; Batho, "The Library of the 'Wizard' Earl," 246–61.

61. Cotgrave, *A Dictionary of the French and English Tongues* (London, 1611), "elabourer."

62. George Chapman, *The Georgicks of Hesiod* (London: H[umphrey] L[ownes] for Miles Partrich, 1618), title-page; "To the Understander," *Achilles Shield*, in *Chapman's Homer: The Iliad*, 548; Burton, *The Anatomy of Melancholy*, vol. II, 86 [2.2.4.1]; Brahe, *De aliis quibusdam instrumentis astronomicus*, in *Tycho Brahe's Description of his Instruments and Scientific Work as given in "Astronomiae Instauratae Mechanica [Wandesburgi, 1598]"*, ed. Hans Raeder, Elis Strömgren, and Bengt Strömgren (Copenhagen: Komission hos Ejnar Munksgaard, 1946), 100.

63. Chapman, *Iliads*, Book xviii, lines 356–58, in *Chapman's Homer: The Iliad*, 382; compare *Achilles Shield*, lines 43–45. On Thetis' footstool, see *Achilles Shield*, line 30; on the dancing maze, see *Achilles Shield*, lines 291–304; *Iliad*, Book xviii, lines 536–47. On Hephaestus' *daidala*, see Detienne and Vernant, *Cunning Intelligence*, 281; Marie Delcourt, *Héphaistos ou La Legende du Magicien* (Paris: Les Belles Lettres, 1982), 22–25; Françoise Frontisi-Ducroux, *Dédale. Mythologie de l'artisan en grèce ancienne* (Paris: F. Maspero, 1975), 55–64.

64. On Bacon's use of aphorisms, see Vickers, *Francis Bacon and Renaissance Prose*, 72–73; 75.

65. Chapman, *Ovids Banquet of Sence*, Preface. Compare Puttenham, *Arte of English Poesie*, Book iii, chapter 3, 143, which defines *Enargia*, from the Greek *argos*, or light, as an ornament that "geveth a glorious lustre and light." On the Stoic conception of *Enargia* as perspicuity, see Williamson, *The Senecan Amble*, 140–42.

66. Chapman, *Ovids Banquet of Sence*, Preface.

67. Chapman, Dedicatory Epistle to Earl Marshall, *Achilles Shield*, in *Chapman's Homer: The Iliad*, 543.

68. *Ibid.*; on Hephaestus' tripods and handmaids; see *Achilles Shield*, lines 65–67; 6–11; compare *Iliads*, Book xiii, lines 334–35, in which the tripods enter, "their motion free, / And back againe go out alone, miraculous to see."

69. Lomazzo, *A tracte containing the artes*, Book i, chapter 1, 15–17; Book ii, chapter 1, 1–2.

70. Chapman, *The Tragedy of Chabot Admirall of France*, in *The Plays of George Chapman: the Tragedies*, ed. Alan Holyday (Cambridge: D. S. Brewer, 1987), 1.i.68–76. On Chapman's use of perspectival metaphors, see Waddington, *The Mind's Empire*, 117–22; Lucy Gent, *Picture and Poetry 1560–1620. Relations between Literature and the Visual Arts in the English Renaissance* (Leamington Spa: James Hall, 1981), 44–54.

71. BL MS Lansd. 121(13), fo. 99a; compare Bourne's *Inventions or Devises*, 97, where he instructs the user of an optical glass not to "stand oblique or awry" to see through the device properly.

72. On "squint-ey'd Envie," see Chapman, "To the Reader," *Homer's Iliads*, line 159, in *Chapman's Homer: The Iliad*, 10. On strabismus, see Banister, *A Treatise of One-Hundred and Thirteene Diseases of the Eyes*, Book iii, chapter 1; Walter Bailey, "A Treatise of the Principall Diseases of the Eyes," in *Two treatises concerning the preservation of eie-sight* (Oxford: Joseph Barnes, 1616), 28. On Zoilus, see Carey Herbert Conley, *The First English Translators of the Classics* (New Haven: Yale University Press, 1927), 82–101; Clarke, *Homer's Readers*, 107.

73. Chapman, "To the Understander," *Achilles Shield*, lines 9–11, in *Chapman's Homer: The Iliad*, 548.

74. Cornelius Agrippa, *Of the Vanitie and Uncertaintie of Artes and Sciences*, tr. J[ames] Sa[nford] (London: Henry Wykes, 1569), chapter 26, 36r; John Donne, "The Broken Heart," in *The Complete English Poems*, ed. A. J. Smith

(London: Penguin, 1986), lines 29–30; Bacon, "The Plan of the Work," in *Novum Organum*, 23.

75. Huygens, *Autobiography*, cited in Alpers, *The Art of Describing*, 17–18.
76. Robert Hues, *Tractatus de Globis et Eorum Usu* (London: Thomas Dawson, 1594), tr. John Chilmead as *A Learned Treatise of Globes* (London: T[homas] P[urfoot], 1639), C2r; Preface. On Hues, see Taylor, *Mathematical Practitioners*, 178; Feingold, *The Mathematicians' Apprenticeship*, 135–38.
77. Henry Cuffe, *The differences of the Ages of mans life together with the originall causes, progresse, and end thereof* (London: Arnold Hatfield, 1607), "Preface to the Reader." Cuffe was secretary to the Earl of Essex, the dedicatee of Chapman's 1598 translations of Homer.
78. Hues, *A Learned Treatise on Globes*, C2r.
79. Donne, "A Valediction: of Weeping," lines 10; 13. On Hariot's work on stereography, see Shirley, *Thomas Harriot*, 85–86; on his study of scientific instruments with Hakluyt, see Fauvel and Goulding, "Renaissance Oxford," chapter 3 of *Oxford Figures: 800 Years of the Mathematical Sciences*, ed. John Fauvel, Raymond Flood, and Robin Wilson (Oxford: Oxford University Press, 2000), 57.
80. Blagrave, *The Mathematicall Jewell*, chapter 1.
81. On the "impalsied" translation of Homer, see Chapman, Dedicatory Epistle to Earl Marshall, *Achilles Shield*; on translation, see his "To the Reader," *Iliads*, lines 125–26, both in *Chapman's Homer: The Iliad*, 545; 10.
82. Chapman, "To the Reader," *Iliads*, lines 95–97.
83. *Ibid.*, line 103.
84. Chapman, "To the Reader," *Iliads*, lines 120–26.
85. *Ibid.*, lines 171–76.
86. Jonson, "To . . . Mr. George Chapman, on His Translation of Hesiod's *Works and Days*," lines 10–11; on Chapman's "farre-fetcht and . . . beyond-sea manner of writing," see "To the Understander," *Achilles Shield*, line 25, in *Chapman's Homer: The Iliad*, 548.
87. Pliny, *The historie of the world: commonly called, The naturall historie of C. Plinius Secundus*, tr. Philemon Holland (2nd edn., London: Adam Islip, 1634), vol. i, Book VII, chapter 21, 167.
88. Powell, *Humane Industry*, chapter 12, 185.
89. Burton, *The Anatomy of Melancholy*, vol. ii, 84–87; 92 [2.2.4.1]; on idleness and scientific virtuosity, see Shapin, *A Social History of Truth*, 51; Houghton, "The English Virtuoso," 60–64.
90. Powell, *Humane Industry*, chapter 1, 8–9.
91. On the instruments made by Cheke and Buckley for Prince Edward and Princess Elizabeth, see Taylor, *Mathematical Practitioners*, 168–69; on royal collections of miniature machines, see Feingold, *The Mathematicians' Apprenticeship*, 196–205; Strong, *Henry, Prince of Wales*, 184–8; Evans, *Rudolf II*, 176–89. On Charles V, see Stirling-Maxwell, *The Cloister Life of Charles V*, 176–77; 477–8; Mignet, *Charles Quint*, 213–15. On Charles I's watch, see Taylor, *Mathematical Practitioners*, 201.

92. Chapman, "To the Reader," *Iliads*, lines 71–80.
93. Stewart, *On Longing*, 38. On the aesthetics of the miniature, see Gaston Bachelard, *The Poetics of Space*, tr. Maria Jolas (Boston: Beacon Press, 1969), 155; Robert Harbison, *Eccentric Spaces: A Voyage through Real and Imaginary Worlds* (New York: Ecco Press, 1976), 22. On Greene's *Tale of Troy* and miniature books, see Louis Bundy, *Miniature Books. Their History from the Beginnings to the Present Day* (London: Sheppard Press, 1981), 11.
94. Chapman, "Preface to the Reader," in *Chapman's Homer: The Iliad*, 15: "I understand the understandings of all other interpreters and commenters in places of [Homer's] most depth . . . in whose exposition and illustration if I abhorre from the sence that others wrest and racke out of him, let my best detractor examine how the Greeke word warrants me."
95. Guido Pancirolli, *De Rerum Memorabilium*, tr. as *The History of Many Memorable Things Lost* (London, 1715), chapter 10 ("Of Clocks"), 334.
96. Plutarch, "Of the Common Conceptions Against the Stoics," in *Morals*, 1102–06.
97. Peacham, *The Compleat Gentleman*, chapter 9, 85–86; chapter 17, 155.
98. Henry Vaughan, "The Sphere of Archimedes out of Claudian," in *Henry Vaughan: The Complete Poems*, ed. Alan Rudrum (New Haven: Yale University Press, 1976), 361. Vaughan also translated Hugo Grotius' epigram upon Drebbel's perpetual motion machine. On the epigram, see Puttenham, *The Arte of English Poesie*, Book 1, chapter 27, 54.
99. Thomas Campion, "De Horologio Portabili," in *Epigrammatum libri II* (London: E. Griffin, 1619), Book 1, Epigram 151, 1; Campion, Preface to his *Book of Ayres*, in David Lindley, *Thomas Campion* (Leiden: E. J. Brill, 1986), 54.
100. Notably Jean Hagstrum, *The Sister Arts: the Tradition of Literary Pictorialism and English Poetry from Dryden to Gray* (Chicago: University of Chicago Press, 1958), 66–70; Heffernan, *Museum of Words*, 23; W. J. T. Mitchell, *Picture Theory: Essays on Verbal and Visual Representation* (Chicago: University of Chicago Press, 1994), 151–2; Peter Wagner, ed., *Icons – Texts – Iconotexts: Essays on Ekphrasis and Intermediality* (Berlin: Walter de Gruyter, 1996), editor's introduction, 3–5.
101. Peacham, *The Compleat Gentleman*, chapter 9, 85.
102. On Platter's *plaisir du conter* see Steven Mullaney, "The Rehearsal of Cultures," in *The Place of the Stage: License, Play, and Power in Renaissance England* (Chicago: University of Chicago Press, 1988), 60.
103. Guillaume de Salluste, Sieur Du Bartas, *His Devine Weekes and Workes*, tr. Joshua Sylvester (London, 1605, rpt. Delmar, FL: Scholars' Facsimiles and Reprints, 1977), "The sixth Day of the first Weeke," 221.
104. Francesco Colonna, *Hypnerotomachia Poliphili: The strife of love in a Dreame*, tr. R[oger] D[allington] (London: William Holme, 1592), C3v.
105. *Itinerario di Antonio Tiepolo*, cited in García-Diego, *Juanelo Turriano*, 59.
106. Stewart, *On Longing*, 47. On the construction of the cathedral clock at Strasbourg, completed in 1574, see M. Schickelé, *L'Horloge astronomique de la cathédrale de Strasbourg* (Strasbourg: Imprimerie de l'Alsacien, 1922).

107. Burton, *The Anatomy of Melancholy*, vol. II, 86–88 [2.2.4.1].

108. Coryate, *Crudities*, "The Character of the famous Odcombian, or rather Polytopian, Thomas the Coryate," b r, and "Incipit Glareanus Vadianus. A Sceleton or bare Anatomie of the Punctures and Iunctures of Mr. Thomas Coryate of Odcombe," l 2r.

109. BL MS Lands. 100 (19) [Steven Powle, Description of Strasborough Clocke Tower, dated 1581], fos. 156–57. Edmund Burke, *A Philosophical Inquiry into the Origin of our Ideas of the Sublime and the Beautiful*, ed. Adam Phillips (Oxford: Oxford University Press, 1990), Book II, chapter 7, 66.

110. BL MS Lands. 100 (19), fos. 156–57.

111. Evans, *Rudolf II and his World*, 274; on Henry's interest in model ships, see Thomas Birch, *The life of Henry prince of Wales, eldest son of King James I* (London: A. Millar, 1760), 80.

112. Marsilio Ficino, *Platonic Theology*, tr. Josephine L. Burroughs in her "Ficino and Pomponazzi on Man," *Journal of the History of Ideas* 5:2 (April 1944), 227–42: 235.

113. Foucault, *Discipline and Punish*, 136–39.

114. On Queen Elizabeth's dress, see Joan Evans, *Nature in Design: a Study of Naturalism in Decorative Art from the Bronze Age to the Renaissance* (London: Oxford University Press, 1933), 98; on insects in Spenserian epic, see Judith Dundas, *The Spider and the Bee. The Anatomy of Spenser's Faerie Queene* (Urbana: University of Illinois Press, 1985), 3–12; Spenser, *The Faerie Queene*, II.xii.77.

115. Pliny, *Natural History*, Book XI, chapter 2, 310.

116. Richard Leigh, "Greatness in Little," lines 47–52, in his *Poems, Upon Severall Occasions* (London, 1675), 39.

117. On Aldrovandi, see Findlen, *Possessing Nature*, 210; on *Schüttelkasten*, see Bredekamp, *The Lure of Antiquity*, 47–48.

118. Thomas Moffett, *The Theater of Insects*, in Edward Topsell, *The History of four-footed beasts and serpents . . . whereunto is now added. The theater of insects, or, Lesser living creatures* by T. Moffett (London: E. Cotes, 1658), 83; compare Pliny, *Natural History*, Book XI, chapter 2, 311.

119. Moffett, *Theater of Insects*, in Topsell, *History*, 260. On the "dancing maze," see Chapman, *Achilles Shield*, line 292. On the "ring" composition of Homeric epic, see Keith Stanley, *The Shield of Homer. Narrative Structure in the Iliad* (Princeton: Princeton University Press, 1993), 9.

120. Sandys, "Upon the Eighth Booke of Ovid's *Metamorphosis*," in his *Ovids Metamorphosis English'd*, 291.

121. Bacon, *De Sapientia Veterum*, "Daedalus, or Mechanique," 94. On Renaissance labyrinths, see Hermann Kern, *Labyrinthe* (Munich: Prester Verlag, 1982); Giancarlo Maiorino, *The Portrait of Eccentricity: Arcimboldo and the Mannerist Grotesque* (University Park, PA: Pennsylvania State University Press, 1991), 94–99.

122. Thomas Moffett, *The silkwormes, and their flies: lively described in verse . . . For the great benefit and enriching of England* (London: Valentine Simmes, 1599), 34.

123. *Ibid.*, "To the most renowned Patronesse . . . Marie Countesse of Penbrooke."

124. *Ibid.*, 34–5.

125. *Ibid.*, 35.

126. On the definition of a machine as the means by which "things possessing little weight" are able to "move heavy weights," see Aristotle, *Mechanical Problems*, 331–32.

127. George Chapman, "The Occasion of this Imposed Crowne," in *The Crowne of all Homer's Workes, Batrachomyomachia* (London: John Bill, 1624).

128. W[illiam] Fowldes, *The Strange, Wonderfull, and bloudy Battell between Frogs and Mise* (London: S. S[tafford] for John Bayly, 1603), E3r.

129. Thomas Browne, *Musaeum Clausum, or Bibliotheca Abscondita*, in *The Complete Works of Sir Thomas Browne*, 4 vols., ed. Geoffrey Keynes (Chicago: University of Chicago Press, 1964), vol. iii, 119.

130. Huygens, *Autobiography*, cited in Alpers, *The Art of Describing*, 18.

131. T. C. [Thomas Combe], *An Anatomie of the Metamorpho-sed A JAX*, Part 2 of *A New Discourse of a Stale Subject, or the Metamorphosis of Ajax*, ed. Elizabeth Story Donno (New York: Columbia University Press, 1962), 187. On the collaboration between Harington and Combe, see *ibid.*, introduction, 23–52.

132. *Ibid.*, 195–96; 192.

133. Harington, *Prefatory letter from Philostilpnos* and *Misacmos' answer to the letter*, in *The Metamorphosis of A JAX*, 57–58.

134. Harington, *The Metamorphosis of A JAX*, Prologue, 68, 160; Chapman, *Iliads* (1611), Book xxiii, lines 615–16; 673–78, in *Chapman's Homer: The Iliad*, 471–73.

135. Chapman, *Homer's Odysseys*, Book viii, line 459, in *Chapman's Homer: The Odyssey*, ed. Allardyce Nicoll (2nd edn., Princeton: Princeton University Press, 1998), 141.

136. On the handmaids of gold, see Chapman, *Iliads*, Book xviii, line 372; on Vulcan's lameness, see *Achilles Shield*, line 38; Heffernan, *Museum of Words*, 16.

137. Powell, *Humane Industry*, chapter 12, 181–83.

138. Pliny, *Natural History*, Book xi, chapter 24, 324.

139. Chapman, *Homer's Odysseys*, Book viii, lines 395–98, in *Chapman's Homer: The Odyssey*, 139.

140. Pliny, *Natural History*, Book xi, chapter 24, 324.

141. See Cotgrave, *A Dictionarie of the French and English Tongues*, "subtil," Eeee 6r.

142. Vives, *De Tradendis Disciplinis*, tr. Watson, 73–75.

143. See his *Trattato dell'Oreficeria*, in Benvenuto Cellini, *I Trattati dell'Oreficeria e della Scultura*, ed. Carlo Milanesi (Florence: Felice le Monnier, 1857), 25; 27–28; 42.

144. Chapman, *Ovids Banquet of Sence*, Preface to Matthew Roydon; Peacham, *Graphice*, Book i, chapter 2, 7; Nicholas Hilliard, *The Arte of Limning*, ed. R. K. R. Thomas and T. G. S. Cain (Edinburgh: Carcanet, 1992), 76; 80.

145. For these descriptions of lustrous objects, see Chapman, *Achilles Shield*, lines 211; 298–99; 317; 313–14, in *Chapman's Homer: The Iliad*, 555–58.

146. Lomazzo, *A tracte containing the artes*, Book IV, chapter 11, 149; chapter 15, 158. On the term *poikile*, see Detienne and Vernant, *Cunning Intelligence*, 18–20; on Thetis' feet, see Chapman, *Achilles Shield*, line 321; *Iliads*, Book XVIII, line 327, where she is the "silver-footed Queene."

147. Jonson, "To the Memory of My Beloved, the Author Mr William Shakespeare," line 68, in *Complete Poems*, ed. Parfitt, 265; Spenser, *The Faerie Queene*, 1.ii.9; 1.i.35.

148. Bacon, *Advancement of Learning*, Book I, 24; Montaigne, "Of Vaine Subtilties, or Subtill Devices," in *Essayes*, Book I, chapter 54, 269; Cardano, *De la Subtilité*, Book XV, 297.

149. Cardano, *De la Subtilité*, Book XV, 318v–323r.

150. On the "dialectic of vision and concealment" in Renaissance culture, see Maus, *Inwardness and Theater in the English Renaissance*, 29.

151. William Caxton, *The Recuyell of the Historyes of Troye*, 2 vols., ed. Oskar Sommer (London: D. Nutt, 1894), vol. II, 331.

152. Chaucer, *The Squire's Tale*, lines 181–223. On Chaucer's treatment of natural magic, see Eamon, "Technology as Magic," 171–212; Joyce Lionarons, "Magic, Machines, and Deception: Technology in the Canterbury Tales," *Chaucer Review* 27 (1993), 377–86.

153. Thomas Hood, *A copie of the speache: made by the mathematicall lecturer unto the worshipful companye present. At the house of the worshipful M. Thomas Smith . . . the 4th of November, 1588* (London: Edward Allde, 1588), A2v.

6 INHUMANISM: SPENSER'S IRON MAN

1. Robert Devereux, "The Passion of a Discontented Minde," in *Poems of Edward de Vere, 17th Earl of Oxford and Robert Devereux, 2nd Earl of Essex*, ed. Steven May. *Studies in Philology* 77 (1980), 229–30.

2. Spenser, "A Letter to the Authors . . . to the Right, noble, and Valorous, Sir Walter Raleigh," in *The Faerie Queene*, ed. Roche, 15. All further references in the text are to this edition.

3. Braden, *Anger's Privilege*, 71.

4. Montaigne, "Of the Parthians Armes," in *Essayes*, Book II, chapter 9, 358–59.

5. Johnson, *Essaies*, Essay 8; on Lipsius, see Salmon, "Stoicism and Roman Example," 203.

6. William Sherman, "Thomas Digges," *DLB*, vol. CXXXVI, 77–79; Oestreich, *Neostoicism*, 85.

7. Shakespeare, *Henry V*, III.2.80–81, in *Complete Works*, 867. Thomas Digges, *Foure paradoxes, or politique discourses concerning militarie discipline* (London: H[umphrey] Lownes, 1604), 40–41; *The historie of Xenophon . . . Whereunto is added a comparison of the Roman manner of warres with this of our time, out of Justus Lipsius*, tr. John Bingham (London: John Haviland for Ralphe Mabb, 1623), Epistle Dedicatorie. On the mechanical projects of Digges and Leicester, see Alan Haynes, *The White Bear. Robert Dudley, the Elizabethan Earl of Leicester* (London: Peter Owen, 1987), 122–23; Feingold, *The Mathematicians' Apprenticeship*, 207.

8. Barnabe Rich, *A right excelent and pleasaunt dialogue, betwene Mercury and an English Souldier contayning his supplication to Mars* (London: John Day, 1574), H3r–v.

9. Roger Williams, *A Briefe Discourse of Warre* (1590), in *The Works of Sir Roger Williams*, ed. John X. Evans (Oxford: Clarendon Press, 1972), 39. On Williams' military service, see Evans, introduction to the *Works*, lvii; lxxvii.

10. John Smythe, *Certain Discourses concerning the Great Mistaking of the Effects of Divers Sorts of Weapons* (London, 1590), rpt. as *Certain Discourses Military*, ed. J. R. Hale (Ithaca: Cornell University Press, 1964), 66. On the unreliability of the gun, see Bert Hall, *Weapons and Warfare in Renaissance Europe: Gunpowder, Technology, and Tactics* (Baltimore: Johns Hopkins University Press, 1997), "The End of Knighthood," 130–38; 141–51; J. R. Hale, *War and Society in Renaissance Europe* (New York: St. Martin's Press, 1985), 50.

11. Castiglione, *Book of the Courtier*, Book II, 109.

12. On the demise of single combat, see Hale, *War and Society*, 1–49.

13. On the waning of the chivalric tournament, Malcolm Vale, *War and Chivalry: Warfare and Aristocratic Culture in England, France, and Burgundy at the End of the Middle Ages* (Athens: University of Georgia Press, 1981), 174 and throughout. On the disappearance of the battle, see Michael Howard, *War in European History* (Oxford: Clarendon Press, 1976), 26–27 and 34–37; Hale, *War and Society*, 31–38.

14. *Acts of the Privy Council*, October 26, 1595, "The Musters in Cambridgeshire," 27–28, in *Acts of the Privy Council of England*, n.s. vol. xxv (London: Her Majesty's Stationery Office, 1890); Whigham, *Ambition and Privilege*, 75.

15. David Norbrook, *Poetry and Politics in the English Renaissance* (London: Routledge, 1984), 109; 132.

16. Mervyn James, "At a Crossroads of the Political Culture," in his *Society, Politics, and Culture*, 429. On Essex's place in Book v's allegory, see Norbrook, *Poetry and Politics*, 124–39; Goldberg, *James I and the Politics of Literature*, 3–21; Ray Heffner, "Essex and Book v of *The Faerie Queene*," *English Literary History* 3 (1936), 67–82.

17. Spenser, *The Faerie Queene*, "A Letter of the Authors," 15. On Spenser's ambivalence towards Essexian militarism, see Michael West, "Spenser and the Renaissance Ideal of Christian Heroism," *PMLA* 88 (1973), 1013–32.

18. On the idea of the *gemina persona*, see Kantorowicz, *The King's Two Bodies*, 7–20.

19. *De Gli Elementi D'Euclide Libri Quindici*, tr. Federico Commandino (Urbino: Domenico Frisolino, 1575), "I Prolegommeni di M. Federico Commandino." On Talus as *lex talionis*, see Geoffrey Wagner, "Talus," *English Literary History* 17 (1950), 79–86; John Erskine Hankins, *Source and Meaning in Spenser's Allegory* (Oxford: Clarendon Press, 1971), 171–73; James Nohrnberg, *The Analogy of the Faerie Queene* (Princeton: Princeton University Press, 1976), 409–25; Jane Aptekar, *Icons of Justice: Iconography and Thematic Imagery in Book v of Spenser's Faerie Queene* (New York: Columbia University Press, 1969), 39–57.

20. "Junius Brutus," *Vindiciae Contra Tyrranos* ("A Defense of Liberty against Tyrants"), ed. Harold Laski (Gloucester: Peter Smith, 1963), 145.

21. Spenser, *A View of the Present State of Ireland*, ed. W. L. Renwick (Oxford: Clarendon Press, 1970), 106.

22. For similar arguments, see Wagner, "Talus," 85; Kenneth Gross, *Spenserian Poetics: Idolatry, Iconoclasm, and Magic* (Ithaca: Cornell University Press, 1985), 89.

23. On Book v as a critique of Elizabeth's "soft attitude" towards the Irish, see Walter S. H. Lim, "Figuring Justice: Imperial Ideology and the Discourse of Colonialism in Book v of *The Faerie Queene* and *A View of the Present State of Ireland*," *Renaissance and Reformation* 19 (1995), 45–70: 57; see also Clark Hulse, "Spenser, Bacon, and the Myth of Power," in *The Historical Renaissance: New Essays on Tudor and Stuart Literature and Culture*, ed. Heather Dubrow and Richard Strier (Chicago and London: University of Chicago Press, 1988), 329–30; Andrew Hadfield, "Spenser, Ireland, and Sixteenth-Century Political Theory," *Modern Language Review* 89 (1994), 5.

24. Spenser, *A View*, 33.

25. *Ibid.*, 12.

26. *Ibid.*, 159.

27. Jean Bodin, *The six bookes of a common-weale . . . done into English, by Richard Knolles* (London: Adam Islip, 1606), Book IV, chapter 6, 509.

28. "Giustitia Rigorosa," in Ripa, *Nova Iconologia*, vol. I, 223. On the relation of this emblem to *The Faerie Queene*, see Aptekar, *Icons of Justice*, 56–57.

29. Cervantes, *Don Quixote*, Part II, chapter 49; Erasmus, Adage 3359 [Chalcenterus], in *Opera Omnia*, vol. II, part 8, ed. R. Hoven (Amsterdam and Lausanne: Elsevier, 1997), 56.

30. Shakespeare, *Measure for Measure*, I.iv.57–58, in *Complete Works*, 412.

31. Hesiod, *Works and Days*, in *Hesiod, Homeric Hymns, and Homerica*, tr. H. G. Evelyn-White (Cambridge, MA: Harvard University Press, 1982), 13, lines 143–51.

32. *Lawes and Orders of Warre, established for the Good Conduct of the Service in Ireland* (1599), Godwyn Pamphlets 1114 (State Tracts, 1592–1641), 5.

33. Thomas Digges, *Stratioticos*, Book III, chapter 1, N r.

34. Diogenes Laertius, *Lives of the Ancient Philosophers*, 2 vols., tr. R. D. Hicks (Cambridge, MA: Harvard University Press, 1979), vol. II, 139.

35. Du Vair, *The Morale Philosophie of the Stoicks*, 69–70.

36. Shakespeare, *Antony and Cleopatra*, v.ii.238–40, in *Complete Works*, 1342; Chapman, *Bussy D'Ambois*, v.iii.125–26; 143–45. On the recognition that *apatheia* denotes callousness as well as wisdom, see Diogenes Laertius, *Lives*, vol. II, 117–18.

37. Theophrastus, *De Lapidibus*, ed. and tr. Earle R. Caley and John F. C. Richards (Columbus: Ohio State University Press, 1956), 54; compare Albertus Magnus, *De Mineralibus*, ed. and tr. Dorothy Wyckoff (Oxford: Clarendon Press, 1967), 233–34.

38. Thomas Dekker, *London's Tempe, or the Field of Happiness* (London, 1629), rpt. in *Early English Poetry, Ballads, and Popular Literature of the Middle Ages*, vol. x (London: Percy Society, 1844), 46; 49.

39. *Ibid.*, 49; Plato, *Ion*, tr. W. R. M. Lamb, in *Plato III* (Cambridge, MA: Harvard University Press, 1952), 533D–E.

40. Pliny, *The Historie of the World*, Book XXXVI, chapter 16, 586.

41. Shakespeare, *Antony and Cleopatra*, III.7.70–71, in *Complete Works*, 1322.

42. Braden, *Anger's Privilege*, 30.

43. For Bacon's observations about Essex, see Briggs, "Chapman's *Seaven Bookes of the Iliades*," 64–65; Richard McCoy, *The Rites of Knighthood: the Literature and Politics of Elizabethan Chivalry* (Berkeley and Los Angeles: University of California Press, 1989), 88.

44. Thomas Coningsby, *Journal of the Siege of Rouen*, August 17, 1591, rpt. in *Camden Miscellany* I, Old Series, 39 (London: Camden Society, 1847), 14–15.

45. Braden, *Anger's Privilege*, 30; 71.

46. For Calvin's assertion that Stoicism is a "stonie philosophie," see his *Institutes of the Christian Religion*, ed. John T. McNeill and tr. Ford Lewis Battles, 2 vols. (Philadelphia: Westminster, 1960), III. viii. 9, vol. I, 709, and the discussion by Monsarrat in *The Light from the Porch*, 73.

47. Chapman, *The Revenge of Bussy D'Ambois*, III.iv.116–22.

48. Hall, "The Patient Man," in his *Heaven upon Earth and Characters of Vertues and Vices*, 100.

49. On anti-Stoic sentiments during the Renaissance, see Robert Ornstein, *The Moral Vision of Jacobean Tragedy* (Madison: University of Wisconsin Press, 1965), 41 and throughout; Monsarrat, *The Light from the Porch*, esp. chapter 3, 51–108.

50. Seneca, *De Constantia Sapientis*, III.5; X.4, in *Seneca: Moral Essays*, 3 vols., tr. John Basore (Cambridge, MA: Harvard University Press, 1998), vol. I, 57; 81. On Senecan notions of constancy and their influence on Renaissance philosophical thought, see Miles, *Shakespeare and the Constant Romans*, 49; Monsarrat, *The Light from the Porch*, 90.

51. Braden, *Anger's Privilege*, 89; 30; 93.

52. Desiderius Erasmus, *Praise of Folly*, tr. Betty Radice (London: Penguin, 1987), 106. On the "fictitious" nature of the passionless sage, see Monsarrat, *The Light from the Porch*, 7.

53. Calvin, *Institutes of the Christian Religion*, III.8.9, vol. I, 709; Plutarch, "That the Stoickes deliver more strange opinions, than do the Poets," in *Morals*, 1055. Plutarch's reference is to Kaineus, a soldier made "of a metall harder than the diamond" and mentioned by Pindar, *Threnos* 6.8, in *Pindar*, 2 vols., tr. William Race (Cambridge, MA: Harvard University Press, 1997), vol. II, 365.

54. Braden, *Anger's Privilege*, 93.

55. Heinrich Bullinger, *The Decades* (1577), 4 vols., tr. H. I. and ed. Thomas Harding (Cambridge: Cambridge University Press, 1849–52), vol. II, 56–7; *The Workes of Lucius Annaeus Seneca*, tr. Thomas Lodge (London: William Stansby, 1614), "To the Courteous Reader."

56. Calvin, *Institutes*, III.viii.9–10, vol. I, 709–10; Bullinger, *Decades*, vol. II, 56.

57. Edward Reynolds, *A treatise of the passions and faculties of the soule of man* (London: R. H[earne and John Norton], 1640), 48.

58. Owen Felltham, *Resolves, divine, morall, politicall* (London: George Purslowe for Henry Seile, 1623), Book 1, chapter 62, 190–91; Richard Greenham, *Grave Counsels*, in *The workes of the reverend and faithfull . . . M. Richard Greenham* (London: Felix Kingston, 1599), 43; Cornwallis, "The Resolved Christian," in *Essayes*, 270.

59. Erasmus, *Praise of Folly*, 106; Thomas Gataker, Sermon on Amos 6.6, in *Certaine sermons, first preached . . . by M. Thomas Gataker . . . And now gathered together into one volume* (London: John Haviland, 1637), 31–33; on the anti-Stoic sentiments of Renaissance humanists such as Giannozzo Manetti, see Eugenio Garin, *Italian Humanism*, tr. Peter Munz (New York: Harper & Row, 1965), 57.

60. Richard Hooker, *Laws of Ecclesiastical Polity*, ed. George Edelen, in *The Works of Richard Hooker*, 5 vols., ed. W. Speed Hill (Cambridge: Belknap Press, 1977), vol. 1, Book 1, chapter 10, part 1, 96.

61. John Milton, *Areopagitica*, in *John Milton: Complete Poems and Major Prose*, ed. Merritt Y. Hughes (New York: Odyssey Press, 1957), 728.

62. For this interpretation of Malengin, see *The Works of Edmund Spenser: a Variorum Edition*, ed. Ray Heffner (Baltimore: Johns Hopkins University Press, 1936), *The Faerie Queene, Book v*, commentary to Canto 10, v–xix, 233–35.

63. Thomas Heywood, *Troia Britanica: or, Great Britaines Troy* (London: W. Jaggard, 1609), Canto 1, 4.

64. On weaponry in Renaissance epic, see Michael Murrin, *History and Warfare in Renaissance Epic* (Chicago: University of Chicago Press, 1994); Michael Leslie, *Spenser's "Fierce Warres and Faithfull Loves": Martial and Chivalric Symbolism in The Faerie Queene* (Cambridge: D. S. Brewer, 1983), chapters 1–3; Louis Montrose, "Spenser's Domestic Domain: Poetry, Property, and the Early Modern Subject," in *Subject and Object in Renaissance Culture*, 84–85; 119–24.

65. Castiglione, *The Book of the Courtier*, Book 1, 53.

66. George Peele, "The Honor of the Garter," in *Life and Minor Works*, ed. D. H. Horne (New Haven: Yale University Press, 1952), 247.

67. Williams, "A Briefe Discourse," in his *Works*, 29–32; on changes in arming, see Evans, introduction, cxvi–cxxiii.

68. Smythe, *Certain Discourses Military*, 42–44.

69. Du Vair, *The Morale Philosophie of the Stoicks*, 61–62.

70. On Chapman's Achilles, see Richard Ide, *Possessed with Greatness: the Heroic Tragedies of Chapman and Shakespeare* (Chapel Hill: University of North Carolina Press, 1980), 24–25; Briggs, "Chapman's *Seaven Bookes of Iliads*." In his dedication of the 1598 *Seaven Bookes*, Chapman calls Essex "the Most Honored now Living Instance of the Achillean vertues eternized by divine Homere."

71. Castiglione, *The Book of the Courtier*, Book 1, 47.

72. On the "preposterous" nature of the battle against the Souldan, and the "ominous implications" of the role reversals between Artegall and Talus, see West, "Spenser's Art of War," 669; 670.

73. *Foure bookes of husbandry, collected by M. Conradus Heresbachius . . . conteyning the whole arts and trade of husbandry . . . Newely Englished . . . by Barnabe Googe* (2nd edn., London: John Wight, 1586), Book 1, 41v.

74. On the "mysterious personality" of the gun, see Hale, *War and Society*, 50; on the construction of the wheel-lock pistol, see Hall, *Weapons and Warfare*, 191.

75. West, "Spenser's Art of War," 679. On Philip's *impresa* and Spenser's interpretation, see Aptekar, *Icons of Justice*, 80–83.

76. Plato, *Meno*, 97 D–E, in *Plato IV*, tr. W. R. M. Lamb (Cambridge, MA: Harvard University Press, 1952), 361; compare Aristotle, *Politics*, 1253b. On Daedalus and Spenser's Talus, see Nohrnberg, *Analogy*, 417.

77. Jacques Ellul, cited in Langdon Winner, *Autonomous Technology: Technics-Out-of-Control as a Theme in Political Thought* (Cambridge, MA: M.I.T. Press, 1977), 42.

78. Conrad Kyeser, *Bellifortis*, 2 vols., ed. Götz Quarg (Düsseldorf: Verlag, 1967), vol. 1, 117. On Kyeser, see Gille, *Engineers of the Renaissance*, 58–66; Eamon, "Technology as Magic," 186–89.

79. Biringuccio, *Pyrotechnia*, cited in Hale, *Renaissance War Studies*, 407; compare the arguments in Hale, "War and Public Opinion in Renaissance Italy," in *Renaissance War Studies*, 359–87; West, "Spenser's Art of War," 681–84.

80. Plato, *Minos*, 320 C–D, in *Plato: VIII*, tr. W. R. M. Lamb (Cambridge, MA: Harvard University Press, 1952), 417; Apollodorus, *The Library*, 2 vols., tr. J. G. Frazer (Cambridge, MA: Harvard University Press, 1995), vol. 1, 1.ix.26, 117; Apollonius Rhodius, *Argonautica*, IV.1637–71, tr. R. C. Seaton (Cambridge, MA: Harvard University Press, 1988), 407–09. On Spenser's use of these sources, see Norhrnberg, *Analogy*, 412–13.

81. Ovid, *Metamorphoses*, Book VIII, 236ff; Apollodorus, *The Library*, III.xv.8–27.

82. John Banister, *The Historie of Man, sucked from the sappe of the most approved Anathomistes* (London: John Daye, 1578), 35.

83. Desiderius Erasmus, *Knucklebones, or the Game of Tali*, in *The Colloquies of Erasmus*, tr. Craig Thompson (Chicago: University of Chicago Press, 1965), 436.

84. Klaus Theweleit, *Male Fantasies*, 2 vols., tr. Stephen Conway (Minneapolis: University of Minnesota Press, 1987–89), vol. 1, 93.

85. Apollonius, *Argonautica*, IV.1645–49; Apollodorus, *The Library*, 1.ix.26.

86. On these and other "spectacles of dismemberment" in Book V, see Lim, "Figuring Justice," 54.

87. Aristotle, *Parts of Animals*, IV.10, in *Aristotle: Parts of Animals*, tr. A. L. Peck (Cambridge, MA: Harvard University Press, 1937), 373; the passage is discussed in Goldberg, *Writing Matter*, 91.

88. Peter Apian, *Instrument Buch* (Ingolstadt, 1533), L3v; Joseph Boillot, *Modelles Artifices de Feu et Divers Instruments de Guerre* (Chaumont: Quentin Mareschal, 1598), A3r.

89. On Amboise Paré's designs for prosthetic hands and arms see David Wills, *Prosthesis* (Stanford, CA: Stanford University Press, 1995), 246. On the artificiality of the Renaissance hand, see Goldberg, *Writing Matter*, 63; 105.

90. James VI and I, *Basilikon Doron*, 60.
91. Ducci, *Ars Aulica*, 3.
92. Taccola's work, which exists in two separate manuscripts, has been reprinted in Taccola, *Liber Tertius de Ingeneis ac edifitiis non usitatis*, ed. James Beck (Milan: IC Polifilo, 1969) and in Frank Prager and Giustina Scaglia, *Taccola and his Book De Ingeneis* (Cambridge, MA: M.I.T. Press, 1972); for Taccola's giraffe and porcupine, see *De Ingeneis*, ed. Prager and Scaglia, 136; 132. On Taccola, see also Gille, *Engineers of the Renaissance*, 68–71.
93. On Louis XII's *impresa*, see Mario Praz, *Studies in Seventeenth-Century Imagery* (2nd edn., Rome: Edizioni di Storia e Letteratura, 1964), 65.
94. Dallington, *Aphorisms Civill and Militarie*, Aphorism 55.
95. Emmanuele Tesauro, *Il Cannocchiale Aristotelico, O sia Idea delle Argutezze Heroiche . . . Contenente ogni genere di Figure, & Inscrittioni Espressive di Arguti, & Ingegniosi Concetti* (Venice: Paolo Baglioni, 1655), 10th Proposition, 64–65.
96. Charron, *Of Wisdome*, chapter 57, 208.
97. Montaigne, *An Apologie for Raymond Sebond*, in *Essayes*, Book II, chapter 12, 536.

CONCLUSION

1. Murrin, *The Veil of Allegory: Some Notes Toward a Theory of Allegorical Rhetoric in the English Renaissance* (Chicago: University of Chicago Press, 1969), 142.
2. François Rabelais, *Quart Livre*, in *Oeuvres complètes*, ed. Guy Demerson (Paris: Editions du Seuil, 1973), chapter 62, 710–11.
3. Montaigne, "Of Constancie," *Essayes*, Book I, chapter 12, 35–36.
4. Vannoccio Biringuccio, *Pyrotechnia* (Venice, 1540), ed. and tr. Cyril Stanley Smith and Martha Teach Gnudi (Cambridge, MA: M.I.T. Press, 1943), Book X, 149; 440.
5. John White, *A rich cabinet, with variety of inventions: unlock'd and open'd, for the recreation of ingenious spirits at their vacant hours Being receipts and conceits of several natures, and fit for those who are lovers of natural and artificial conclusions* (London: William Whitwood, 1651), receipts 25 and 26, K3r–K4v.
6. John Babington, *Pyrotechnia or, A discourse of artificiall fireworkes . . . together with sundry such motions, both straight and circular, performed by the helpe of fire* (London: Thomas Harper for Ralph Mab, 1635), chapter 33; Dedication to the Earl of Newport, "Master of his Maiesties Ordnance."
7. Donne, "An Anatomy of the World," lines 129–30, in *Complete English Poems*, 274.
8. In James Shirley's *Triumph of Peace* (London: John Norton, 1633), 19, a creak is heard "as if there were some danger by some piece of the Machines falling," while Gian Lorenzo Bernini, *The Inundation of the Tiber*, depicts an artificial flood diverted away from the audience at the last possible moment. On Bernini's use of stage machinery, also see his *The Impresario*, ed. and tr. Donald Beecher and Massimo Ciavolella (Ottawa: Dovehouse Editions, 1985), II.i and

introduction, 10–13; Donald Beecher, "Gianlorenzo Bernini's *The Impresario*: artist as supreme trickster," *University of Toronto Quarterly* 53 (1984), 236–47. On the mechanical errors in *The Masque of Squires*, see John Orrell, "The Agent of Savoy at *The Somerset Masque*," *Review of English Studies* 28 (1977), 301–04. On the frequency of set machinery disasters, see Nicola Sabbatini, *Practica di Fabricar Scene e Machine Ne'Teatri*, rpt. in *The Renaissance Stage: Documents of Serlio, Sabbatini and Furttenbach*, ed. Bernard Hewitt (Coral Gables: University of Miami Press, 1958), Book 1, chapter 37, 90–98; Strong, *Henry, Prince of Wales*, 86–97.

9. Bernini, *The Impresario*, 11.i, tr. Beecher, 43.

10. Edward Coke, *Fourth Part of the Institutes of the Laws of England: Concerning the Jurisdiction of Courts*, cited in Stephen White, *Sir Edward Coke and "the Grievances of the Commonwealth," 1621–1628* (Chapel Hill: University of North Carolina Press, 1979), 51.

11. Thomas Tymme, *A silver watch-bell The sound wherof is able . . . to win the most profane worldling . . . that in the end he may obtaine everlasting salvation* (London: T. C[reede] for William Cotton, 1605), chapter 1, 24–25.

12. Donne, "An Anatomy of the World: The First Anniversary," line 213.

13. Caus, *Les Raisons des Forces Mouvantes*, "Au Roy Tres Chrestien"; "Epistre au bening Lecteur."

14. Smythe, *Instructions*, 97.

15. Flavio Biondo, *Historiarum ab inclinato Ro. imperio. decades III*, in his *Opera* (Basel: Hier. Froben and Nicol. Episcopium, 1559), 394.

16. Jean Nicot, *Thresor de la Langue Françoise Tant Ancienne que Moderne* (1621; rpt. Paris: A. and J. Picard, 1960), 384.

17. Rabelais, *Pantagruel*, in *Oeuvres*, chapter 16, 280. On the connections between Panurge and Odysseus, see Terence Cave, "Panurge and Odysseus," in *Myth and Legend in French Literature: Essays in Honour of A. J. Steele*, ed. Keith Aspley, David Bellos, and Peter Sharratt (London: Modern Humanities Research Association, 1982), 47–59; Gérard Defaux, "Un héritage encombrant: Ulysse Polytropon," chapter 3 of his *Le Curieux, le glorieux et la sagesse du monde dans la première moitié du XIVe siècle* (Lexington, KY: French Forum, 1982).

18. Peter Dear, *Revolutionizing the Sciences: European Knowledge and its Ambitions, 1500–1700* (Princeton: Princeton University Press, 2001), 99.

19. Rabelais, *Gargantua*, in *Oeuvres*, Book 1, chapter 24, 118; English translation cited from *The Complete Works of François Rabelais*, ed. and tr. Donald M. Frame (Berkeley: University of California Press, 1991).

20. Elias, "State Formation and Civilization," in *The Civilizing Process*, 462.

21. Jonson, *Pleasure Reconciled to Virtue* (London, 1618), in *Works*, vol. VII, 479–81.

22. Rabelais, *Quart Livre*, in *Oeuvres*, chapter 57, 736; English version cited from *Works*, 561.

23. On the "Renaissance computer" and early modern "knowledge technology," see *The Renaissance Computer: Knowledge Technology in the First Age of Print*, ed. Neil Rhodes and Jonathan Sawday (London and New York: Routledge, 2000), esp. Introduction, 7–9. On "technologies of the self," see Michel

Foucault, "Technologies of the Self," in *Technologies of the Self: A Seminar with Michel Foucault*, ed. Luther H. Martin, Huck Gutman, and Patrick H. Hutton (Amherst: University of Massachusetts Press, 1988), 18. My closing arguments are indebted to Donna Haraway's observation that cyborgs and other postmodern machine/human hybrids "can suggest a way out of the maze of dualisms in which we have explained our bodies and our tools to ourselves," thus offering us a "powerful infidel heteroglossia." See her *Simians, Cyborgs, and Women. The Reinvention of Nature* (London and New York: Routledge, 1991), 181.

Index